Extreme DAX

Take your Power BI and Microsoft data analytics skills to the next level

Michiel Rozema

Henk Vlootman

BIRMINGHAM—MUMBAI

Extreme DAX

Copyright © 2022 Packt Publishing

All rights reserved. No part of this book may be reproduced, stored in a retrieval system, or transmitted in any form or by any means, without the prior written permission of the publisher, except in the case of brief quotations embedded in critical articles or reviews.

Every effort has been made in the preparation of this book to ensure the accuracy of the information presented. However, the information contained in this book is sold without warranty, either express or implied. Neither the authors, nor Packt Publishing or its dealers and distributors, will be held liable for any damages caused or alleged to have been caused directly or indirectly by this book.

Packt Publishing has endeavored to provide trademark information about all of the companies and products mentioned in this book by the appropriate use of capitals. However, Packt Publishing cannot guarantee the accuracy of this information.

Producer: Suman Sen
Acquisition Editor – Peer Reviews: Saby Dsilva
Project Editor: Rianna Rodrigues
Content Development Editor: Lucy Wan
Copy Editor: Safis Editing
Technical Editor: Aditya Sawant
Proofreader: Safis Editing
Indexer: Manju Arasan
Presentation Designer: Pranit Padwal

First published: January 2022

Production reference: 1070122

Published by Packt Publishing Ltd.
Livery Place
35 Livery Street
Birmingham
B3 2PB, UK.

ISBN 978-1-80107-851-1

www.packt.com

Contributors

About the authors

Michiel Rozema is one of the world's top Power BI experts and lives in the Netherlands. He holds a master's degree in mathematics and has worked in the IT industry for over 25 years as a consultant and manager. Michiel was the data insight lead at Microsoft Netherlands for 8 years, during which time he launched Power BI in the country. He is the author of two Dutch books on Power Pivot and Power BI. Michiel is one of the founders of the Dutch Power BI user group, organizer of the Power BI Summer School, and has been a speaker at many conferences on Power BI. He has been awarded the Microsoft MVP award since 2019 and, together with fellow MVP Henk Vlootman, he runs the consultancy company Quanto, which specializes in Power BI.

Henk Vlootman is a senior global Power Platform, Power BI, and Excel business consultant. Every year since 2013, Henk has received the Microsoft MVP award for his outstanding expertise and community leadership. Henk is one of the founders of the Dutch Power BI user group, organizer of the Power BI Summer School, and has been a speaker at many conferences on Power BI all over the world. He is also the author of two Excel and two Power Pivot/Power BI books. He started his career in 1992 with his own company, then as an Excel consultant. Nowadays he runs the consultancy company Quanto, which specializes in Power BI, together with fellow MVP Michiel Rozema.

About the reviewer

Greg Deckler is a Microsoft MVP for Data Platform and an active member of the Columbus Ohio IT community, having founded the Columbus Azure ML and Power BI User Group (CAMLPUG) and presented at many conferences and events throughout the country. An active blogger and community member interested in helping new users of Power BI, Greg actively participates in the Power BI community, having authored over 180 Power BI Quick Measures Gallery submissions and over 5,000 solutions to community questions. Greg is Vice President of Cloud Services at Fusion Alliance, a regional consulting firm, and assists customers in gaining competitive advantage from the cloud and cloud-first technologies like Power BI. Greg has authored three books on Power BI: *Learn Power BI*, *DAX Cookbook*, and *Power BI Cookbook, Second Edition*. Finally, Greg has also built an external tool for Power BI Desktop called Microsoft Hates Greg's Quick Measures, and he posts Power BI videos on YouTube.

I would like to thank my son, family, and the entire Power BI community for all of their support.

Table of Contents

Preface

In this book, you'll take your Power BI and Microsoft data analytics skills to the next level. You'll discover the true power of DAX and learn how to build advanced DAX solutions for practical business scenarios.

Who this book is for

If you are an analyst with a working knowledge of DAX in Power BI or other Microsoft analytics tools, this book will help you upgrade your DAX knowledge and work with analytical models more effectively.

This book is not for beginners and practical experience with DAX is necessary.

What this book covers

Chapter 1.1, *DAX in Business Intelligence*, discusses the field of business intelligence and the central role of analytical models in modern BI solutions. Power BI models are ideally suited for use as such models, not least because of the power of DAX.

Chapter 1.2, *Model Design*, discusses the foundational concepts of the Power BI model. You learn what makes a Power BI model fundamentally different from other data management products and what an optimal design looks like.

Chapter 1.3, *Using DAX*, summarizes the different uses of DAX in Power BI models: calculated columns, calculated tables, measures, security rules, and queries. We also give you some best practices for working with DAX.

Chapter 1.4, Context and Filtering, covers row context, query context, and filter context, and the role contexts play in the evaluation of DAX formulas. We discuss how contexts can be transformed using the CALCULATE function, by removing filters and adding filters to an existing context. In addition, we look at time intelligence functions, DAX table functions, the deep connection between tables and filters, and DAX variables.

All of these are foundational concepts in exploring more advanced analyses with DAX. After this important chapter, *Part 2* of this book is focused on applying all the concepts discussed so far to real-life business cases, many of them based on the projects we've worked on across the years.

Chapter 2.1, Security with DAX, demonstrates many aspects of securing Power BI models and the power of DAX for doing so. We discuss the versatility of row-level security, security roles, and securing hierarchies, attributes, and aggregation levels through combinations of modeling, DAX, and row-level security.

Chapter 2.2, Dynamically Changing Visualizations, covers how to use helper tables and the SWITCH function to capture user input. We demonstrate how to dynamically change data binding with DAX to create highly dynamic visuals. Depending on your intended use, a helper table can be as simple as a few rows with options, or a larger list based on other data in the Power BI model.

Chapter 2.3, Alternative Calendars, shows you how to implement time intelligence when your calendar looks different than the standard Gregorian calendar that a Power BI model assumes. We close the chapter off with an alternative to relative date filters in Power BI reports, which is more flexible and can handle selections in non-standard calendars as well.

Chapter 2.4, Working with AutoExist, focuses on *which* calculations are done to populate a visual from a Power BI model. Understanding how AutoExist works will help you to find out why you sometimes do not see results you are expecting in a visual. It also helps to avoid performance problems in reports that are the result of using too many columns from too many tables in one visual.

Chapter 2.5, Intercompany Business, discusses two main business challenges: intercompany business and consolidated views, and invoices to be sent on open sales orders. We discuss how to keep thorough track of context, how to tailor DAX measures to visualizations, and strategies for approaching advanced analyses.

Chapter 2.6, Exploring the Future: Forecasting and Future Values, teaches you about financial metrics for analyzing the future of investments. We discuss the common metrics of Future Value, Present Value, Net Present Value, and Internal Rate of Return, and their equivalents in DAX, including XNPV and XIRR. We also introduce what-if parameters and see how to use them in complex calculations.

Chapter 2.7, Inventory Analysis, deals with analyzing inventory data, although the kind of analysis in this chapter can be applied to all sorts of status-oriented data. We discuss different ways to model this kind of data, how to calculate inventory status at some point in time, and how to compare actuals with targets. You will also see different ways to look into the future, including a linear regression in DAX.

Chapter 2.8, Personnel Planning, discusses ways to analyze the need for personnel (in terms of full-time equivalents, or FTEs) when undertaking projects. From a technical perspective, you will learn ways to work with multiple fact tables that must be considered in combination to provide useful results. The challenge is not only to come up with correct results, but to find the optimal way to compute those results as well.

To get the most out of this book

As mentioned, in this book we assume that you already have practical experience with DAX and are looking to extend your knowledge, applying DAX to a range of more complex scenarios. For this reason, we do not generally explain the way a DAX function and its arguments are used, unless we need to for a specific case; this information can easily be found on the internet.

All models can be found on the book's GitHub site at `https://github.com/PacktPublishing/Extreme-DAX`. Each chapter contains a link to the PBIX file(s) used in the chapter. We recommend that you use the PBIX files to help you follow along with the chapters.

You can use the latest version of Power BI Desktop to open the PBIX files. When relevant, each figure in a chapter, representing a visualization and the code used, can be found in the PBIX file.

Download the example code files

The code bundle for the book is hosted on GitHub at `https://github.com/PacktPublishing/Extreme-DAX`. We also have other code bundles from our rich catalog of books and videos available at `https://github.com/PacktPublishing/`. Check them out!

Download the color images

We also provide a PDF file that has color images of the screenshots/diagrams used in this book. You can download it here: `https://static.packt-cdn.com/downloads/9781801078511_ColorImages.pdf`.

Conventions used

There are a number of text conventions used throughout this book.

CodeInText: Indicates DAX expressions in the text. For example: "The inactive relationship will save us a lot of ALL('Calendar') clauses in our DAX code."

A block of code is set as follows:

```
Total Sales =
CALCULATE(
    SUM(fProjectSales[Budget]),
    USERELATIONSHIP(fProjectSales[StartDate], 'Calendar'[Date])
)
```

When we wish to draw your attention to a particular part of the text, the relevant lines or items are set in italics. For instance: "Note that we made the relationship between fProjectSales and Calendar *inactive*. This is done because most calculations will probably not group projects by their start date, but spread results over a period of time *beginning* with the start date of a project."

Warnings or important notes appear like this.

Tips and tricks appear like this.

Get in touch

Feedback from our readers is always welcome.

General feedback: Email feedback@packtpub.com, and mention the book's title in the subject of your message. If you have questions about any aspect of this book, please email us at questions@packtpub.com.

Errata: Although we have taken every care to ensure the accuracy of our content, mistakes do happen. If you have found a mistake in this book, we would be grateful if you would report this to us. Please visit http://www.packtpub.com/submit-errata, selecting your book, clicking on the Errata Submission Form link, and entering the details.

Piracy: If you come across any illegal copies of our works in any form on the Internet, we would be grateful if you would provide us with the location address or website name. Please contact us at copyright@packtpub.com with a link to the material.

If you are interested in becoming an author: If there is a topic that you have expertise in and you are interested in either writing or contributing to a book, please visit http://authors.packtpub.com.

Share Your Thoughts

Once you've read *Extreme DAX*, we'd love to hear your thoughts! Scan the QR code below to go straight to the Amazon review page for this book and share your feedback.

https://packt.link/r/1801078513

Your review is important to us and the tech community and will help us make sure we're delivering excellent quality content.

Part I

Introduction

1.1

DAX in Business Intelligence

Without a doubt, information is nowadays one of the most valuable assets of any organization. We all know this as consumers: companies are lining up to get our personal data. Not because any of us are so interesting individually (though we're sure you are a very interesting person!), but the combination of data from many consumers enables companies to get valuable insights to drive their business forward.

This is not only true for commercial companies. Public institutions, hospitals, and universities also benefit from information to better run their core processes. In any case, information is the foundation of progress and innovation.

But getting from data to information to insights can be a tedious process. It involves combining data from different sources, discovering hidden structures and correlations, and considering the context of data. This is why the field of business intelligence, or data analytics, has traditionally been exclusive to IT professionals. Which is not optimal, as it is really about *business* insights.

This book is all about one of the hottest tools for data analytics in existence today: **DAX (Dynamic Analysis eXpressions)**. As a reader, we assume that you have some experience with DAX and that you are looking to improve your skills. As the foundation for this, it is important to understand what DAX is for and what it is *not* for. Additionally, you must learn to avoid doing things elsewhere that can be done better with DAX.

This chapter covers some general concepts that will help you lay this foundation. We cover the following topics:

- The Five-Layer model for business intelligence
- Enterprise BI and end-user BI
- Where DAX fits in, and where to find it
- Tools to develop models and DAX
- Powered by DAX: visual, interactive reports
- How to approach solution development
- The digital transformation cycle

The Five-Layer model for business intelligence

To be able to discuss analytics in a structured and comprehensive way, we have developed a simple framework that describes the main components and responsibilities in an analytics solution. We have given it an equally simple name: the **Five-Layer model**.

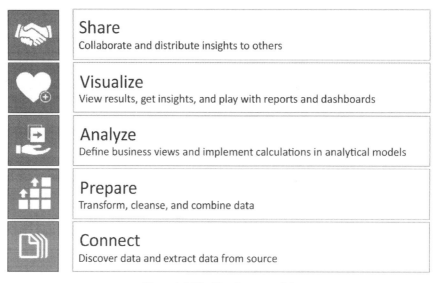

Figure 1.1: The Five-Layer model

The first and lowest layer, **Connect**, is the starting point of analytics: if you want to analyze data, those data must come from somewhere. They could reside in Excel sheets, text files, large business databases, or somewhere on the Internet.

These raw data aren't typically in the right format to be able to analyze, especially when they come from different sources. Therefore, you need to **Prepare** your data. Preparation can take many forms, like imposing certain data types, transforming data, building data history, or matching data based on key attributes.

Creating nice and clean datasets in the Connect and Prepare layers can take a lot of effort. A lot. Building a data warehouse, a typical IT component in the Prepare layer, often leads to development projects spanning multiple years. The sad thing about this is that by the time the data warehouse is complete, the world has changed and the data warehouse does not comply anymore.

When data has been put in a workable format, you can start with proper analysis of the data in the **Analyze** layer. This is really the heart of the analytics solution. Building analytical models allows you to slice and filter data, compute aggregations of all sorts, and add calculations to provide specific insights.

The **Visualize** layer is all about creating reports and dashboards visualizing the results of analytical models. We have called this layer Visualize and not simply Output as, to really provide insights, helping a user focus on the important results is as important as providing results at all. Classic reports consisting of pages and pages of details are not very insightful, and force the user to export the whole report to Excel where they can aggregate the data. Really providing insight usually involves effective visualization of the most important outcomes of the analysis, while giving the user the option to answer the questions arising from the insight by viewing additional visuals on a lower detail level.

The top layer, **Share**, consists of platforms and processes aimed at providing access to reports and dashboards to the right people, while shielding them from those who shouldn't have access.

Whether you build your analytics solution in Excel, use Power BI, develop a corporate business intelligence system, or use no automated system at all, you will have to cover the five layers in some way. In a good analytics solution, the layers are clearly separated, and the processing of data is done in the right layer. Doing this has a lot of advantages, like avoiding implementing the same logic multiple times. Proper implementation of the Five-Layer model makes it relatively easy to cope with changes in, for example, source systems.

As you will see later in this chapter, DAX lives in the Analyze layer, with strong ties to both the Prepare and Visualize layers. We will talk about visualizations in a separate section, but first, let us discuss the question *who does what in BI?*

Enterprise BI and end-user BI

Organizations are becoming ever more data-driven. An organization that assesses performance on **key performance indicators**, or **KPIs**, uses dashboards reflecting the status for each KPI. These dashboards are typically highly standardized: the organization has reflected on the business strategy, business processes, how to measure the KPIs, and how to report on them. An automated dashboard with KPIs is relatively stable and will not change much, and is typically built and maintained by a central IT department or BI competence center.

The next level of being a data-driven organization is that *every* decision taken can be based on insights from relevant data. This means that the need for a more dynamic form of analytics arises, one that can answer ad hoc questions. This form of analytics is marketed as **self-service BI** and promises that everyone can build a BI solution without the help of a central IT department. From the Five-Layer model, it is clear why this is not realistic: few end users are able or have the time to solve the complexities of all the layers. The ideal situation is when the central IT department and end users complement each other, each focusing on their specific strengths.

We use the terms **enterprise BI** and **end-user BI** to distinguish between the two forms of analytics. **Enterprise BI** is the form of analytics built and maintained by IT. It uses large-scale server or cloud platforms and serves many users at the same time. Solutions are built in professionally managed projects that focus on data quality, availability of the platform, and well-defined processes.

End-user BI is done by business users. They have a direct need for insights in their daily job and look for fast and accessible ways to get these insights. Many of them start building their analytics solutions in Excel, but the complexity of the Excel documents leads to an ever-increasing time investment for keeping the data up to date and maintaining and extending the solution. Excel is not capable of coping with growing data volumes. To solve this, Microsoft has extended the features of Excel to turn it into a real end-user BI platform, with Power Query and Power Pivot as powerful new tools to prepare and analyze data. These tools have evolved into what is now **Power BI**.

The beauty of the Microsoft platform for analytics is that the tools for enterprise BI and end-user BI work seamlessly together. The technology underlying Power BI is a driving force behind this. In fact, it is now possible to mix the two formerly opposed sides of BI into one architecture with different levels of self-service capabilities:

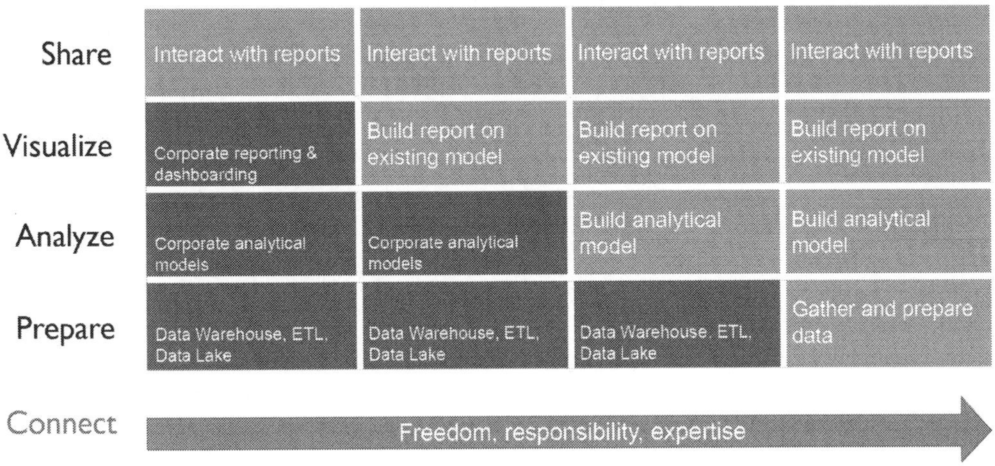

Share	Interact with reports	Interact with reports	Interact with reports	Interact with reports
Visualize	Corporate reporting & dashboarding	Build report on existing model	Build report on existing model	Build report on existing model
Analyze	Corporate analytical models	Corporate analytical models	Build analytical model	Build analytical model
Prepare	Data Warehouse, ETL, Data Lake	Data Warehouse, ETL, Data Lake	Data Warehouse, ETL, Data Lake	Gather and prepare data
Connect	Freedom, responsibility, expertise →			

Figure 1.2: The integration of enterprise and end-user BI

The Five-Layer model is a useful framework for positioning these self-service capabilities. Users who express a need for self-service BI can have that on different layers in the model. They may create their own visualizations on top of existing (corporate) analytical models; they may build their own analytical models using centrally prepared datasets; or they may gather their own data, combine that with corporate data, and create most of the solution by themselves. They may even use artifacts created by other end users to build upon.

It should be clear that when moving down in the five layers, the complexity of the work done tends to increase. Therefore, this not only requires more advanced expertise, but it also adds to the responsibility of complying with corporate guidelines and standards. Central IT or BI needs to facilitate selected end users to create their own solutions. When implemented correctly, this leads to a situation where all people in the organization benefit from insights optimally. We call this vision **collective analytics**.

Power BI offers several features that enable the implementation of collective analytics. One of these features is DAX, which is instrumental in empowering business users not only to create their own analytic solutions, but also be strongly involved in developing enterprise solutions. We will talk about the latter in the *How to approach solution development* section later in this chapter, but let us first take a look at what DAX is and where it is found in a BI solution.

Where DAX fits in, and where to find it

In an analytics solution based on the Microsoft platform, DAX is used in the Analyze layer. DAX lives inside analytical models as the formula language to define calculations and other logic. In fact, models and DAX are really two sides of the same coin: the design of the model impacts the complexity of the DAX code, and your skills in DAX determine your model designs (we will elaborate on the core concepts of data models in *Chapter 1.2, Model Design*).

The power of DAX is in its strong data aggregation capabilities. The DAX language contains many functions and constructs for defining a variety of aggregations to generate results that lead to the insights needed. In the past, many types of aggregations could not be created directly but had to be implemented through specifically preparing data. For instance, computing a year-to-date sales total can be done in DAX with a single function, while in Excel or traditional reporting tools, separate indicators are needed to denote which sales transactions belong to the year-to-date period. The end result, while more complex to implement, is still less dynamic than the DAX solution, which provides historical year-to-date figures as well.

This means that, with DAX, the effort that goes toward data preparation is much lower than in traditional BI solutions. As the DAX syntax and many core concepts are similar to those in Excel, the DAX language is relatively easy to learn for Excel users. This doesn't mean, though, that DAX is easy to *master*: when working with DAX, you will find that the complexity of the questions to be answered with DAX calculations steadily increases. And with that, you will need to create ever more sophisticated DAX code. This book will give you many examples of advanced applications of DAX, which will hopefully help you solve your DAX problems.

All core Microsoft data products now offer the capability to build an analytical model including DAX. It is confusing, however, that in each product the naming of the model is different. Below, we give an overview of models and DAX in different Microsoft products.

Excel

Since version 2010, Microsoft Excel offers analytical data modeling capabilities in the form of **Power Pivot**. Power Pivot, also called a **Data Model** in Excel, is the analytical model based on DAX.

Power BI

The shining star in the Microsoft data platform is Power BI. It was introduced first as an add-on to Office 365 but was turned into a separate service in 2015. The analytical model in Power BI is called a **Power BI dataset**, or a **dataset** for short, and is the home for DAX.

Power BI datasets and other Power BI artifacts are run within the Power BI cloud service accessible through the Power BI website, `powerbi.com`. Some other access points to the Power BI service are available, like the Power BI mobile app, Microsoft Teams, and even custom applications through a special version of the Power BI service called Power BI Embedded. Alternatively, Power BI Report Server is server software designed for customers that cannot or do not want to use the cloud service.

SQL Server Analysis Services

Microsoft's data server platform, SQL Server, contains an analytics component called **Analysis Services (SSAS)**. Starting as OLAP Services around the millennium, SSAS has been a classical OLAP (for *Online Analytical Processing*) server for years and is now called **Multidimensional**. With SQL Server 2012, a second flavor of analytical capabilities was introduced, called **Tabular**, which is the analytical model based on DAX.

You may wonder about the differences between the two technologies in SSAS. This is not the book for going deep into all the details here, but the most fundamental thing is that SSAS Multidimensional is based on "classical" relational database technology. This technology is not designed to aggregate and perform calculations on large amounts of data, and a Multidimensional model, or cube, simply performs all these calculations beforehand during model processing. The effect of this is that a Multidimensional model is far less flexible and dynamic than a Tabular model, simply because all aggregation levels and calculation results are computed during model processing. On the contrary, the power of DAX is being able to perform calculations on the fly, meaning a much more dynamic analytics experience, as a report designer is not restricted by aggregation levels implemented by the model designer.

Azure Analysis Services

Azure Analysis Services (AAS) is a fully managed analytics cloud service based on the same Tabular engine as SSAS. The difference, obviously, is that AAS runs in the cloud. The result is that your organization doesn't have to worry about the maintenance of the hardware and databases. It is also a flexible solution, since the resources can be scaled to meet the needs of the moment.

The analytical model with DAX clearly exists under many different names: Power Pivot, Data Model, dataset, or Tabular model.
This poses a challenge for this book when we need to refer to the analytical model. As our primary focus is on Power BI, we will use the term **Power BI model** throughout this book, or simply **model** when there is no risk of confusion. The term "analytical model" is used only for the conceptual model in the Five-Layer model.

Tools to develop models and DAX

You have multiple options to choose from as your tool to work with DAX, depending on the target platform for the model:

- For a Power Pivot model, you use Excel with the Power Pivot add-on.
- For a Power BI dataset, you use Power BI Desktop.

It is interesting to note that there are in fact three versions of Power BI Desktop. One can be downloaded from the Power BI website, `powerbi.com`. The second is installed from the Windows Store and is automatically updated just like any other app from the store. When you realize that Power BI Desktop gets a new release nearly every month, these automatic updates are a real plus, although it can sometimes be annoying when a new release changes things you do not expect. If you want to, you can install both versions on the same computer. The third version of Power BI Desktop, which can be downloaded from the Power BI website as well, is a special edition for use with Power BI Report Server.

- For a Tabular model in SSAS or AAS, you use Visual Studio, which offers many features for professional development, like integration with version control systems, scripting, and compatibility.
- For a Power BI dataset in Power BI Premium, you can choose between Power BI Desktop and Visual Studio. This is possible through the XMLA endpoint, a technique implemented in Power BI Premium that gives a Power BI dataset the exact same outside appearance as a Tabular model.
- In addition, there are several community-based tools available like Tabular Editor and DAX Studio. These can even be integrated into Power BI Desktop.

For this book, we choose to use "plain" Power BI Desktop, as this is a free app that you probably already have. Every reader of this book can easily download Power BI Desktop and use the example files provided in the book's GitHub repository at `https://github.com/PacktPublishing/Extreme-DAX`.

Powered by DAX: visual, interactive reports

In discussing the Five-Layer model, we already briefly touched upon the importance of visual reporting. But effective visual reporting is only possible through the power of DAX-based models.

Creating visual output is paramount to generating real insights versus a lot of information only. Just take the example below:

SKU	Sales_Invoiced	Sales_Ordered	Costs_Invoiced	Costs_Ordered
Plain Z-block ZZ9-Y28437			14,392	7,000
Plain Z-block ZZ9-U28242		7,789	7,158	3,579
Plain Z-block ZZ9-T26881	397,505	20,000	26,963	13,482
Plain Z-block ZZ9-S64558	397,505	5,000	6,741	3,370
Plain Z-block ZZ9-R40552		0		
Plain Z-block ZZ8-Y18897	14,638	0	0	0
Plain Z-block ZZ8-U88875		0	26,167	12,727
Plain Z-block ZZ8-T61179		0	0	0
Plain Z-block ZZ8-S36266	102,555	21,848	33,041	16,802
Plain Z-block ZZ7-Y20451	60,877	11,470	48,411	23,504
Plain Z-block ZZ7-U37943	2,316,010	18,893	0	0
Plain Z-block ZZ7-T56946	373,786	53,481	141,109	70,711
Plain Z-block ZZ7-S23177	4,165,307	0	0	0
Plain Z-block ZZ7-R27880	603,548	107,124	379,770	188,075
Plain Z-block ZZ6-Y64561	70,576	17,396	69,854	34,748
Plain Z-block ZZ6-U54228	6,082,221	643,833	1,112,547	555,126
Plain Z-block ZZ6-T77239	3,167,617	302,802	729,264	370,290
Plain Z-block ZZ6-S11071	3,740,085	211,956	474,656	222,601
Plain Z-block ZZ6-R61826	225,502	0	0	0
Total	**392,931,619**	**413,196,311**	**614,578,321**	**312,851,914**

Figure 1.3: Some sales data in a table visual

Can you spot the problem or opportunity this company has? If so, you are very good at numbers! Most people, though, are much more visually inclined. The picture below provides the same insight in a visual way:

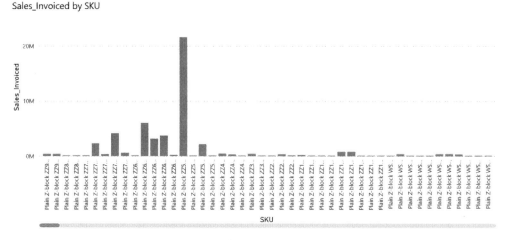

Figure 1.4: The same sales data presented more visually

It is obvious now that one of the SKUs is doing significantly better than the others. That is an interesting and valuable insight: if we can make the other SKUs reach the same performance, the overall results of the company will dramatically improve. This insight also leads to something else: you want to know what it is about this SKU that makes it so great. Is there a single large customer that ordered this SKU? Are there specific geographies where the SKU is sold? And what about the margin on this SKU; perhaps it sells well because we priced it too low?

This is a fundamental cause-and-effect that happens all the time when you create deep insights through visual reports. Insights lead to new questions. The answers to these questions are new insights, which, in turn, lead to other questions.

How can this effect be addressed? The traditional way has been to provide as much information as possible in a single report. The reason for this was that it takes time to render a report. Power BI approaches this in a fundamentally different way, made possible by the power of DAX, by adding *interaction* to reports:

Figure 1.5: The Visualize-Interact cycle

Interaction allows the consumer of a report to dig into the initial insights and find the answers to their follow-up questions, making the move from straightforward reporting to analyzing in an organic way. For this to work, the report needs to be able to provide new visualizations in the blink of an eye. For a Power BI visual report, which retrieves all content from a Power BI model, this means that the model must be equally fast in providing results to the report. The performance of the model is a result of its structure and the DAX code that you implement. So, there is a direct link between your DAX code and the user experience of your reports!

How to approach solution development

Power BI models and DAX enable a different way to develop BI solutions with much deeper involvement from businesspeople. This leads to solutions that deliver insights that optimally add value to the business.

The traditional, IT-centric way to create BI solutions is to start with connecting to data sources and preparing data. At first glance, this sounds like the right thing to do; after all, we need good data to have good and valuable insights.

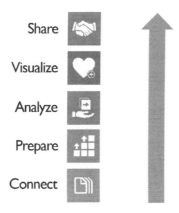

Figure 1.6: The traditional BI solution development approach

This approach is typically materialized in the development of an enterprise data warehouse. The idea behind having a data warehouse is to store all of the organization's data in a single place, and to use that as the foundation for all reporting.

It should be clear that this can be a major undertaking, as organizations have many different systems, with lots of different data in them. The data warehouse is traditionally implemented as a relational database system, which means that all of the enterprise data must fit in the database structure, or schema, of the data warehouse.

The variety of data causes the schema of a data warehouse to be highly complex. Moreover, whenever a source system changes, or a new system is introduced, the data in the new system must match the schema of the data warehouse, or the data warehouse must be changed to accommodate the new data. As a consequence, data warehouse projects are notorious for their duration and high costs. Many careers are built on data warehouses and, unfortunately, many careers have been broken on them as well.

There is a more fundamental flaw in the traditional approach. By starting with source systems and working upward through the Five-Layer model, you miss the invaluable business context about the insights that are actually needed. Even while most data warehouse projects aim to include business needs and contexts in the process, in reality, the business fades into the background in many, and perhaps most, projects that are approached this way. The technical complexity is just too much to let the business be involved deeply. Often, the result is that when the data warehouse is finally finished (or rather, taken into production for the first time), it is already behind the real business needs of that moment.

While waiting for the corporate reports to be available, the organization has already deployed a "shadow IT" tactic to retrieve the insights needed. People take any tool at hand (usually Excel) and any data that they can put their hands on, and build analytics solutions themselves. While this is a solution to a problem – the urgent need for insights – it doesn't help the organization in the long run. The quality of the data, and therefore the validity of the insights generated, remains questionable. The risk of making incorrect decisions based on these insights is high.

Using Power BI models to accelerate BI solution development

Instead of the approach described above, Power BI enables working both upward and downward through the Five-Layer model.

Figure 1.6: The solution development approach Power BI enables

With this approach, we use Power BI not only as the target platform for the solution, but also as a tool to streamline the project itself. By doing this, you leverage the specific capabilities of Power BI: fast creation of reports providing tangible insights, based on wherever the data is. The nature of Power BI models and DAX is foundational for these capabilities.

The approach is based on two basic principles:

1. We do not know exactly what we need
2. Our data is not correct

The consequence of these principles is that it is impossible to get it right the first time. Rather, you should deploy an iterative way of working to fail fast and improve fast.

We do not know exactly what we need

This principle means that you do not expect the business owner, or yourself for that matter, to be able to provide correct specifications for the reports. If you have ever undertaken a BI project, you will recognize this. Even those who claim they know exactly how things should be will overlook some details.

Even if they do not, there will be a misunderstanding in how to implement the specifications in the solution, if only because the person developing the solution does not have the same business context.

As a consequence, it is not effective to spend a lot of time gathering requirements or writing down specifications and getting them approved. You just know that the first report will be wrong, so the better way is to do it wrong as fast as possible. As it turns out, it is much easier to point out the errors and flaws in something that actually exists than to write down all the details in an abstract way.

You can formalize this approach by working in multiple iterations with a joint session at the end to show prototypes and gather feedback. (We like to call these *business design sessions* to highlight the nature of them: they are not feedback sessions or demos, but joint efforts to achieve the right results.) Depending on your skills in Power BI and DAX, you can take two or more days to work on a prototype. The results of a business design session are taken as input for the next iteration.

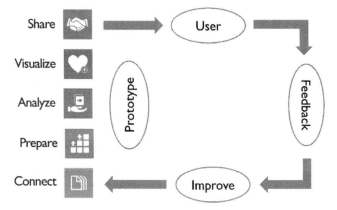

Figure 1.7: Iterative requirements capturing

The result of this is a report that is truly jointly developed and optimally aligned with business needs. Moreover, the report and underlying analysis model is an exact specification of the data that the lower layers in the Five-Layer model should provide.

Our data is not correct

This second principle is most probably not new to you. Of course our data is not correct! The reason for this is that real-world business processes are much messier and more complex than anyone could model.

And, when you consider that IT systems are designed with an image in mind of what a business process *should* look like, it is clear that a system to automate a business process faces a fundamental dilemma. Either the system implements a strict data quality policy, in the sense that one can only enter data that conforms to the designed processes (and therefore fails to capture each and every case in that process), or the system provides flexibility to capture all instances of the business process, and necessarily allows for data that does not fit the designed ideal flow.

The latter option is what is chosen most of the time. This means that a typical business system allows for exceptions, custom fields that users leverage to enter custom information, and different kinds of bypasses. As a consequence, data from business systems does not always conform to your expectations. And things become worse when your business data is in spreadsheets or other files!

In traditional BI solutions, messy data is hard to detect and solve. The reason is that, typically, the BI system only contains aggregated data or the technology does not support the exploration of data on a detailed level by business users. This is where Power BI comes in: the technology of Power BI models is so powerful that in many situations, data can be loaded into the model without being aggregated. The visual and interactive reports provide insights through sophisticated (DAX) aggregations, while allowing you to zoom in to the deepest levels of detail.

In an iterative approach to BI solution development, results after the first few iterations are typically full of errors. Knowledgeable businesspeople are generally capable of discovering these errors quite easily. At first, flaws in the aggregations implemented are discovered this way; but in later iterations, the quality of the data comes to light. Being able to see detailed data in a Power BI report is a huge help in driving the adoption of, and trust in, new BI solutions.

The digital transformation cycle

So far, we have focused on what is needed to go from "raw" data to insights, and the role of DAX-powered Power BI models in this process. We have seen that business value does not come from merely connecting and preparing data, but that it is the insights from visual, interactive reports that provide value.

However, no organization will get better from just staring at nice-looking reports. What really matters, of course, is what you do with the insights. In other words: you need to take action to reap the benefits of a BI solution. You will also want to measure the effects of these actions, either in an automated way or by letting users enter feedback into some kind of system. The result of that is, again, data.

This leads to a cycle of *digital transformation*, or data-driven business improvement:

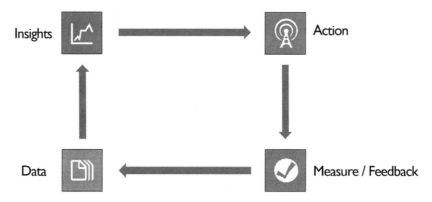

Figure 1.8: The digital transformation cycle

While Power BI shines in the process of going from data to insights, it is not designed to cover the other half of the transformation cycle. That part requires different capabilities, like facilities to enter or update data, and technology to connect systems and people.

It is for this reason that Microsoft made Power BI a part of a broader platform called the **Power Platform**. The Power Platform addresses the full digital transformation cycle with the same basic design principles: a central role for the business user, easy entry, and sheer power to cover demanding business requirements.

The Power Platform consists of three main components next to Power BI:

- **Power Apps** provides an environment to develop business applications in a low-code manner, for use on smartphones or through a web browser. These can be used to edit or add data.

- **Power Automate** allows for automating process flow between a variety of systems, services, and user-oriented applications. A flow could, for instance, be triggered by an incoming email, ask for confirmation by a business owner, and automatically update data and trigger the refresh of a Power BI model and connected reports.

- **Power Virtual Agents** offers a platform to create user-friendly interaction with the Power Platform through AI-powered chatbots. With these, a user can enter data or kick off actions through a conversation-style interaction instead of having to learn a specific app interface.

Although these are all separate components of the Power Platform, tight integration exists between them. For example, you can create a Power BI report with an embedded Power Apps app to allow users to change data in a context-aware manner, right from where the insights are. In the same way, Power Automate flows can be embedded in Power BI reports to allow for taking action based on insights.

Summary

In this chapter, we discussed the field of business intelligence and the central role of analytical models in modern BI solutions. Power BI models are ideally suited for use as such models, not least because of the power of DAX.

You have learned about two capabilities of DAX that have a profound impact on the way BI solutions can be designed and developed:

- DAX enables sophisticated calculations for a variety of aggregations of data; aggregations that, in the past, needed a lot of preparation of customized data. Therefore, DAX allows for shifting the focus from data (with all the tedious work involved) to the logic to generate business insights.

- DAX as a language is set up in a way that allows businesspeople who are mostly familiar with Excel to work on the BI solution themselves, to varying degrees. This means that much more alignment with business priorities can be achieved.

As Power BI models and DAX are two sides of the same coin, it is important to know how to balance the two to achieve optimal results. Simply put, you should do with DAX whatever DAX is particularly good at, and not solve these things in data, and vice versa, that is, not using DAX to prepare or generate data.

The next few chapters elaborate on these topics. In *Chapter 1.2, Model Design*, we discuss the dos and don'ts of designing Power BI models. *Chapter 1.3, Using DAX*, focuses on how to use DAX for best results. *Chapter 1.4, Context and Filtering*, continues on this theme, exploring the most important concepts to understand when writing DAX calculations. *Part 2* of this book contains many examples, mostly from real-life customer projects, that demonstrate the power of DAX and the balance between DAX and Power BI models.

1.2
Model Design

Being effective with DAX starts with designing a good analysis model. In this chapter, we address a number of modeling-related topics that are important to understand for strong model designs.

The topics in this chapter include:

- The way the Power BI engine stores data
- Choosing the right data types
- Relationships
- What structure to strive for in your models

To achieve good models, you will need to adapt to the appropriate way of thinking. This is a change needed both when you start working with Power BI coming from a background in Excel, and when you have a background in relational databases. When you are used to working in Excel, the concept of relationships in an analysis model specifically takes time to comprehend; but even when you have a database background, there are many things that are different as well. One of the difficulties in designing for Power BI is that the concepts seem familiar to database professionals, when in reality, they are fundamentally different. We therefore discuss many of these differences in this chapter.

Columnar data storage

The power of the Power BI model comes primarily from a smart data storage mechanism. Power BI models are, in fact, databases in the sense that they organize and store data. But the internals are very different from other database technologies you may be familiar with.

Relational databases

The traditional, corporate way of working with data is with a **relational database management system (RDBMS)** like Microsoft SQL Server. In an RDBMS, tables of data are defined with a fixed number of data columns per table. Each column must have a data type, like integer, text, or decimal number, and from this information, the RDBMS can derive how much space is needed to store a single row of data, or record, and how many rows can be stored in a disk-based data file. This concept makes an RDBMS an effective choice for applications that *process transactions*, like sales transactions from a web shop or transactions in a company's financial ledger.

The concept of an **index** in an RDBMS makes finding a specific record fast and efficient, which means that processing transactions on existing records can also be implemented effectively with an RDBMS. Tables can be linked through relationships (hence the name RDBMS), which makes sure that data in these tables are consistent; for example, an RDBMS will block the insertion of a sales transaction involving an unknown customer.

The RDBMS is a mature concept and many optimizations for it have been invented and implemented. As a result, most traditional analytics platforms rely on RDBMS technology as well. However, the needs of an analytical solution are completely different from those of a transactional system. In analytics, you are typically not interested in retrieving all data from a single row, but in retrieving data from many rows at the same time, and only from one or a few columns. To retrieve information from a single column, the RDBMS still needs to read complete rows from storage. Also, aggregating data from many rows is something an RDBMS is not designed to do and so will be relatively slow.

Figure 1.2.1 visualizes this; storing data by row (identified by the numbers) leaves no possibility of efficiently retrieving all the required column's values:

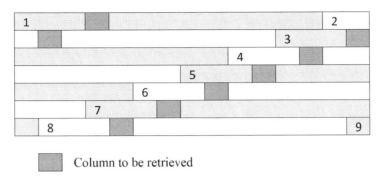

Column to be retrieved

Figure 1.2.1: Retrieving column values from row-based storage is inefficient

Columnar databases

The Power BI model transposes the concept of an RDBMS by storing data not on a per-row basis, but per column. The rationale behind this is that in an analytical solution, often only a couple of columns have to be read from storage, but for all available rows. This is most efficient when all data in the same column are stored near each other.

Another reason is that in real-life situations, many values in a single column are the same; for example, millions of sales transactions are for only thousands or tens of thousands of products. A columnar database can therefore highly compress data by only storing a specific value once and keeping track of which rows it belongs to.

The high compression rate that columnar databases achieve opens up the possibility of keeping the whole database in memory, meaning that all data resides in the internal memory of the computer or server the database runs on, instead of being stored in files on disk. Keeping data in memory accelerates data retrieval even more.

The columnar model means data aggregation is done very efficiently. Instead of, for instance, summing all separate values in a column, the columnar database engine can simply take each distinct value and multiply that by the number of rows the value appears in. In short, the Power BI model's database engine is designed from scratch to support the typical workloads that come with data analytics: handling large amounts of data with specific characteristics and performing aggregations and calculations across these.

There is, however, one caveat here: in the end, you still need to know which values in different columns go together in one row. It is not enough that product 103 has been sold; you need to know how much it was sold for, to which customer, and on what day. To enable this, the model must keep lists of pointers that keep track of which value goes in which row, for any column. The overhead from this obviously grows when more columns are added to a table. "Narrow" tables are therefore more efficient than "broad" tables in a Power BI model.

Data types and encoding

The Power BI model works with a limited number of data types. Choosing the right data type for your data is important, as it determines the way your data is stored, or *encoded*, and how efficiently the model can process your data. Below is a list of all the data types recognized by Power BI:

- **Text**: The most generic data type is Text. Virtually all data can be stored as Text. When loading data through Power Query, the generic Power Query data type Any is converted to Text in the Power BI model. This causes numerical columns to be stored as Text when you forget to explicitly make the type conversion in Power Query. (You can, of course, change the data type in the model, which will automatically add a type change step in Power Query.)

- **Whole Number**: The data type Whole Number is used, as you would guess, to store whole numbers. Because of the way the Power BI model stores and compresses data, this is one of the most efficient data types available.

- **Decimal Number**: This data type is the most versatile of the number data types. It can store almost anything, from very small to very large numbers, and with fractional values. You can store numbers with up to 15 digits.

- **Fixed Decimal Number**: The Fixed Decimal Number type, sometimes called Currency, is a data type for storing fractional number values with four decimals. You can store numbers with up to 19 digits, including the four decimals. This means that this data type has a smaller reach than the Decimal Number type. The Fixed Decimal Number type is typically used to store currency amounts, but can be used for any value that doesn't need many decimals.

- **Date/Time, Date, Time**: The Power BI model stores date and time values with a similar structure as Excel. This means that values are decimal numbers, with the whole number part representing the date, and the decimals representing the time.

The difference compared to Excel is in the base reference date: in a Power BI model, the number 1 corresponds to December 31, 1899, while in Excel, the number 1 corresponds to January 1, 1900 (both at midnight). The decimal adds the time as a fraction of a 24-hour day; for example, the value 2.5 represents January 1, 1900, at noon.

You have three choices for storing your date/time data. The Date/Time data type stores both dates and times. The Date data type stores only dates, meaning that this data type is equivalent to whole numbers. The Time data type only stores the time part, or decimals.

- **True/False**: The True/False or Boolean data type can only store two values: True and False. Though of limited use, data is stored very efficiently using this type.

- **Binary**: The Binary data type is used to store data that cannot be represented as text, like image data or documents. It is not possible to perform aggregations or calculations with this data type, but it may be used for storing images for use in reports.

Selecting the best data types for your data is paramount for an efficient model. The Power BI model aims to store the unique values in a column as efficiently as possible. We have long passed the time when we needed to care about bits and bytes when working with computers, but when designing a model, it still helps to consider the individual 0s and 1s that computers work with. The model will determine how many bits are needed to store your values; as all data is kept in memory, every bit saved helps.

As an example, suppose you have a column with whole number values between 0 and 10. In digital notation, the number 10 is represented as 1010, or 4 bits. The set of values can thus be encoded in words of 4 bits, directly representing the values. This approach is called **value encoding**. In our modern computers with 64-bit processors, using 4 bits is already much more efficient than storing the values as 64-bit numbers.

Value encoding is possible for data types that are whole numbers "under the hood": Whole Number, Date, True/False, and also Fixed Decimal. Fixed Decimal benefits from the *fixed* number of four decimals: it is basically a whole number divided by 10,000. The DAX engine is, in fact, capable of doing basic transformations before doing value encoding, like subtracting the same number from all values encountered.

Other data types cannot be directly represented as whole numbers, and the database still needs to find a way to store values in a minimum number of bits. This is done by keeping a numbered list of values and storing the numbers instead of the values. This is called **hash encoding**. Hash-encoded columns work less efficiently than value-encoded columns, as the database needs to do the translation between numbers and values each time the column is used.

It is important to keep in mind that the Power BI model chooses the best encoding given the data type and values in a column. This means that even when you use a whole number-based data type, you could still end up with hash encoding. To give an extreme example, when you have a column containing not only numbers between 0 and 10, but also the number 1,000,000, the number of bits needed to store these values directly is so much larger that the engine will decide to use hash encoding instead.

We see this happen in real projects quite regularly, in particular when it comes to storing dates. Suppose you have a table with employees, containing the date they entered the company but also the date they quit. For all current employees, the end date is of course empty; though, often, a specific future date is set instead of keeping the field empty. This is a valid approach, but if you choose a date like December 31, 9999, you will certainly lose the benefits of value encoding for your date columns. Instead, use a value that is not too far into the future, like December 31, 2029 (depending on your scenario, of course).

Relationships

One of the most misunderstood elements in Power BI models is the concept of relationships. Whether you are working with Power BI coming from an Excel background, or you have been educated in relational databases, relationships in Power BI models require an approach that is different from what you are familiar with.

Data in Excel

Let us zoom in on data in Excel first. The concept closest to a database in Excel is that of Excel tables. You could consider an Excel table as a "flat" database. This way of storing data has many disadvantages.

As an example, the figure below shows data as it may be stored in an Excel worksheet:

Full Name	Job Role	Date of Birth	Order Date	Amount
Taylor, Giuliana	Sales Manager Finance	20 May 1975	2-4-2018	120
Campbell, Aki	Business Development manager	28 October 1980	3-4-2018	244
Brown, Arun	Senior Consultant	16 February 1968	5-4-2018	3154
Stewart, Amaris	System Developer	2 May 1982	31-3-2018	355
Stewart, Amaris	System Developer	2 May 1982	8-5-2018	521
Stewart, Amaris	System Developer	2 May 1982	12-4-2018	78
Taylor, Giuliana	Consultant	20 May 1975	11-5-2018	224
Collins, Chet	Finance Manager	22 November 1965	28-3-2018	1528
Clark, Elke	Consultant	5 September 1993	9-4-2018	1205

Figure 1.2.2: A table in Excel

This table contains order amounts and dates for sales orders, which are sold by employees. There are multiple issues with flat databases:

- Clearly, all information about an employee (like job role and date of birth) is duplicated with each order sold by that employee. So, a lot of information is stored redundantly, which takes up a lot of storage space.

- Storing information multiple times increases the risk of errors in the data.

- When some attributes of an employee change, like her job role, the changes have to be put through in all rows associated with that employee.

- Things get worse when there are multiple attributes of the same kind for an entity. In our example, Giuliana seems to have two job roles. Each of Giuliana's sales orders is associated with only one job role, which may or may not make sense from a business point of view: when we aggregate sales by job role, the result for "Consultant" will only contain one of Giuliana's orders.

- One of the biggest issues arises when data is coming from multiple sources. Let's imagine that we do not only have sales data, but also targets. It takes a lot of effort to combine data from these sources into one flat table of data. In fact, Excel users spend most of their time setting up the single flat data table they need to work with pivot tables.

In Excel, there is really no workaround for these issues. That is, except when you start using Power Pivot, the Power BI model equivalent in Excel. Before discussing the Power BI approach, let's look at how data is handled in a relational database.

Data in relational databases

In a relational database, or RDBMS, the data is separated into multiple tables. Typically, these tables are associated with entities that are relevant to the organization, like Customer, Employee, Product, and others. Each row in a table has an identifier, or **key**, that allows for consistently referring to the row from other tables; for instance, in a table with sales orders, the keys for customer and product can be included instead of all the attributes for the customers and products involved:

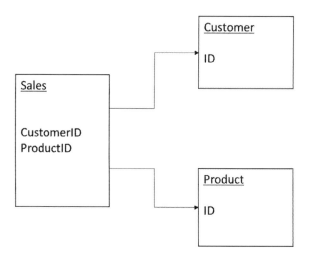

Figure 1.2.3: Relationships in an RDBMS

Obviously, it doesn't make sense to register a sales order without a customer key or with an unknown key. That is why, in an RDBMS, you can define relationships between tables to denote which columns in a table refer to the key in other tables. The RDBMS then enforces that a column on which a relationship is defined only contains known keys of the related table. It blocks the insertion or mutation of a record with a value that doesn't appear in the related table. In other words, an RDBMS relationship acts as a *constraint* on the data stored and is used to enforce *referential integrity.*

Power BI's relational model

In a Power BI model, relationships are links between tables. At first sight, they are comparable to relationships in an RDBMS but, in reality, they are fundamentally different.

The basis of a relationship in a Power BI model is a data table with a unique key. Another table with the same key values can be related to it, but in this table, the key values need not be unique. This type of relationship is called **one-to-many**, meaning that there is one table where a key appears exactly once, and another table where the same key can appear many times. You may call the column with unique keys a **primary key column**, and the column with non-unique keys a **foreign key column**, just like with relational databases.

The structure of a Power BI model, with its tables and relationships, can be viewed in a diagram view, like the one from Power BI Desktop in the figure below:

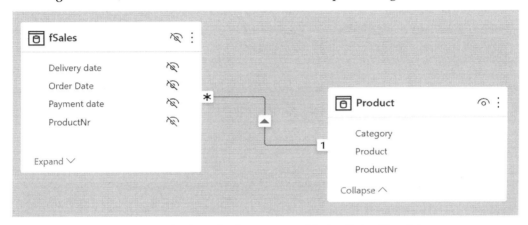

Figure 1.2.4: A relationship between two tables in a Power BI model

There are two fundamental differences between relationships in a Power BI model and relationships in an RDBMS. The first is referential integrity. While a relationship in an RDBMS acts as a constraint on the data, a relationship in Power BI does not do this. Frankly, Power BI couldn't care less whether or not your data is consistent. When the foreign key column contains values that do not appear in the primary key column, the relationship can still be defined.

The model will link each unknown foreign key value to a blank row (as in the figure below). This row will not be visible in the model but can become visible in a report.

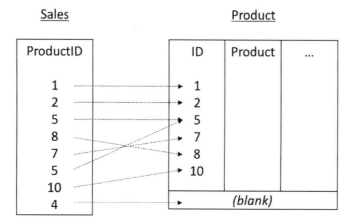

Figure 1.2.5: Unknown values are related to a blank row

One advantage of this is that you don't have to worry about the order in which data tables are loaded or refreshed, whereas in an RDBMS this is something to consider carefully. The drawback, of course, is that you have to be careful when creating relationships, specifically if you do that through dragging and dropping fields in the diagram view. Power BI will not complain when you drop a field on the wrong target, creating a relationship that doesn't make sense whatsoever.

The other fundamental difference between relationships in Power BI and in relational databases is *filter propagation*. A relationship in a Power BI model actively filters data. More specifically, when some rows in one table are selected, the related rows in the other table are automatically selected as well (in the direction of the arrow). This is a core design principle of the Power BI model, with many implications for designing DAX calculations.

In an RDBMS, a relationship does not have this behavior. When querying an RDBMS, the user must specify which tables to combine on which (primary key and foreign key) columns. This makes querying an RDBMS very flexible, but it also forces the RDBMS to do a lot of work for each query. As a result, retrieving data from many tables and therefore processing a lot of relationships can become slow.

Relationship properties

When you create a relationship between tables in a Power BI model, you can set several properties on the relationship that drives its behavior. These properties are directly related to a relationship's main purpose, filter propagation.

Active and inactive relationships

To enable relationships to do filter propagation, there must be an unambiguous connection between tables. Suppose that for a sales transaction, both the order date and the payment date are registered. When relationships exist from both columns to a Calendar table, and a row is selected in the Calendar table, it would not be clear which sales transactions should be selected: the transactions that were ordered on that date, or those that were paid, or both?

To deal with this, the Power BI model allows only one *active* relationship between two tables. This also applies when tables are connected via other tables: only a single active relationship path is allowed. In *Figure 1.2.6*, it is the relationship between the columns fSales[Order Date] and Calendar[Date]. When you define a relationship that creates a second path, that relationship is made inactive. Inactive relationships are shown in the diagram view with a dashed line.

In *Figure 1.2.6*, this will be the relationship between the columns fSales[Delivery date] and Calendar[Date] and the columns fSales[Payment date] and Calendar[Date]:

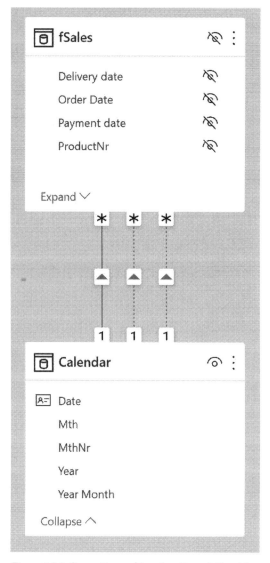

Figure 1.2.6: One active and two inactive relationships

An inactive relationship can be activated for a specific calculation using the USERELATIONSHIP DAX function.

Warning: Activating relationships with the USERELATIONSHIP function will lead to errors in DAX calculations when row-level security (RLS) is defined on the table containing the primary key. The reason for this is that security filters are propagated through relationships, just like any other filter. Inactivating the relationship that propagates the security filter and activating another relationship causes ambiguity about what should be selected.

Because of this, it is important to design your model with care, keeping in mind possible (future) security requirements. Do not overuse inactive relationships. For an in-depth exploration of securing your models, refer to *Chapter 2.1, Security with DAX*.

Cross filter direction

Filter propagation through relationships is normally done only from the primary table to the foreign table. In the diagram view, the direction of filter propagation, or cross filtering, is shown through a small arrow in the middle of the relationship line:

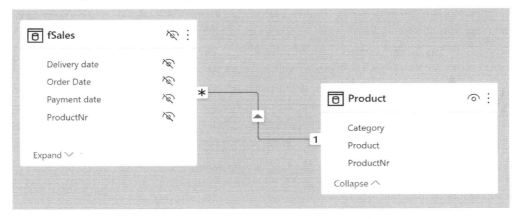

Figure 1.2.7: The cross filter direction of a relationship

It is possible to change the cross filter direction so that filter propagation happens in both directions. This is done in the **Edit relationship** dialog by setting the cross filter direction to **Both**. This may seem like a convenient setting to apply by default, but do not do this! In fact, double cross filtering relationships should be used only in specific scenarios. Try to avoid them, otherwise, or you will end up with strange behavior in reports, many inactive relationships, and highly complex DAX calculations.

One specific scenario in which to use relationships with double cross filter direction is when implementing many-to-many relationships. For instance, assume a model with customers and branch offices. Customers are serviced from one or more branch offices and, conversely, branch offices service multiple customers:

Figure 1.2.8: Customers and Branch offices

Both the Customer and Branch office tables have unique key columns, but neither of them can have a column with a foreign key: each row must be linked to multiple rows in the other table. The solution to this is to have an intermediate table with all relevant combinations of customer keys and branch office keys. Now, two relationships can be created from the combination table to the Customer and Branch office table, respectively:

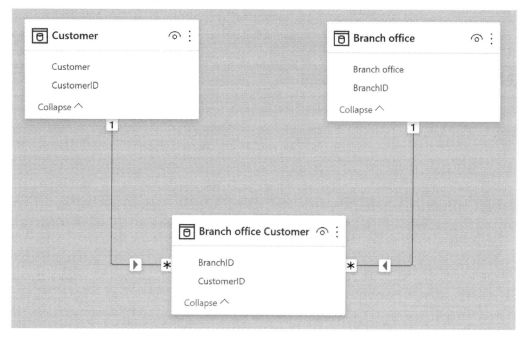

Figure 1.2.9: An intermediate table

However, the relationships do not yet correctly cross filter from Customer to Branch office and vice versa: you can select a row in the Customer table and the relationship will propagate the selection to the combination table. But this selection is not propagated to the Branch office table.

The solution is to set both relationships to the both-ways cross filter direction. Now, when selecting a row in the Customer table, the relationship propagates this selection in the default direction to the combination table and the other relationship propagates this to the Branch office table. Conversely, when selecting a row in the Branch office table, the relationship propagates the selection to the combination table and the selection is then propagated to the Customer table.

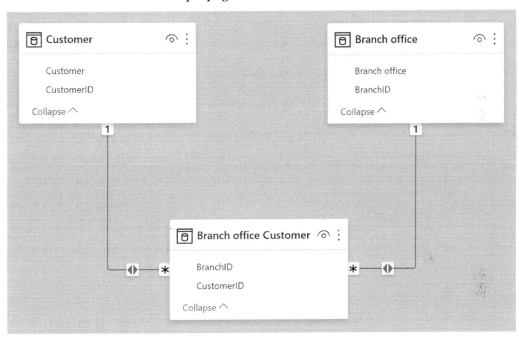

Figure 1.2.10: Implementing a many-to-many relationship through an intermediate table

The caveat here appears when you relate one of the tables, say the `Customer` table, to a table with sales transactions. Necessarily, with each sales transaction, the `Customer` key is recorded. The setup allows for selecting a customer – for instance, MegaBike – and viewing the total sales for MegaBike. However, it is not possible to view sales for MegaBike from a specific branch office: when you select a branch office, the total sales for MegaBike are returned whenever they are linked to the branch office. When you report on total sales by branch office, the MegaBike sales will be part of each branch office that MegaBike is related to.

In this scenario, the better modeling option is almost always to relate both the `Customer` and the `Branch office` tables to the sales table directly, without using the combination table to relate both tables together.

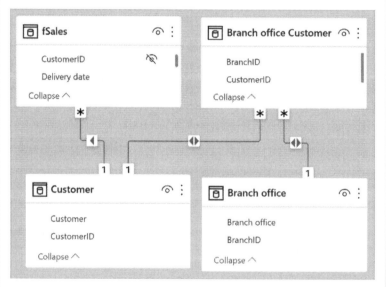

Figure 1.2.11: Using cross filtering between the Branch office Customer and Customer and Branch office tables

Cardinality

The default relationship in a model is one-to-many, with a table containing a (unique) primary key, and another table containing the same values as foreign keys, which are not unique. The official name for this relationship property is the relationship **cardinality**.

Relationships can have other cardinalities as well. A trivial one is **many-to-one**, which is really the same as one-to-many with the position of the two tables reversed.

A relationship can have **one-to-one** cardinality, meaning that the keys are unique on both sides of the relationship. One-to-one relationships have both-ways cross filter direction by default. As a consequence, the two tables act as a single table in almost all circumstances. You should avoid one-to-one relationships in your model: instead, combine the two related tables into a single table unless you have specific reasons to keep them separated (see *Chapter 2.4, Working with AutoExist,* to learn what these reasons could be).

The last option for relationship cardinality is **many-to-many**. In this case, neither of the two related tables contain unique keys. Again, you may have specific reasons to use this kind of relationship. We strongly advise against using many-to-many relationships, as these will easily lead to bad modeling. The section *RDBMS principles to avoid in Power BI models* later in this chapter elaborates on many-to-many relationships.

Effective model design

The concepts of relationships and filter propagation enable powerful analytics in Power BI models. It is important to think about the design of a model: which tables should the model contain, and which columns need to be in those tables? Which relationships are needed? In short, what is the overall structure of the model? The choices you make in model design will determine what results the model will be able to deliver.

Star schemas and snowflakes

A best practice for analytics using relational databases is to work with a specific database structure, known as a **star schema**. The basic ideas of star schemas apply to Power BI models as well.

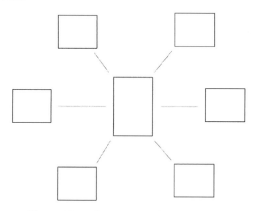

Figure 1.2.12: Generic star schema structure

The central tables in a star schema model are the **fact tables**. These tables contain things that have happened, will happen, or should happen; like sales transactions, financial ledger transactions, customer inquiries, student enrollments, sales opportunities, and others.

Through foreign key columns, the fact tables are related to tables describing different entities relating to the facts, like customers, products, cost centers, students, dates, and others. In the star schema concept, these tables are called **dimensions**; in a Power BI model, however, we prefer to call them **filter tables**, for reasons explained below.

The columns in filter tables are used to filter the results in a report, by using them as row labels in a matrix or table visual, on a chart axis, or as a slicer field. A fact table contains the data that is aggregated in the report. Each key value can appear multiple times in a fact table, corresponding to multiple facts that happened on the same day, or for the same customer, and so on.

In a pure star schema model, there are no relationships between filter tables. When filter tables are related to other filter tables, the resulting model structure is called a **snowflake**:

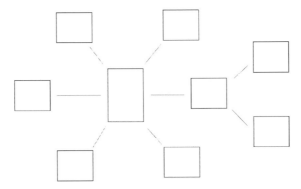

Figure 1.2.13: A snowflake schema

The issue with star schemas

Among RDBMS professionals, snowflake schemas are generally considered to be an inferior design. A lot of design effort is put into creating a pure star schema. Many Power BI consultants come from an RDBMS background and apply what they learned in relational databases to Power BI. As a consequence, you will hear "*Build a star schema!*" all the time when gathering information on Power BI modeling.

The somewhat provocative title of this section is to have a discussion about what is really important in Power BI modeling. The fact is, a Power BI model is *not a* relational database; what is confusing, however, is that many concepts and terms used look similar to the RDBMS world. This invites the Power BI model designer to apply learnings from relational databases to Power BI models. The problem is that this generally leads to suboptimal models.

It is important to realize that the concept of star schemas was developed when there was no such thing as a columnar database. An RDBMS star schema minimizes the number of joins to be solved when querying the database, which is important as relational databases tend to get into trouble when needing to join many tables at once, on a lot of rows of data. This is the typical workload of a data warehouse, which was traditionally used as the source for reporting. By "traditionally," we mean before the time of Power BI models – nowadays, the data warehouse, when available, is just the source of data for Power BI models and, in importing data to a model, hardly any join will be needed.

The question "*why a star schema?*" is typically answered in the context of "*as opposed to a normalized, transactional schema.*" Indeed, business intelligence, with its need for aggregations on many, many rows of data, is a totally different workload to transaction processing, with its need for inserting or updating individual rows of data while guarding the consistency of the data. For analytics, a star schema-based model is an absolute necessity.

Many people, however, translate this, in a rather purist way, to "*do not use a snowflake model.*" Or, put differently, each dimension table should be directly related to a fact table. While there may be reasons for this in a data warehouse that is queried directly for reporting, it cannot be stated generically for Power BI models. The technology of the Power BI model works far better with relationships and, on top of that, the compression of data is so strong that using a snowflake model does not need to be a problem. As a rule of thumb, a star schema is a good starting point when designing your model, but don't bother spending a lot of effort to avoid having a snowflake model.

Why this long exposition on star schemas versus snowflake schemas? This is because it is the primary indication of cluelessly applying traditional data warehouse ideas to Power BI. In our consultancy work, we regularly have to deal with IT departments doing this, and it takes a lot of time and effort to explain that, indeed, Power BI is fundamentally different. We deliberately use different terminology for some elements of a Power BI solution to underline the differences and to make things easier to understand for business users.

In the next section, we discuss several ways in which suboptimal Power BI solutions appear from applying traditional RDBMS and data warehouse principles.

RDBMS principles to avoid in Power BI models

In the previous section, we warned against applying learnings from the RDBMS world to Power BI models mindlessly. Below, we discuss several specific examples.

Interdependent dimensions

What is a dimension? In data warehousing, a dimension is a table containing descriptive attributes about facts stored in a fact table. The name *dimension* is derived from the concept in mathematics and physics; here, a dimension is an independent parameter that describes an object, like height or width.

This, as well as the term *multidimensional modeling* to describe the old way of doing analytics (before column store solutions existed), suggests that dimensions in a data warehouse are meant to be independent entities. We encounter a lot of data warehouse schemas, however, with dimensions that are closely related. For example, you may encounter a `Customer` dimension table as well as a Market `Segment` dimension table. If a customer can belong to multiple market segments, the dimensions are indeed independent; but in many organizations, a customer belongs to a single segment.

This is not an issue in a data warehouse, but in a Power BI model it is. Imagine you have a Power BI report with slicers for market segment and customer. Your users will rightfully expect that when they select a segment, the customer slicer will only show the customers for the segment chosen. In other words, your model needs to propagate a filter on `Market Segment` to the `Customer` table, and vice versa. With a default one-to-many relationship with a single cross filter direction, this is not going to happen; the solution is to enable both-ways cross filtering on the relationships, resulting in a model like the following:

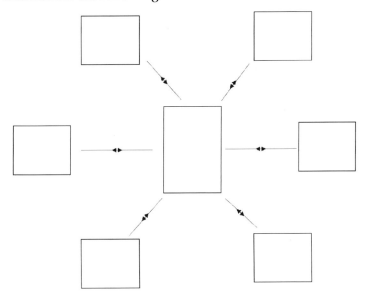

Figure 1.2.14: Interdependent dimensions require both-ways cross filtering

However, this is a severe case of bad modeling in Power BI, and you will find out why when you try to add a second fact table: it is impossible to do that while keeping all relationships active. A better design would be to cluster filter tables that belong together and let only one of them have a relationship with the fact table (with a single cross filter direction). If needed, the relationships between the filter tables in a cluster can be implemented with a double cross filter direction, as in *Figure 1.2.15*.

A big advantage of this is that multiple key columns in the fact table can be eliminated.

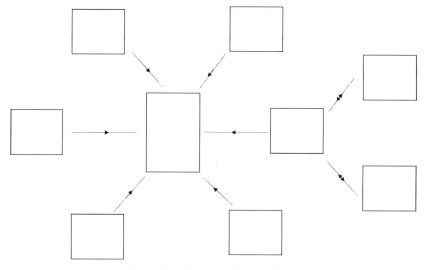

Figure 1.2.15: Clustered filter tables

 In this book, we use the name *filter table*, and not *dimension table*, for three reasons: first, to avoid the suggestion that we are doing traditional RDBMS-based modeling; second, because multiple filter tables may belong to a single cluster and thus are not independent; and third, to use a name that makes sense for the business user and better aligns with the core concept of filters in Power BI.

You could, of course, argue that the filter tables in a cluster could be combined into one large table, which would turn the model into a proper star schema. Indeed, you could, but you do not necessarily need to do this. Moreover, there are reasons to not do it: you can spend your time better by addressing business questions, you may have other fact tables with a different granularity needing to relate to one of the filter tables specifically (like a target per segment), and the entities may be more easily recognizable to business users than when combined in a single large table.

One fact table only

This one is quite basic: sometimes, we meet people who heard about the star schema requirement and interpret that as "*you should have a single fact table.*" While this would solve the problem with many double cross filter relationships, it requires a lot of work creating that single fact table, and leads to a fact table with a lot of columns. There is no problem with having multiple fact tables in your model!

Data warehouse as the single source of truth

From the discussion above, it should be clear that there is no technical necessity for Power BI to have a (relational) data warehouse in place with a thoroughly designed database schema. As the data warehouse would only serve tables of data to Power BI models, you do not really need the *schema-first* architecture of a relational data warehouse. Indeed, you could work with a simpler *data-first* architecture like a data lake.

In many situations, however, you will find that a data warehouse is available. This usually comes with the requirement that *"all business logic must be implemented in the data warehouse."* From the point of view of Power BI, this is not the best approach.

The main flaw in this policy is that a data warehouse has only one way of communicating with the outside world: in the form of data. A report typically contains data that is aggregated in either a basic or highly sophisticated way (the second part of this book is only about advanced ways of aggregating data). The fact is, many results needed in a report cannot be established by standard aggregations like a sum or average of values in a column. It is therefore impossible to implement all business logic in the data warehouse.

Many data warehouse implementations at least aspire to implement as much business logic as possible. The problem here is, again, that the data warehouse can only communicate in the form of data. This leads to fact tables with many columns, each a specific business rule or aggregation. But what you do not want to have in a Power BI model is fact tables with many columns!

Interestingly, there is a database-like technology that is capable of communicating both through data and through aggregation logic: the Power BI model!

Since it is possible to connect to Power BI datasets in DirectQuery mode, it is now possible to use a Power BI model as the central hub for data *and* aggregations, and derive other models from it. In other words: if there can be a single source of truth, it is probably a Power BI model.

Using many-to-many relationships

One thing you should definitely avoid at all costs is creating a direct relationship between two fact tables. As fact tables seldom contain columns with unique values, this relationship will be of many-to-many cardinality. (If your fact table does contain a column with unique, or nearly unique values, you should ask yourself if your model needs this column.)

Not only will such a relationship lead to unexpected results, as filter propagation is hard to track this way, but the model will struggle with performance as well. This is because there are probably far too many rows being related. The performance impact of a relationship is highly correlated with the number of unique values in the primary key, or *one* side of the relationship. Do not let this number become too big; we use a maximum of about 100,000 rows as a rule of thumb.

Another, only slightly better use case for many-to-many relationships is to relate fact tables with filter tables that have a different granularity. For instance, if your model contains a `Product` table with a `Category` column that groups multiple products, sales facts are probably stored at the product level. Targets, or sales forecasts, may be given on the level of product category. Power BI allows for creating a many-to-many relationship between the target fact table and the `Category` column in the `Product` table:

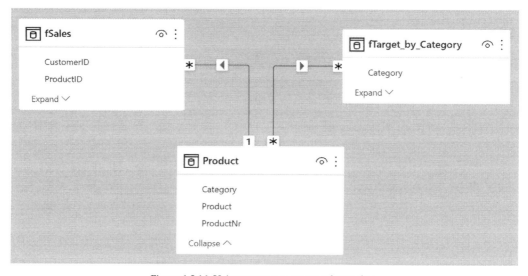

Figure 1.2.16: Using a many-to-many relationship

While this works without problems, we do prefer implementing this using an intermediate filter table containing categories as unique rows:

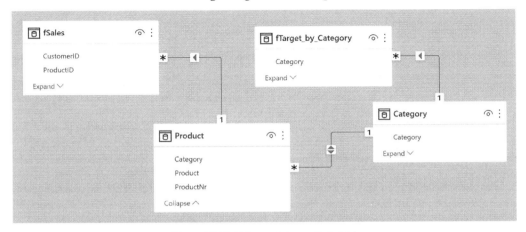

Figure 1.2.17: Using an intermediate table

By using an intermediate table, all structure is implemented through regular, one-to-many relationships that have consistent behavior and for which the DAX engine is optimized. One difference, for instance, is that many-to-many relationships do not cause a blank row to be added to the filter table when an unknown value is encountered; this can lead to unexpected results. After all, inconsistency in data is generally visible in the output of a Power BI model through blank labels, which are caused by blank rows. Without these blanks, inconsistencies remain hidden.

The use of clusters of filter tables discussed before is a natural way to deal with granularity differences in fact tables using regular relationships.

Memory and performance considerations

The design of a Power BI model highly impacts its size, and size is highly correlated with performance. In this section, we share some best practices to optimize the performance of your model, as a recapitulation of the topics discussed in this chapter. As a rule of thumb, smaller models with respect to size are faster. You can use the file size of the Power BI model as an indication; you can also get a more detailed view of size and performance by using specific community-driven tools like DAX Studio.

Keep in mind the following guidelines while designing your Power BI model:

- **Having fewer columns is better**. The Power BI model achieves a high compression rate of data due to the columnar database concept. However, it still needs to keep track of which values belong together in a row. The more columns a table has, the more overhead the model needs to know what goes where. So, keep the number of columns per table as small as possible.

  What we see a lot of people do is just load all columns of a source table into the Power BI model, out of convenience (or laziness, you could say). Take into account that it's easier to add a column when you need it than to find out which columns aren't being used and remove them later on. A model never shrinks organically!

- **Use the right data types**. Internally, the Power BI model optimizes data storage at the level of bits. All optimizations of the columnar database are based on this. It means that any data type that is not a whole number has to be treated differently using a dictionary of values. This doesn't mean that only the Whole Number data type is efficient to use; multiple data types are treated as whole numbers internally, like Date, Fixed Decimal Number, and True/False.

  The data type consideration also applies to relationships, so use one of the whole number types for relationships when possible.

- **Having many rows is no issue, but watch out for many values**. Again, due to the columnar database concept, the Power BI model can store a lot of rows efficiently. It will determine the most optimal way to store the values in a column, but more distinct values need more space. The number of unique values in a column is by far the most important thing to keep an eye on!

  Often, an obvious way to save memory is to remove unique keys in fact tables. Many transactional systems provide a unique identifier for each transaction and, when loaded, these are among the most "expensive" columns in a Power BI model. We have had cases where simply removing one unique column from the largest fact table reduced the size of the model by over 90%!

  As with data types, the number of distinct values has an impact on relationships as well. The number of primary key values of a relationship should be relatively small. If you have a relationship with hundreds of thousands or even millions of unique key values, you should be looking for a different structure in your model.

- **Avoid outliers**. In many source systems, developers use special values for denoting the planned absence of real data, or other reasons. The special values are often outliers to ensure they are not confused with real data; like "December 31, 9999". These outliers can cause the Power BI model to store a column using a dictionary as with the less efficient data types, even if the values themselves are whole number values. This is because when storing values as whole numbers, the model has to account for all possible values between the smallest and the largest value in the column, and it may be more efficient to go for a dictionary instead.

  To avoid this, leave these values blank or choose a special value that is close to the actual values.

- **Do you really need all that history?** An obvious way to have a smaller model is to load less data. We have encountered many cases in which a source system keeps a long history of data. This is especially true when using a data warehouse as a data source for the Power BI model. You may load sales transactions from the year 2000 onward, but ask yourself: who is going to analyze the sales data from before 2010 or 2015? It may be better to have a separate model for the few archeologists who want to carve out wisdom from the past, and have a richer, more elaborate model for daily use containing only a few years of history.

- **In some cases: split columns**. In extreme situations, it may be useful to split columns to end up with two columns, each having fewer distinct values. This could happen with composite keys, for example, a product code consisting of a category code and a sequence number: "A82.019". Separate category code and sequence number columns would have far fewer distinct values each and may be stored more efficiently. This approach has obvious drawbacks in more complex handling and, also, the composite column may be needed for a relationship; so only do this when you really, really need it.

Many of these considerations have more impact when the data volume of your model gets bigger. But it is good to keep them in mind even with a small model; after all, it is harder to change things when problems arise.

Summary

In this chapter, we have discussed the foundational concepts of the Power BI model. You have learned what makes a Power BI model fundamentally different from other data management products (the in-memory column store) and what the consequences are for what an optimal design looks like.

A good Power BI model has an effective structure with fact tables, filter tables, and relationships between them. Making good design choices when it comes to structure and data types, as well as carefully considering what your data looks like from the perspective of granularity, unique values, and value distribution, leads to a model that performs well. And perhaps more importantly, such a model forms a good basis for rich calculations in DAX.

In the next chapter, we will look at the ways DAX can be used in Power BI models.

1.3

Using DAX

The real power of Power BI models is in calculations using the DAX language. While many Power BI users focus on the model and try to avoid DAX entirely, anything that goes beyond simple, basic aggregations of data requires DAX calculations. And you will surely encounter the need for more sophisticated calculations in Power BI sooner rather than later. The typical way things go is that the first well-designed Power BI report leads to more and ever more complicated questions to ask about your data.

Part 2 of this book aims to give you inspiration on what can be achieved using DAX and how to approach a business problem with DAX. Before we dive into *Part 2*'s scenarios, we still have some fundamentals to cover. In this chapter, we briefly touch upon the different uses of DAX in Power BI. These uses are:

- Calculated columns
- Calculated tables
- Measures
- Security filters
- DAX queries

We also discuss how to create date tables with DAX. The chapter concludes with some general best practices for the use of DAX.

 A PBIX file with examples accompanies this chapter. The file, `1.3 Using DAX.pbix`, can be downloaded from this link: `https://github.com/PacktPublishing/Extreme-DAX/tree/main/Chapter1.3`.

Calculated columns

A **calculated column** is a column of data that is added to a table in the Power BI model by performing a DAX calculation. A basic example is to calculate the value of a sales transaction by multiplying the number of products sold by the price per product (note that column names are written between square brackets in DAX):

```
Amount = [Quantity] * [Price]
```

Below is the resulting calculated column:

CustomerID	ProductID	Price	Quantity	OrderDate	Amount
		1 Amount = [Quantity] * [Price]			
1500	503	0.07	3	12/31/2014	0.22
1938	206	6.29	12	12/31/2014	75.48
1868	206	8.16	20	12/31/2014	163.25
1836	206	3.86	20	12/31/2014	77.10
1796	206	4.67	48	12/31/2014	224.04
1826	202	36.25	18	12/31/2014	652.46
1950	202	29.12	15	12/31/2014	436.73
1904	202	28.44	11	12/31/2014	312.84
1928	203	45.55	16	12/31/2014	728.84
1808	203	31.80	67	12/31/2014	2,130.43

Figure 1.3.1: A calculated column

Calculated columns are a straightforward way to add some intelligence to the Power BI model. If you come from an Excel background, this probably has the most natural feel to it, as putting formulas in columns is the way most Excel users have learned to work in Excel. But our strong recommendation is: *DO NOT* use calculated columns, unless you have very good reasons to do so. There are a couple of reasons why:

- A calculated column creates new data, which takes up space in the model. As was discussed in the previous chapter, more columns make the model larger and slower.

- If, for whatever reason, you need to delete a table from your model and add it again in some changed way (and you will definitely find yourself in this situation at some point), you will lose all calculated columns and will have to rebuild them.

- The columns used for a calculation, like the [Quantity] and [Price] columns in the preceding example, need to stay in the model but would possibly have no other use. In the example, ask yourself what you would do with the [Price] column. Compute the average price per product, perhaps? The answer is no: the average price should be weighted by the number of products sold, so a straightforward average of the [Price] column would be incorrect. Instead, you would divide the total sales amount by the total number of products sold, and you don't need the [Price] column for that.

- The results of the calculations in a calculated column are static: they are computed only when defining the column and when the Power BI model is refreshed. This is in opposition to the dynamic nature of DAX and Power BI reports in general.

The issue with calculated columns is that, most often, the things you do with them fall into the category of data preparation, or the *Prepare* layer in the Five-Layer model discussed in *Chapter 1.1, DAX in Business Intelligence*. There are better tools for doing data preparation than the Power BI model, like Power Query. An optimal model would contain the columns [Quantity] and [Amount] in a sales transaction table, not [Price].

There are some exceptions to the rule of not using calculated columns, which you may encounter when you work on more advanced scenarios with DAX:

- Sometimes, when creating a complex DAX calculation, you will find that part of it is in fact static, in that it could indeed be implemented as a calculated column. If this is a complex calculation that needs to be done over and over again, you may gain significant performance by implementing it as a calculated column. However, you should first consider creating the column in the *Prepare* layer!

- Some calculations that should result in a model column are very hard to do in *Prepare* with, for instance, Power Query, while being straightforward using an appropriate DAX function. In this case, you would save on both development time and data refresh performance by implementing these calculations as a calculated column. This situation typically occurs when the column values needed are the result of some sophisticated aggregation. However, if you run into this situation, first ask yourself if the problem can be solved without a calculated column!

In short, you should not use a calculated column unless you have very good reasons to, as an exception.

Calculated tables

Calculated tables are comparable to calculated columns: they add data to a Power BI model, but now in the form of a complete table. To create a calculated table, you most often need special DAX table functions. You will encounter many DAX table functions in *Part 2*; for a general introduction to table functions, see *Chapter 1.4, Context and Filtering*.

To create a simple calculated table in a Power BI model, you can use the table constructor. The expression below, consisting only of a list of values between braces, creates a table with one column:

```
Example = {1, 2, 3}
```

The result of this formula is a table named `Example`, with a single column of [`Value`]:

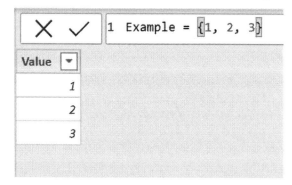

Figure 1.3.2: A calculated table made with the table constructor

Note that the table constructor does not give much control over the table that is created. The column is named `Value` and the data type of the `Value` column is derived from the values provided (which is, of course, fairly accurate most of the time). When the values provided are different types of data, a data type is chosen that can store all the values. For example:

```
Example2 = {1, 2, "3"}
```

This formula produces a table in which the `Value` column has the Text data type.

The table constructor does allow the creation of tables with multiple columns by providing lists of values by row, between parentheses:

```
Example3 = { (1, "Red"), (2, "Green"), (3, "Blue") }
```

This is the resulting table:

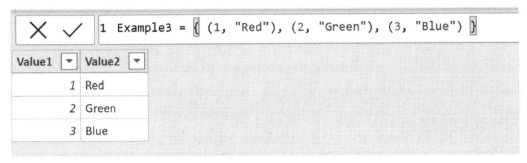

Figure 1.3.3: The table constructor with two columns

A table with properly named columns and tightly controlled data types can be obtained using the DATATABLE function. The arguments to this function are a series of pairs of column names and data types, and a list of values for the rows of the table. DATATABLE has two quirks: first, the data types have different names than the ones used in the Power BI model (INTEGER for whole number, STRING for text, and so on), and the values in one row must be contained in braces instead of parentheses like in the table constructor. The table in *Figure 1.3.3*, but with nicer names, can be constructed using DATATABLE with the formula below:

```
Example4 =
DATATABLE(
    "Number", INTEGER,
    "Color", STRING,
    {
        {1, "Red"},
        {2, "Green"},
        {3, "Blue"}
    }
)
```

Calculated tables are often used to create Date or Calendar tables in a Power BI model. These are discussed later in this chapter.

Some of the issues with calculated columns also apply to calculated tables: a calculated table increases the Power BI model's size, and you are probably doing something that is really data preparation. However, contrary to a calculated column, a calculated table is not tightly coupled to other elements of the model. When you remove columns or tables that the calculated table uses to compute, you will get an error; but adding the tables or columns again will solve this.

In general, our recommendation is to not use calculated tables when they can be taken care of in the *Prepare* layer of the Five-Layer model. When you don't have access to *Prepare* capabilities, for example, when you are working with a centrally-managed data warehouse, you can use calculated tables for tables that are not offered by the data warehouse, or that would not be practical to store in the data warehouse.

Measures

Measures, or in some earlier model versions, **calculated fields**, are without a doubt the most powerful element of Power BI models. In fact, most of the work we do on Power BI models comes down to designing and implementing DAX measures.

When using a numeric column from a fact table in a Power BI report, the column values will be aggregated. The basic aggregations available are *sum*, *average*, *minimum*, *maximum*, *count*, *distinct count*, and some statistical aggregations like *standard deviation*, *variance*, and *median*. The basic aggregations differ depending on the data type; for a Date column, for instance, you can choose *earliest* and *latest*, *count*, and *distinct count* only. When you use columns this way, the Power BI model creates an **implicit measure** in the background: an aggregation function that returns the selected aggregation of the values in the column.

In real life, many of the required insights come down to aggregations that cannot be expressed in terms of basic aggregations. Many people, both Excel users and data warehouse developers, build (calculated) columns to try to create data that will provide the results they need, while still only needing one of the basic aggregations. For example, in both Excel models and data warehouses, you may encounter an indicator that denotes whether or not a row of data falls in the "current year-to-date" category. Again, this is a static solution that will not let you, say, retrieve the year-to-date results of two months ago.

DAX allows you to define your own *custom aggregations* by writing DAX formulas to create **explicit measures**. As an example, the weighted average price discussed in the previous calculated columns section can be implemented as a DAX measure with the formula below:

```
Average Price = SUM(fSales[Amount]) / SUM(fSales[Quantity])
```

In this formula, the assumption is made that the table with sales transactions is called fSales.

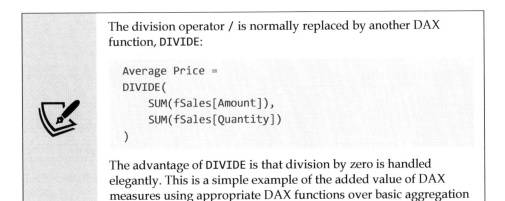

> The division operator / is normally replaced by another DAX function, DIVIDE:
>
> ```
> Average Price =
> DIVIDE(
>     SUM(fSales[Amount]),
>     SUM(fSales[Quantity])
> )
> ```
>
> The advantage of DIVIDE is that division by zero is handled elegantly. This is a simple example of the added value of DAX measures using appropriate DAX functions over basic aggregation of columns.

DAX measures should be your default option for adding intelligence to your Power BI model. A measure does not add data to the model and therefore keeps the model lean and fast. However, as the calculation is done on demand when a user views a report, it is important to put effort into creating the most efficient calculations. In *Part 2*, we focus not only on how to solve business scenarios with DAX measures, but also on how to create efficient DAX measures.

For working with DAX in general, but with DAX measures in particular, there are some fundamental concepts that are critical to understand. Among these are the concepts of DAX context, DAX filtering through context transformation, and DAX table functions. These concepts are discussed in *Chapter 1.4, Context and Filtering*.

DAX security filters

DAX can also be used for implementing security within a Power BI model. When a user retrieves a report, they will be able to see all results provided by the model through that report. In many cases, there is a need to restrict what the user sees, based on their role or identity. For instance, consider the DAX *security expression* below:

```
Customer[Region] = "Europe"
```

When set for a specific security role, this DAX security filter will cause users in that role to only see customers in the Europe region, together with data related to those customers.

Chapter 2.1 further introduces security with DAX.

DAX queries

The last way to use DAX is as a query language. You will not need this when working with Power BI visual reports, but classic, RDBMS-oriented reporting tools mostly rely on retrieving custom datasets from databases to render reports. A common data source for these is a data warehouse or other database; but a Power BI model in the form of a published Power BI dataset can be used in this way as well. Note that at the time of writing, you need to have a Power BI Premium license, either per capacity or per user, to do this.

A specific use case for DAX queries is in Power BI paginated reports. These are developed using the Power BI Report Builder (as opposed to Power BI Desktop, which is the tool for all other use cases) and can connect to a published Power BI model.

When making the connection, you need to provide a DAX query to retrieve a set of data from the Power BI model:

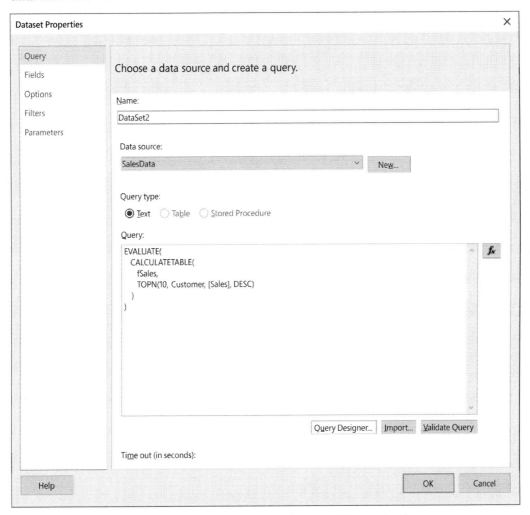

Figure 1.3.4: Writing a DAX query in the Power BI Report Builder

If you use Power Pivot in Excel, you can use DAX queries as a way to retrieve data from the Power Pivot model, as an alternative to the default pivot table output.

Like calculated tables, DAX queries need a table expression. In this case, the function EVALUATE is used to, well, evaluate the table expression and return the table. The expression below returns the complete Customer table:

```
EVALUATE( Customer )
```

In the table expression, all DAX functions can be used, including DAX measures that can be used to retrieve specific aggregated results from the model. The only restriction is that the end result of the formula must be a table.

Date tables

Most, if not all, Power BI models contain data that is related to dates. A **date table** (or calendar table, or whatever you like to call it) is therefore a common ingredient of a Power BI model. A date table has a special place in the model, because of DAX time intelligence functions (more on these in *Chapter 1.4, Context and Filtering*).

A date table must have one row per day for an uninterrupted period of time. Typically, this period should be large enough to cover all the rows in your fact tables. It is advisable to start and end the date table on year start and end, respectively. The date table must have a date column, being the unique key of the table (you may choose the name of this column yourself). Other columns in the table are attributes for each day, like year, month, quarter, weekday, and so on.

Power BI models have an **Auto date/time** feature which, when turned on, creates a hidden date table for each column in the model that has the date or date/time data type, supplemented with a year/month hierarchy.

If you have not yet done so, turn off this feature now! It is the cause of bloated models and performance problems. The value of these hidden tables, although convenient for users who do not want to bother about modeling, is non-existent for any experienced user. A Power BI report that delivers consistent results with a single selection of, say, year, needs a proper date table anyway.

Better still, in the Power BI Desktop options, turn off the **Auto date/time for new files** option to get rid of these tables forever.

Your table containing dates can be formally marked as such using the **Mark as date table** option. With this, the column containing dates is marked as the official date column:

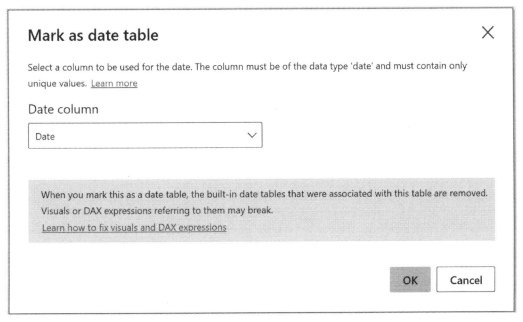

Figure 1.3.5: Marking a table as the date table

In *Chapter 1.4*, you will learn about the effects of marking a table as a date table when we discuss time intelligence functions.

Creating a date table

Technically, a date table is not different from other tables. You may have calendar data available somewhere; in this case, you can just import the date into the Power BI model. There are also ways to create a date table just from some input parameters (for instance, which years the table should span) in Power Query, which we will not cover in this book.

Here, we focus on how to create a date table as a calculated table based on a DAX formula. There are two DAX functions available that are specifically aimed at doing this: CALENDAR and CALENDARAUTO. Both functions return a one-column table containing dates.

CALENDARAUTO explores the whole model and finds the first and the last dates from any column with the Date or Datetime data type (calculated columns and columns in calculated tables excluded). The range of dates starts with the beginning of the year of the first date found and continues until the end of the year of the last date found. While this sounds convenient, you have to realize that when a model contains, for instance, birth dates or strange outliers like December 31, 2199, a huge table spanning decades or even centuries will be created.

The better option is therefore CALENDAR. This function takes two arguments, the first and last dates of the table to be created:

```
CALENDAR(
    DATE(2021, 1, 1),
    DATE(2023, 12, 31)
)
```

As the result of these functions is a single Date column, you will need to add more columns to create a proper date table. This can be done with calculated columns, but you can do it in one formula using the ADDCOLUMNS function that does just that, adding columns:

```
Date =
ADDCOLUMNS(
    CALENDAR(
        DATE(2021, 1, 1),
        DATE(2023, 12, 31)
    ),
    "Year", YEAR([Date]),
    "Month", FORMAT([Date], "mmmm", "En-US"),
    "MonthNr", MONTH([Date]),
    "Year/Month", FORMAT([Date], "yyyy-mm")
)
```

In the formula above, ADDCOLUMNS takes the result of the CALENDAR function and adds columns to it. You have to provide both a name for each column and an expression that provides the corresponding value. The formula provides a nice example of the use of the FORMAT function, which can be used to apply a variety of formats based on, in this case, a date value, while optionally providing the locale to be used as well.

The result of the formula is below:

Date	Year	Month	MonthNr	Year/Month
1/1/2021	2021	January	1	2021-01
1/2/2021	2021	January	1	2021-01
1/3/2021	2021	January	1	2021-01
1/4/2021	2021	January	1	2021-01
1/5/2021	2021	January	1	2021-01
1/6/2021	2021	January	1	2021-01
1/7/2021	2021	January	1	2021-01

Figure 1.3.6: A date table created with a DAX formula

In a real-world model, the start and end dates of the date table need to be dynamic to reflect the loading of new data. You could, for instance, find the latest date in the fSales table using MAX(fSales[OrderDate]) and use that value as the end date of the date table. You could also find the last day of the year of the last order date in the fact table using DAX. We do not elaborate on this any further here.

Best practices in DAX

When working with DAX, you will benefit from following some best practices. Applying these will help you create fast models, make it easier to maintain your models in the long term, and allow you to better support others who create Power BI reports or other output from your models.

Think in terms of DAX measures primarily

If we did not make ourselves clear enough above: your main DAX tool should be DAX measures. These are highly dynamic, do not make the model larger, and there is no calculation you cannot do through a measure.

As a rule of thumb, calculated columns and calculated tables are a no-go, until you have very good arguments for using them!

Build explicit measures

We recommend creating explicit DAX measures instead of using numeric columns from (fact) tables directly in visual reports. There are several reasons for this:

- A measure is created by the Power BI model anyway when you use a column in a report, and it is easy to do this yourself.

- An explicit measure can be given its own clear name, like `Total sales` instead of `Amount` or, in Power Pivot in Excel, `Sum of Amount`.

- The measure can also be given its own output format that is applied everywhere the measure is used. For instance, you may choose to show `Total sales` without a currency sign, without decimals, but with thousands separators. This can be a different format than the one derived from the data type.

- Explicit measures can be used as building blocks for more complex calculations (see below). Implicit measures are either not available, or are not convenient to use because they cannot be changed.

Not using numeric columns from fact tables directly has the added benefit that you do not risk using incorrect aggregations. As the `Average Price` measure discussed earlier shows, it is easy to make mistakes just by adding a column to a visual.

Use base measures as building blocks

In a DAX formula, measures can be called in order for the results of those measures to be used in the calculation. Building your set of DAX measures using basic measures (the simplest aggregations of numeric columns in fact tables) as building blocks helps to gradually create more complex calculations.

Using base measures saves you from having to think about how to calculate basic results over and over again. We see many people doing this. Moreover, base measures allow for easily adapting business logic. More often than not, some additional business logic shows up during a later stage of developing a Power BI solution. For instance, at first you may be told that *"sales is the sum of all invoice amounts."* But when the first results of the Power BI model become visible, you will hear *"oh wait, invoices of type X do not count in sales and should be excluded."* With a base measure, all you would have to do is exclude type X invoices in the base measure's formula. Without this, you would need to go over all your sales-related measures to redo the logic.

Hide model elements

You may design a Power BI model thinking that you are the only one creating the reports as well. But in practice, other people may start to use your model for building their own reports. For both them and you, it is good to hide elements of the model that would obscure the useful tables, columns, and measures:

- Foreign key columns of a relationship should be hidden: the same values are available as a primary key, which will correctly filter the other side.

- Technical (key) columns with no use for reporting should be hidden.

- We recommend hiding the fact tables: all foreign key columns should be hidden, and numeric columns should not be used directly but through explicit measures. You may have other columns in your fact tables; consider moving them to an appropriate filter table or removing them completely. (Some columns in a fact table may only be used to filter without being exposed to a user; they can stay in the fact table.)

- DAX measures that are only used as intermediate calculations for more complex DAX measures should be hidden.

Strategically hiding elements of the Power BI model will avoid confusion and reduce the number of questions that you, as the model designer, will get because "*the model doesn't work.*"

Do not mix data and measures – use measure tables instead

A DAX measure always has a **home table**, which is the table under which the measure is shown to the model designer. More importantly, it is where the report designer sees the measure in the model's **Fields** pane when creating a Power BI report. We see many people placing measures under the fact table that contains the column being aggregated. While this is doable for simple, straightforward measures, like basic aggregations, we advise against this practice for the following reasons:

- More sophisticated measures will aggregate columns from different tables, creating ambiguity around which table is the correct home table.

- More importantly, as with calculated columns, if you ever need to delete a table and recreate it, you will lose all the measures under that table.

What we do recommend is to store all measures in one or more dedicated **measure tables**. These are tables that do not contain data, but only host measures. A measure table is one of the exceptions to the "no calculated tables" rule. The simplest way to create a measure table is as a calculated table with the formula below:

```
Results = ROW("ZZ", "OK")
```

This creates a table, called Results, containing one column, ZZ, with one row of data. The value in the ZZ column in that single row is the text "OK". The single column is needed, as a table without at least one column is not a table; but when you hide that column, Power BI will recognize this as a measure table and place it at the top of the **Fields** pane. This makes measures easy to find. The column is called ZZ to have it appear at the bottom of the list of measures in the table. This column, and the value in it, are never used, so you can replace "OK" with anything you like. Below is the result:

Figure 1.3.7: A measure table in Power BI Desktop's Data view (left) and Report view (right)

You can create a measure table in Power Query as well, for instance, through the **Enter Data** option. This works the same way: hide the data column and add a measure to have the table move to the top of the **Fields** pane.

At the time of writing, though, there is a minor difference in the icon used for the measure table: when the table is imported through Power Query, a specific measure table icon is used, but when you create it as a calculated table, the generic icon for calculated tables is used:

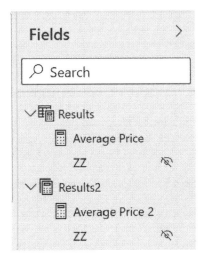

Figure 1.3.8: Calculated (top) and imported (bottom) measure tables

For complex models, you can use display folders to group measures. You can even decide to have multiple measure tables. For example, we have sometimes used a separate measure table for all basic measures that only serve as building blocks for higher-level calculations. By doing this, all building block measures can be hidden or made visible at once (you only need to hide the zz column by hand).

Table types

It is advisable to make a clear distinction between the types of tables we have discussed in this and the previous chapter. In addition to the three types already discussed, there is yet another table type, the *helper table*:

- **Fact tables** contain main data to aggregate, but no columns used in reports, and are hidden.
- **Filter tables** (or dimension tables, if you will) contain all attributes on which to filter results from the model.

- **Measure tables** contain no data, but only DAX measures, and are found at the top of the field list.

- **Helper tables** are small tables used to drive specific report behavior, like the selection of the time period reported. You will learn more about helper tables in *Chapter 2.2, Dynamically Changing Visualizations*.

You don't need to distinguish between these table types by giving them specific names. We are not a fan, for instance, of adding a `dim` prefix to a filter table name: `dimCustomer`, `dimCalendar`, and so on. This is not very friendly to users of your model, who are left to wonder what `dim` could mean. You should present elements of the Power BI model in a way that speaks for itself as much as possible. Hiding fact tables, using measure tables, and giving filter tables descriptive names creates a situation where the **Fields** pane contains available (calculated) results at the top, and all attributes to filter those results below, nicely grouped into logical sets (that you as the model designer know to be tables).

Summary

In this chapter, you have seen the different uses of DAX in Power BI models: calculated columns, calculated tables, measures, security rules, and queries. The main takeaway is that DAX measures are (or should be) the primary way of generating valuable results from a model, and indeed, for the majority of the remainder of this book we will focus on DAX measures. We have given you some best practices for working with DAX: avoid calculated columns, use explicit DAX measures, create simple DAX measures and use these as building blocks for more advanced calculations, use measure tables, and hide elements of a model that could confuse the report designer (even if that is yourself).

The next chapter deals with probably the most important concepts to understand when working with DAX: context and filtering. After that, we will be ready to explore advanced DAX business cases in *Part 2*.

1.4
Context and Filtering

The single most important concept to understand when writing DAX calculations is **context**. Context is what separates DAX, as a dynamic analysis language, from Excel functions or SQL queries – or Power Query scripts, for that matter. While all of these only return different results when the data changes (with some exceptions like when using parameters), a single DAX formula can provide many different results depending on where and how you use it: the context.

DAX context is also the key to achieving advanced results with DAX. After you have overcome typical beginner's mistakes, like not knowing what DAX functions to use, incorrect syntax, or forgetting parentheses, issues with context are the most common problem when working with DAX. We will even go as far as to state:

Every problem in DAX comes from context, and every solution is found by closely examining context.

This statement is seldom negated!

In this chapter, we discuss foundational topics surrounding context that are a necessity for understanding all the content in *Part 2* of this book. This is what this chapter covers:

- Introduction to DAX context
- DAX filtering: using CALCULATE
- Time intelligence
- Changing relationship behavior

- Table functions in DAX
- Filtering with table functions
- DAX variables

This chapter will be relatively light on examples, as the chapters of *Part 2* demonstrate all aspects of DAX context in depth.

The Power BI model

The examples in this chapter are taken from a simple Power BI model. The model consists of one fact table, fSales, with some filter tables:

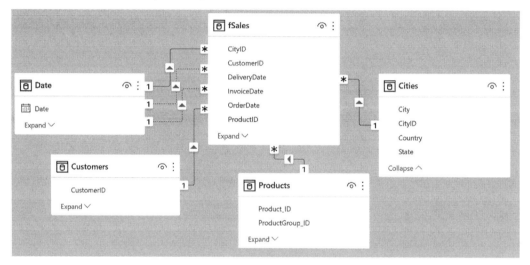

Figure 1.4.1: The sample Power BI model

 The model file for this chapter, 1.4 Context and filtering. pbix, can be downloaded from https://github.com/ PacktPublishing/Extreme-DAX/tree/main/Chapter1.4.

Introduction to DAX context

The generic term for DAX context is **evaluation context**: it is the context in which a DAX formula is evaluated, leading to a specific result. We like to distinguish between three types of context:

- Row context
- Query context
- Filter context

In most Power BI documentation and publications, only two types of context are identified: *row* and *filter context*. The term *query context* has been used in relation to Power Pivot in Excel since way before Power BI came into being (yes, we're that old), and we have kept using it. In our experience from DAX courses, distinguishing between query context and filter context helps people to understand more complex scenarios.

Let's look at each context type in more detail.

Row context

Row context is the type of context you work with when creating calculated columns. A DAX formula defining a calculated column is evaluated for each row in the table. The result of the calculation is, typically, specific to each row. The reason for this is that values in other columns from the same table can be used in the calculation; these values can be different in each row. For instance, a calculated column in the fSales table to compute margin as the difference between sales amount and costs would look like this:

```
Margin = fSales[SalesAmount] - fSales[Costs]
```

You can immediately spot that this formula is used for a calculated column by the direct reference to the columns. This can only be done within a row context, and this is what makes this context type different from other types. (In simple calculated column formulas, the fSales prefix is often omitted.)

Note that this direct reference only works for column values in the current row (the row for which the formula is currently evaluated): to retrieve values from other rows, you will need to take a completely different approach. This is a fundamental difference with calculations in Excel, where is it quite common to take a value from "*the row above this one.*" It is easy to understand why, when you realize that there is no strict order between the rows in a table in a Power BI model.

There are only a few DAX functions specifically designed to work in a row context. If the table containing the calculated column is related to another table, in each row you can retrieve the corresponding value from a column in the other table using the RELATED function. The formula below leverages a relationship between the fSales[OrderDate] and Date[Date] columns to retrieve the year for each row:

```
Year = RELATED('Date'[Year])
```

The result is a Year column in the fSales table:

OrderDate	ProductID	UnitAmount	SalesAmount	Year
12/21/2020	215	25	222.50	2020
12/21/2020	215	38	1,623.38	2020
12/21/2020	215	14	149.52	2020
12/21/2020	215	12	576.73	2020
12/21/2020	215	2	42.72	2020
12/21/2020	215	8	85.44	2020
12/21/2020	215	11	411.18	2020
12/21/2020	215	15	320.40	2020
12/21/2020	215	50	801.01	2020

Figure 1.4.2: Adding a Year calculated column (some columns removed for readability)

There is one restriction required for RELATED to work: the relationship must have unique values in the "other" table – in this example, the Date table. After all, the formula must result in a single value.

When the cardinality of the relationship is reversed, you can use the RELATEDTABLE function. For example, if you wanted to add a calculated column to the Date table with the number of sales transactions on each day, the formula below would do the trick:

```
Number of Transactions = COUNTROWS(RELATEDTABLE(fSales))
```

The RELATEDTABLE above results, for each row in Date, in the set of rows in fSales that are related to that row. As this is a table, it cannot be used directly as values in the calculated column; in this case, we use COUNTROWS to simply count the number of rows in that table.

Although RELATEDTABLE is meant for use in a row context, it is fundamentally different from RELATED in that it uses a different context type under the hood.

 As discussed in *Chapter 1.3, Using DAX*, we discourage the use of calculated columns. This does not mean that you will not have to deal with row context. Row context plays an important role in DAX table functions as well. More on that later in this chapter.

We'll move on to the other context types now. There are some peculiarities about row context that can be made clear after we have discussed query and filter context.

Query context

You work with query context when you use DAX measures. Like row context before, query context is what makes a DAX measure return a specific result. The difference, of course, is that we are not working within a single table. In short, query context refers to the set of rows in a Power BI model that are selected and over which the DAX formula is evaluated. It helps to distinguish between two separate, although closely related, elements in query context:

- A **selection** refers to the set of rows in each table in the model that are selected in a specific context.
- **Filters** are what cause rows to be selected.

In a query context, the filters come from elements in a (Power BI) report. These come in various sorts: slicers, filters in the filter pane, labels in a visual, or selected items in another visual. Each of these forms a specific rule on a column; for instance, in the figure below, the slicer induces a filter on the Year column: *Year equals 2019*. There can be many filters on different columns, and there may even be multiple filters on the same column. Together, the filters determine which rows are selected in each table: all rows that satisfy every filter rule.

 There is a thorough discussion of visual filters in *Chapter 2.4, Working with AutoExist*.

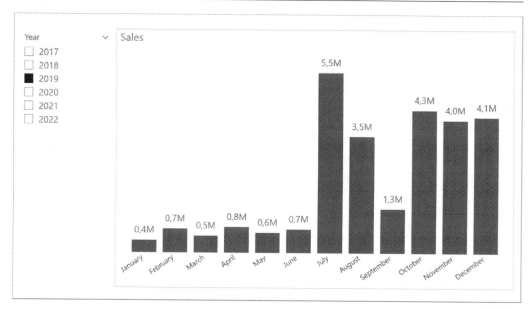

Figure 1.4.3: A simple Power BI report

In a query context, relationships between tables play an important role: that of *filter propagation*. This means that a filter on a column in one table is propagated by the relationship to the other table, in the relationship's crossfilter direction:

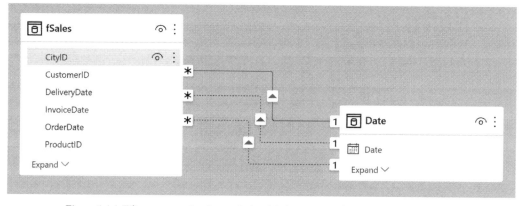

Figure 1.4.4: Filter propagation by a relationship happens in the direction of the arrow

Strictly speaking, it is not the filter itself that is propagated, but rather the effects of the filter: in the related table, only rows that correspond to rows that satisfy the filter rule are selected. This is, of course, exactly the behavior that is needed: when a slicer is set on the year 2019 like in *Figure 1.4.3*, we want to see results for 2019, which means that all calculations should only be done on rows in the fact table that correspond to dates in 2019.

Because of the nature of query context, you cannot directly use columns in a formula like you can in a row context. The formula below, as a measure, is not accepted by the editor:

```
Report Year = 'Date'[Year]
```

It results in an error message: **A single value for column 'Year' in table 'Date' cannot be determined**. The reason is that, conceptually, the selection could contain multiple values. This is true even when the column contains only one unique value, or when the table contains only one row.

Filter context

Filter context looks similar to query context, with one important exception: filter context is a context changed by DAX code, for example, by adding or changing filters in a query context. The central DAX function that is used for this is CALCULATE (or its sibling CALCULATETABLE). The way changing context with CALCULATE works is discussed in depth in the *DAX filtering: Using CALCULATE* section later in this chapter.

What makes filter context difficult is that you cannot determine the filters in the context from the visual, like you can with query context. Working with filter context requires a level of abstract thinking and meticulously keeping track of which filters are active in a specific situation. For the same reason, measures that create and use filter context can be confusing to the report users and should therefore be applied with care, by using self-explanatory measure names, for example.

Being able to change context opens up a plethora of possibilities not available with merely row context and query context. It allows us to obtain results that do not correspond with the query context, and that can be used to provide advanced insights, like comparing sales for a product with sales of all products, comparing this year's sales to last year's, extrapolating trends into the future, and so on. In fact, none of the scenarios discussed in *Part 2* of this book are possible without filter context.

The general approach to creating sophisticated insights with DAX can be described as follows:

1. Study the (possible) query contexts your calculation will be evaluated in.
2. Determine what filter context is needed to return the required result.
3. Determine how to go from query context to filter context.

To master DAX, you should acquaint yourself with this way of thinking, which is fundamentally different from retrieving data with SQL, programming, or doing calculations in Excel.

Detecting filters

Filters in an evaluation context cause the selection of rows in the tables of a model. When you consider the effect of this on a single column, several things can happen. It could be that no selection is made, such that all values in the column are in the context. It could also be that a subset of values is selected. This can be caused by a filter on that column, in which case we say that the column is filtered *directly*, or it can be caused by a filter on another column in the same table or a filter in another table, which is propagated by a relationship. No matter where that filter comes from, we say that the column is *indirectly* filtered or crossfiltered.

DAX contains a number of functions to detect the filters in the context and their effect. Each function takes a column reference, say column A, as an argument:

- ISFILTERED: Whether there is a filter directly on column A.
- ISCROSSFILTERED: Whether a filter on any column in the model causes a selection in column A.
- HASONEFILTER: Whether a (direct) filter on column A selects *exactly one* value.
- HASONEVALUE: Whether a filter on any column in the model causes a selection of *exactly one* value in column A.
- ISINSCOPE: Whether *exactly one* value is selected in column A, caused by a filter on column A that comes from inside the visual. This function is designed to detect the current drill-down level in a visual that allows for drill-down.

These functions can be of help if you want to investigate what the context looks like. They can also be used to implement specific DAX measure behavior, although there are pitfalls along the way. You can find some examples in *Chapter 2.1, Security with DAX*.

Comparing query and filter context to row context

Now that we have covered query and filter context, we can look at row context from a different perspective. As an example, suppose you create a calculated column in the fSales table with the formula below:

```
TotalTax = SUM(fSales[Tax])
```

You will find that in the resulting `TotalTax` column, each row contains the same value. The `SUM` function calculated the total of *all* rows in the table, even though we are in row context for a single row. To DAX beginners, this is often a surprising find. Let's look at another example, this time a calculated column in the `Date` table:

```
TotalShipping = SUM(fSales[ShippingCosts])
```

Again, you will find that same result in every row, even though there is a relationship between the `fSales` and `Date` tables. Shouldn't the relationship cause the calculation to return the total shipping costs for each day separately?

These examples teach us something about the nature of row context. The `TotalShipping` example suggests that in a row context, relationships do not propagate selections. This is a useful rule of thumb to work with, but the reality is a bit more subtle. In a row context, DAX specifically allows for using column values from the same table; outside of that, nothing is selected or filtered. In a calculated column, there are no filters on any column in the table. As a consequence, relationships have nothing to propagate. This means that when you refer to another table, like the `TotalShipping` calculation does, you work with the complete table. Even when you refer to the table which the calculated column is in, like in the `TotalTax` calculation, you are looking at all rows.

As a consequence, if you are in a row context but need a relationship to propagate, you must find a way to *change the row context to a filter context*. And for that, you must use the `CALCULATE` function.

DAX filtering: Using CALCULATE

Changing context using DAX code is one of the most powerful features of DAX. The DAX `CALCULATE` function, which is used for **context transformation**, is arguably the most important DAX function. By specifying filter expressions in `CALCULATE`, you can control the subsets of rows your formula works on. This can be done by adding or replacing filters, but also by removing filters from the context. As relationships play an important role in context by propagating filters, activating or inactivating relationships or changing their filter propagation behavior is a form of context transformation as well.

Let's start with a sample DAX measure:

```
SalesLargeUnitAmount =
CALCULATE(
    SUM(fSales[SalesAmount]),
    fSales[UnitAmount] > 25
)
```

This measure returns the sales on transactions in which more than 25 units were sold. The first argument of CALCULATE is the calculation to be performed, in this case, the sum of the SalesAmount column in fSales. All other arguments – and there can be many – are filter arguments.

> DAX allows you to write a formula without explicitly using the CALCULATE function when the calculation is in a separate measure. For instance, with a basic sales measure:
>
> ```
> Sales = SUM(fSales[SalesAmount])
> ```
>
> The sample measure we saw previously can also be rewritten as:
>
> ```
> SalesLargeUnitAmount =
>     [Sales] (fSales[UnitAmount] > 25)
> ```
>
> We advise against this syntax, as formulas using an explicit CALCULATE are more readable, especially in more complex formulas.

To understand how CALCULATE works, you should keep in mind that the function performs four basic steps in order:

1. The existing context (either row or query context, or another filter context) is changed into a filter context.
2. Existing filters, if any, on columns (or entire tables) referred to in the filter arguments are removed.
3. New filters are added.
4. The expression in the first argument is evaluated in the new filter context.

Several specific DAX functions can be used in filter arguments to change this behavior, but let us first focus on these steps, working with the SalesLargeUnitAmount measure as an example.

Step 1: Setting up a filter context

The first thing to do for CALCULATE is to create an environment in which filters can be changed. When we start in a query or filter context, we already have that environment, so there is nothing to do. So, for our SalesLargeUnitAmount measure, this step is trivial. When we start in a row context, however, the differences are huge.

The transition from row context to filter context is achieved by creating a filter on each column in the table that prescribes the value in that column to be the column's value in the current row (remember that a row context is always about a single row). The result is a filter context where the current row is selected. In addition to this, if there are relationships from this table to other tables, these relationships now have filters to propagate, and therefore we can expect subsets of rows to be selected in those other tables as well.

For example, we can change the formula for the TotalTax calculated column used earlier by wrapping it in CALCULATE (note that we use CALCULATE without any filter argument here):

```
TotalTax2 = CALCULATE(SUM(fSales[Tax]))
```

For each row, the formula changes row context into filter context. The SUM function now works on the selected rows, which is only the current row. In other words, the result is just the value of the Tax column in the row itself:

Tax	TotalTax	TotalTax2
6,011.49	4,358,171,557.25	6,011.49
4,007.66	4,358,171,557.25	4,007.66
4,293.92	4,358,171,557.25	4,293.92
858.78	4,358,171,557.25	858.78
858.78	4,358,171,557.25	858.78
858.78	4,358,171,557.25	858.78
13,454.30	4,358,171,557.25	13,454.30
13,454.30	4,358,171,557.25	13,454.30

Figure 1.4.5: The effect of CALCULATE in a calculated column

In the case of the TotalShipping calculated column, in the Date table, the same thing happens:

```
TotalShipping = CALCULATE(SUM(fSales[ShippingCosts]))
```

The row context in the Date table is transformed into a filter context that has filters on each column of the table. This time, the relationship between the fSales and Date tables can propagate the selection, causing the set of rows in fSales to be selected that correspond to the current row in Date:

Date	Year	Month	Month Name	Number of Transactions	TotalShipping
Wednesday, April 29, 2020	2020	4	April	176	207,393.42
Thursday, April 30, 2020	2020	4	April	112	109,006.97
Friday, May 1, 2020	2020	5	May	160	185,256.18
Saturday, May 2, 2020	2020	5	May	224	282,413.38
Sunday, May 3, 2020	2020	5	May	272	361,922.66
Monday, May 4, 2020	2020	5	May	192	250,798.15
Tuesday, May 5, 2020	2020	5	May	256	292,352.95
Wednesday, May 6, 2020	2020	5	May	80	104,958.11
Thursday, May 7, 2020	2020	5	May	176	178,446.53
Friday, May 8, 2020	2020	5	May	176	200,070.26

Figure 1.4.6: CALCULATE causes relationships to propagate filters

The result of adding CALCULATE is that we now have a correct TotalShipping amount per day.

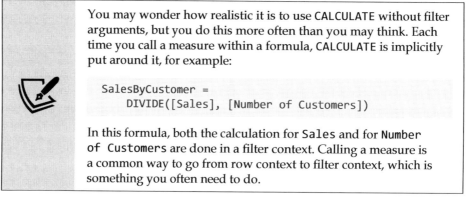

You may wonder how realistic it is to use CALCULATE without filter arguments, but you do this more often than you may think. Each time you call a measure within a formula, CALCULATE is implicitly put around it, for example:

```
SalesByCustomer =
    DIVIDE([Sales], [Number of Customers])
```

In this formula, both the calculation for Sales and for Number of Customers are done in a filter context. Calling a measure is a common way to go from row context to filter context, which is something you often need to do.

Now that the initial filter context is in place, CALCULATE can take the next step.

Step 2: Removing existing filters

The second step in the working order of CALCULATE is to remove filters from the new filter context. The process is straightforward: each column that is referenced in one of the filter arguments is checked for filters. If a filter exists on that column, it is removed.

In our example `SalesLargeUnitAmount` measure, the single filter argument is:

```
fSales[UnitAmount] > 25
```

This filter argument leads CALCULATE to remove any existing filter on the
`fSales[UnitAmount]` column.

What is sometimes forgotten is that columns that are *not* mentioned in filter
arguments keep their filters (when they exist). And as you do not have full control
over what the original context looks like, you should take care in going over the
different scenarios your measure may be used in. You may need to remove more
filters than you initially expect. You will find an example of the impact that other
filters can have after we have covered all four steps.

The behavior of CALCULATE in *step 2* can be changed by using the KEEPFILTERS
function. This function causes CALCULATE to skip *step 2* for the filter argument you
apply KEEPFILTERS to, for example:

```
SalesLargeUnitAmount KeepFilters =
CALCULATE(
    [Sales],
    KEEPFILTERS(fSales[UnitAmount] > 25)
)
```

In this formula, whenever there is an existing filter on the `UnitAmount` column, it is
kept, *and* a new filter is added in *step 3*.

Step 3: Applying new filters

The third step that is performed by CALCULATE is applying new filters. As in *step 2*,
the function goes over its filter arguments and takes these as instructions for creating
new filters. In the example, the filter argument

```
fSales[UnitAmount] > 25
```

causes a new filter to be created on the `UnitAmount` column, selecting all values larger
than 25.

In understanding CALCULATE, it is very helpful to remember that *step 2* and *step 3* are applied in that order. The order of the filter arguments themselves is irrelevant. As a simple example:

```
Sales373_374 =
CALCULATE(
    [Sales],
    Products[ProductID] = 373,
    Products[ProductID] = 374
)
```

Many beginners in DAX expect this formula to return sales for product 374, reasoning that the filter is first set on ProductID 373, and then on 374. In reality, this measure will always return blank, because two filters on ProductID are added, which require the column to equal both 373 and 374. There are no rows in the Products table that satisfy these rules and the TotalSales measure will therefore return a blank value (assuming there is a relationship propagating filters from the Products table to the fSales table).

You may consider this a trivial example; however, in a slightly different form, it fools many:

```
Sales373OrWhat =
CALCULATE(
    [Sales],
    Products[ProductID] = 373,
    ALL(Products)
)
```

Like for the previous example, the correct way to understand what happens is to realize that filters are removed for each filter argument before new filters are added. The result is sales for ProductID 373.

Step 4: Evaluating the expression to calculate

The last step in the working order for CALCULATE is easy: after setting up a filter context, removing filters, and adding new filters, the expression in the first argument can be evaluated in the new context. This is the proof of the pudding, of course, as this is where we can really see what the effect of all the context transformations is.

As an example of how filter manipulation can be tricky, take the matrix visual below.

Group	Sales373	SalesRearWheel525	Sales
⊞ **Oil filters**			**190,215,158**
⊞ **Other**			**11,497,355,884**
⊟ **Rear wheel**	**735,209,424**	**735,209,424**	**2,391,842,110**
228	735,209,424		21,543,669
239	735,209,424		1,606,503,554
373	735,209,424	735,209,424	735,209,424
466	735,209,424		5,569,759
467	735,209,424		23,015,703
⊞ **Transport**			**415,907,579**
Total	**735,209,424**	**735,209,424**	**14,495,320,732**

Figure 1.4.7: Output for example measures

In this matrix, we show information about products using the Group and ProductID columns as labels. We focus specifically on product 373 in product group Rear wheel. The name of this product, which is in the Product column, is REAR WHEEL STEEL #525. We want to be able to compare each product's sales with product 373's sales. You could think of this as product 373 being the most strategic product for our company, and we want to express each product's sales as a percentage of the sales of product 373.

To accomplish a comparison, we need a calculation that returns sales for product 373 in each row of the visual. We try this using two measures:

```
Sales373 =
CALCULATE(
    [Sales],
    Products[ProductID] = 373
)
```

As well as:

```
SalesRearWheel525 =
CALCULATE(
    [Sales],
    Products[Product] = "REAR WHEEL STEEL #525"
)
```

The Sales measure is in the visual so you can better see what is happening. In most of the rows in the visual, two filters exist in the query context: one on the Group column, and one on the ProductID column. The exceptions are the subtotal rows (with a filter on Group only) and the grand total row (with no filters).

Clearly, the two measures using CALCULATE return different results. Why this difference? As Sales373 references the ProductID column in the filter argument, any existing filter on that column is removed (*step* 2) before the new filter is added (*step* 3). On the visual's row for product 239, for instance, the filter "*ProductID equals 239*" is removed and the filter "*ProductID equals 373*" is added. As a result, the calculation returns sales for product 373.

Something else happens in the SalesRearWheel525 measure. Here, the filter argument references the Product column, so any existing filter on the Product column is removed (*step* 2). After that, the new filter is added (*step* 3). Looking at product 239 again, the query context contains filters on Group and ProductID. The measure does not remove these, but adds the new filter on the Product column. The selection in the resulting filter context is all the rows in the Product table that satisfy all three filters; in other words, no rows are selected and the result is blank, unless the three filters happen to point to the same product. This is true only for product 373 itself, which is why that is the only row in the visual that shows a result.

The same reasoning explains why the Sales373 measure does not return results in groups other than Rear wheel: when a filter on Group selects another group, the combination with ProductID 373 (the newly added filter) leads to an empty selection on the Product table.

Removing filters with ALL functions

Both measures from the previous section have the same problem, of course, depending on the context. To create a measure that always returns the sales for product 373, regardless of what selection of products is made in the query context, we must get rid of any filter that may get in the way.

It is important to have precise control over which filters are removed. To enable this, a category of DAX functions is available that we call the ALL functions. The differences between these functions are in which filters are removed:

- **ALL**: This function can take one or more column references or a table reference as arguments. It removes filters from the columns specified, or from all columns from the table referenced. If you really want to, you can use ALL without arguments to remove all filters from the entire Power BI model. Examples:

```
ALL(Cities[Country])
ALL(Cities[Country], Cities[State])
ALL(Cities)
ALL()
```

 When using ALL on a table, the columns that filters are removed from include columns in related tables. For instance, ALL(fSales) would remove filters from the Cities table as well when there is a many-to-one relationship between fSales and Cities. See also ALLCROSSFILTERED.

- **ALLEXCEPT**: This function can be used as an alternative to ALL with many column arguments. Instead of mentioning all columns you want to remove filters from, you specify a table and the columns in that table that should keep their filters. Filters from all other columns in the table are removed. Example:

  ```
  ALLEXCEPT(Cities, Cities[Country])
  ```

- **ALLNOBLANKROW**: When you use ALL, the resulting context includes all values from the specified columns. This includes values from a possible blank row that is added to the table because of an incomplete relationship (see *Chapter 1.2, Model Design*; these values are necessarily blank). If you do not want these blank values to be included in the context, you should use ALLNOBLANKROW instead of ALL. This function takes one argument, either a column or a table. Example:

  ```
  ALLNOBLANKROW(Cities[Country])
  ```

- **ALLSELECTED**: This is a special ALL function, as it is the only function that is aware of the origin of filters. ALLSELECTED removes filters, but only when these filters originate from labels within the visual where the measure is used. External filters, like those coming from slicers, page filters, or other visuals, are left untouched. This function is used to create measures that aggregate selected items within a visual, for instance, to compute a percentage that always adds up to 100% in the total for the visual. The function takes a table, one or more columns, or nothing, as arguments. Example:

  ```
  ALLSELECTED(Cities[Country])
  ```

- **ALLCROSSFILTERED**: This function was introduced for use in composite Power BI models, or models that include a mix of direct query and import tables, or different direct query connections. Relationships between tables of different origin in such a model are "weak" and do not provide the standard behavior: ALL(fSales) would not remove filters from the Cities table when fSales is a direct query table and Cities is imported. The ALLCROSSFILTERED function takes a table reference as an argument and will remove filters from both that table and related tables, even when relationships are weak. In a standard import model, you do not need to use ALLCROSSFILTERED. Example:

```
ALLCROSSFILTERED(fSales)
```

There is an alternative DAX function you can use to remove filters within a CALCULATE statement: REMOVEFILTERS. This function takes one or more columns or an entire table as an argument, for instance:

```
CALCULATE(
    [Sales],
    REMOVEFILTERS(Cities)
)
```

This function was introduced as an easier-to-understand alternative to ALL. We prefer the shorter ALL, and never use REMOVEFILTERS.

By carefully choosing one or more ALL functions, you can make CALCULATE do exactly what you want. Remember that we wanted to create a measure that always returns sales for product 373; in other words, we know exactly what we want the filter context to look like. We do not have control over what filters exist in the query context we start with, but we do have control over what filters are removed. Consider this updated measure:

```
SalesRearWheel525_ALL =
CALCULATE(
    [Sales],
    Products[Product] = "REAR WHEEL STEEL #525",
    ALL(Products)
)
```

With this formula, *any* existing filter from the Products table is removed before adding the filter on the Product column. The difference is clear:

Group	Sales373	SalesRearWheel525	SalesRearWheel525_ALL	Sales
⊞ Oil filters			735,209,424.43	190,215,158
⊞ Other			735,209,424.43	11,497,355,884
⊟ Rear wheel	735,209,424	735,209,424	735,209,424.43	2,391,842,110
228	735,209,424		735,209,424.43	21,543,669
239	735,209,424		735,209,424.43	1,606,503,554
373	735,209,424	735,209,424	735,209,424.43	735,209,424
466	735,209,424		735,209,424.43	5,569,759
467	735,209,424		735,209,424.43	23,015,703
⊞ Transport			735,209,424.43	415,907,579
Total	735,209,424	735,209,424	735,209,424.43	14,495,320,732

Figure 1.4.8: Using ALL

Not only is the result for product 373, the REAR WHEEL STEEL #525, returned for the other products, the result is even returned when the query context filters other product groups. With this, we have the essential building block for expressing any product's sales relative to product 373's sales, with a simple division:

```
Sales% = DIVIDE([Sales], [SalesRearWheel525_ALL])
```

With a combination of filter arguments and ALL functions, many powerful DAX measures can be created. Some filters are more difficult to create and specify than others, however, and among these are filters that deal with the calendar. This is why DAX contains a special category of functions for this purpose, which we discuss in the next section.

Time intelligence

There are probably hardly any Power BI models that do not include some analysis over time. We want to compare current results with those of last year, for instance. Many other calendar-related insights may also be needed, like year-to-date results, rolling totals, or growth rates from any other past period of time. The difficulty is that the Gregorian calendar is quite messy: most years have 365 days, but some have 366, and months can have anywhere between 28 and 31 days.

These calendar complexities notwithstanding, calendar-based analysis is simply about filtering to change context. Consider the year-to-date sales chart below:

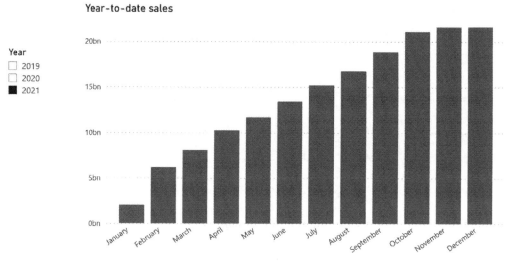

Figure 1.4.9: A year-to-date chart

By definition of year-to-date, what you see in, say, the August column, is the total sales in the period of January 1, 2021 up until August 31, 2021. However, the query context for this column contains a filter on year (2021) and month (August), causing a selection of August 1 to August 31, 2021. Clearly, the context must be transformed along the way to be able to return the year-to-date total sales.

In the calculation for year-to-date sales, you would therefore expect the use of CALCULATE with some filter arguments:

```
SalesYTD =
CALCULATE(
    [Sales],
    ... (some filter argument)
)
```

Indeed, DAX time intelligence functions implement filter arguments in CALCULATE to deal with the complexities of the calendar. The year-to-date filter is provided by the DATESYTD function:

```
SalesYTD =
CALCULATE(
    [Sales],
    DATESYTD('Date'[Date])
)
```

The DATESYTD function works on the basis of the query context on the date table. Its recipe looks like this:

1. Retrieve the last date in the context.

2. Determine the year this date falls in, and the first day of that year.

3. Create a filter on the Date[Date] column, selecting everything from the first day of the year to the last date in the context.

   With the new context, CALCULATE can do its job evaluating, in our example, the Sales measure. But wait: the DATESYTD filter argument references the Date column, but in the chart in *Figure 1.4.9*, there are filters on the Year and Month columns! This is a very common situation, and therefore, DATESYTD takes one more step:

4. Add an implicit ALL('Date') filter argument.

This last step is common to all time intelligence functions, and saves us from having to add explicit ALL functions all the time.

 The implicit ALL('Date'[Date]) clause is only added when you have formally marked your table with dates as the Power BI model's date table, or when the relationships from fact tables to your date table are created on columns with the Date data type. Although the time intelligence functions can therefore work correctly without a formal date table declaration, we strongly recommend using this declaration anyway.

As mentioned, time intelligence is a very common need. For this reason, several time intelligence functions offer shorter, easier-to-use versions as well. The DATESYTD function, used in combination with CALCULATE, can be replaced by the TOTALYTD function:

```
SalesYTD_short =
TOTALYTD(
    [Sales],
    'Date'[Date]
)
```

This formula is exactly the same, although syntactically different. While that may be an advantage, the downside is that, to many beginners in DAX, this function looks like it calculates a year-to-date *total*. In reality, the only thing TOTALYTD does is change the context. It may return a year-to-date average or year-to-date anything; it all depends on the measure or expression used as the first argument.

For the sake of completeness, it is possible to use DATESYTD and TOTALYTD for fiscal years that start at another date than January 1. DATESYTD allows for a second argument, which it should be able to derive a day in the year from, like "8/31" or "2020/9/30"; this is taken as the *last* day of the year. For reasons we have never really understood, in TOTALYTD this argument is the fourth argument, which means that you must include a third argument. This is an additional filter. You can safely use ALL('Date'[Date]) here, as that is implicitly added anyway.

Next to DATESYTD, the time intelligence functions used the most are:

- SAMEPERIODLASTYEAR: As the name says, the function takes the current context and moves it back exactly one year. This is, of course, what you need to compute year-on-year growth numbers. Surprisingly, there is no shortcut version of the function. The sales for last year could be calculated with:

```
SalesLY =
CALCULATE(
    [Sales],
    SAMEPERIODLASTYEAR('Date'[Date])
)
```

- DATESINPERIOD: This function can be used to return a period starting at (or ending on) a certain reference date, and with a specified length expressed in units of days, months, quarters, or years. This is the function you need to compute rolling totals. For example, the 12-month rolling total of sales (thus looking back 12 months) is calculated using the formula below. Here, MAX('Date'[Date]) is used to retrieve the last day in the context as the reference date:

```
SalesRollingTotal =
CALCULATE(
    [Sales],
    DATESINPERIOD(
        'Date'[Date],
        MAX('Date'[Date]),
        -12, MONTH
    )
)
```

When working with time intelligence functions, it is important to keep in mind that each time intelligence function transforms the context on the date table; nothing else. This means that any table in the model that is not related to the date table will not be impacted by this context transformation. It also means that you will get unexpected results when your date table is "short." For example, if your date table starts with the year 2020 and you use the SAMEPERIODLASTYEAR function in a context that selects dates in February 2020, the result will be an empty context on the calendar. That will lead to a blank result for the measure, even if the fact table you aggregate over does have dates in 2019 or earlier.

Changing relationship behavior

In *Chapter 1.2*, *Model Design*, you learned that there can be multiple relationships between tables, but only one of those relationships can be active. The same is true for relationship paths between tables: a Power BI model allows for only one active path between any two tables in the model. This is of course only useful if the inactive relationships can be made active if you need to. You can do this by using the function USERELATIONSHIP.

The function USERELATIONSHIP is used by including it as a filter argument in CALCULATE. This may seem surprising, but it really makes sense. A relationship between a fact table and a filter table ensures that a selection in the filter table propagates to the fact table. Activating another relationship means that that relationship now propagates the selection to the fact table, with the effect that different rows in the fact table are selected. In other words: activating another relationship means changing the context for the calculation. And changing context is what CALCULATE is for.

USERELATIONSHIP takes two arguments, which are references to the columns between which the relationship is defined that must be activated. For example, if the active relationship between the fSales and Date tables is on fSales[OrderDate], but you want to use the relationship on fSales[InvoiceDate] instead, this is the formula to do that:

```
TotalInvoiced =
CALCULATE(
    [Sales],
    USERELATIONSHIP(fSales[InvoiceDate], 'Date'[Date])
)
```

It should be clear that the meaning of the calculated results changes when you use another relationship. While the Sales measure returns the amount ordered, the TotalInvoiced measure returns the amount invoiced. The former would be used for revenue analysis, while the latter may help in cashflow analysis (in which calculations on actual payments would be a crucial addition). This depends, of course, on the business definitions in the organization of what sales actually are.

Another way of changing relationship behavior is to change the filter propagation behavior of the active relationship. The DAX function for this is CROSSFILTER, which is, again, used in a filter argument in CALCULATE.

Like USERELATIONSHIP, CROSSFILTER takes the two columns involved in a relationship as arguments. In a third argument, you can set the filter propagation direction, or cross filter type, of the relationship. There are five cross filter types that can be used:

- **OneWay**: Propagate filters in the default direction: from the table with the primary (unique) key to the table holding the foreign (non-unique) key.
- **Both**: Propagate filters in both directions.
- **None**: Do not propagate filters at all.
- **OneWay_LeftFiltersRight**: Propagate filters in one direction, from the column in the first argument to the column in the second argument.
- **OneWay_RightFiltersLeft**: Propagate filters in one direction, from the column in the second argument to the column in the first argument.

To give an example of the use of CROSSFILTER, suppose you want to know to how many states products were sold. The model contains relationships between the fSales, Cities, and Date tables:

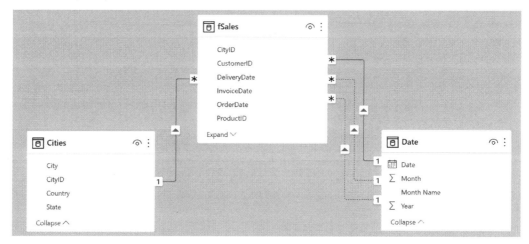

Figure 1.4.10: Model diagram for sales by city

From the model diagram, notice that we could select a month, and all sales transactions in that month would be selected through the active relationship. We cannot directly count the number of states, however: the relationship between Cities and fSales only propagates filters from Cities to fSales, while we need filter propagation in the other direction. In that case, the selected rows in the fSales table would lead to the corresponding rows in the Cities table being selected, and we could then count the number of states.

Clearly, the filter propagation direction of the relationship must be changed. The DAX formula is this:

```
StatesSoldTo =
CALCULATE(
    DISTINCTCOUNT(Cities[State]),
    CROSSFILTER(fSales[CityID], Cities[CityID], Both)
)
```

With the DISTINCTCOUNT function, we count the unique values in the State column. But before that is done, CROSSFILTER causes a selection of rows in the Cities table based on which rows are selected in the fSales table.

Table functions in DAX

There is a lot you can do with basic aggregation functions like SUM and AVERAGE, in combination with DAX filtering using CALCULATE. But the DAX language goes beyond that. This section is about table functions, which open up an ocean of more advanced calculations in DAX. In *Part 2* of this book, you will find that many of the business scenarios discussed involve DAX table functions.

Table aggregations

To start, let's look closely at a simple aggregation in DAX:

```
Sales1 = SUM(fSales[SalesAmount])
```

The SUM function in this formula traverses the fSales table and retrieves the value in the SalesAmount column from each row. All these values are summed up to provide the end result.

 Because of the special way a Power BI model encodes and stores data (see *Chapter 1.2, Model Design*), this may not be what happens technically. Logically, however, this is what SUM does, and that is what we are interested in here.

Now, suppose the SalesAmount column is a calculated column, created with the following formula:

```
SalesAmount = fSales[UnitAmount] * fSales[SalesPrice]
```

As both the UnitAmount and SalesPrice columns are in the fSales table as well, a valuable question to ask is: can we calculate sales without using the SalesAmount column? After all, we strongly prefer not to have calculated columns in the model. The calculation we are looking for should again traverse the fSales table, but instead of retrieving the value in the SalesAmount column, it should take the values from the UnitAmount and SalesPrice columns and multiply one by the other. The DAX function to use here is SUMX:

```
Sales2 =
SUMX(
    fSales,
    fSales[UnitAmount] * fSales[SalesPrice]
)
```

While the SUM function only accepts a column reference as its argument, SUMX needs to be provided with a table, fSales in the example above, and in the second argument, an expression to be calculated for each row in the table. We call SUMX a **table aggregation function**; you may also encounter the name **iterator**, as SUMX iterates over the table in its first argument.

Most basic aggregation functions have a table aggregation equivalent, like SUMX, AVERAGEX, MINX, MAXX, COUNTX, COUNTAX, PRODUCTX, and CONCATENATEX. As is obvious from this list, table aggregation functions are recognized by the X at the end of the function name. Lesser-known table aggregation functions include statistical functions like MEDIANX, PERCENTILEX, and STDEVX (the last two functions come in two flavors, which we will not elaborate on here).

A simple table aggregation function is COUNTROWS, which returns the number of rows in a table and has no non-table equivalent. The function RANKX is the table equivalent of the RANK.EQ function.

The example above is helpful if you want to eliminate calculated columns. But the real power of table aggregation functions lies in the fact that you can use any table you want as the first argument. For example, suppose you want to create a measure that returns the average sales per city. For this, the calculation should not iterate over the fSales table, which contains individual sales transactions, but over the Cities table:

```
SalesPerCity =
AVERAGEX(
    Cities,
    [Sales]
)
```

We will discuss what happens exactly in this calculation, but let us first further elaborate on the tables that can be used. Not only can any table in the model be used in a table aggregation function, but you can even create your own specific tables to work with. We call these **virtual tables** (as *calculated tables* is already taken by the Power BI model).

Using virtual tables

In the previous section, you saw a formula to calculate the average sales per city. Now, suppose we want to compute the average sales per state. With the same approach as the `SalesPerCity` measure, we would need a table with one row for each state to iterate over. This table is not readily available in the model, as `State` is just a column in the `Cities` table. We must therefore construct this table ourselves, and although in this simple case we could add a `State` table to the model (as a calculated table, for instance), the preferred way to do it is by creating a **virtual table**. This table will only exist during the evaluation of the measure.

There is a broad set of DAX functions available to create virtual tables. The general complexity of working with these functions is that their result is a table. This means that there is no standard output mechanism available to view the results, like how you can create a Power BI visual to view the results of a DAX measure. Creating a calculated table in the Power BI model with the same function could be helpful, but in any case, working with DAX table functions requires a certain level of abstract thinking.

To start with our state challenge, the function `VALUES` takes a column reference as its argument and returns a table with unique values from that column. For example:

```
VALUES(Cities[State])
```

This table expression returns a table with the unique `State` values. An equivalent function is `DISTINCT`, which also returns unique values from a column; the difference is that `DISTINCT` does not include a blank value in the blank row coming from an incomplete relationship (see *Figure 1.2.5* in *Chapter 1.2, Model Design*). It is up to you to decide whether or not that blank value should be in the result.

The formula for sales per state is:

```
SalesPerState =
AVERAGEX(
    VALUES(Cities[State]),
    [Sales]
)
```

There is a whole group of DAX functions returning tables, which we will not list here comprehensively. The most commonly used functions are below:

- SUMMARIZE: Although this is a very versatile and complex function that is able to generate complete pivot table-like results, this is not the way SUMMARIZE is used within DAX measures. This function is very useful as an extension to VALUES: while VALUES returns the unique values in one column, SUMMARIZE can return the unique combinations of values in more than one column. For example, the unique combinations of CityID and ProductID values from the fSales table can be retrieved with the following (note that you have to provide the table itself in the first argument):

  ```
  SUMMARIZE(fSales, fSales[CityID], fSales[ProductID])
  ```

- FILTER: This function has two arguments: the first is a table (either an existing table in the model or the result of another table function), and the second is an expression that is evaluated for each row in the table. The expression should result in either true or false, and FILTER includes only the "true" rows in the result. For instance, the expression below returns cities in Germany:

  ```
  FILTER(Cities, Cities[Country] = "Germany")
  ```

- TOPN: Like FILTER, TOPN returns a subset of the rows of a table. The highest, or lowest, rows of a table are returned, based on some criteria. You provide the number of rows, the table from which to take the rows, the value on which to rank each row, and whether you want them to be sorted from high to low or low to high. For instance, to create a table with the 15 customers that have the highest sales:

  ```
  TOPN(15, Customers, [Sales], DESC)
  ```

- CROSSJOIN: These functions create a single table from two input tables. CROSSJOIN returns a table that simply contains a row for each combination of rows from the input tables. The example below returns a table with all combinations of products and cities, containing all the columns from the Cities and Products tables:

  ```
  CROSSJOIN(Cities, Products)
  ```

- GENERATE: Like CROSSJOIN, this function returns a table that is a combination of input tables. In this case, the second argument is a table expression that is evaluated for each row in the table in the first argument. If this expression happens to return an empty table for a specific row, that row is not included in the result. Alternatively, you can use GENERATEALL, which does include such a row, but with blank values in the columns of the table expression. For example, the expression below returns a table with cities and products that have been sold to customers in those cities, again including all the columns from the Cities and Products tables:

```
GENERATE(Cities, FILTER(Products, [Sales] > 0))
```

You will encounter a few other table functions in *Part 2*, which we will introduce when we need them.

Context in table functions

The GENERATE example above may be intuitively clear, but if you look closer, it is really a quite complicated example. To understand what an expression like this one does, it is important to know how DAX context works in table functions. Let's use the GENERATE example in a complete measure formula:

```
AvgUnitAmount1 =
AVERAGEX(
    GENERATE(
        Cities,
        FILTER(
            Products,
            [Sales] > 10000
        )
    ),
    AVERAGE(fSales[UnitAmount])
)
```

The purpose of this measure is to calculate the average number of products sold per sales transaction (the UnitAmount) for all sales transactions on products in cities where those products sold more than 10,000. Can you spot the errors in this formula?

When we use this measure in a Power BI visual, it is evaluated in a query context. This context can be anything; it may contain one or more filters on columns in the Power BI model.

The AVERAGEX function has two arguments, and these arguments are themselves evaluated in different contexts:

- The first argument, a table expression, is evaluated in the same context as the AVERAGEX function itself.

- The second argument, a scalar expression, is evaluated *in row context* for every row in the table in the first argument.

You may have already noticed this from the Sales2 measure discussed earlier, which uses direct column references in the second argument of SUMX. The row context here provides the possibility of directly using columns in the table to calculate with. In fact, the row context is stacked on top of the query context, while in the row context in a calculated column, there are no filters at all; in this case, the filters from the query context are still there.

Common errors made when using virtual tables are related to row context in table aggregation functions. A simple example is below:

```
ThisDoesntWork =
SUMX(
    VALUES(fSales[UnitAmount]),
    fSales[Tax]
)
```

While this formula uses two columns from the fSales table, the Tax column cannot be directly referenced as the row context is not in the fSales table, but in the result of the VALUES function. This result is a table with only one column, fSales[UnitAmount]; only this column can be used directly.

The table functions FILTER, TOPN, and GENERATE discussed above work in the same way: the table argument is evaluated in the context in which the function is called; the other argument is evaluated in a row context. In the case of GENERATE, this means that we have a table expression evaluated in a row context.

For the formula for AvgUnitAmount1 above, we have a whole stack of contexts that come into play. Let's break them down step by step:

1. AVERAGEX: Evaluated in query context.

2. GENERATE: Evaluated in the same context as AVERAGEX.

3. Cities: Still evaluated in the same context.

4. FILTER: Evaluated in row context in the Cities table.

5. Products: Evaluated in the same context as FILTER.

6. [Sales]: As this is a call to another measure, an implicit CALCULATE causes a filter context to be created. For each call, we are at one row in Cities and one row in Products. In the filter context, filters on each column in the Cities and Products tables are added. The result is thus the sales for that product, in that city.

7. AVERAGE: This is evaluated in row context in the table returned by GENERATE, which is a subset of combinations of cities and products.

So where is the error in this formula?

It is in the last step: although this step is evaluated for the correct combinations of cities and products, it is evaluated in row context. This means that only the filters already present in the query context have an impact on the AVERAGE calculation. The current city and product do not impact the calculation, as there are no (additional) filters on the Cities and Products tables to select the current city and product. The way to solve this problem is to turn the row context into a filter context, just like what was done in *step 6*. We can do this by adding CALCULATE:

```
AvgUnitAmount2 =
AVERAGEX(
    GENERATE(
        Cities,
        FILTER(
            Products,
            [Sales] > 10000
        )
    ),
    CALCULATE(AVERAGE(fSales[UnitAmount]))
)
```

> In most cases, it would be better to put the average unit amount calculation in a separate measure, as this will probably be needed elsewhere. You then have to write the logic of the calculation only once, and the call to this measure would take care of the row context transition automatically.

In designing more complex measures in DAX, it is crucial to meticulously keep track of context and context transformations.

There is another, mathematical error in this formula: we calculate the average over the city/product combinations of the average unit amount. This is not necessarily equal to the average unit amount of all sales transactions for these city/product combinations. To solve this, we need to use a different approach; but let us focus on performance first.

Performance considerations using table functions

There are a couple of things to keep in mind when using virtual tables in DAX. The overall goal is always to provide results as fast as possible, so performance should always be a consideration.

First, it is important to realize that virtual tables need to be constructed in memory by the DAX engine. This means that the larger the virtual table, the more memory is needed and the higher the risk of lower performance. You may even run into **Not enough memory to perform this calculation** errors. For this reason, you should ask yourself whether the table you use could be made smaller: specifically, do you need all the columns included in the table?

In the AvgUnitAmount2 measure above, this is clearly not the case. The virtual table created by GENERATE contains all columns from both the Cities and the Products table. But for the result of the calculation, only the unique keys in the tables are really needed: they determine which rows in fSales are selected, and thus determine the value of the Sales measure. An optimized version would be:

```
AvgUnitAmount3 =
AVERAGEX(
    GENERATE(
        VALUES(Cities[CityID]),
        FILTER(
            VALUES(Products[ProductID]),
            [Sales] > 10000
        )
    ),
    CALCULATE(AVERAGE(fSales[UnitAmount]))
)
```

The second thing to consider is the number of rows in the virtual table. While this is obviously also a factor in the total size of the table, it determines the number of iterations in a table aggregation as well.

For instance, if the purchasing price of a product is stored in the `Products` table, you could calculate the total purchasing amount based on the `fSales` table:

```
TotalPurchased1 =
SUMX(
    fSales,
    fSales[UnitAmount] * RELATED(Products[PurchasePrice])
)
```

Instead, you could optimize the number of iterations by letting `SUMX` iterate over the `Products` table instead of the `fSales` table. Or even better, iterate over the unique `PurchasePrice` values:

```
TotalPurchased2 =
SUMX(
    VALUES(Products[PurchasePrice]),
    Products[PurchasePrice] * CALCULATE(SUM(fSales[UnitAmount]))
)
```

In this variant, all transactions corresponding to a `PurchasePrice` value are aggregated at once. Mind the `CALCULATE` here to go from row context to filter context and filter the correct sales transactions.

Memory usage and the number of iterations is a reason why the `CROSSJOIN` function is often not an attractive function to use in DAX measures. The number of rows returned by `CROSSJOIN` can be huge, which can easily lead to memory problems. When you include `CROSSJOIN` in a table aggregation, like the following (A and B being two arbitrary table expressions):

```
SUMX(
    CROSSJOIN(A, B),
    [Sales]
)
```

It is often more efficient to not use `CROSSJOIN` at all:

```
SUMX(
    A,
    SUMX(
        B,
        [Sales]
    )
)
```

A yet more efficient approach is not to iterate at all, but to use virtual tables for filtering instead. This is the topic of the next section.

Filtering with table functions

One of the most profound insights when working with DAX is the deep connection between tables and filtering. In this section, you will learn what this connection is, and how to leverage it.

Using CALCULATETABLE

As we discussed earlier in this chapter, table expressions used in table aggregation functions like SUMX are evaluated in the same context as the table aggregation function itself. This is not always what you want: sometimes, you need a different context. DAX provides a function for precisely this purpose: CALCULATETABLE.

Like its cousin CALCULATE, CALCULATETABLE changes context before evaluating an expression. In CALCULATE, this expression must return a scalar value; in CALCULATETABLE, it must be a table expression. Apart from that, the function works with the same four-step process:

1. Set up a filter context.
2. Remove existing filters from columns or tables referred to in the filter arguments.
3. Add new filters as specified in the filter arguments.
4. Evaluate the table expression in the first argument.

Often, CALCULATE and CALCULATETABLE can be used interchangeably. Take, for instance, the formula below:

```
AveragePerCity_Canada1 =
AVERAGEX(
    CALCULATETABLE(
        VALUES(Cities[CityID]),
        Cities[Country] = "Canada"
    ),
    [Sales]
)
```

You can rewrite this measure as a straightforward CALCULATE formula:

```
AveragePerCity_Canada2 =
CALCULATE(
    AVERAGEX(
        VALUES(Cities[CityID]),
        [Sales]
    ),
    Cities[Country] = "Canada"
)
```

Both calculations return the average sales per city for Cities in Canada (depending on the query context, of course). But be warned: there are technical differences between the two. In the first formula, the Cities[Country] = "Canada" filter is applied to the evaluation of the Cities table, while in the second formula, the filter is applied to both the Cities table and the Sales measure evaluations. While this difference does not impact the results of the measure in this case, you may use more advanced measures instead of Sales that are impacted by this difference.

 Like CALCULATE, CALCULATETABLE creates a filter context. When used in a calculated column, in each row new filters are added to select that row. When evaluating a related table in the new context, the relationship now has filters to propagate and the related table will be filtered to only the rows that are linked to the current row. This is why the RELATEDTABLE function, which is used to retrieve the related part of another table, is nothing more than the CALCULATETABLE function without filter arguments.

Using CALCULATETABLE, it is possible to add filters to table evaluations. Interestingly, you can use tables to add filters as well.

Filters and tables

Now that we have covered table functions, it is time to go back and take a new look at filters. Earlier, we introduced filters in query and filter context as "rules" on columns in the Power BI model, like "Cities[Country] *must equal France or Germany*." You can view this rule as providing the values that the Country column should contain; or, taking yet another perspective, view it as a single-column table with two rows, containing "France" and "Germany".

In fact, this is exactly how filters work, and how the CALCULATE function works: by adding tables that define which values in columns are selected, possibly replacing existing tables that implement a filter. The foundational principle is this:

> *Every filter is a table, and every table can be used as a filter.*

This principle means that any simple filter argument in CALCULATE can be rewritten as a table. Consider, for instance, the formula below:

```
SalesFranceGermany =
CALCULATE(
    [Sales],
    Cities[Country] IN {"France", "Germany"}
)
```

The filter argument here is the equivalent of the table expression below:

```
FILTER(
    ALL(Cities[Country]),
    Cities[Country] IN {"France", "Germany"}
)
```

So, the meaning of this filter is literally: of all the Country values, select only "France" and "Germany".

This explains why a formula like the one below works:

```
CALCULATE(
    [Sales],
    Cities[Country] = "France"
    || Cities[Country] = "Germany"
)
```

Although this is not the simplest filter argument, it is just the equivalent of:

```
FILTER(
    ALL(Cities[Country]),
    Cities[Country] = "France"
    || Cities[Country] = "Germany"
)
```

Most of the DAX functions we introduced as filter functions are really table functions, as you can already see from the FILTER expression above, which uses ALL as a table function. Indeed the ALL functions are table functions: ALL(Cities[Country]) is a one-column table containing all unique countries, and ALL(Cities[Country], Cities[State]) is a two-column table containing all unique combinations of country and state that are found in the Cities table.

 Not all functions used in filter arguments are table functions: USERELATIONSHIP and CROSSFILTER change relationship behavior and do not create tables. KEEPFILTERS changes the behavior of CALCULATE, but cannot be used to create a table. REMOVEFILTERS, which functions like ALL in a filter argument, cannot be used to create a table.

Even the time intelligence functions are table functions when we exclude the shortcut versions like TOTALYTD. Each creates a one-column table containing the dates in the specified period. This means that you could use these functions in table aggregation functions, for example, to calculate the year-to-date average sales per day:

```
AverageSalesPerDay_YTD =
AVERAGEX(
    DATESYTD('Date'[Date]),
    [Sales]
)
```

The more exciting use of the *filter is table* principle is that you can use any (virtual) table as a filter within a CALCULATE function. As an easy example, suppose you want to have a measure that returns the total sales in the country or countries your selected Cities are in. If you are sure that in the query context for this calculation, the Country column is filtered, then the formula is not difficult:

```
SalesWholeCountry1 =
CALCULATE(
    [Sales],
    ALLEXCEPT(Cities, Cities[Country])
)
```

This calculation removes all the filters from the Cities table, except for from the Country column. So, if the query context contains the filters "*City is Atlanta*" and "*Country is United States*," the resulting filter context has only the filter "*Country is United States*" left.

However, if the query context has only the filter "*City is Atlanta*" to begin with, we are in trouble: removing this filter gives us the whole world! To solve this, we need to "reinject" a "*Country is United States*" filter into the context, and it should be derived from the `City` filter. This can be done with a table filter:

```
SalesWholeCountry2 =
CALCULATE(
    [Sales],
    ALL(Cities),
    VALUES(Cities[Country])
)
```

To see what is happening here, it is important to realize that *filter arguments are evaluated in the same context as the* `CALCULATE` *table itself*. In a query context where only one city is selected, the `VALUES(Cities[Country])` expression returns a single-column table with the country that city is in. This is exactly the filter that we need to implement the required calculation.

As another example, the formula below calculates the sales amount of the 10,000 largest customers:

```
SalesLargestCustomers1 =
CALCULATE(
    [Sales],
    TOPN(10000, ALL(Customers), [Sales], DESC)
)
```

Note that we use `ALL(Customers)` here to be sure that we don't have filters in the query context limiting the customers we are considering. The `TOPN` function returns the 10,000 largest customers (as a subset of the `Customers` table, including all columns – you may want to eliminate unneeded columns here!). This table is then used as a filter.

This formula makes it clear why using table filters should be preferred over using table aggregations. Consider the table aggregation alternative for this measure:

```
SalesLargestCustomers2 =
SUMX(
    TOPN(10000, ALL(Customers), [Sales], DESC),
    [Sales]
)
```

Now ask yourself: how many times is the Sales measure called in the evaluation of this calculation? It depends, of course, on the number of customers we have in our Customers table. Let's assume that we have 60,000 customers. The TOPN function must call Sales for each customer to determine who the largest customers are. After that is done, the SalesLargestCustomers1 measure only needs one additional call to Sales: the TOPN table is applied as a filter, creating the context for the largest customers. The SalesLargestCustomers2 measure, however, traverses the TOPN table and calls Sales for each row. In other words, this measure calls Sales 70,000 times in total, whereas the SalesLargestCustomers1 measure only calls it 60,001 times! The DAX engine may optimize things here, but the difference will be significant.

Using tables as filters becomes even more powerful when you realize that, unlike filters in a query context, table filters can have multiple columns. This means that we now have a solution for our problematic AvgUnitAmount3 measure from earlier in this chapter:

```
AvgUnitAmount4 =
CALCULATE(
    AVERAGE(fSales[UnitAmount]),
    GENERATE(
        VALUES(Cities[CityID]),
        FILTER(
            VALUES(Products[ProductID]),
            [Sales] > 10000
        )
    )
)
```

Instead of the average of averages that came with the table aggregation over the GENERATE expression, this time, we use GENERATE to provide a filter that selects combinations of cities and products that have sales over 10,000. We then calculate the average unit amount for all sales transactions that correspond to the selected city/product combinations. Not only do we now have the correct average calculation, but we have also eliminated iterating over the GENERATE table as well, which will help in further improving the performance of this measure.

Using TREATAS

There is one important constraint when using table filters: the tables must effectively filter the tables over which the calculation is done. Just adding a table as a filter that has nothing to do whatsoever with the rest of the model will not do anything.

For instance, the formula below does not return sales for the United Kingdom:

```
UKSales_wrong =
CALCULATE(
    [Sales],
    ROW("Country", "United Kingdom")
)
```

Why does this not work? The Power BI model has no way to determine that with the arbitrary table created with the ROW function, which has a column named Country, it should filter the Cities table, which contains a Country column as well. You could say, *"well, the name is the same so the DAX engine could assume that this is what the formula is meant to do"*; but that would lead to very unpredictable results in models that may have the same column names in many different tables.

To be able to be used as a filter, the DAX engine should be able to identify that the virtual table is connected to a table, or some columns, from the model. This connection is called **lineage**, and in short, it means that when creating a virtual table, DAX keeps track of what the original columns were where the columns in the virtual table originated from. Let's look at the GENERATE expression once again:

```
GENERATE(
    VALUES(Cities[CityID]),
    FILTER(
        VALUES(Products[ProductID]),
        [Sales] > 10000
    )
)
```

It is clear that Cities[CityID] is a column in the model, and as VALUES takes the unique values from that column, VALUES(Cities[CityID]) has lineage to it. In the same way, VALUES(Products[ProductID]) has lineage to the ProductID column in the Products table. GENERATE creates a table containing combinations of values from the two VALUES expressions, so each column in the resulting table has lineage to the respective model column.

Most table functions retain the lineage of the columns they provide. Some functions, however, allow for forming tables in a strange way, which can be problematic when it comes to lineage. For instance, the UNION function allows for combining tables by taking rows from two source tables that may have conflicting lineage. If so, columns in the result table do not have lineage to any existing column in the model.

In some cases, you want the lineage of the virtual table to be different than it is by default. DAX offers a solution through the TREATAS function, which forces the model to consider the columns in a table to have a specific lineage.

TREATAS is another example of a function that is exclusively used in CALCULATE, or CALCULATETABLE, filter arguments. The formula below correctly calculates UK sales (although there are easier ways to accomplish this):

```
UKSales_correct =
CALCULATE(
    [Sales],
    TREATAS(
        ROW("Country", "United Kingdom"),
        Cities[Country]
    )
)
```

Note that TREATAS does not require the name of the column to be the same. We could have named the column in the ROW expression anything we wanted. TREATAS works with multi-column tables as well; in this case, you should specify a model column for each column in the table. You can find a comprehensive example of the use of TREATAS in *Chapter 2.5, Intercompany Business*.

DAX variables

DAX table functions and filtering greatly enhance the complexity of calculations that can be done with DAX. The flip side is that formulas can become quite long. More importantly, with all the different contexts in play, it can be problematic to obtain correct results.

DAX variables make life much easier when designing advanced DAX code. The name is somewhat odd, as the purpose of DAX variables is that you can evaluate something once, and use it later in other circumstances (other contexts, typically) without worrying about the evaluation of the variable. In other words, a DAX variable is used as a constant!

A variable is declared using the VAR keyword. Multiple variables can be declared, and the declaration of a variable can use the value of another variable declared earlier. Declarations of variables are closed off by the RETURN keyword:

```
VAR ThisValue = 5
RETURN
...
```

It is good to know that DAX variables can be used in any expression in a DAX formula. A variable can contain a scalar value, but it can also be a table. The (rather ridiculous) formula below is correct DAX code:

```
VariableTest =
VAR Variable1 = 3
VAR Variable2 = Variable1 + 5
RETURN
CALCULATE(
    VAR Variable3 = MAX(fSales[UnitAmount])
    RETURN
    SUM(fSales[Tax]) + Variable2 + Variable3,
    VAR Variable4 = 4
    VAR TableVariable =
            FILTER(
                    ALL(fSales[UnitAmount]),
                    fSales[UnitAmount] = Variable4
            )
    RETURN
    TableVariable
)
```

The location of the variable declaration in the formula determines the context in which the variable is evaluated. For instance, the Variable3 variable above is evaluated in the filter context formed by applying the TableVariable table filter to the original query context for this measure. If Variable3 had been declared right after Variable2, it would have been evaluated in the query context. Note that Variable4 and TableVariable are used in a filter argument of the CALCULATE function; both are evaluated in the original query context.

Each variable has its own scope, which means that it cannot be used outside of the expression that it is declared in. In the formula above, Variable3 cannot be used to define TableVariable; Variable3 is the first argument of CALCULATE and outside of that, it is unknown. Conversely, Variable4 and TableVariable cannot be used in the first argument of CALCULATE. Variable1 and Variable2 are part of the expression of the whole formula and can be used anywhere.

DAX variables can help to simplify the flow of a calculation, but they can also make your formulas more readable, simply through the use of clear variable names. Let us revisit the AvgUnitAmount4 measure once again:

```
AvgUnitAmount4 =
CALCULATE(
    AVERAGE(fSales[UnitAmount]),
    GENERATE(
        VALUES(Cities[CityID]),
        FILTER(
            VALUES(Products[ProductID]),
            [Sales] > 10000
        )
    )
)
```

Using variables, this formula can be simplified:

```
AvgUnitAmount5 =
VAR LargeCityProductCombinations =
    GENERATE(
        VALUES(Cities[CityID]),
        FILTER(
            VALUES(Products[ProductID]),
            [Sales] > 10000
        )
    )
RETURN

CALCULATE(
    AVERAGE(fSales[UnitAmount]),
    LargeCityProductCombinations
)
```

Always remember that DAX variables are constants! The variant below is not correct:

```
AvgUnitAmount_wrong =
VAR LargeProducts =
    FILTER(
            VALUES(Products[ProductID]),
            [Sales] > 10000
        )
VAR LargeCityProductCombinations =
    GENERATE(
        VALUES(Cities[CityID]),
        LargeProducts
    )
RETURN

CALCULATE(
    AVERAGE(fSales[UnitAmount]),
    LargeCityProductCombinations
)
```

By putting the FILTER expression in a variable, we have turned it into a constant table. However, in the GENERATE function, we want the product list to be determined anew for each city.

Summary

In this chapter, you have learned about row context, query context, and filter context and the role that contexts play in the evaluation of DAX formulas. We have discussed how contexts can be transformed using the CALCULATE function, by removing filters and adding filters to an existing context. In addition, we looked at time intelligence functions, which provide filters specifically tailored to the Gregorian calendar.

We then focused on DAX table functions, which give us the ability to aggregate over tables and the use of custom-made, virtual tables within DAX formulas. Using virtual tables provides a wealth of analytics capabilities on top of what is already possible using "standard" DAX functions and filtering. We talked about the deep connection between tables and filters, which allows for using any table as a filter. And, finally, DAX variables were discussed, which make it easier to implement complex logic in DAX and add to the readability of DAX code as well.

All of these are foundational concepts you need for exploring more advanced analyses with DAX. After this pivotal chapter, *Part 2* of this book is focused on applying all the concepts discussed to real-life business cases. Our aspiration is that by going through these cases, you will get to appreciate and understand the power of DAX even more, and that you are inspired to tackle your own business questions using DAX calculations.

Chapter 2.1, Security with DAX, is dedicated to security in Power BI models. As you will see in this chapter, knowledge of DAX, context, and filtering already finds many applications when designing security.

Part II

Business cases

2.1
Security with DAX

When working with data, chances are you deal with confidential data that must be secured. Even within an organization, some people should be able to see more than others. In a Power BI model, there are sophisticated ways to apply security. From this chapter, you will learn how to do this.

Note that we will not cover security in the distribution or sharing of reports and dashboards in Power BI. Instead, we focus on security within Power BI models. The typical scenario here is that two users of the same report see different report content, depending on their security settings.

This chapter covers the topics below:

- Securing a Power BI model with row-level security
- Configuring security on hierarchical data
- Securing attributes, or individual columns in a table
- Securing aggregation levels for calculated measures

 We will be using several models in this chapter that you can find in the GitHub repo for this book. Download the model files from `https://github.com/PacktPublishing/Extreme-DAX/tree/main/Chapter2.1` to help you follow along with the chapter, or to explore in your own time.

Introduction to row-level security (RLS)

With **row-level security** (**RLS**), you can restrict users from seeing all data that is in a Power BI model. RLS is the main form of security in a Power BI model. It is called *row*-level because you define which rows in each table in the model are visible to the user. Note that because RLS is set on the model level, any report that visualizes results from that model will satisfy the security policy defined on it.

Before diving in, let's make something clear: when you need a secure solution, you *have* to use RLS (or a related concept called object-level security, which we will discuss later in this chapter). There's just no way around it. Do not try to implement security through sharing reports (or not sharing, rather). You cannot oversee what will happen to the use of your model in the future: people may get self-service access to the Power BI model, get added to security groups by accident, or other things may happen. For the same reason, do not try to secure results through DAX measures that only return results when some condition is met: people who can build reports on top of the model can easily circumvent these. The rule of thumb should be: each user *could* have access to the model and should not see things that are prohibited.

Security roles

RLS is based on security roles. Think of a security role as a separate implemented security policy. You could have a security role for individual salespeople, for instance, in addition to a security role for C-level executives and one for human resource managers.

Security roles are part of the design of a Power BI model. Role membership, in contrast, is not; only after publishing a model can you add users to a role. You can have as many security roles as you wish, but there are some very important considerations to make, which we will cover in this section.

Security roles are defined and maintained through the **Manage roles** window:

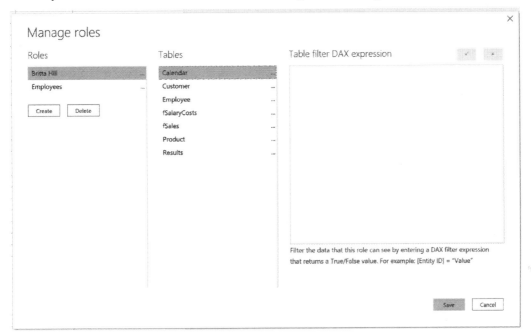

Figure 2.1.1: The Manage roles window

Once you publish a model in which a security role is defined, no one can access the data until they have been added to one of the security roles – unless you are an admin, member, or contributor in the workspace where the model has been published.

In the Power BI service, you can see whether security roles have been defined by the appearance of a **Security** option in the context menu on the dataset:

Figure 2.1.2: Finding the Security option

People can be added to security roles individually, through their email address, or as a (security) group.

Note that adding someone to a security role does not give her access to the dataset as a whole, so you have to give access on two levels:

- Access to the dataset (through a shared report, workspace membership, and/ or build permission on the dataset itself)
- Inclusion in a security role

DAX security filters

Once you create a security role, it's time to define the actual security policy the role will implement. You do this by declaring DAX **security filters** on one or more tables in the model. Note that DAX security filters are declared by role and by table; you can have different security filters on the same table, as long as they are in different security roles.

A DAX security filter determines which rows a user in this security role will see in the table. You can compare a DAX security filter to a calculated column that is added to the table and that has values *true* or *false*. For example:

```
Product[Category] = "Components"
```

When defined on the `Product` table, this filter will return `TRUE` for each product row that has `"Components"` as its `Category` value, and `FALSE` for all other products. The filter will be added to each and every measure evaluation, effectively only returning results for products in the `Components` category.

You don't need to set security filters on each table because the relationships in your model propagate filters from one table to another. This is true for the evaluation context for a measure, but also for security filters. This means that you can effectively secure your model with just a few security filters – but be aware that changes in the model may break the security policies!

In *Figure 2.1.3*, you see a simple example with a relationship (1) and two tables (2). With a security role `SelectCanada`, which filters the `Country` column on Canada (3), the `fSales` table is filtered through the relationship:

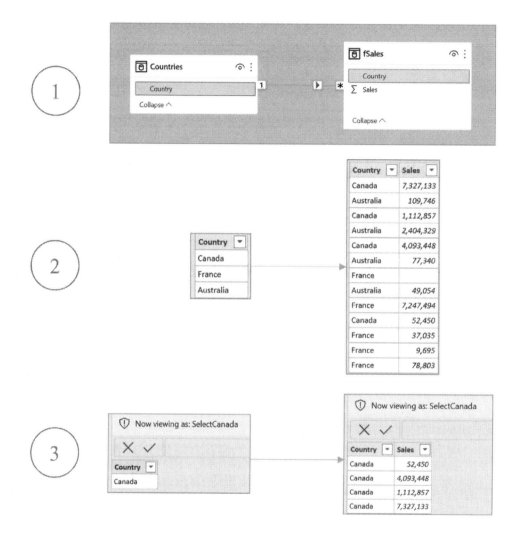

Figure 2.1.3: Security filters propagate through a relationship

When working with relationships that have a bidirectional cross filter setting, or **Both** as Power BI calls it, special attention is needed when defining RLS. The default behavior for these relationships is that they propagate security filters in only one direction: the direction the relationship would have if it had the cross filter property set to single, or from the one-side to the many-side.

You can enable security filter propagation in both directions through the **Edit relationship** window:

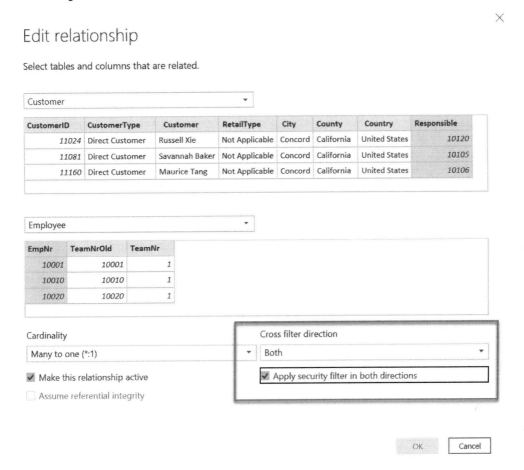

Figure 2.1.4: The Edit relationship window

Dynamic row-level security

A static security filter like Product[Category] = "Furniture" is not that useful in real life. RLS becomes a lot more useful when it's dynamic, meaning that the security filters are derived from who the user is.

 The examples in this section can be found in the 2.1 Row-level security.pbix file.

Who the user is can be retrieved using a couple of functions, of which the most consistent is USERPRINCIPALNAME. This DAX function returns the email address of the user, which should then be used to derive the right security logic.

An older DAX function, USERNAME, returns the user's email address when in the Power BI service, but in Power BI Desktop, or in an Analysis Services instance, it returns the username. As looking up the user's identity is quite hard this way, USERPRINCIPALNAME was introduced to make this a little easier.

When you use Power BI Embedded, you can configure security on the level of the application that the Power BI report is embedded in (this is called **app owns data**). In this case, there is no user as such but, instead, the app can provide an identifier (the **secret**) to Power BI when calling the report. The secret can be a user-level identifier, but it can also be an identifier on another level, like organization or department. In this case, USERPRINCIPALNAME retrieves the secret with which you can derive the security filters.

You do not normally use the email address as the user ID throughout the model, but a number, either an employee number from an HR system or a generated key. Either way, you will need a separate table with a mapping between the email address and user ID. In simple models, you can have a relationship between this table, let's call it UserSecurity, and the table containing user data; or you can even filter the Employee table directly using the email address.

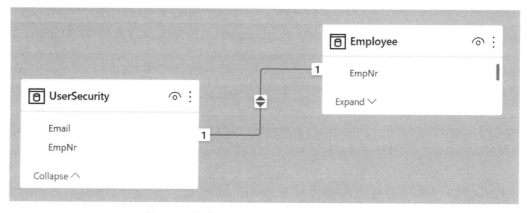

Figure 2.1.5: The UserSecurity and Employee tables

In larger and more complex models, only securing an Employee table is probably not enough. In this case, it makes sense to have a separate UserSecurity table that is not related to any other table in the model.

This is because you will run into having multiple relationship paths from the UserSecurity table to several tables and will therefore need to have inactive relationships.

When working with a standalone UserSecurity table, you need to retrieve the user ID from the table as part of a DAX security filter. For instance, to secure the Employee table, the DAX security filter would be:

```
VAR ThisUser =
    LOOKUPVALUE(
        UserSecurity[EmpNr],
        UserSecurity[Email],
        USERPRINCIPALNAME()
    )
RETURN
[EmpNr] = ThisUser
```

Notice that you can use DAX variables in a DAX security filter. The variable ThisUser retrieves the EmpNr value from the UserSecurity table, using USERPRINCIPALNAME() as the value to look for. After RETURN, the filter checks whether the EmpNr value in the current row of the Employee table is equal to the ThisUser variable, effectively filtering to only the row for the current user.

Remember that the UserSecurity table contains sensitive data, and consider whether this table needs to be secured itself! You could set a specific security filter on the UserSecurity table:

```
FALSE()
```

This filter would make none of the rows in the table visible to the user. This works only when the UserSecurity table is not related to other tables, as this filter should not be propagated to the rest of the model.

> Remember that security filters are applied simultaneously and therefore do not depend on each other, just like filter arguments in the CALCULATE function. This means that when you use the filter above to hide all rows in the UserSecurity table, it is still possible to do a lookup in the table to retrieve the current user in another security filter. And inversely, you cannot use the security filter on a table to derive logic for a security filter on another table.

Modeling considerations for RLS

The use of RLS brings with it some constraints on what you can do from a modeling perspective. Specifically, you will find that some uses of inactive relationships become impossible.

Consider, for example, the model below. This model contains a fact table, fHours, containing hours worked by employees. Employees work on projects, in which case we speak of *direct hours*; but they also spend their time on other things: meetings, leave, sickness, and so on, which are called *indirect hours*. Each project has a project manager, who is also an employee.

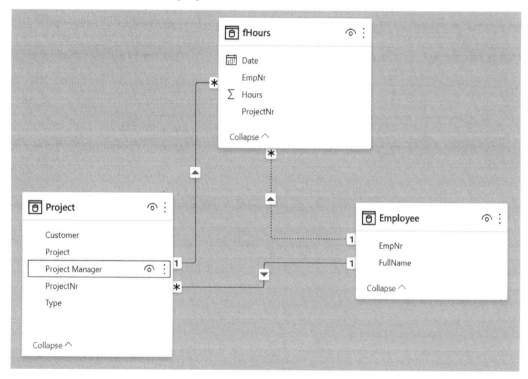

Figure 2.1.6: fHours, Project, and Employee tables

 You can find this example in `InactiveRelationship.pbix`.

In this model, direct hours can be reported by project and through projects, by project manager; indirect hours can be reported by employees directly. So, there are two ways the Employee table is related to the fHours table and, therefore, we need an inactive relationship somewhere. In this case, the relationship between fHours and Employee is chosen to be inactive.

What measures can you create to retrieve the number of direct hours from this model? The basic formula is simple:

```
Direct Hours = SUM(fHours[Hours])
```

Since the indirect hours in the fHours table are not linked to a project, a blank row will be added to the Project table. This blank row will show up in reports as a blank project whenever a measure yields a result for that blank project, which the formula above does. You can make the formula a bit more sophisticated by testing for this situation and filtering out results that are really about indirect hours:

```
Direct Hours =
CALCULATE(
    SUM(fHours[Hours]),
    NOT(ISBLANK(fHours[ProjectNr]))
)
```

Calculating indirect hours works the same way, but now we're interested in rows without a ProjectNr value. The relationship between fHours and Employee also needs to be activated:

```
Indirect Hours =
CALCULATE(
    SUM(fHours[Hours]),
    ISBLANK(fHours[ProjectNr]),
    USERELATIONSHIP(fHours[EmpNr], Employee[EmpNr])
)
```

With these measures, you can report direct and indirect hours by employee (note
that `Direct Hours` are the hours on projects the employee is the project manager of):

FullName	Direct Hours	Indirect Hours
Adams, Doug	6482	1778
Allen, Alethea	10779	3663
Anderson, Eimear	13435	2218
Bailey, Faustina	13825	2455
Baker, Ambrocio	12924	1491
Baker, An	7539	1765
Bell, Atsuko	10315	1841
Bell, Kai	6974	3160
Brown, Arun	17237	2148
Brown, Bourey	5519	2929
Campbell, Aki	7761	2259

Figure 2.1.7: Direct and indirect hours by employee

Suppose, now, that you want to secure this model. Let's create a simple security role
that only returns results for Doug Adams. For this, there needs to be a DAX security
filter on the `Employee` table:

```
[FullName] = "Adams, Doug"
```

When this security role is active, you will see that the visual is not populated but returns an error instead:

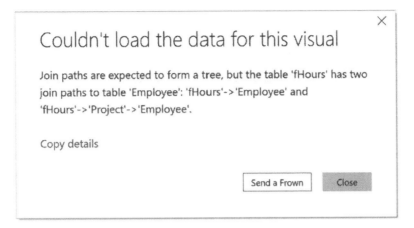

Figure 2.1.8: Couldn't load the data for this visual error message

This seems to be a strange error message. The fHours table has two join paths to the Employee table – but the idea behind USERELATIONSHIP is that the active path is not used, right? Well, this is true when it comes to context in measure evaluation, but not for security filters.

In fact, you should be happy that this error occurs, because what we're trying to do here is to remove or change security on the fHours table. The normal situation is that we only see rows in fHours linked to projects that Doug is the project manager of. With USERELATIONSHIP, we tell the model to ignore those settings and give us access to other rows. The model doesn't allow that and keeps the data secure. After all, being able to do this would mean that users who have self-service capabilities, which include writing custom measures, could override security filters and compromise the security of the model.

This behavior is fundamental, and it means that you can easily run into trouble when security is an afterthought in the design of your model. The message here is not that inactive relationships should always be avoided, but that it is important to recognize potential issues in the future when security may be needed.

There is no single way of solving this problem; it all depends on what your analytical needs are. You may, for instance, split the fact table in two, with one fact table for direct hours and one for indirect hours:

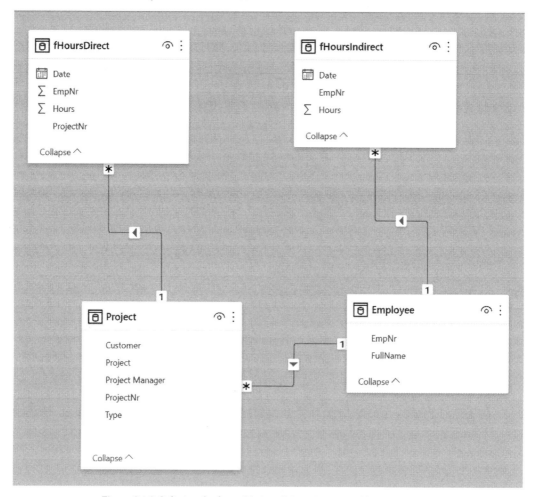

Figure 2.1.9: Splitting the fact table into fHoursDirect and fHoursIndirect

This solution, however, doesn't allow for reporting direct hours by employee (as someone who works on the project, not as the project manager).

Another option would be to duplicate the `Employee` table and add a `Project Manager` table this way:

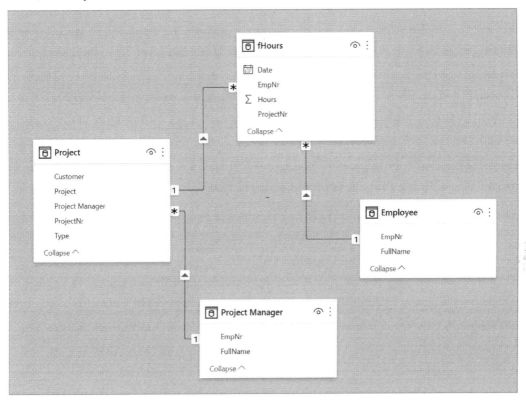

Figure 2.1.10: Adding a Project Manager table

This solution would require DAX security filters on both the `Project Manager` and the `Employee` table.

Testing security roles

When you design and implement security policies, you will want to test these as well. Conveniently, both Power BI Desktop and the Power BI service have a **View as roles** feature that allows you to view the data as visible in a specific role.

With the **View as roles** option, it is also possible to impersonate a specific user and test what this user sees. In Power BI Desktop, this is straightforward: in the **View as roles** window, select both the role you want to test and the option **Other user**.

Here, you can enter the email address of the user you want to test:

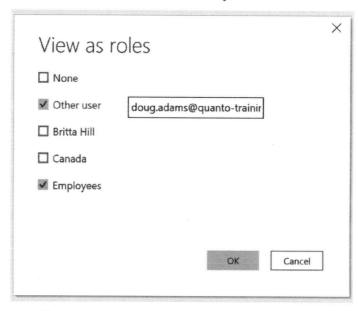

Figure 2.1.11: The View as roles window in Power BI Desktop

In the Power BI service, it works in basically the same way, although the "Other user" option is somewhat hidden. When you select **Security** on a dataset, click the three dots at the right of a security role and select **Test as role**:

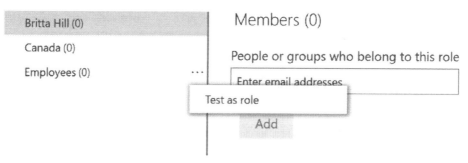

Figure 2.1.12: The Test as role option in the Power BI service

When viewing the report in a role, click once again on the role, now in the blue **Now viewing as:** bar. There, you have the option to enter the email address of the user you want to impersonate:

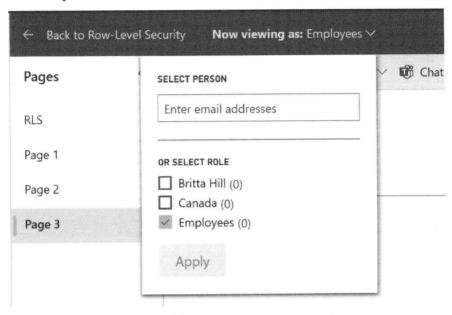

Figure 2.1.13: Selecting someone to impersonate

There is one constraint in testing RLS: you cannot easily test reports with a live connection to a published Power BI model, meaning that they are not in the same file as the model. This is a problem, as "live connection" is a common way of deploying reports. In the next section, we describe an approach to testing RLS with live connection reports, enabling the tester to impersonate any user.

Testing live connection reports

In many organizations that deploy Power BI reports, help desks get questions from users saying things like "*I don't see any data in my report,*" or "*I should see X and Y, but only see X; oh, and also Z.*" Or, even worse, "*John should see only X, but sees everything.*" Often, these problems are due to the user being in the wrong role (or inadvertently having edit rights on the Power BI model), but these questions can also lead to new insights into required changes to the security policies. In any case, it is useful to be able to impersonate a user to test what they actually see in reports.

Keeping in mind that you want to be able to do this on production reports (the versions actually in use throughout the organization), it is imperative that the impersonation itself is secure. In other words, it should be restricted to specific users (support personnel, for instance) and not be accessible to the common user. Additionally, it should be easy to switch impersonations in a production environment; meaning it should work with the reports and underlying Power BI models that are in use.

The solution to this contains a number of specific elements:

- A query parameter used to set the impersonation: pImpersonation
- A specific test account: PBITestUser (this should be an account with an email address in your organization, and a Power BI licence)
- A Power BI workspace for testing: PBITest

Let's walk through it.

Impersonation model

We start with a very simple model. The only element of this is a query parameter, pImpersonation.

1. In Power BI Desktop, start a new model.
2. Click **Transform Data** to start the Power Query Editor.
3. Click **Manage Parameters / New Parameter** to enter a query parameter.
4. Call the parameter pImpersonation and make sure to uncheck the **Required** box. Set the **Type** as **Text**, add a **Description**, and leave **Current Value** empty for now:

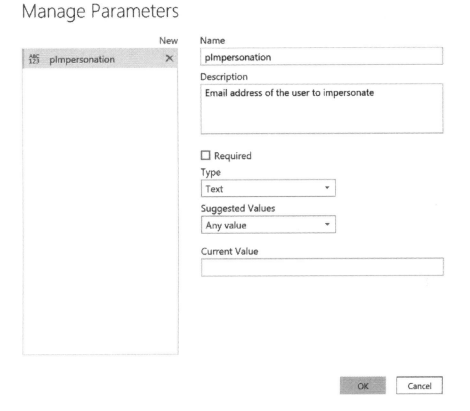

×

Manage Parameters

	New	Name
ABC 123 plImpersonation	×	plImpersonation

Description

Email address of the user to impersonate

☐ Required

Type

Text ▾

Suggested Values

Any value ▾

Current Value

OK   Cancel

Figure 2.1.14: Entering a query parameter in the Manage Parameters window

5. Click **OK** to exit the **Manage Parameters** window. A parameter query is now created. In the **Queries** pane, it is shown in italics as parameters are not loaded into the Power BI model. But in this case, we do want to load it! Right-click on the query, and set **Enable Load**. The query is now shown in upright text.

6. Select **Close & Apply**. Power BI loads the parameter into the model, resulting in a one-column table with an empty row:

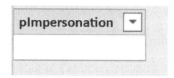

Figure 2.1.15: The pImpersonation table

7. Save the model, giving it the name Impersonation, and publish it to the **PBITest** workspace.

 For your convenience, you can download this model from GitHub; its name is 2.1 Impersonation.pbix.

Adding the pImpersonation table to the model

In the original Power BI model that needs to be tested, you can now add a DirectQuery connection to the pImpersonation table with the following steps. The model will become a composite model.

1. Open the model in Power BI Desktop, and click **Power BI Datasets** in the ribbon.

2. You can now select the Power BI model to connect to. Select the **Impersonation** dataset from the **PBITest** workspace.

3. The pImpersonation table is now added to the model. You cannot view the data in the table, but you can create a visual with the pImpersonation column to see what is in it (it's blank, for now).

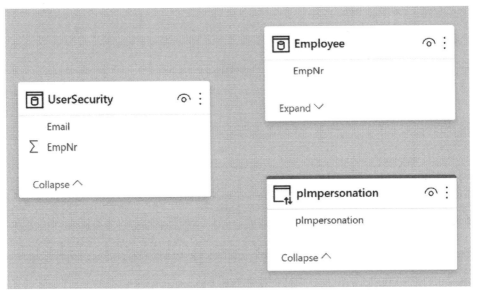

Figure 2.1.16: pImpersonation table added to the model

Adding a test security role

Next, you create a new security role, UserTest, that will consider the value of pImpersonation. If it contains a valid email address, the security filters will take that email address to impersonate a user. If the value is blank, no security filters are applied.

As an example, below is the adapted security filter for the Employee table:

```
VAR Impersonation = SELECTEDVALUE(pImpersonation[pImpersonation])
VAR User =
    LOOKUPVALUE(
        UserSecurity[EmpNr],
        UserSecurity[Email],
        Impersonation
    )
RETURN
ISBLANK(User) || [EmpNr] = User
```

The first variable, Impersonation, uses SELECTEDVALUE to retrieve the value of the pImpersonation parameter (which is a column in this model). SELECTEDVALUE is normally used to retrieve a value from a column if and only if there is just one (unique) value in that column; in our case, there is always only one value as we have just one row in the pImpersonation table.

The second variable, User, tries to retrieve an EmpNr value from the UserSecurity table using LOOKUPVALUE. Note that UserSecurity is used to translate user email addresses to user IDs; if an EmpNr value is found, the rest of the security filter works with that value.

Note that when pImpersonation is a blank value or an invalid email address, LOOKUPVALUE will return BLANK. This is the case where we want no filtering to be done. The last line of the code, ISBLANK(User) || [EmpNr] = User, implements just that: when the variable User is blank, ISBLANK(User) is true for each row in the table. If it is not, the formula only returns true for the row where the column EmpNr contains the User value retrieved.

Making it all work

With the new security role in place, the model can now be published. For the impersonation to work, you'll still have to take care of a couple of things:

1. Add the PBITestUser account to the UserTest security role.
2. Add PBITestUser to the PBITest workspace where the Impersonation dataset is published.
3. Share the (live connection) report to be tested with PBITestUser.
4. Do not give full access to the underlying model to PBITestUser!

To impersonate a user and test the report, PBITestUser should log in to Power BI, navigate to the Impersonation dataset, and change the pImpersonation parameter value under the dataset's Settings to the email address to be impersonated. **Do not forget that the Impersonation dataset needs to be refreshed after changing the parameter value!** As the parameter is the only thing in the model, refreshing will take only a second. Next, navigate to the report that is shared with PBITestUser.

Because the report's model has a DirectQuery connection to Impersonation, the changed parameter value will be directly available. The security role will pick up the email address and filter the report accordingly. Note that security filters are normally applied when a user connects to a model for the first time during a session; when you change the parameter while viewing the report, it will not pick up the new value. Instead, navigate away from the report and wait a while (about 10 minutes is enough in our tests).

This method is secure as long as PBITestUser is the only account in the UserTest role. As no other role uses the pImpersonation value, the Impersonation dataset doesn't even need to be secured – it's only an email address, after all.

To test different security roles this way, you could create a specific test role for each security role that has been defined on the model. This way, you can even test what happens when a user is a member of multiple roles by adding PBITestUser to the respective test roles.

 We used a separate test workspace to host the Impersonation dataset, but you may want to solve this in another way. The important thing is that the test user must have read access to this dataset, and must not have full access to the model to be tested (like by being an admin on the workspace where the model is located). This is because as a workspace admin, member, or contributor, security roles are not applied.

So far, we have discussed the possibilities and pitfalls in securing data based on a user's identity. This assumes that the data are directly relatable to the user in some way. In many situations, this is not enough, as the user is part of a larger organization with a specific structure. The section below deals with these situations.

Securing hierarchies using PATH functions

In most organizations, data is not directly related to a single user who has access to it. Instead, there is a group of people that each have access to different sets of data. Managers have access to the data of employees reporting to them, for instance. DAX contains a set of functions to deal with parent-child hierarchies like these: the PATH functions.

Hierarchical tables

First, let's take a look at a typical organization structure, in this case, that of QuantoBikes, our example company. QuantoBikes is organized into several divisions aligned with continents, and each division consists of multiple teams.

The organization map is pictured below:

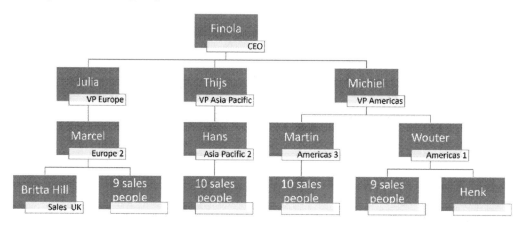

Figure 2.1.17: QuantoBikes organization map

In the Employee table, this organizational hierarchy is registered by having a column called MngrNr, or Manager Number. This column contains the employee number for each employee's direct manager; only the CEO does not have a manager:

EmpNr	MngrNr	Role	M/F	Name	Surname	FullName
10001		CEO	F	Finola	Martin	Martin, Finola
10010	10001	Vice President Americas	M	Mike	Tulips	Tulips, Mike
10101	10010	Unit Manager Americas 1	M	Lisa	Young	Young, Lisa
10102	10010	Unit Manager Americas 2	M	Bob	Murphy	Murphy, Bob
10103	10010	Unit Manager Americas 3	M	Jay	Robinson	Robinson, Jay
10104	10101	Employee	F	Eulalie	Lee	Lee, Eulalie
10105	10101	Employee	M	Bodhi	Hernandez	Hernandez, Bodhi
10106	10101	Employee	M	Leo	Johnson	Johnson, Leo
10107	10101	Employee	F	Ceridwen	Morgan	Morgan, Ceridwen

Figure 2.1.18: The Employee table for QuantoBikes

Power BI assumes that an employee does not have more than one direct manager, which is a fair assumption. You may have to deal with hierarchies with multiple parents (a family tree, for instance); these are cases too complex to solve with PATH functions alone. We will not cover these in this book.

The hierarchy could consist of multiple trees when multiple rows in the table contain a blank value in the parent column.

Introducing PATH functions

With two columns in a table encoding a parent-child hierarchy, you could traverse the table going from, in our example, employee to manager, to the manager's manager, and all the way to the top of the hierarchy. DAX contains a small set of functions that do this for you and provide useful information about the hierarchy.

PATH

`PATH(Employee[EmpNr], Employee[MngrNr])` must be evaluated in row context on the `Employee` table. It takes the two columns describing the hierarchy as arguments and returns the path from the top of the hierarchy to the current `EmpNr`. The result is a text string with a concatenation of all `EmpNr` values separated by the pipe character. For example, the path for Leo Johnson (employee 10106) is:

```
10001|10010|10101|10106
```

Note that the path is always text, even when the hierarchy columns are numeric.

PATHCONTAINS

The function `PATHCONTAINS` takes a path and a value as arguments and returns `TRUE` when the value is included in the path. So, taking Leo Johnson as an example again,

```
PATHCONTAINS(
    <Leo's path>,
    10010
)
```

would return `TRUE`.

PATHLENGTH

The function `PATHLENGTH` returns the number of items in a path. In other words, it returns the level in the hierarchy at which the current item appears.

```
PATHLENGTH(<Leo's path>)
```

The above would return 4.

PATHITEM

The function PATHITEM takes a path and a number N as arguments, and returns the Nth item from the hierarchy, counting from the start (or the top of the hierarchy).

```
PATHITEM(<Leo's path>, 3)
```

The above returns 10101.

PATHITEMREVERSE

The function PATHITEMREVERSE does the same thing as PATHITEM, but counts from the end of the path, or the bottom of the hierarchy.

```
PATHITEMREVERSE(<Leo's path>, 3)
```

The above returns 10010, which is the number of Leo's skip-level manager.

Note that PATHITEM and PATHITEMREVERSE return text values, even when the path was originally created from numeric values.

 The normal use of the PATH functions is to create a path with PATH and use that as input for the other functions. You can, however, create a path string in whatever way you like. The PATH functions don't have any hidden knowledge about the way the paths were created; they just work on a text string and search for pipe characters.

Using PATH functions in RLS

You can use the PATH functions to implement more sophisticated security logic when your data has a hierarchical structure. Suppose you want to implement the security policy that a manager has access to the data of all employees reporting to her, directly or indirectly. To do this, start by creating a column in the Employee table containing the hierarchical path for each employee:

```
Path = PATH([EmpNr], [MngrNr])
```

The DAX security filter on the `Employee` table would again start by retrieving the employee number of the logged-in user:

```
VAR ThisUser =
    LOOKUPVALUE(
        UserSecurity[EmpNr],
        UserSecurity[Email],
        USERPRINCIPALNAME()
    )
```

The next step would be simply to check if the current user is in the path of an employee:

```
RETURN
PATHCONTAINS([Path], ThisUser)
```

The function `PATHCONTAINS` returns `TRUE` when the logged-in user is in the path of the employee, and `FALSE` otherwise. The result of the security filter is, therefore, that all employees in the hierarchy under the user (and no one else) are visible.

Advanced hierarchy navigation in RLS

By using `PATH` functions in a clever way, you can implement all kinds of advanced security rules. For example, let's implement the policy that a manager may view data for all employees reporting to him, and all employees reporting to his peers. In other words:

- If John is a manager, he can view data for himself and all of his (direct or indirect) reports.
- If John is a manager, he can view data for employees reporting to his peers (who are the employees directly reporting to his manager).
- John cannot view data for his manager or his peers.
- If John is not a manager, he can only view his own data (even if one of his peers has people reporting to her).

We will need quite some code to implement this policy, and will use DAX variables to keep track of what we are doing. The code covers the steps below:

1. Determine if John is a manager.
2. Make a first selection by determining which employees report to John's manager.

3. Remove John's peers from the selection.

4. Make the resulting group of employees visible to John.

First, let's see how to find out that John is not a manager. This is not straightforward, as the path only works upwards, so we don't have the organizational tree under an employee readily available. But we can traverse the Employee table and count how many times John appears in a path. Someone who is not a manager would only appear in their own path, not in that of others. To use the PATH functions, we first need to retrieve John's employee number from the UserSecurity table. Here is the DAX code:

```
VAR ThisUser =
    LOOKUPVALUE(
        UserSecurity[EmpNr],
        UserSecurity[Email],
        USERPRINCIPALNAME()
    )
VAR IsManager =
    IF(
        COUNTROWS(
            FILTER(Employee,
                PATHCONTAINS(Employee[Path], ThisUser)
            )
        ) > 1,
        TRUE(),
        FALSE()
    )
```

The variable IsManager is TRUE whenever the user is a manager. We could proceed to find people reporting to John, but according to our policy, all employees that John may view are reporting, directly or indirectly, to John's manager. It therefore makes sense to start by testing whether John's manager is in the path of the employee. We use LOOKUPVALUE to retrieve the MngrNr value for the logged-in user (the variable ThisUser) and then use PATHCONTAINS to check if John's manager appears in the employee's path:

```
VAR ThisUserMngr =
    LOOKUPVALUE(
        Employee[MngrNr],
        Employee[EmpNr],
        ThisUser
    )
VAR ReportsToManager = PATHCONTAINS([Path], ThisUserMngr)
```

If we were to use the variable `ReportsToManager`, we would select too many employees to view. We should skip John's manager and John's peers. To do this, it is helpful to work with the organizational levels that John and his manager work at; only employees at least two levels lower than John's manager may be viewed by John. You can use the PATHLENGTH function to do this:

```
VAR ThisUserPath =
    LOOKUPVALUE(
        Employee[Path],
        Employee[EmpNr],
        ThisUser
    )
VAR MngrLevel = PATHLENGTH(ThisUserPath) - 1
```

Note that the security filter is evaluated for each row in the `Employee` table, but each time, we want to find the level of John's manager. With this information, we can derive which employees should be visible:

```
VAR ShouldBeVisible =
ReportsToManager
    && PATHLENGTH([Path]) >= MngrLevel + 2
```

But wait: there is one employee where `ShouldBeVisible` results in `FALSE`, while the employee should indeed be visible: John himself. So, we need a slightly altered variable:

```
VAR ShouldBeVisible =
    (ReportsToManager
    && PATHLENGTH([Path]) >= MngrLevel + 2)
    || [EmpNr] = ThisUser
```

We can now complete the security filter, bringing everything together:

```
RETURN
IF(
    IsManager,
    ShouldBeVisible,
    [EmpNr] = ThisUser
)
```

There is only one case where things go wrong, and probably not the least important one: the CEO, who has no manager, would only get to see herself. This is because the ThisUserMngr variable is BLANK, and therefore no employee is identified as reporting to her: after all, no path contains a blank value, so the variable ReportsToManager is FALSE for any employee. Conveniently, we have another variable to detect this case: MngrLevel is zero when the user has no manager. The final filter should therefore be implemented with:

```
RETURN
SWITCH(TRUE(),
    MngrLevel = 0, TRUE(),
    IsManager, ShouldBeVisible,
    [EmpNr] = ThisUser
)
```

The SWITCH statement here first checks if the user is the CEO and if so, renders all employees visible; then, it checks if the user is a manager, and applies the manager security rules. If the user is neither CEO nor manager, it lets the user only see himself.

Now that you have seen row-level security in action, we will discuss how to use RLS to implement even more sophisticated security policies: securing attributes and, later in this chapter, securing aggregation levels.

Securing attributes

In this section, we will take a wholly different look at security in Power BI models. In the previous sections, we focused on ways to restrict the visibility of *rows* in tables of the model. This is the most common security need but, sometimes, other forms of security are needed. If you think of row-level security as "horizontal" security, looking at your data, then it makes sense to consider the possibility of "vertical" security. In other words, can we secure columns, or attributes?

The case for secured attributes

Securing a Power BI model with RLS is only really needed when the model is used by a broader audience. If you have a model used only by C-level executives, you probably won't need to have RLS at all, as each user is allowed to see all the data. Only when the audience grows larger does the need arise to segment the data based on geography, customer segment, or organizational structure, as discussed in the previous sections.

In the same way, if you have models that only apply to a specific business process, like sales and opportunity management, you probably do not need to secure specific attributes. The model might contain, for instance, the names of salespeople and their responsibilities, but maybe not their pay level, date of birth, or social security number. When data concerning different business processes are combined in one model, like sales and human resource management, you need to include additional attributes that may not be shared with every user.

Object-level security and its restrictions

One way of securing attributes is **object-level security**. This comes in two forms:

- **Table-level security** makes an entire table disappear from view in a security role.
- **Column-level security** makes one or more columns in a table disappear.

We consciously use the word *disappear* here; when, for instance, the Product table is secured using table-level security, the model acts as if there is no Product table at all. The same happens when a column is secured using column-level security.

We're not covering every aspect of object-level security here, in part because it is implemented without using DAX, what this book is about, and more importantly, because we cover a more exciting way of securing attributes in the next sections. There is certainly a case for using object-level security. The official documentation states that it restricts access to "sensitive" table names and column names, and you may have data that is so private that even knowing that it exists should be restricted to only those who need to know (a filter table UFO Type comes to mind here, but more serious examples are certainly available).

However, the disappearance of tables and columns poses a problem for Power BI models and reports. When a secured table has relationships to other tables, you may have to create other relationship paths for users that don't have access to the secured table. More importantly, a Power BI report that references secured columns, or columns from secured tables, will break and raise errors to users without access to those columns or tables.

In other words, using object-level security forces you to partition your reports into versions for users with access to secured objects and versions for users without that access.

And with that, you could wonder if you're not better off with a separate model for the secured data – after all, it will only be used by a custom report anyway.

 Although OLS is supported in Power BI models, it cannot be configured with Power BI Desktop currently.

Dynamically securing attributes: introducing value-level security

We now introduce a slightly different form of securing attributes, which allows for serving both users with and without access to secure attributes with the same report. We coined the term **value-level security** as it is a blend of row-level and column-level security. With value-level security (OK, **VLS** for short) you can give a user access to the values of a column in some rows, but not in others.

With VLS, you could implement security policies like "*Managers can see the pay levels of employees who report to them, but not the pay levels of employees who report to their peers, even while they can still see those employees and their sales numbers.*" In a completely different subject, another example could be "*Teachers can see their students' names, numbers, and grades, but only tutors can see their students' addresses. Teachers who are a tutor for some students may see their address, but not that of other students.*"

You may want to implement this using DAX measures. While this may be a start, it is not a secure solution in the long run. Users who receive the build permission on the Power BI model in order to create their own reports (a strong use case for Power BI) can also create their own DAX measures. In doing so, they have access to everything that is in the model and that is not secured. This means that any security implemented through a measure can be circumvented by creating another measure.

More importantly, a serious model can contain tens or hundreds of measures. When each measure needs to be equipped with the logic to implement security on attributes, you lay the foundation for errors and high maintenance costs. Instead, we want to have a solution that will work with any measure that works on the model.

Implementing VLS demands a sophisticated combination of modeling and DAX security filters. In the sections below, we will go through these.

 The example model for this section is `2.1 Value-level security.pbix`.

Value-level security: modeling

The first thing to do when designing a VLS solution is to wonder what a secured report will look like. An error message is not what we want, so the visual in the figure below is the best option. In this example, SSNs are shown for some employees, and values are left blank for others:

FullName	SSN	Sales
Bell, Kai		28,576,085.10
Brown, Arun	58568416	6,145,905.24
Brown, Bourey		4,477,075.12
Campbell, Aki		7,624,145.65
Campbell, Benjamin		8,228,672.33
Carter, Antonella		48,060,095.42
Clark, Chaoxiang	50923350	5,800,699.00
Clark, Elke		14,203,206.40
Collins, Bingwen	42983059	6,917,897.79
Collins, Chet		4,210,427.47
Cook, Fenna		202,007.42

Figure 2.1.19: A VLS-secured report

The important thing to notice here is that secured values are not visible in the report; but in this example, as the column SSN is a label and not the result of a measure, there must be a value in the model to be shown in the visual. This could be empty text, or the value BLANK, or something else, and that value must be in a row in a table.

Now, if you realize that for some users, the values should be visible and for others, not, the logical step is to split the table to be secured, in this case Employee, into two parts: one for publicly accessible columns (subject to RLS restrictions, of course), and another one containing the private columns:

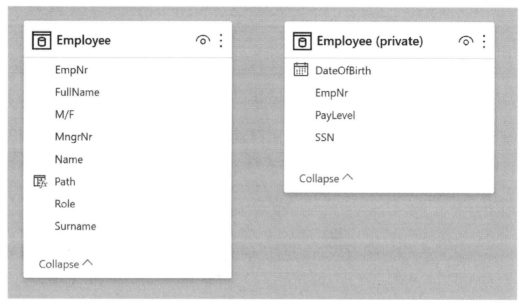

Figure 2.1.20: Splitting the Employee table into public and private parts

We still need to be able to link corresponding rows to each other. You can indeed do that, as we have the EmpNr column in both tables. You could create a relationship between the two tables, and this relationship would even be one-to-one. But that doesn't help us, and it certainly won't give us blank values for the private columns; rather, it brings us back to the situation with just one table.

The solution is to add rows to the private table. In the case of the Employee table, the Employee (private) table must contain twice the number of rows as the Employee table, divided into two sets. One set of rows contains all values for EmpNr, as well as all the private data; we'll call these the **positive** rows.

The other set of rows also contains all values for EmpNr, but *blank* values (or whatever other option you choose) in the private columns; we'll call these the **negative** rows. An additional column, Private, helps to distinguish between positive and negative rows. The picture below shows this schematically:

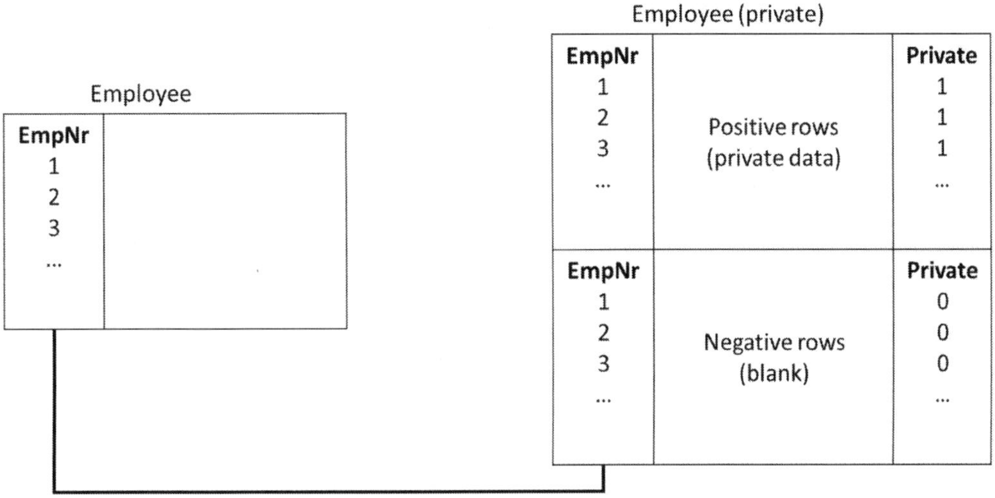

Figure 2.1.21: Adding rows to the Employee (private) table

The Employee (private) table is linked to the Employee table by a many-to-one relationship, with Employee (private) being at the "many" side of the relationship. The relationship needs to have bidirectional cross filtering enabled. When selecting an employee by FullName, for instance, you want to have the private data of that employee be selected. And vice versa: when selecting a Pay level, you want all employees with that pay level to be selected. So, filters need to be propagated from Employee to Employee (private) and vice versa.

The intermediate table can easily be created using an M script (this script assumes you have an sEmployee query that provides the basic data for the Employee table and that itself is not loaded into the model):

```
let
    Source = sEmployee,
    PositiveRows = Table.SelectColumns(Source,
{"EmpNr", "SSN", "DateOfBirth", "PayLevel"}),
    AddPrivate = Table.AddColumn(PositiveRows,
"Private", each 1, Int64.Type),
    NegativeRows = Table.SelectColumns(Source,
{"EmpNr"}),
    AddPrivate2 = Table.AddColumn(NegativeRows,
"Private", each 0, Int64.Type),
    Combine = Table.Combine({AddPrivate, AddPrivate2})
in
    Combine
```

This script creates two copies of the sEmployee table, one with the private columns and one with the EmpNr column only. A Private column is added to both copies with the value 1 or 0, respectively; finally, the two copies are appended.

It may be useful to add additional columns. For instance, if you want to use the organizational hierarchy in the security policy for private attributes, it makes sense to include the MngrNr column in both copies as well.

Make sure *not* to enable the **Apply security filter in both directions** setting on the relationship. As you will see in the next section, we are going to secure the private attributes with a security filter on Employee (private). This is in addition to a security filter on Employee. The model does not allow a security filter to be propagated against the default direction in this case.

Value-level security: security filters

When you create some output with columns from the Employee and Employee (private) tables, you will notice that you get two copies of output for each employee: one with the actual private attributes (the positive copy) and another one with blank private attributes (the negative copy). This is because of how we designed the Employee (private) table.

FullName	SSN	Sales
Baker, Ambrocio		8,795,933.89
Baker, Ambrocio	64397266	8,795,933.89
Baker, An		6,049,866.35
Baker, An	63093208	6,049,866.35
Bell, Atsuko		4,067,526.02
Bell, Atsuko	62452047	4,067,526.02
Bell, Kai		28,576,085.10
Bell, Kai	65872791	28,576,085.10
Brown, Arun		6,145,905.24
Brown, Arun	58568416	6,145,905.24
Brown, Bourey		4,477,075.12

Figure 2.1.22: Seeing two output rows for each employee

But this means that you can now use row-level security to select which copy you want to show. For each employee whose private attributes should be visible, make sure the corresponding positive row in `Employee (private)` is visible, but hide the negative row. For each employee whose private attributes should not be shown, hide the positive row in `Employee (private)`, with non-blank private attributes, and make the negative row visible.

The DAX formula for the security filter on `Employee (private)` would look like this:

```
(
    <when to show>
    && [Private] = 1
)
|| (
    NOT(<when to show>)
    && [Private] = 0
)
```

We'll call the first <when to show> clause the **positive** clause and the other one the **negative** clause. For example, to show private attributes only for employee 10203, the filter would be:

```
(
    [EmpNr] = 10203
    && [Private] = 1
)
|| (
    [EmpNr] <> 10203
    && [Private] = 0
)
```

This expression is true for the single row with EmpNr = 10203 and private data, and also for the rows with other values for EmpNr and blank values. For all other rows in Employee (private), the expression is false and the rows are hidden.

As you can see, for each employee exactly one row in Employee (private) is visible. Employees who should not be visible at all can be hidden by setting a security filter on the Employee table as usual. If you were to set a security filter [MngrNr] = 10201 on Employee, you would get the result in the picture below (Faustina Bailey is employee 10203):

FullName	SSN	Sales
Bailey, Faustina	51719541	29,400,154.13
Campbell, Benjamin		8,228,672.33
Clark, Elke		14,203,206.40
Flores, Aziza		18,043,800.76
Gomez, Zachary		15,287,240.74
Green, Elettra		9,362,221.73
Lewis, Araceli		12,439,119.97
Nelson, Avril		13,026,817.45
Ramirez, Milo		22,202,694.78
Reed, Cybele		12,975,664.97

Figure 2.1.23: Viewing an employee's SSN

Value-level security: advanced scenarios

In the security filters on the private table, you can apply everything possible in DAX, as usual. As an example, to implement the security policy "*a manager can see private attributes of her direct reports, but not of indirect reports,*" you would start by having the MngrNr and Path in the Employee (private) table. The first step in the table's security filter is to retrieve the user:

```
VAR ThisUser =
    LOOKUPVALUE(
        UserSecurity[EmpNr],
        UserSecurity[Email],
        USERPRINCIPALNAME()
    )
```

Next, the path of the user and the organizational level is determined:

```
VAR ThisUserPath =
    LOOKUPVALUE(
        'Employee (private)'[Path],
        'Employee (private)'[EmpNr],
        ThisUser
    )
VAR ThisUserLevel = PATHLENGTH(ThisUserPath)
```

The restriction "*only direct reports*" comes down to employees who are reporting to this user (the user appears in their path) and who are direct reports (their level is one below the level of the user). In DAX:

```
PATHCONTAINS([Path], ThisUser)
&& PATHLENGTH([Path]) <= ThisUserLevel + 1
```

Note that <= is used here (as opposed to just =) to include ThisUser, who is the only employee in her own path with the same level as her (by definition, ThisUser is not in the path of any employee with a level smaller than, or hierarchically above, ThisUserLevel, so no higher managers are included). The filter on Employee (private) will therefore be:

```
RETURN
(
    PATHCONTAINS([Path], ThisUser)
    && PATHLENGTH([Path]) <= ThisUserLevel + 1
    && [Private] = 1
)
||
```

```
(
    NOT(
        PATHCONTAINS([Path], ThisUser)
            && PATHLENGTH([Path]) <= ThisUserLevel + 1
    )
    && [Private] = 0
)
```

Do not forget to apply NOT to both the PATHCONTAINS clause and the PATHLENGTH clause: mind the parentheses!

So far, we have assumed that there is one set of employee attributes that is private, and that a user who may see a private attribute of some employees can see all their private attributes. You can go one step further and define multiple sets of private attributes, for instance, to separate public attributes from contact details for use by peers, and from HR attributes that can only be viewed by managers. Be careful, however: it quickly complicates your model beyond what can be managed and, of course, these things take their toll on the performance of your model too.

But if needed, you can duplicate the structure to accommodate multiple sets of private attributes. You would have to create a model as pictured below:

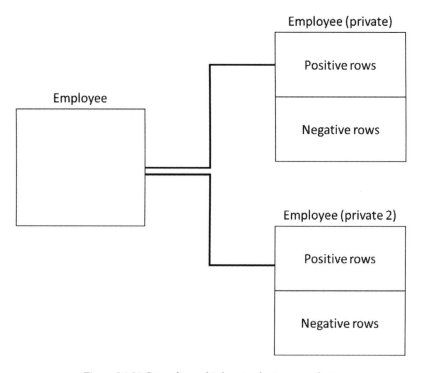

Figure 2.1.24: Setup for multiple sets of private attributes

Both private tables are linked directly to the public table. Having set this up, you can secure both sets of private attributes individually by applying RLS filters to the respective tables. Again, RLS on the public table determines which rows are visible at all.

How to develop in models with value-level security

One big issue with VLS is that developing reports against a VLS-enabled model becomes messy. As we saw in the previous section, when you have full access to a model, you will get duplicates of rows whenever you use a private attribute in a report.

When working in the model itself, one easy approach would be not to load the negative rows of the private tables. This way, you will see all private attributes, but at least you'll get no duplicates. The best way to do this is to use a parameter to set whether or not to load the negative rows. With this, you can switch all private tables at once by changing the parameter value.

Another approach is to create a Development table with a Private column containing values 0 and 1. You can then create relationships from all the private tables to the Development table on the Private columns. This allows you to set a filter in a report (Development[Private] = 1) to switch off all negative rows. This way, you can easily switch from within a report without having to expose the private tables themselves:

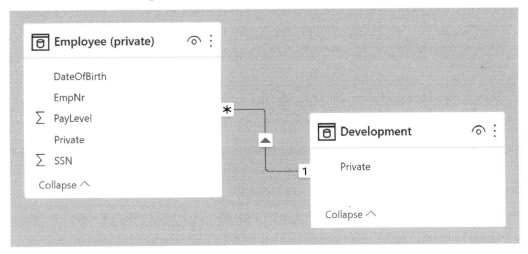

Figure 2.1.25: Creating a Development table with a relationship to private tables

With these approaches, you will be able to build reports while seeing data just like a user would. You still need to make sure that users do not see all data because they have edit rights on the Power BI model.

Another application of row-level security is to secure aggregation levels, which the next section is about. You can use a similar approach to securing attributes, although there are some caveats.

Securing aggregation levels

Yet another element in securing a Power BI model is related to aggregation levels. There could be a policy like *"salary costs may be viewed by team, but individual employees' salaries can only be viewed by their direct manager."* In this section, we explore options to secure viewing results on different aggregation levels.

Measures cannot be secured, fact tables can

We've mentioned it already earlier in this chapter: implementing security through DAX in measures is not secure. You should always design your model with a possible self-service user in mind, who will be able to write her own measures against the model. Through these, any security feature of your hard-wrought measures can be circumvented.

Instead, security must rely on the model structure and RLS only. This means that not every security policy that you can think of can be implemented. For instance, your users could ask for sales by individuals, but sales margin by team only. As both measures work on data from the same fact table, it is not possible to do this. In other cases, data is taken from different fact tables (for instance, one with sales by individual, one with salary costs by team).

Restricting fact table granularity

The most secure way of making sure that, say, salary costs can only be viewed by team and not by employee, is not to load these data at the employee level. You could create a salary costs fact table with rows per team. The obvious question here is how to give authorized users access to salary costs at the employee level anyway. You may do this with another dataset.

One of the lesser-used features of Power BI is **cross-report drillthrough**. It is a feature that is not so easy to implement, as it heavily depends on how your models and reports are published in the Power BI service. We will not cover cross-report drillthrough in detail here, but the concept is that when you enable it and reports are in the same workspace, you can enable drillthrough actions in a report that jump not to another page in the same report, but to a page in another report.

To get cross-report drillthrough to work, all that is needed is that fields in both reports used for the drillthrough action have the same name, so that Power BI can recognize them as being equal. The interesting thing here is that these reports don't have to use the same underlying model. This means that you can have a report with salary costs by team, and perform a drillthrough to a detailed report that shows salary costs by employee in a specific team. The model underlying the detailed report can implement its own security policies, so unauthorized users can be blocked from seeing the detailed data.

Securing aggregation levels with composite models

Composite models are Power BI models with a mix of DirectQuery fact tables and imported fact tables. The imported tables can be aggregated versions of the DirectQuery ones. This feature is designed to be able to report and analyze many billions of rows of data, and is based on the (plausible) assumption that users rarely need a look at lower detail levels in their data. Depending on the question asked, the model will choose to retrieve results from the aggregated table or, when needed, from the DirectQuery one. The selection is made automatically based on the aggregation level that is requested. To secure aggregation levels, this is not what we want; instead, we want to base this selection on security rules.

Fortunately, this can be done. You could have one fact table with salary costs at the team level, say fSalaryTeam, and another one with salary costs at the employee level, fSalaryEmployee. With RLS, you can shield fSalaryEmployee from unauthorized users, or even give users access to fSalaryEmployee for only some part of the data, like that relevant to their own team.

In the remainder of this section, we'll use a security role with access to the Europe division in the Teams table and to the Europe 2 team (with TeamNr = 9) in the fSalaryEmployee table as a simple example:

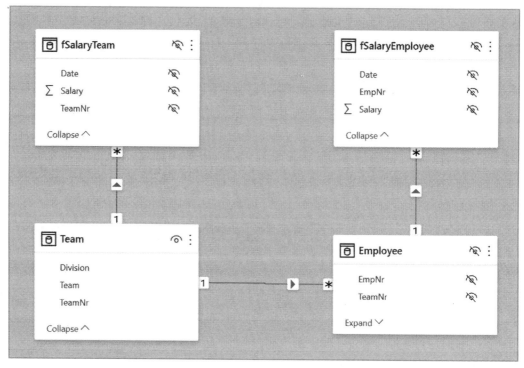

Figure 2.1.26: fSalaryTeam, fSalaryEmployee, Team, and Employee tables

The security filters are:

```
[Division] = "Europe"      // in table Teams
RELATED(Employee[TeamNr]) = 9     // in table fSalaryEmployee
```

 The model file for this section is 2.1 Aggregation security 1.pbix.

The challenge here is that you need to change the DAX code for measures; not to implement the security itself, but to seamlessly switch from one fact table to the other. Ideally, you would want one measure that takes salary costs from fSalaryTeam when evaluated on the team level or higher, but calculates over fSalaryEmployee when evaluated on the detailed level.

This challenge comes down to determining what the evaluation context for the measure looks like. In *Chapter 1.4, Context and Filtering*, you have seen several DAX functions that can help with that (ISFILTERED, ISCROSSFILTERED, and so on). Using these functions, you can build a measure that switches from one fact table to another. It is hard, though, to get it right, and some unexpected situations occur. Your first try might be the formula below:

```
Salary Costs =
IF(
    HASONEVALUE(Employee[EmpNr]),
    SUM(fSalaryEmployee[Salary]),
    SUM(fSalaryTeam[Salary])
)
```

This looks OK: whenever exactly one employee number is selected, in whatever way, calculate the salary from the fSalaryEmployee table, or else, calculate it from the fSalaryTeam table. The function HASONEVALUE is often used by inexperienced DAX developers, mainly in constructions like the following:

```
IF(HASONEVALUE(Table[Number]),
    VALUES(Table[Number]) * 5
)
```

Aside from the fact that there are better ways to extract a single value from a column, the HASONEVALUE (and, similarly, HASONEFILTER) functions have one property that is often overlooked: they return true when *exactly one* value is selected in the column. They return false when that number is larger than one, but also when it is zero!

The picture below shows the output from the Salary Costs measure in our example security role:

Division	Salary Costs
⊟ **Europe 1**	**851,268**
Bell, Kai	851,268
Hill, Britta	851,268
Jackson, Eabha	851,268
Kelly, Eric	851,268
Parker, Celestina	851,268
Rivera, Esperanza	851,268
Rodriguez, Freja	851,268
Scott, Axel	851,268
Stewart, Amaris	851,268
Thomas, Asher	851,268
Thompson, Amy	851,268
Wilson, Alexander	851,268
⊟ **Europe 2**	**819,972**
Bailey, Faustina	819,972
Bell, Kai	95,628
Campbell, Benjamin	819,972
Clark, Elke	819,972
Flores, Aziza	819,972
Total	**2,040,780**

Figure 2.1.27: Salary Costs output

Notice how many employees seem to have the same salary costs, and that they are actually equal to the salary costs of the team. Notice also that an employee like Kai Bell seems to be in two teams! In fact, we see all employees *not* belonging to a team appearing with the result for the team as a whole. The reason for that is that HASONEVALUE returns zero in those cases, causing the measure to choose fSalaryTeam to calculate over. For an in-depth discussion about why these employees are evaluated, see *Chapter 2.4, Working with AutoExist*.

Now, you may try to use ISFILTERED instead of HASONEVALUE in the DAX formula. But it does not help to report salary costs by, for instance, pay level. It would be better to determine if the selection is a subset of a team, and switch to employee-level data in that case.

One way to do this is to simply count the employees and compare the number with the total number of employees in the team:

```
Salary Costs =
IF(
    COUNTROWS(Employee) =
    CALCULATE(
        COUNTROWS(Employee),
        ALL(Employee),
        VALUES(Team[TeamNr])
    ),
    SUM(fSalaryTeam[Salary]),
    SUM(fSalaryEmployee[Salary])
)
```

The picture below shows sample output for this measure, both on employee name and on gender (both of which are columns in the Employee table):

Division	Salary Costs
⊟ **Europe**	**2,040,780**
⊞ **Europe**	**369,540**
⊞ **Europe 1**	**851,268**
⊟ **Europe 2**	**819,972**
Bell, Kai	95,628
Hill, Britta	66,612
Jackson, Eabha	67,740
Parker, Celestina	78,456
Rivera, Esperanza	67,644
Rodriguez, Freja	90,888
Scott, Axel	111,228
Stewart, Amaris	93,708
Thomas, Asher	77,004
Wilson, Alexander	71,064
Total	**2,040,780**

Division	Salary Costs
⊟ **Europe**	**2,040,780**
⊞ **Europe**	**369,540**
⊞ **Europe 1**	**851,268**
⊟ **Europe 2**	**819,972**
F	465,048
M	354,924
Total	**2,040,780**

Figure 2.1.28: Salary Costs for Europe 2 by employee name and gender

The security role only shows the Europe division and Salary Costs at the employee level for team Europe 2. As you can see from the output, Salary Costs by team are returned for all teams within Europe; this clearly shows that these results are taken from the fSalaryTeam table. Salary Costs by individual employee are only returned for team Europe 2; for other teams, the measure correctly retrieves data from the fSalaryEmployee table but receives nothing because the security filter does not allow that. When reporting Salary Costs by gender, we are not looking at individual employees. Still, the measure recognizes that an aggregation level below the team level is requested and takes results from the fSalaryEmployee table.

Combining aggregation security with value-level security

It is possible to combine securing the aggregation level with securing private data with RLS, but there are some additional things to take care of when you do this. The extended model would look like this:

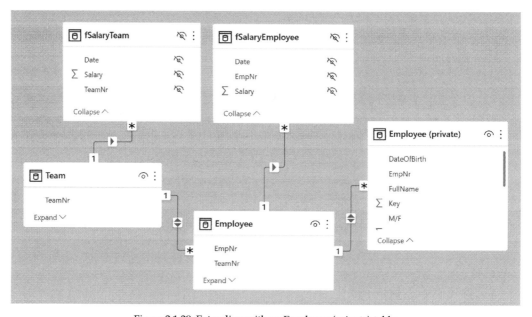

Figure 2.1.29: Extending with an Employee (private) table

If you were to change the output to Salary Costs by team and pay level, you would notice that you get the Salary Costs per team for each pay level. The reason, of course, is that our approach to determining whether a complete team is in context is falling flat now that we are using another table. An additional ALL clause should be added to the formula:

```
Salary Costs =
IF(
    COUNTROWS(Employee) =
    CALCULATE(
        COUNTROWS(Employee),
        ALL(Employee),
        ALL('Employee (private)'),
        VALUES(Team[TeamNr])
    ),
    SUM(fSalaryTeam[Salary]),
    SUM(fSalaryEmployee[Salary])
)
```

With this, the measure returns correct results:

Division	Salary Costs
⊟ **Europe**	**2,040,780**
⊟ **Europe**	**369,540**
⊞ **Europe 1**	**851,268**
⊟ **Europe 2**	**819,972**
29	201,996
30	71,064
33	155,460
34	280,224
35	111,228
Total	**2,040,780**

Figure 2.1.30: Salary Costs by team and pay level

Always remember that half of the rows in the private table must be hidden to avoid duplicate output (for the figure above, the security filter [Private] = 1 was applied).

You can, of course, implement more sophisticated rules now. If you want to secure higher pay levels, for instance, you may use this security filter on Employee (private):

```
([Paylevel] <= 33 && [Private] = 1)
||
([Paylevel] > 33 && [Private] = 0)
```

The result of this, combined with the division and team filters discussed above, is the following:

Division	Salary Costs
⊟ **Europe**	**2,040,780**
⊟ **Europe**	**369,540**
⊟ **Europe 1**	**851,268**
⊟ **Europe 2**	**819,972**
29	201,996
30	71,064
33	155,460
Total	**2,040,780**

Figure 2.1.31: Salary Costs by team and pay level, with higher pay levels secured

Note that we don't see any results for pay levels above 33, but also that the numbers don't add up. Shouldn't we get a blank line here with the results for levels 34 and up? When you take a close look at the security filter, you'll notice that the negative clause doesn't do anything. There are no rows in Employee (private) with Paylevel 34 or higher and Private = 0: after all, the whole point of the rows indicated with Private = 0 is that the other columns are blank! This means that we're not hiding one-half of the rows, but many more.

If you like the output as it is, that's fine, of course. If not, you would have to determine which employees have those higher pay levels, and filter based on their employee numbers. When doing this (we used a lazy enumeration of some employee numbers), the blanks show up:

Division	Salary Costs
⊟ **Europe**	**2,040,780**
⊟ **Europe**	**369,540**
	369,540
⊟ **Europe 1**	**851,268**
	851,268
⊟ **Europe 2**	**819,972**
	391,452
29	201,996
30	71,064
33	155,460
Total	**2,040,780**

Figure 2.1.32: Salary Costs by team and pay level, with higher pay levels secured and blanks shown

As you can see, it's not easy to get everything to work exactly how you would expect it; we now see blanks not only in team Europe 2, but in the other teams as well. After all, we do have access to these teams; all employees in those teams are grouped under the blank pay level, so the Salary Costs measure's logic determines that we're looking at all employees of the team and returns the team's salary costs.

By fine-tuning the security filter on Employees (private), you could even further control this and let the blank output only appear for team Europe 2. We'll leave that for you to detail out.

Securing an aggregation level as an attribute

Above, we've discussed securing an aggregation level on a per-fact table basis. Another way to approach aggregation-level security is to consider the aggregation level as an attribute. This way, all connected fact tables and, as a consequence, all measures, are subject to the security policy. This is less flexible than our previous approach, but the upside is that you don't have to write specific DAX measures, and it's easier to set up.

 The model file for this section is 2.1 Aggregation security 2.pbix.

The basic idea here is that when we want to secure output on the individual employee level, we could just treat every employee attribute as private. In other words, the public `Employee` table would only contain the keys (`EmpNr` and `TeamNr`, in our example) and all other columns would move to the `Employee` (private) table. With the value-level security approach introduced in this chapter, the employee data can then be secured.

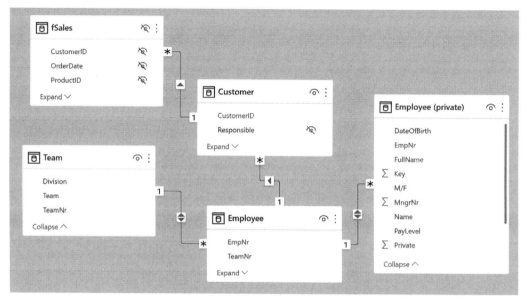

Figure 2.1.33: Leaving only the keys in the Employee table

Suppose you want to implement the security policy "*only data for the Europe division can be viewed; and only for team Europe 2 can it be viewed on the employee level.*" This can be done with two security filters on the `Team` and `Employee` (private) tables. On the `Team` table:

```
[Division] = "Europe"
```

On the Employee (private) table (using the fact that team Europe 2 has TeamNr 9, which can be found in the Employee table):

```
(RELATED(Employee[TeamNr]) = 9 && [Private] = 1)
||
(RELATED(Employee[TeamNr]) <> 9 && [Private] = 0)
```

With a straightforward Sales measure, you get the result in the picture below:

Division	Sales
⊟ **Europe**	**356,543,039.67**
⊟ **Europe**	**38,240,468.58**
	38,240,468.58
⊟ **Europe 1**	**155,169,593.24**
	155,169,593.25
⊟ **Europe 2**	**163,132,977.84**
Bell, Kai	28,576,085.10
Hill, Britta	5,395,875.37
Jackson, Eabha	15,110,324.82
Parker, Celestina	16,936,659.43
Rivera, Esperanza	18,618,870.70
Rodriguez, Freja	37,643,209.02
Scott, Axel	9,130,149.63
Stewart, Amaris	9,484,343.70
Thomas, Asher	14,808,215.18
Wilson, Alexander	7,429,244.89

Figure 2.1.34: Results of the security policy using VLS

You can extend this to, again, securing certain attributes of employees by splitting the Employee (private) table and creating an Employee (very private) table (although we would recommend a different naming scheme by this point). This is the exact same principle as the solution to having different sets of private attributes discussed before.

Both tables are related to the original Employee table:

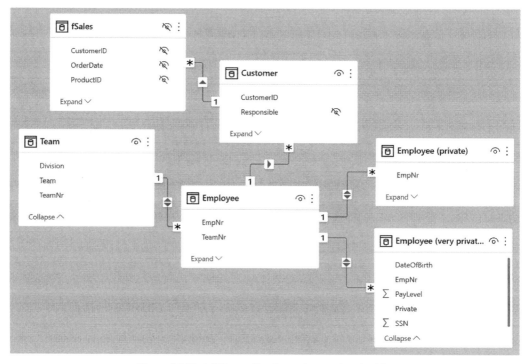

Figure 2.1.35: Adding an Employee (very private) table

You can now apply a different security filter to the Employee (very private) table, for example, to only allow access to very private data of employee 10220, using the positive/negative filter structure:

```
([EmpNr] = 10220 && [Private] = 1)
||
([EmpNr] <> 10220 && [Private] = 0)
```

The result in a table visual is in the picture below:

Division	Team	FullName	SSN	Sales
Europe	Europe			38,240,468.58
Europe	Europe 1			155,169,593.25
Europe	Europe 2	Bell, Kai		28,576,085.10
Europe	Europe 2	Hill, Britta		5,395,875.37
Europe	Europe 2	Jackson, Eabha		15,110,324.82
Europe	Europe 2	Parker, Celestina	73110445	16,936,659.43
Europe	Europe 2	Rivera, Esperanza		18,618,870.70
Europe	Europe 2	Rodriguez, Freja		37,643,209.02
Europe	Europe 2	Scott, Axel		9,130,149.63
Europe	Europe 2	Stewart, Amaris		9,484,343.70
Europe	Europe 2	Thomas, Asher		14,808,215.18
Europe	Europe 2	Wilson, Alexander		7,429,244.89
Total				**356,543,039.67**

Figure 2.1.36: Accessing the very private data of an employee

This approach to securing an aggregation level is not 100% secure, because the fact table still uses the granularity on the employee level. A self-service user could write measures to retrieve results for a specific employee with a formula like:

```
Sales 10201 =
CALCULATE(
    [Sales],
    fSales[EmpNr] = 10201
)
```

To be able to do this, the user would have to know that the number 10201 is used and what it stands for. If you implement this method, you should at least not use business keys, such as employee numbers, that are well known in your organization.

Summary

In this chapter, you have seen many aspects of securing Power BI models. Row-level security is a versatile feature, mainly because you can use DAX to implement sophisticated security filters.

Careful design is needed when implementing security in Power BI models, mainly due to the possibility of having multiple security roles, and because users may be a member of multiple roles. Not all security roles can effectively be combined in the same model, and security therefore even impacts decisions to split models.

With DAX, you can retrieve a user's identity and use that to determine what data is visible, allowing for highly personalized security settings. You can even navigate an organization's hierarchical structure using DAX PATH functions.

You have also learned that through effective combinations of modeling, DAX, and row-level security, you can achieve other forms of security, like value-level security to secure attributes, and securing aggregation levels.

The overall conclusion is this: DAX has tremendous power not only as a calculation language, but also to implement security policies.

In the next chapter, we will focus on a wholly different topic: visualizations, and how to make these even more dynamic than Power BI visuals already are.

2.2
Dynamically Changing Visualizations

Visualizations in a Power BI report use data from the Power BI model in two ways. First, values from *columns* are used to populate visual elements like the axis in a column chart, row labels in a table visual, or selection items in a slicer. We use the term **label** to generically refer to these elements. Second, aggregated data from the model, typically in the form of *DAX measures*, provides the results that a visual represents. While it is not visually clear, the buckets or wells that are used to bind a visual to data fields distinguish between these two types of data usage. For instance, the buckets **Axis** and **Legend** demand label data and the **Values** bucket needs aggregated data:

Figure 2.2.1: Field buckets for a Power BI visual

While Power BI provides many ways to create compelling reports out of the box, sometimes you want to go beyond these. This chapter presents approaches to dynamically change both ways of data binding through DAX. The two ways of binding data (columns and measures) each require their own DAX approach. It is even possible to combine both to create highly dynamic visuals.

In this chapter, we will cover the following topics:

- Dynamic measures
- Dynamic labels and axes
- Creating helper tables
- Combining dynamic labels with dynamic measures

Let's get started by introducing the Power BI model we will use.

The business case

A bicycle company, QuantoBikes, uses a Power BI model in order to keep track of their sales. Based on the data in the fSales table, the board has defined three key performance indicators (KPIs): the **sales per month**, the **year-to-date sales**, and the **12-month rolling sales**. These KPIs can be analyzed by order date, invoice date, or delivery date, which are also available in the fSales table. Additionally, the board is interested in the sales by product, country, and retail type. The data for this information is stored in three different tables: Products, Customers, and Cities.

 You can download the model file for this chapter, 2.2 Dynamically changing visualizations.pbix, from https://github.com/PacktPublishing/Extreme-DAX/tree/main/Chapter2.2.

The relationships between the different tables are depicted below:

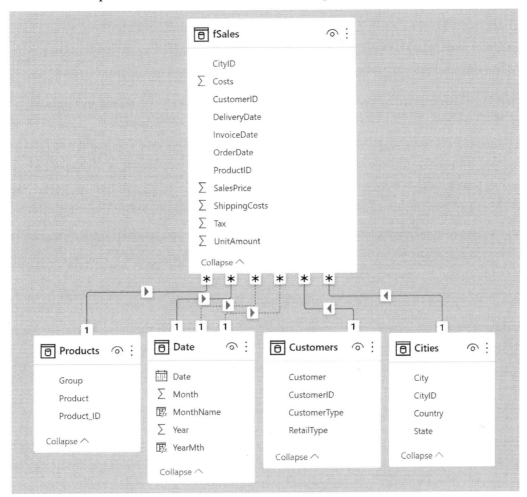

Figure 2.2.2: The model diagram

The Date to fSales relationships consist of one *active* relationship from Date[Date] to fSales[InvoiceDate] and two *inactive* relationships from Date[Date] to fSales[OrderDate] and from Date[Date] to fSales[DeliveryDate]. All other relationships are between the ID columns with the same name in both tables.

Many different views on the sales data are requested. Putting a separate visual for each view on the same report page would result in a cramped report, which is not that insightful. Another approach would be to divide the views over different pages in the report, which makes it hard to find the views you want to see.

The alternative is to make the visuals in the report dynamic, allowing the user to simply choose the view by, for instance, selecting an option in a slicer. What we want to accomplish is to create DAX measures that:

- Allow the user to change the calculation applied
- Allow the user to change both the calculation applied and the date column used in the sales table
- Allow the user to change the labels
- Combine all of the above into one visualization

Dynamic measures

A visual is bound to a measure by adding the measure to an appropriate bucket, like the **Value** bucket in a column chart. What we want to achieve is to let the user select a KPI using a slicer and adapt the measure to that selection. As measure binding is static (we cannot dynamically replace the measure with another measure), we need to create a DAX measure that responds to the slicer selection.

For this dynamic measure to work, a couple of things are needed:

1. We need to create basic measures for each KPI.
2. In order to use a slicer, we need to create a helper table with the KPI description.
3. We need to create a new measure that, based on the selection, selects the corresponding basic KPI measure.

Let us start with the basics.

The basic KPI measures

First, we create the three basic DAX functions for our KPIs:

1. The **sales per month** will be calculated by the DAX table function SUMX:

   ```
   Sales = SUMX(
           fSales,
           fSales[UnitAmount] * fSales[SalesPrice]
       )
   ```

   If you need more information about DAX table functions, see *Chapter 1.4,
   Context and Filtering*.

2. For the **year-to-date sales** measure, we use the time intelligence DAX
   function TOTALYTD:

   ```
   YTD Sales = TOTALYTD([Sales],'Date'[Date])
   ```

   If you need more information on DAX time intelligence functions, see *Chapter
   1.4*.

3. The last basic measure to calculate the **12-month rolling sales** uses a
   combination of the DAX filter function CALCULATE and the time intelligence
   function DATESINPERIOD. If you need more information on DAX filter
   functions, see *Chapter 1.4*. We will adjust this basic calculation to our specific
   needs during the process:

   ```
   12 mth Sales =
   CALCULATE(
       [Sales],
       DATESINPERIOD(
           'Date'[Date],
           MAX(fSales[OrderDate]), -12, MONTH)
   )
   ```

When using DATESINPERIOD, special consideration should be given to the reference date (MAX(fSales[OrderDate]) in the formula above). This date is the last date in the 12-month period returned by DATESINPERIOD.

In historical overviews, the reference date is the last day of the selected period, or MAX('Date'[Date]). For example, the 12-month rolling total for April 2020 is the sales for the 12 months ending with April 30, 2020. For a current view, this may not be the best option. For example, when today's date is January 13, 2022 and the context for the calculation selects January 2022, it would return sales for the period between February 1, 2021 and January 31, 2022. This includes almost half a month without sales, assuming no future sales are in our data. The result is a strange dip in the rolling total for the current month that only gradually improves when the month advances.

When orders are placed almost every day, using MAX(fSales[OrderDate]) solves this problem. When, again, today's date is January 13, 2022, the last order may be from January 12, 2022, and the running total is calculated over the period between January 13, 2021 and January 12, 2022.

An alternative would be to use MIN(MAX('Date'[Date]), TODAY()), although in this case, you would need to solve the problem of all future months returning the current rolling total. After all, a context selecting January 2048 would still return the rolling total for today.

Creating a helper table

If we want the user to have a slicer in the report to select one of the KPIs, we need to have a column in the model to populate the slicer. When this column does not exist, we have to create a table for this, called a **helper table** or, alternatively, a **control table**.

The helper table that we need looks like this:

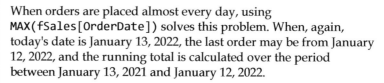

Code	Sort	Description
1	1	Sales
2	2	YTD Sales
4	3	12 mths rolling

Figure 2.2.3: The helper table

Our helper table contains three columns:

- The first column is named Code. It is used to determine the selection. We always use whole powers of 2 to populate this column, in other words, 1, 2, 4, 8, and so on. The reasoning behind this sequence is explained below.

- The second column is named Sort. It contains whole numbers, beginning with 1 in the first row and increasing by one with each row. You can use this column to sort the Description column (through the **Sort by column** option) whenever you do not want the items to be sorted alphabetically.

- The third column contains the Description. This is the column used in the slicer. You can, of course, use a name that aligns better with the selection made, like Time period in this case.

The helper table can be created as a calculated table using a DAX formula. The table should be given an appropriate name:

```
Time period =
DATATABLE(
    "Code", INTEGER,
    "Sort", INTEGER,
    "Description", STRING,
    {
        {1, 1, "Sales"},
        {2, 2, "YTD Sales"},
        {4, 3, "12 mths rolling"}
    }
)
```

Before we create the dynamic DAX measure, let us discuss how to use the helper table. The helper table does not have relationships with other tables in the model. When the Description column is used in a slicer, a selection in the slicer causes a filter on the column. As a result, the corresponding row is selected. Note that the user can select multiple rows when the slicer is not set on single select explicitly.

In the model, we now have a query context on the helper table and we can use DAX to determine what selection was made. If you use the DAX SUM function on the Code column, the powers of 2 make sure that each combination of selected items corresponds to a unique sum of Code values. For example, a sum of 5 can only be the result of selecting both **Sales** and **12 mths rolling**. Therefore, based on the result of SUM('Time period'[Code]), we can decide which calculation to choose.

There are other DAX functions that can be used here, like SELECTEDVALUE, which detects whether exactly one value in a column is selected. You should still use the Code column, though, to avoid having to change DAX code when someone decides that the descriptions should be changed. Our "powers of two" approach enables scenarios in which the selection of two or more items is allowed.

Creating a dynamic DAX measure

Now that we know how to detect a slicer selection on the helper table, we can use a SWITCH function to select the correct basic measure.

The DAX formula for this dynamic measure is:

```
DynHelperSales =
VAR SelectSales = SUM('Time period'[Code])
RETURN

SWITCH(SelectSales,
    1, [Sales],
    2, [YTD Sales],
    4, [12 mth Sales]
)
```

Let us look more closely at the SWITCH function. This function takes a first argument, Expression, followed by an arbitrary number of Value/Result argument pairs, and closes off with an optional Else argument.

The function evaluates the Expression and compares it consecutively with the Values. When the Expression and a Value are equal, the corresponding Result is returned. If not, the Expression is compared to the next Value. When none of the Values are equal to Expression, the function returns Else, or a blank value if Else is omitted.

In our example, we do not use the Else argument. So, if a selection is made that does not result in a value that is in the SWITCH list, the measure returns a blank.

As not selecting anything is equivalent to selecting all items, not using a slicer on Time period at all will result in blank results. For users who build their own reports on this Power BI model, this can be confusing. For this reason, you may consider adding an Else clause as a default, like [Sales].

The pictures below show sample output using this measure in a visual:

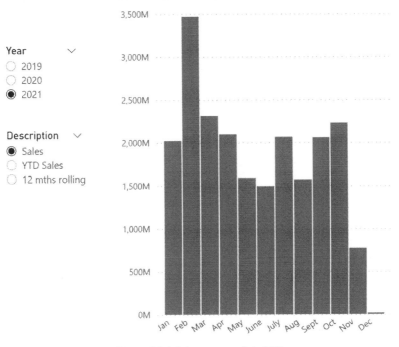

Figure 2.2.4: Sales per month in 2021

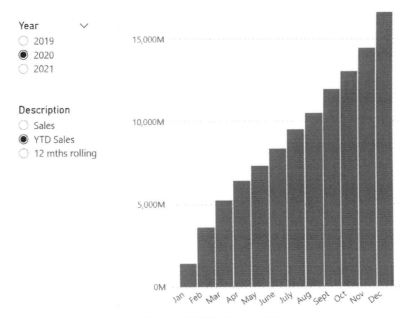

Figure 2.2.5: YTD Sales in 2021

Creating a dynamic visual using a helper table and dynamic DAX measure greatly enhances the experience of the user, who is now able to personalize part of the report. We can go one step further and combine this selection with a similar method to select the date used in the sales table. In doing so, a user can switch easily between a financial view (invoices), sales view (orders), and operations view (delivery).

Selecting both the calculation and date columns dynamically

In the previous section, we developed a DAX measure to dynamically switch between sales by period, year-to-date sales, and 12-month rolling total sales. We now want to apply a similar approach in a slightly different way, to dynamically select a relationship to use. To give you an idea of what we want to achieve, we have added two visualizations:

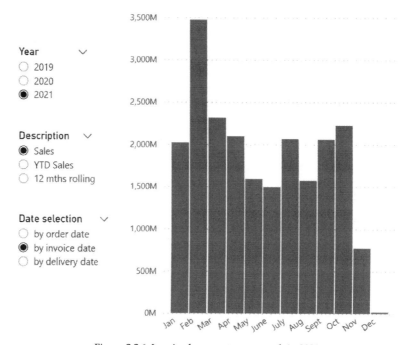

Figure 2.2.6: Invoiced amounts per month in 2021

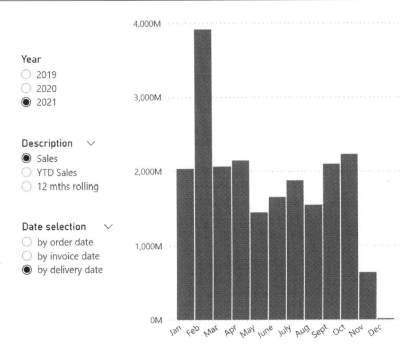

Figure 2.2.7: Value of delivered orders by month in 2021

What do we want to do? In the fSales table, we have three date columns: InvoiceDate, OrderDate, and DeliveryDate, each of which has a relationship with the Date table. By default, the active relationship on the InvoiceDate column is used. We want to use a slicer to dynamically activate one of the other relationships.

There is one caveat here: we created the 12-month rolling total based on OrderDate. Since the values in the other date columns are probably different, we need to adjust the DAX formula for the 12-month rolling total to use the proper date column.

Again, we need a helper table to allow us to choose between the date columns. The DAX formula is similar to the formula for the first helper table, with a different third column:

```
Date selection =
DATATABLE(
    "Code", INTEGER,
    "Sort", INTEGER,
    "Date selection", STRING,
    {
        {1, 1, "by order date"},
        {2, 2, "by invoice date"},
```

```
            {4, 3, "by delivery date"}
        }
    )
```

The DAX measure `DynHelperSales2` starts by determining the choices made in both helper tables:

```
DynHelperSales2 =
    VAR SelectSales = SUM('Time period'[Code])
    VAR SelectDate = SUM('Date selection'[Code])
RETURN

SWITCH(SelectSales,
    1, SWITCH(SelectDate,
        1, CALCULATE([Sales],
                USERELATIONSHIP(fSales[OrderDate],'Date'[Date])
            ),
        2, [Sales],
        4, CALCULATE([Sales],
                USERELATIONSHIP(fSales[DeliveryDate],'Date'[Date])
            )
        ),
    2, SWITCH(SelectDate,
        1, CALCULATE([YTD Sales],
                USERELATIONSHIP(fSales[OrderDate],'Date'[Date])
            ),
        2, [YTD Sales],
        4, CALCULATE([YTD Sales],
                USERELATIONSHIP(fSales[DeliveryDate],'Date'[Date])
            )
        ),
```

To respond to both helper table selections, two `SWITCH` functions need to be nested. The outer `SWITCH`, on `SelectSales`, is the time period selector as used in the previous section. The inner `SWITCH`, on `SelectDate`, activates the corresponding relationship. Note that `USERELATIONSHIP` has not been used in the option 2 inside the nested `SWITCH`. Since the relationship with the `InvoiceDate` column is the active one, the `USERELATIONSHIP` is not needed here.

The rolling total option needs extra care, as we need to work from another reference date. Instead of calling the generic `[12 mth sales]` measure, the logic is different for each option.

Each CALCULATE function now has two filter arguments: one provides the rolling total period with the correct reference date, the other selects the correct relationship.

```
    4, SWITCH(SelectDate,
        1, CALCULATE([Sales],
                DATESINPERIOD(
                    'Date'[Date],
                    MAX(fSales[OrderDate]),
                    -12,
                    MONTH
                ),
                USERELATIONSHIP(fSales[OrderDate],'Date'[Date])
            ),
        2, CALCULATE([Sales],
                DATESINPERIOD(
                    'Date'[Date],
                    MAX(fSales[InvoiceDate]),
                    -12,
                    MONTH
                ),
                USERELATIONSHIP(fSales[InvoiceDate],'Date'[Date])
            ),
        4, CALCULATE([Sales],
                DATESINPERIOD(
                    'Date'[Date],
                    MAX(fSales[DeliveryDate]),
                    -12,
                    MONTH
                ),
                USERELATIONSHIP(fSales[DeliveryDate],'Date'[Date])
            )
        )
    )
)
```

When you use this measure in the column chart, you can select both the time period and the kind of sales (determined by the date relationships), allowing for output like in *Figures 2.2.6* and *2.2.7*.

The DAX formula can be rewritten in a way that avoids nested SWITCH functions. For this, we use SWITCH in a slightly different way than is normally done. The common usage is to provide some value (typically, the result of some calculation) and then provide several options for static values to compare it with.

But you can flip this around: provide a static first value, and calculated values to compare with. This takes advantage of the fact that SWITCH does all comparisons in order of the arguments and will stop at the first match.

In the formula below, the first argument for SWITCH is the static value TRUE(). We then include tests on combinations of the selections, and the first test to return TRUE() is executed:

```
DynHelperSalesOption =
VAR SelectSales = SUM('Time period'[Code])
VAR SelectDate = SUM('Date selection'[Code])
RETURN

SWITCH(TRUE(),
    SelectSales = 1 && SelectDate = 1,
        CALCULATE([Sales],
            USERELATIONSHIP(fSales[OrderDate],'Date'[Date])),
    SelectSales = 1 && SelectDate = 2,
        CALCULATE([Sales],
            USERELATIONSHIP(fSales[InvoiceDate],'Date'[Date])),
    SelectSales = 1 && SelectDate = 4,
        CALCULATE([Sales],
            USERELATIONSHIP(fSales[DeliveryDate],'Date'[Date])),
    SelectSales = 2 && SelectDate = 1,
        CALCULATE([YTD Sales],
            USERELATIONSHIP(fSales[OrderDate],'Date'[Date])),
    SelectSales = 2 && SelectDate = 2,
        CALCULATE([YTD Sales],
            USERELATIONSHIP(fSales[InvoiceDate],'Date'[Date])),
    SelectSales = 2 && SelectDate = 4,
        CALCULATE([YTD Sales],
            USERELATIONSHIP(fSales[DeliveryDate],'Date'[Date])),

    SelectSales = 4 && SelectDate = 1,
        CALCULATE([Sales],
            DATESINPERIOD('Date'[Date],
            MAX(fSales[InvoiceDate]), -12, MONTH),
            USERELATIONSHIP(fSales[OrderDate], 'Date'[Date])),

    SelectSales = 4 && SelectDate = 2,
        CALCULATE([Sales],
            DATESINPERIOD('Date'[Date],
            MAX(fSales[InvoiceDate]), -12, MONTH),
            USERELATIONSHIP(fSales[InvoiceDate], 'Date'[Date])),
```

```
    SelectSales = 4 && SelectDate = 4,
        CALCULATE([Sales],
            DATESINPERIOD('Date'[Date],
            MAX(fSales[InvoiceDate]), -12, MONTH),
            USERELATIONSHIP(fSales[DeliveryDate], 'Date'[Date]))
    )
```

With this, we have a measure that includes multiple dynamic options in one formula. You can, of course, extend this with more selections in additional helper tables; enumerating all combinations in a single SWITCH expression avoids you having to nest even more levels of SWITCH.

Having dynamic values in visuals is one thing. Having the dynamic selection of labels in a visual is another, providing even more flexibility to the report user. This is the topic of the section below.

Dynamic labels

Consider the following challenge. Your Power BI report contains a column chart with sales by city. The users of your report want to have the option to select other labels for this chart, allowing them to view sales by, say, retail type or product group. Since you have already provided them with some slicers to select the measure used in the visual, you want to use a slicer to select the chart label as well.

 As this book is about DAX, we solve this problem with DAX. There are other options in Power BI: you could use bookmarks to show different charts, or allow the report user to select other fields from the model with personalized visuals. All options have pros and cons, like ease of use, the need to change DAX code, and the possibility of using a slicer or other report element to make the selection. We do not elaborate on the other options here.

In this section, a helper table and custom DAX measures are used to solve this challenge.

Solution overview

The fundamental difference between dynamic labels and the dynamic measures discussed earlier is that labels in a visual cannot be populated through calculated results. Instead, the label uses values from a single column in the model.

But the labels we want to provide come from three different tables in the model:

- Country, a column in the Cities table
- RetailType, a column in the Customers table
- Group, a column in the Products table

All values in these columns need to be in a single column to use them in a visual. To accomplish that, we will create a special helper table with two columns. The first column contains an indicator of which type of label (Country, RetailType, or Group) is in a row, and the second column contains the values from the three columns. The first column can be used to select the label type. A DAX measure will then implement a dynamic relationship to one of the three original tables.

Creating a helper table

The helper table is created as a calculated table based on a DAX formula. The figure below shows part of the table to give you an impression of what we aim to create:

Code	Country	LabelType
1	Australia	Countries
1	Canada	Countries
1	Germany	Countries
1	France	Countries
1	United Kingdom	Countries
1	United States	Countries
2	Value Added Reseller	RetailType
2	Warehouse	RetailType
2	West	RetailType
2	Limited	RetailType
2	East	RetailType
2	Ltd.	RetailType
2	Not Applicable	RetailType

Figure 2.2.8: The HelperAxes table

In the formula to create this calculated table, three DAX variables are defined that each create one part of the helper table. This is the first variable:

```
HelperAxes =
    VAR Country =
    CROSSJOIN(
        ROW("Code", 1),
        ROW("LabelType", "Countries"),
        VALUES(Cities[Country])
    )
```

The `CROSSJOIN` function combines multiple tables into one table that contains all columns from the input tables, and all combinations of rows in the input tables. In this case, we create a new table from three input tables:

- `ROW("Code", 1)` is a table with one row and a `Code` column containing the value 1

- `ROW("LabelType", "Countries")` is a one-row table as well, this time containing the value "Countries"

- `VALUES(Cities[Country])` is a one-column table, with possibly more than one row, containing the unique `Country` values

Since both `ROW` functions only create a one-row table, the total number of rows in the `CROSSJOIN` table is the number of unique values of the `Cities[Country]` column.

Similar variables are defined for the other label types to include. At the end, the `UNION` function is used to append the rows of the three (table) variables and create one big helper table:

```
HelperAxes =
    VAR Country = CROSSJOIN(
        ROW("Code", 1),
        ROW("LabelType", "Countries"),
        VALUES(Cities[Country])
        )
    VAR Customer = CROSSJOIN(
        ROW("Code", 2),
        ROW("LabelType", "RetailType"),
        VALUES(Customers[RetailType])
        )
    VAR Product = CROSSJOIN(
        ROW("Code", 4),
```

```
        ROW("LabelType", "Product Group"),
        VALUES(Products[Group])
        )
    RETURN


    UNION(Country, Customer, Product)
```

The name of the second column, Country, is not suitable anymore, since it contains different kinds of information. The name is derived from the Country column in the Cities table. When the table has been made, double-click on the header name and change the name Country to AxisValues.

Creating a DAX measure using dynamic labels

Now that we have a helper table to support dynamic labels, we need a DAX measure that selects the type of label to be used in a visual based on user input. Note that we don't really change labels; we just make sure that the measure only returns results for the label values corresponding to the selected label type. The visual will not show labels without any value. To give you an idea of what we want, below are the results of the DynAxis measure we are going to create.

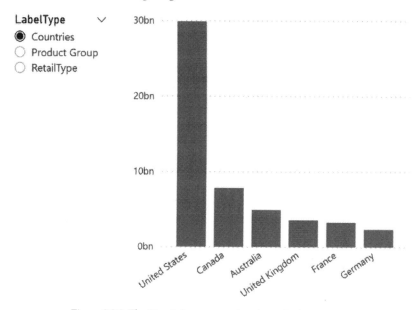

Figure 2.2.9: The DynAxis measure showing sales by country

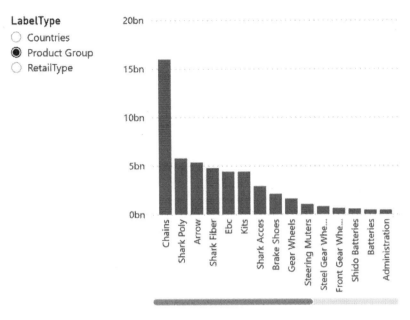

Figure 2.2.10: The DynAxis measure showing sales by product group

Like in the measure for dynamic calculations, we use `SWITCH` to determine the selection made:

```
DynAxis =
SWITCH(
    SELECTEDVALUE(HelperAxes[Code]),
    1,
    CALCULATE([Sales],
        TREATAS(VALUES(HelperAxes[AxisValues]), Cities[Country])
    ),
    2,
    CALCULATE([Sales],
        TREATAS(VALUES(HelperAxes[AxisValues]), Customers[RetailType])
    ),
    4,
    CALCULATE([Sales],
        TREATAS(VALUES(HelperAxes[AxisValues]), Products[Group])
    )
)
```

Note that there are now multiple rows with the same value in the `Code` column. To correctly determine the selection, we have to use `SELECTEDVALUE` to retrieve the unique code values selected, and then determine the actual values.

The DAX function TREATAS performs the real magic here. TREATAS takes a list of values and applies these as a filter to another column. The two columns do not need to be related in any way. You can interpret this as TREATAS creating a virtual relationship. Because of the way the DAX formula is structured, for each choice in label type, a virtual relationship to another table is created (Cities, Customers, or Products). "Real" relationships on these tables propagate the filter onto other tables in the model.

Look again at the figures at the start of the section for the result of the DAX measure in a visual. The slicer filters on the LabelType column from the helper table, while the AxisValues column is used on the *y*-axis of the chart.

The helper table and DAX measure successfully implement a dynamic *y*-axis. The obvious question now is: *can we also add the slicers for time period and sales type that were implemented in the dynamic calculation section?* This is, in fact, not hard to do, although it comes with some work.

Combining dynamic labels and dynamic calculations

If you want to combine the dynamic labels and the dynamic calculations in one visual, you need to use a logical combination of the DAX logic we have seen so far. We can still use SWITCH to determine selections made by the user, but keep in mind that the number of options grows fast. In our case, we have three helper tables, each with three options, meaning 3 x 3 x 3 = 27 options inside the SWITCH function. That is a lot of DAX code to write! Here are examples of the results:

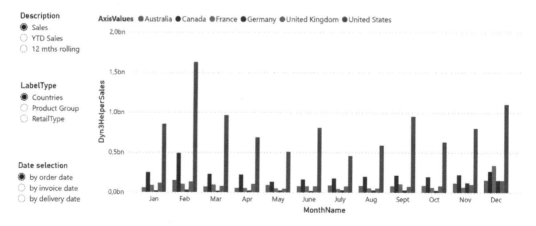

Figure 2.2.11: Sales by countries and order date

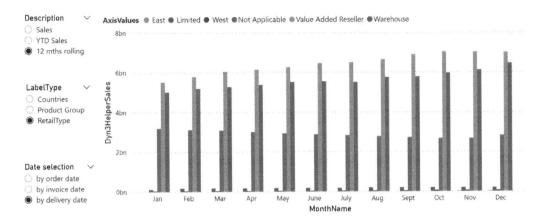

Figure 2.2.12: 12-month rolling sales by retail type and delivery date

It would be too much to include all this code on these pages. Instead, you can find the code in the model for this chapter. For now, let us take a look at some parts of the calculation. Below is the start of the DAX formula with three variable declarations to capture the choices of the user:

```
DynHelperSales3 =
    VAR SelectSales = SUM('Time period'[Code])
    VAR SelectDate = SUM('Date selection'[Code])
    VAR SelectAxis = SELECTEDVALUE(HelperAxes[Code])
RETURN
```

The SWITCH function again uses the SWITCH(TRUE() approach we saw earlier. The first option looks like this:

```
SWITCH(TRUE(),
    SelectSales = 1 && SelectDate = 1 && SelectAxis = 1,
        CALCULATE(
            [Sales],
            USERELATIONSHIP(fSales[OrderDate], 'Date'[Date]),
            TREATAS(VALUES(HelperAxes[AxisValues]), Cities[Country])
    ),
```

Again, all options need to evaluate to TRUE() or FALSE(); SWITCH only executes the first option that is true. The option shown here is:

- The [Sales] measure, because SelectSales equals 1
- The relationship on OrderDate, as SelectDate is 1

- A virtual relationship using TREATAS on Cities[Country] as a result of
  SelectAxis = 1

In comparison, the option for 12-month rolling total sales on delivery date by retail type uses this DAX code:

```
SelectSales = 4 && SelectDate = 2 && SelectAxis = 2,
        CALCULATE(
            [Sales],
            DATESINPERIOD(
                'Date'[Date],
                MAX(fSales[InvoiceDate]),
                -12,
                MONTH
            ),
            USERELATIONSHIP(fSales[InvoiceDate],'Date'[Date]),
            TREATAS(
                VALUES(HelperAxes[AxisValues]),
                Customers[RetailType]
            )
        ),
```

Although the complete formula is very long, all options have a similar structure. Note again that SWITCH evaluates options in order until one is true; the order in which you include the options in the SWITCH expression is completely up to you. It helps to keep a logical order, but you may gain performance slightly by positioning the most common option as the first one.

Summary

In this chapter, you have learned how to use helper tables to capture user input. Depending on your intended use, a helper table can be as simple as a few rows with options, or a larger list based on other data in the Power BI model. In most cases, helper tables have no relationships with other tables in the model. User input in the form of a selection in a slicer can be captured in DAX measures. The SWITCH function is used to select the appropriate calculation based on the user input.

Keep in mind that when using multiple helper tables for dynamic selections, it is better to use an extended SWITCH statement than to work with nested SWITCH functions. Be aware that nesting can also occur through calling another measure that does its own SWITCH. Piling up dynamic selectors like this can eventually lead to performance issues.

In the next chapter, we dive deeper into calendar-based analysis. While we have used several time-intelligence DAX functions in this chapter, many organizations cannot use them because they work with a type of calendar that is not natively supported by DAX.

2.3
Alternative Calendars

Few Power BI models are not concerned with dates. The proper way to handle time-based analysis in a Power BI model is to have a date or calendar table. It allows you to evaluate results not only by the periods of time you select, but also to compare results with the same result in the previous year, calculate year-to-date totals, or do other comparisons over time. In *Chapter 1.3, Using DAX*, the date table in a Power BI model was discussed. In *Chapter 1.4, Context and Filtering*, we covered DAX time intelligence functions that provide a wealth of time-based filter options.

The built-in DAX time intelligence functions assume that you use the common Gregorian calendar. As you know, this calendar organizes days into months with a variable number of days, quarters consisting of three months, and years containing four quarters. Many businesses do not work with the Gregorian calendar, but use a calendar that is primarily week-based instead. In such a calendar, days roll up in weeks, weeks are combined into periods containing a variable number of weeks, quarters contain three periods, and years contain four quarters as usual.

This type of calendar is very common in companies with a continuous production process. Using a week-based calendar has several advantages in this case, like being able to compare some period with the same period in the previous year, while knowing that both periods contain exactly the same number of days.

This chapter deals with calendar-based analysis for week-based calendars. You will explore the following topics:

- Conceptual differences between week-based calendars and the Gregorian calendar
- Creating a week-based calendar table
- Time intelligence analysis on week-based calendars
- Keeping your report current

Week-based and Gregorian calendars

Let us first zoom in to what makes a week-based calendar fundamentally different from the Gregorian calendar, and what varieties exist in week-based calendars. We will choose one variety to work with in the remainder of this chapter.

What is a week-based calendar?

While in both week-based and Gregorian calendars, the day is the smallest unit, there is a huge difference in how days are grouped into larger units. While the Gregorian calendar knows about weeks, a week is not a proper hierarchical level in the calendar: most months are about 4½ weeks long, except for February (and not even in leap years). Even February usually starts somewhere in the middle of a week.

A week-based calendar uses the week as a proper hierarchical level from which all higher levels are defined. A week-based calendar does not have a month; instead, weeks are grouped into periods.

The advantage of a week-based calendar is that the end date of a period is always the same (last) day of a week. Since each period has a predictable length of a fixed number of weeks, this calendar type is very useful for manufacturing planning. The disadvantage of a week-based calendar is that it misses one day in the (Gregorian) year (7 days x 52 weeks = 364 days). To account for that, every five years a 53rd week is added. This can make comparisons in the last period of the year difficult.

The table below lists the differences between the Gregorian and week-based calendars:

Gregorian calendar	Week-based calendar
Month-based	Week-based with periods consisting of whole weeks
Month starts on a random weekday	Week (and periods) always start on the same weekday
Months have different numbers of days, which makes comparisons difficult	Periods follow a simple, repeating structure with mostly the same number of days
Year and month can be read and extracted from the date, as we commonly refer to dates in their Gregorian representation, like January 4, 2023	Calculations are needed to derive week number, period, and even year from the date
Sometimes a year lasts one day longer	Sometimes a year lasts one week longer

Table 2.3.1: Gregorian versus week-based calendars

Week numbers

In a week-based calendar, weeks are the second hierarchical level, after days. The basis of a week is a set of seven days, although, depending on the definition used, some weeks have fewer days. The number of weeks in a year is 52 normally, but as a Gregorian year is 52.143 weeks long, in some years week 53 is added to compensate.

There are different definitions of week numbers, based on regional practices. The ISO 8601 definition, widely used in Europe, has the following characteristics:

- Each new ISO week starts on a Monday.
- An ISO week can start in one (Gregorian) year and end in the next year. For instance, ISO week 52 in 2021 starts on Monday, December 27, 2021, and ends on Sunday, January 2, 2022.
- By definition, January 4 always belongs to ISO week 1. Alternatively, the first Thursday of the year always belongs to ISO week 1.

The week number definitions used in the USA are different; they are characterized by the following:

- Each week starts on a Sunday.
- January 1 always belongs to week 1.
- As a consequence, the first and the last week of a given year have, in general, less than 7 days. In *Figure 2.3.1*, you see that week number 1 in 2022 consists of one day, and week 53 ends on Friday, December 31 2021:

Days	WeekNum ISO	WeekNum USA
Saturday, December 25, 2021	51	52
Sunday, December 26, 2021	51	53
Monday, December 27, 2021	52	53
Tuesday, December 28, 2021	52	53
Wednesday, December 29, 2021	52	53
Thursday, December 30, 2021	52	53
Friday, December 31, 2021	52	53
Saturday, January 1, 2022	52	1
Sunday, January 2, 2022	52	2
Monday, January 3, 2022	1	2
Tuesday, January 4, 2022	1	2
Wednesday, January 5, 2022	1	2
Thursday, January 6, 2022	1	2
Friday, January 7, 2022	1	2
Saturday, January 8, 2022	1	2
Sunday, January 9, 2022	1	3
Monday, January 10, 2022	2	3
Tuesday, January 11, 2022	2	3
Wednesday, January 12, 2022	2	3
Thursday, January 13, 2022	2	3

Figure 2.3.1: The differences between ISO and USA week numbers

Power BI provides a DAX function called WEEKNUM that returns the week number of a given date. The second argument of this function allows you to switch between different week number definitions. We will only focus on options 1 and 21 here:

- Use 1 and the start of the week will be on Sunday (USA definition).
- Use 21 and the ISO week number will be returned.

The WEEKNUM function will automatically deal with years that contain 53 weeks.

Periods

In the Gregorian calendar, months have varying numbers of days but a year always has 12 months. This makes months a popular reporting level. Using 52 or 53 weeks per year for reporting is less convenient; that is why an additional hierarchical level is defined in a week-based calendar: the **period**. A period contains a whole number of weeks (the calendar is week-based, after all), and a year contains a fixed number of periods.

These prerequisites lead to various options, like:

- Periods of 4 weeks each, with 13 periods in a year
- Periods of 4 or 5 weeks each, with 12 periods in a year

The first option has the advantage of fixed period lengths, but the periods are less aligned with the Gregorian months, which makes this calendar less intuitive for many people. On top of that, as 13 is a prime number, the year cannot be divided into larger parts than periods, like quarters.

The more common option is to divide the year into 12 periods. Each period has 4 or 5 ISO weeks, although the last period may have week 53 added as well. You can group the periods into different patterns. A 4-5-4 calendar uses a pattern of one 4-week period, one 5-week period, and another 4-week period. Some companies use a 5-4-4 calendar, but the most common choice is to use a 4-4-5 calendar.

In the remainder of this chapter, we will use a 4-4-5 calendar. All calculations are easily adapted to other week-based calendars.

Quarters

A quarter in the Gregorian calendar spans 3 months. In a 4-4-5 calendar, we work with periods, and a quarter now spans 3 periods, or 13 ISO weeks. This is exactly 91 days per quarter. Only the last quarter can contain 7 days more because of week 53. With this exception, comparisons between quarters are based on exactly the same number of days.

Years

The common Gregorian year contains 365 days. The actual time needed for the Earth to orbit the sun is around 365.25 days, so every four years there is a leap year that is one day longer. A year is the period normally used to evaluate business. If you use a 4-4-5 calendar, the start and the end of each year are defined by the first and last week in the year. In the week numbering system used in the USA, the fixed week length is sacrificed to match the start and end of the Gregorian year. In the ISO 8601 week numbering system, things are reversed: here, the alignment with the Gregorian year is sacrificed to keep the fixed week length.

It is a common mistake to use ISO week numbers in a Power BI model in combination with the Gregorian year. When working with the ISO standard, you should not only use the correct week numbering and have periods in your calendar table, but you should also have an **ISO year** that aligns with the week numbers.

The difference is mainly in the first and last days of the year, of course; this is where the ISO 8601 standard puts days in December in week 1 of the new year, or days in January in week 52 (or 53) of the previous year. By definition, the first Thursday in the year is in week 1; this means that on every Thursday in the year, the Gregorian year matches the ISO year.

Creating a week-based calendar table

When you want to use a week-based calendar, you need to have an appropriate date table. In this section, we will construct a date table as a calculated table with DAX. We will give it the name ISO Date, and use the ISO 8601 standard.

 You can download the model file for this chapter, 2.3 Alternative calendars.pbix, from https://github.com/ PacktPublishing/Extreme-DAX/tree/main/Chapter2.3.

Setting up dates

Since the Gregorian calendar is the basis of all date calculations in DAX, we start the calendar formula as a date table based on the Gregorian calendar. The next step is adding columns to translate the Gregorian into a 4-4-5 calendar, followed by some necessary changes. We start with some variables to define the first and last year in the table:

```
ISO Date 1 =
VAR StartYear = 2019
VAR EndYear = YEAR(TODAY())
RETURN
ADDCOLUMNS(
    CALENDAR(DATE(StartYear, 1, 1), DATE(EndYear, 12, 31)),
    "ISOWeek", WEEKNUM([Date], 21)
)
```

The StartYear variable defines the year at which the date table needs to start; we have chosen 2019 here. The EndYear variable retrieves the year of today's date using a combination of the DAX functions YEAR and TODAY.

The CALENDAR function returns a single-column table, in which the column is named Date, containing a contiguous set of dates between the dates provided in the two arguments. Using the DATE function, we have constructed January 1 of the start year, and December 31 of the end year.

Note that you can define StartYear and EndYear in any way you like. Both can be static values, in which case you may be in trouble when more recent data from after EndYear is loaded. You can decide to have the table end at next year instead of the current year by simply using YEAR(TODAY()) + 1. You could also choose to base StartYear on data that is in the fact tables in your model.

The ADDCOLUMNS function is used to – you guessed it – add columns to a table. Next to an input table, this function needs both a name for the columns to be added, and an expression to define what values are in the different rows. This expression, evaluated in row context on the input table, can use values from the columns in the input table. The column added here contains the ISO week numbers.

If you look at the results of this formula, in the ISOWeek column, you'll notice that the first week only has 6 days:

Date	ISOWeek
1/1/2019	1
1/2/2019	1
1/3/2019	1
1/4/2019	1
1/5/2019	1
1/6/2019	1
1/7/2019	2
1/8/2019	2
1/9/2019	2

Figure 2.3.2: Week 1 in 2019 is missing a day

As mentioned earlier, the first ISO week can start in the current (Gregorian) year, but also in the previous year. The same can happen in the last ISO week of the year: the week might end in the next Gregorian year, and we will miss days in the last week. Let's first correct the beginning and the end of the table.

Finding the correct start date

After providing the start and end year for which to create a week-based table, we need to find the correct dates to create a table with full ISO weeks. Unfortunately, this is way more complex than we'd like; we will approach it step by step and find the correct start date first.

The formula needs to calculate the correct start of the first ISO week, regardless of the year. One thing we know is that, by definition, January 4 is always in ISO week 1. We can therefore use January 4 as an approximate start date and derive the exact start date from it:

```
ISO Date 2 =
VAR StartYear = 2019
VAR EndYear = YEAR(TODAY())

VAR ApproxStartDate = DATE(StartYear, 1, 4)
VAR ExactStartDate = ApproxStartDate - WEEKDAY(ApproxStartDate, 3)
```

The ExactStartDate variable uses the WEEKDAY function. This function returns the number of the day within a week. The first argument is a date, the ApproxStartDate in our case. The second argument specifies how the days are counted throughout the week. The argument accepts the values 1 to 3:

- **1:** The first day of the week is a Sunday with number 1 and the last day is a Saturday with number 7.

- **2:** The first day of the week is a Monday with number 1 and the last day is a Sunday with number 7.

- **3:** The first day of the week is a Monday with number 0 and the last day is a Sunday with number 6.

We take option 3, as this allows us to subtract the weekday number from the date to always arrive at a Monday, or the start of the week in which the date falls:

Days	Option 3	ISO Weeknum
Sunday, December 30, 2018	6	52
Monday, December 31, 2018	0	1
Tuesday, January 1, 2019	1	1
Wednesday, January 2, 2019	2	1
Thursday, January 3, 2019	3	1
Friday, January 4, 2019	4	1
Saturday, January 5, 2019	5	1
Sunday, January 6, 2019	6	1
Monday, January 7, 2019	0	2
Tuesday, January 8, 2019	1	2

Figure 2.3.3: Weekday option 3 can help to retrieve the first day of the week

In the figure, you can see that January 4, 2019, was a Friday, with weekday number 4 using option 3. Subtracting 4 from the date, we arrive at Monday, December 31, 2018. So, the first day of ISO year 2019 is the last day of Gregorian year 2018. If we use ExactStartDate as the first day in the calendar table, we are sure that the first week is complete.

Now that we have the correct start date for our table, let's focus on the correct ending of the last year.

Finding the correct end date

The correct end date for our table is harder to find. Again, we start with a Gregorian candidate: December 31. The following figure shows the dates around year-end 2021 and early 2022:

Days	WeekNum ISO	WeekDay
Saturday, December 25, 2021	51	5
Sunday, December 26, 2021	51	6
Monday, December 27, 2021	52	0
Tuesday, December 28, 2021	52	1
Wednesday, December 29, 2021	52	2
Thursday, December 30, 2021	52	3
Friday, December 31, 2021	52	4
Saturday, January 1, 2022	52	5
Sunday, January 2, 2022	52	6
Monday, January 3, 2022	1	0
Tuesday, January 4, 2022	1	1
Wednesday, January 5, 2022	1	2

Figure 2.3.4: The last ISO week of 2021

As can be seen here, the first two days of 2022 are still in ISO week 52 of ISO year 2021. The question is: how can we use what we know about December 31 to derive what the last day of the year is?

Let us list the possible scenarios. December 31 may be in three ISO weeks: week 52, week 53, or week 1 in the next year.

- If the ISO week number is **52** or **53**, we know that this is the last week of the year, and we simply have to find the last day of the week. (In case you were wondering, if the week number is 52, there can be no week 53: that week would start on January 1 or later, and that means that January 4 would be in that week as well. But, by definition, January 4 is in week 1.)

- If the ISO week number is **1**, the next year has already started. In this case, the last day of the year can be found by moving back a full week and then finding the last day of that week.

As every ISO week starts on a Monday, the end of the last ISO week in the table needs to be a Sunday. With WEEKDAY, you can calculate the number of days you need to add: this is 6 minus the weekday number (with option 3).

Let's put this into DAX code now:

```
VAR ApproxEndDate = DATE(EndYear, 12, 31)
VAR ExactISOWeekDate = ApproxEndDate -
        7 * (WEEKNUM(ApproxEndDate, 21) = 1)
VAR ExactEndDate = ExactISOWeekDate -
        (6 - WEEKDAY(ExactISOWeekDate, 3))
```

The (WEEKNUM(ApproxEndDate, 21) = 1) expression returns a Boolean, true or false, but in arithmetic, this is translated to 1 or 0, respectively. If the ISO week number of ApproxEndDate equals 1, it subtracts 7 x 1 days, otherwise it subtracts 0 days. So, only when the ISO week number is 1, we move ExactISOWeekDate to one week before ApproxEndDate. As we now have a date that is guaranteed to be in the last week of the ISO year, we move to the end of that week in the ExactEndDate variable.

Now that we have both the correct start date and end date, we can use all these variables to create our calendar table:

```
ISO Date 2 =
VAR StartYear = 2019
VAR EndYear = YEAR(TODAY())

VAR ApproxStartDate = DATE(StartYear, 1, 4)
VAR ExactStartDate = ApproxStartDate - WEEKDAY(ApproxStartDate, 3)
VAR ApproxEndDate = DATE(EndYear, 12, 31)
VAR ExactISOWeekDate = ApproxEndDate -
        7 * (WEEKNUM(ApproxEndDate, 21) = 1)
VAR ExactEndDate = ExactISOWeekDate +
        (6 - WEEKDAY(ExactISOWeekDate, 3))
RETURN
ADDCOLUMNS(
    CALENDAR(ExactStartDate, ExactEndDate),
    "ISOWeek", WEEKNUM([Date], 21)
)
```

The start and end of the resulting table are as follows:

Date	ISOWeek		Date	ISOWeek
12/31/2018	1		12/24/2021	51
1/1/2019	1		12/25/2021	51
1/2/2019	1		12/26/2021	51
1/3/2019	1		12/27/2021	52
1/4/2019	1		12/28/2021	52
1/5/2019	1		12/29/2021	52
1/6/2019	1		12/30/2021	52
1/7/2019	2		12/31/2021	52
1/8/2019	2		1/1/2022	52
1/9/2019	2		1/2/2022	52

Figure 2.3.5: The start and the end of the ISO Date 2 table

With this, we have a date table with ISO week numbers that contains complete ISO years. This table can now be extended with other columns, like the period number. This is the topic of the next section.

Creating additional columns

An important column to include is the **period**. The structure of a 4-4-5 period calendar means that ISO weeks 1 to 4 belong to period 1, weeks 5 to 8 are in period 2, and the five weeks 9 to 13 are in period 3; and so on until the end of the year. You may want to find some arithmetic trick to compute the period number from the week number, but we will keep it simple and just list all week numbers with their period numbers. The following code is to be used as a calculated column in the table created above.

 You can add these columns in the table formula created earlier. We do not do that here to keep things readable, but you can find the complete formula in the model file. As some of the new columns, such as the Period column described here, use columns that are themselves added as calculated columns or in ADDCOLUMNS, you need nested ADDCOLUMNS functions to accomplish this.

```
Period =
        ( [ISOWeek] IN {1, 2, 3, 4})            *  1 +
        ( [ISOWeek] IN {5, 6, 7, 8})            *  2 +
        ( [ISOWeek] IN {9, 10, 11, 12, 13})     *  3 +
        ( [ISOWeek] IN {14, 15, 16, 17})        *  4 +
        ( [ISOWeek] IN {18, 19, 20, 21})        *  5 +
        ( [ISOWeek] IN {22, 23, 24, 25, 26})    *  6 +
        ( [ISOWeek] IN {27, 28, 29, 30})        *  7 +
        ( [ISOWeek] IN {31, 32, 33, 34})        *  8 +
        ( [ISOWeek] IN {35, 36, 37, 38, 39})    *  9 +
        ( [ISOWeek] IN {40, 41, 42, 43})        * 10 +
        ( [ISOWeek] IN {44, 45, 46, 47})        * 11 +
        ( [ISOWeek] IN {48, 49, 50, 51, 52, 53}) * 12
```

In the code, each (`[ISOWeek]  IN {...}`) expression is either true or false, which is translated into 1 or 0, respectively. In the list of expressions, exactly one is true in any row. For instance, if the ISO week number is 18, the expression `[ISOWeek] IN {18, 19, 20, 21}` is true, while all the others are false. The calculation will return 1 x 5, or period 5.

A simple column to add is the **weekday**:

```
Weekday = WEEKDAY([Date])
```

Another column we want to have is the **ISO year**. This is the code:

```
ISO Year = YEAR([Date] - WEEKDAY([Date], 3) + 3)
```

For this column, we simply apply the logic that we used earlier to find the first day of the week for any date. When we subtract the weekday number with option 3, we get the Monday in the same week. And by definition, this Monday is in the same ISO year as the date itself. However, this Monday could be in a previous Gregorian year; so, to make sure we can use the YEAR function, we add 3 again to move to the Thursday. (Remember that the Gregorian year and the ISO year are the same for each Thursday.)

For the time intelligence calculations later in this chapter, we will find that having a **week counter** in the date table is very helpful. This counter is a value that starts at zero for the first week in the date table and is increased by 1 with every week:

```
WeekCtr = ROUNDDOWN(([Date] – MIN([Date]) / 7, 0)
```

This formula computes the difference between a date and the first date, divides it by 7 to get an approximate number of weeks between them, and rounds down to a whole number. The result of this is a counter that starts at zero in the first week in the table.

Another useful column is a **period counter**. This cannot be calculated from the dates, like WeekCtr above; instead, we use the ISO years and the period number to calculate a unique number:

```
PeriodCtr = ([ISO Year] - MIN([ISO Year])) * 12 + [Period]
```

This calculation is based on the fact that every ISO year has 12 periods. For a day in the first period in 2019, for instance, January 9, 2019, the result of the formula is:

```
(2019 - 2019) * 12 + 1 = 1
```

If you use a date from the first period in the second accounting year, for instance, January 9, 2020, the result is:

```
(2020 - 2019) *12 + 1 = 13
```

This way, we have a continuously increasing sequence.

Finally, we create three columns that are based on one or two of the basic columns. First, the Year-week column combines the ISO year with the ISO week number. The second column, Year-period, combines the ISO year with the period number. The Previous Year column is just the ISO year minus 1 and will prove useful in the time intelligence calculations coming up:

```
Year-week = ([ISO Year] * 100) + [ISOWeek],

Year-period = ([ISO Year] * 100) + [Period]

Previous Year = [ISO Year] - 1
```

The calendar is now ready for use in the remainder of this chapter. Below is some sample data:

Date	Period	ISOWeek	ISO Year	WeekCtr	PeriodCtr	Year-week	Year-perio	Weekday	Previous Y
12/31/2018	1	1	2019	0	1	201901	201901	0	2018
1/1/2019	1	1	2019	0	1	201901	201901	1	2018
1/2/2019	1	1	2019	0	1	201901	201901	2	2018
1/3/2019	1	1	2019	0	1	201901	201901	3	2018
1/4/2019	1	1	2019	0	1	201901	201901	4	2018
1/5/2019	1	1	2019	0	1	201901	201901	5	2018
1/6/2019	1	1	2019	0	1	201901	201901	6	2018
1/7/2019	1	2	2019	1	1	201902	201901	0	2018
1/8/2019	1	2	2019	1	1	201902	201901	1	2018
1/9/2019	1	2	2019	1	1	201902	201901	2	2018

Figure 2.3.6: The start of the ISO Date table

Note that because of the different approach, the WeekCtr and PeriodCtr columns start at different values. This is not a problem, as these columns are only needed to freely move across the date table; their actual values do not matter.

Time Intelligence calculations for week-based calendars

Now that we have created a 4-4-5 calendar table, we can start using this table to do time intelligence analysis. Instead of the common time intelligence calculations like year-to-date or month-to-date, we now need ISO-year-to-date, or period-to-date calculations. Since the standard DAX time intelligence functions are based on the Gregorian calendar, we will need to build our own calculations. To demonstrate the formulas, we will analyze the sales of the company QuantoBikes.

The Power BI model

QuantoBikes wants to monitor its sales. Since it uses a 4-4-5 calendar, all results need to be reported accordingly. These are the insights needed:

- **Year-to-date sales**: The cumulative sales within an (ISO) year.

- **Year-on-year growth**: Comparing sales of a day, week, period, quarter, or year to the results in the same time period of the previous year. As QuantoBikes works with a 4-4-5 calendar, the number of days in each time period is exactly the same.

- **Rolling average sales**: Average sales per ISO week within a rolling window of weeks.

The Power BI model used is very simple: all it contains is a fact table, fSales, and the ISO Date table. The relationship between them is defined on the InvoiceDate column in fSales.

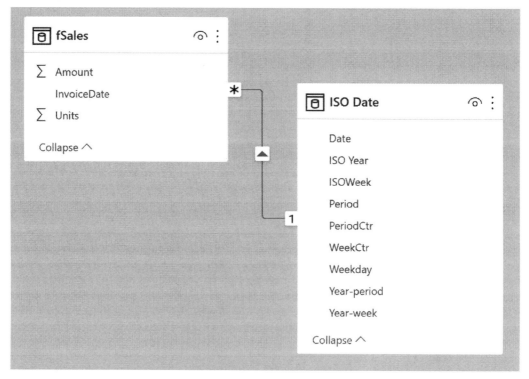

Figure 2.3.7: The Power BI model

Some straightforward results can be computed with basic aggregations:

```
Sales = SUM(fSales[Amount])

Quantity = SUM(fSales[Units])
```

These DAX measures allow us to view, for instance, sales by week:

Sales by ISOWeek

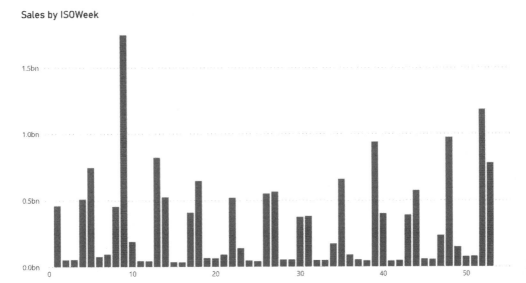

Figure 2.3.8: Sales by ISO week

In the next few sections, we will develop the required time intelligence calculations.

Calculating year-to-date results

The year-to-date calculation returns the cumulative values in a selected year. The equivalent Gregorian time intelligence function is TOTALYTD, or DATESYTD as a filter for use in CALCULATE. Technically, these functions start with the last day in the query context, and create a filter context with all days in the same year up to and including that last day. We must create the same logic in the week-based calendar.

This is the code:

```
SalesYTD =
VAR MaxDate = MAX('ISO Date'[Date])
VAR ThisISOYear = MAX('ISO Date'[ISO Year])
RETURN

CALCULATE(
    [Sales],
    'ISO Date'[Date] <= MaxDate,
    'ISO Date'[ISO Year] = ThisISOYear,
    ALL('ISO Date')
)
```

The MaxDate variable stores the last selected day in the context. The ThisISOYear variable stores the last ISO year, which is the year corresponding to MaxDate.

In the CALCULATE, the [Sales] measure is evaluated in a filter context created by three filter arguments. The 'ISO Date'[Date] <= MaxDate argument causes no dates to be selected after MaxDate. The second filter, 'ISO Date'[ISO Year] = ThisISOYear, makes sure that the selected dates are all in the selected ISO year. The last filter argument, ALL('ISO Dates'), removes other filters from the ISO date table.

The following chart shows SalesYTD for the year 2020 in a column chart with periods on the axis:

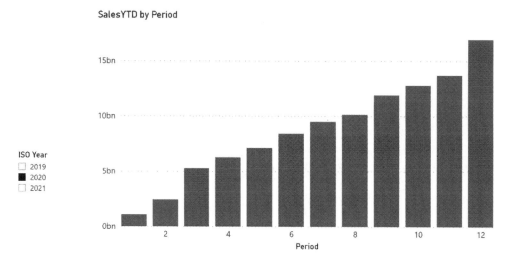

Figure 2.3.9: The year-to-date sales in 2020

In a similar way, a period-to-date calculation can be made. This time, we do not select dates in the same ISO year, but in the same period. The PeriodCtr column is ideal for this:

```
SalesPTD =
VAR MaxDate = MAX('ISO Date'[Date])
VAR ThisPeriod = MAX('ISO Date'[PeriodCtr])
RETURN

CALCULATE(
    [Sales],
    'ISO Date'[Date] <= MaxDate,
    'ISO Date'[Period] = ThisPeriod,
    ALL('ISO Date')
)
```

Here is the result of this measure in a chart:

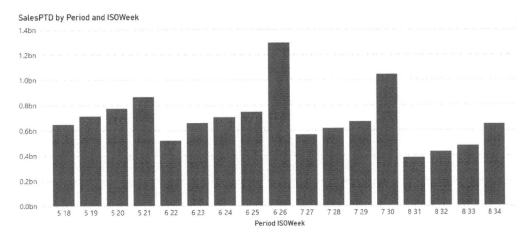

Figure 2.3.10: Period-to-date sales

This chart shows period-to-date sales by week for periods 3 and 4 in 2020. As expected, the values accumulate in later weeks in the same period, but start over in a new period.

Calculating sales growth

To calculate year-on-year growth, we need to compare sales in the "current" year (whatever year we want to view) with sales in the previous year. As the Sales measure already calculates sales in the current year, all we need to do is to create a calculation that returns results for the selected period, but in the previous year. This is the 4-4-5 equivalent of the SAMEPERIODLASTYEAR function.

Since a date selection can span different hierarchical levels of the 4-4-5 calendar, like days, ISO weeks, periods, or ISO years, the formula we build must detect which level is selected. For example, when period 5 of 2021 is selected, we need the formula to calculate results for period 5 in 2020; when week 43 in 2020 is selected, results for week 43 in 2019 must be returned, and so on.

The situation where a single day, or a small set of days, is selected deserves special consideration. There are several approaches to what the corresponding day or days in the previous year are. You could argue that we can just take the same date, so May 3, 2021 would result in May 3, 2020. However, the same date in another year does not necessarily fall in the same week number. Taking the same date would cause inconsistent results.

We will take the following definition: the "last year" equivalent of a day is the day in the previous ISO year that has the same week number and weekday number. This means that May 3, 2021, which is in week 18 and is a Monday, corresponds to April 27, 2020, which is the Monday that is in week 18 in that year.

This definition complicates things even more, as a multi-day selection may be in more than one week. What we need to do is take the week/weekday combinations that correspond to the dates, and move them one year back.

The DAX formula starts with the SWITCH function, followed by the day-level calculation:

```
Sales Last Year =
SWITCH(
    TRUE(),
    ISFILTERED('ISO Date'[Date]),
        VAR PYDates =
            SELECTCOLUMNS(
                'ISO Date',
                "ISOWeek", 'ISO Date'[ISOWeek],
                "Weekday", 'ISO Date'[Weekday],
                "Previous Year", 'ISO Date'[Previous Year]
            )
        RETURN
        CALCULATE(
            [Sales],
            TREATAS(
                PYDates,
                'ISO Date'[ISOWeek],
                'ISO Date'[Weekday],
                'ISO Date'[ISO Year]
            ),
            ALL('ISO Date')
        ),
```

The first argument is TRUE(). This means that the cases in the SWITCH expression are evaluated to determine whether or not they are true. The first option to be evaluated, ISFILTERED('ISO Date'[Date]) in the second argument of SWITCH, examines whether a filter is placed on the day column. If so, the third argument is evaluated and returned.

ISFILTERED requires a direct filter on the 'ISO Date'[Date] column. You should not use ISCROSSFILTERED, since this function would also be triggered when a higher-level column, like Period or ISO Year, is filtered.

The PYDates variable retrieves the selected dates, but not with the ISO year, but the previous year. The SELECTCOLUMNS function simply picks a set of columns from an existing table. In this case, we choose the week number, the weekday number, and the previous year. SELECTCOLUMNS requires us to provide (new) column names for the selected columns. The names we choose do not matter really, because of how we use the table. In the CALCULATE function, TREATAS is used to apply the PYDates table as a filter to the ISO Date table again, but now using the Previous Year values as ISO year values. This gives exactly the same selection of days, but now in the previous year.

If the ISFILTERED('ISO Date'[Date]) clause is false, the next argument is tested:

```
ISFILTERED('ISO Dates'[ISOWeek]),
    VAR PYWeeks =
        SUMMARIZE(
            'ISO Date',
            'ISO Date'[ISOWeek],
            'ISO Date'[Previous Year]
        )
    RETURN
    CALCULATE(
        [Sales],
        TREATAS(
            PYWeeks,
            'ISO Date'[ISOWeek],
            'ISO Date'[ISO Year]
        ),
        ALL('ISO Date')
    ),
```

If there is a filter on the column 'ISO Dates'[ISOWeek], we want to return results for the corresponding weeks in the previous year. The approach is similar to what we did for a selection of days, but this time, we need a table with weeks. The SUMMARIZE function does the trick here, providing a table with the unique combinations of week numbers and previous year values. Again, CALCULATE applies the previous year values as a filter to select ISO year values.

The formula continues in a similar manner for a selection on the `Period` level:

```
        ISFILTERED('ISO Dates'[Period]),
            VAR PYPeriods =
                SUMMARIZE(
                    'ISO Date',
                    'ISO Date'[Period],
                    'ISO Date'[Previous Year]
                )
            RETURN
            CALCULATE(
                [Sales],
                TREATAS(
                    PYPeriods,
                    'ISO Date'[Period],
                    'ISO Date'[ISO Year]
                ),
                ALL('ISO Date')
            ),
```

Here, the set of selected `Period` values with the corresponding previous year is selected and applied as a filter argument in `CALCULATE` in the same way as before. Note that, as the calendar has a consistent structure at the `Period` level, a different approach could be taken as well: you could start with the `PeriodCtr` values selected and subtract 12 from each value to end up in the same period in the previous year. But we will stick with the approach used at lower levels for the sake of consistency within the formula.

Finally, when none of the columns mentioned above are filtered, we are in a situation in which either the ISO year column is filtered, or nothing is filtered at all. In both cases, we return the results of the previous year or years. This means that the last clause is the "else" argument in `SWITCH`:

```
        VAR PYYears =
            VALUES('ISO Date'[Previous Year])
        RETURN
        CALCULATE(
            [Sales],
            TREATAS(
                PYYears,
                'ISO Date'[ISO Year]
            ),
             ALL('ISO Date')
        )
    )
```

As we only use one column now, we can work with `VALUES` instead of `SUMMARIZE` to retrieve the `Previous Year` values in the selection. These values are then used to filter the `ISO Year` column in `CALCULATE`. Note that when nothing is selected, the result depends on which years are in the `ISO Date` table: for instance, when the table contains the ISO years 2019, 2020, and 2021, the previous years are 2018, 2019, and 2020. As 2018 is not in the table, the result will be the sales for 2019 and 2020 combined. This is consistent with the behavior of the `SAMEPERIODLASTYEAR` function.

With this, our last year calculation is finished. To calculate year-on-year growth, we simply compare it with the current sales:

```
Sales Growth % =
VAR ThisYear = [Sales]
VAR LastYear = [Sales Last Year]
RETURN
DIVIDE(ThisYear - LastYear, LastYear)
```

The following charts show some of the results of the `Sales Last Year` measure. The first chart shows results for the first 15 weeks of 2019 and 2020:

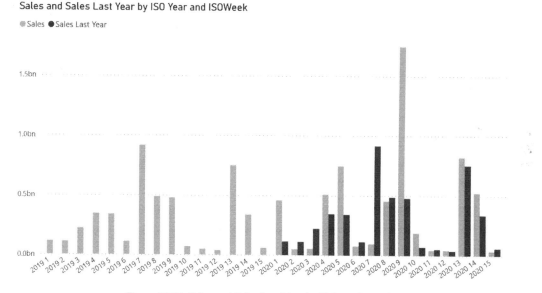

Figure 2.3.11: Sales and Sales Last Year by ISO week number

In the dark-colored `Sales Last Year` columns, it is easy to recognize the pattern of `Sales` in the year before. The same can be seen in a chart by `Period`:

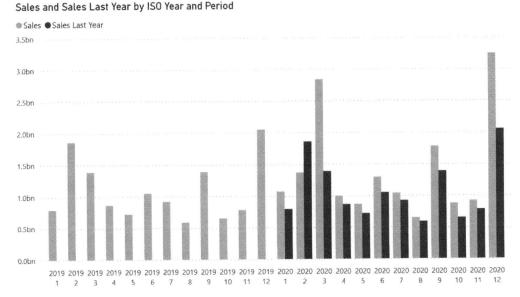

Figure 2.3.12: Sales and Sales Last Year by Period

Here again, the `Sales Last Year` for the periods in 2020 shows exactly the same results as `Sales` in the year 2019.

Moving average by week within an accounting year

If you run a business with a strong seasonality in sales, you may want to report a moving average in order to mitigate the seasonal influences. A **moving average**, also *rolling average* or *running average*, calculates results for a fixed window of time, like 12 months, and divides the result by 12. This way, the result always includes the periods of the year that are traditionally high in sales, or low.

A rolling average can also be used to focus on trends instead of short-term fluctuations in the data. To give a recent example: instead of looking at daily COVID cases, a more realistic view comes from a rolling 7-day average. This period always includes one weekend in which fewer cases are detected than on other days of the week.

Note that the challenge here is in calculating the total result for a rolling time window; the average then comes from dividing by the number of time units. In this section, we will calculate a rolling average of one ISO year on a weekly basis. This means that we determine the last week number in the query context, and calculate results for the time period starting with the week *after* that week number in the previous year, up to and including the last week selected. As the ISO year may contain either 52 or 53 weeks, we then need to determine this number to compute the average by week.

 In the Gregorian calendar calculations, the time intelligence DAX function DATESINPERIOD is used for this type of calculation.

The DAX formula starts by defining a variable that stores the latest Year-week value. Next, the variable RollingWeeks is defined:

```
Moving Average Sales by Week =
VAR MaxWeek = MAX('ISO Date'[Year-week])
VAR RollingWeeks =
CALCULATETABLE(
    FILTER(
        ALL('ISO Date'[Year-week]),
        'ISO Date'[Year-week] > MaxWeek - 100 + 1
        && 'ISO Date'[Year-week] <= MaxWeek
    )
)
```

As the name of the variable describes, you are looking for the set of weeks that are in the correct rolling time period – in our case, a full year. With FILTER, we create a subset of ALL('ISO Date'[Year-week]). We use ALL to exclude any filter placed on the Year-week column.

Now take a closer look at the filter code. To create a rolling list of weeks, we need to find the MaxWeek number in the previous year. For instance, if our selection ends at ISO week 10 in 2020, we want the rolling period to start at week 11 in 2019. Since we do not know whether we have to move 52 or 53 weeks back for a whole year, we use the Year-week column.

You may remember the definition of the Year-week column:

```
([ISO Year] * 100) + [ISOWeek]
```

By this definition, you get the same week number in the previous year when you subtract 100 from the Year-week value. In the example above, week 10 in 2020 has a Year-week value of 202010; subtracting 100 results in 201910, or week 10 of 2019. As we want the rolling period to start one week later, we simply add 1.

The next step is to calculate the sales in the time period we just created:

```
VAR SalesInPeriod =
CALCULATE(
    [Sales],
    RollingWeeks,
    ALL('ISO Date')
)
```

We us the RollingWeeks variable as a table filter here, and remove all other filters on the ISO Date table. The result is all sales during the rolling time period. All that is left to do now is to divide this result by the number of weeks, which can be derived from the RollingWeeks variable by counting the rows of that table:

```
VAR NumberOfWeeks = COUNTROWS(RollingWeeks)
RETURN
DIVIDE(SalesInPeriod, NumberOfWeeks)
```

This is the complete formula:

```
Moving Average Sales by Week =
VAR MaxWeek = MAX('ISO Date'[Year-week])
VAR RollingWeeks =
CALCULATETABLE(
    FILTER(
            ALL('ISO Date'[Year-week]),
            'ISO Date'[Year-week] > MaxWeek - 100 + 1
            && 'ISO Date'[Year-week] <= MaxWeek
    )
)
```

```
VAR SalesInPeriod =
CALCULATE(
    [Sales],
    RollingWeeks,
    ALL('ISO Date')
)
VAR NumberOfWeeks = COUNTROWS(RollingWeeks)
RETURN
DIVIDE(SalesInPeriod, NumberOfWeeks)
```

The following chart shows the moving average results by week in the year 2019:

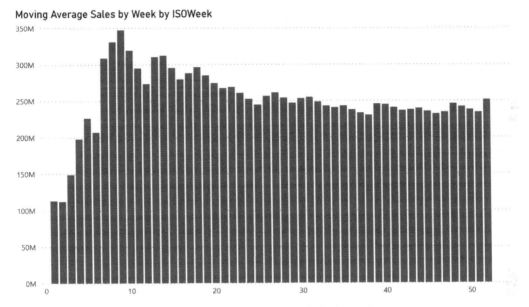

Figure 2.3.13: The moving average of sales by week

Note that the first six weeks show a low rolling average. This is just the effect of slow sales in those weeks. Because of the way we constructed the calculation, a proper average is calculated even in the first weeks of our date table. For instance, the second column from the left is the result of two weeks' sales, divided by 2.

In these few sections, we have shown you some examples of time intelligence calculations with the week-based date table. You can be creative and define other calculations using the same approach and leveraging columns in the date table. In the last part of this chapter, we change gears a bit and discuss how to make a report always show a proper selection of results.

Keeping your report current

In most reports, you want to view the latest results. In a sales report, for instance, you may want to see results for the current and previous months. In a Power BI report, you can place a filter on the year and month to show results for that specific month. However, when a new month starts, each report user will have to change that filter manually to avoid looking at old data.

Power BI reports offer a feature to avoid having to do this: relative date filters. With a relative date filter, set in the reports **Filter** pane, you can set up a rule that is dynamic relative to the current date:

Figure 2.3.14: Relative date filters

While convenient, relative date filters have their limitations. For instance, you cannot set a relative date filter like "*show the last two full months before today.*" Additionally, the relative date filters are based on the Gregorian calendar. When using a week-based calendar, you need to create an alternative to the standard relative date filters. This is the topic of the next section.

The Date Selection table

We want to enable different selections on the date table, comparable to the relative date filter discussed above, only more flexible. The approach for this is to introduce another table – let's call it Date Selection – that contains a column with the selection options as well as a Date column. This table will have a relationship with the date table:

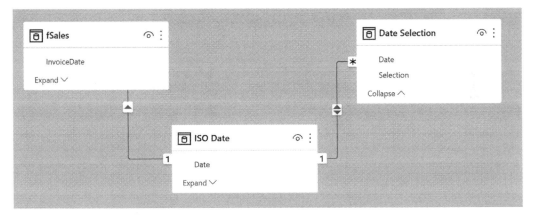

Figure 2.3.15: The Date Selection table

Note that the default filter propagation of the relationship is from ISO Date to Date Selection, but we want filters to propagate in the other direction. So, the cross filter property of the relationship must be set to **Both**.

The `Date Selection` table contains sets of dates for each selection option. As an example, here is the selection option **Last two full weeks** (this table was created on November 15, 2021):

Date	Selection
11/1/2021	Last two full weeks
11/2/2021	Last two full weeks
11/3/2021	Last two full weeks
11/4/2021	Last two full weeks
11/5/2021	Last two full weeks
11/6/2021	Last two full weeks
11/7/2021	Last two full weeks
11/8/2021	Last two full weeks
11/9/2021	Last two full weeks
11/10/2021	Last two full weeks
11/11/2021	Last two full weeks
11/12/2021	Last two full weeks
11/13/2021	Last two full weeks
11/14/2021	Last two full weeks

Figure 2.3.16: Rows in the Date Selection table

By adding a filter on the `Selection` column to a report and setting it to **Last two full weeks**, only the dates in this range will be selected in the `ISO Date` table.

To create the `Date Selection` table, we must start by creating a copy of the `ISO Date` table. Let's call this `SelectDate`. For this table, we use exactly the same formula used for the `ISO Date` table.

The reason why we need to create a separate date table is that the rows in the `Date Selection` table will be derived from the date table. Technically, the relationship causes the `Date Selection` table to be a fact table, with `ISO Date` (from which it is created) as a filter table.

This causes a circular dependency error:

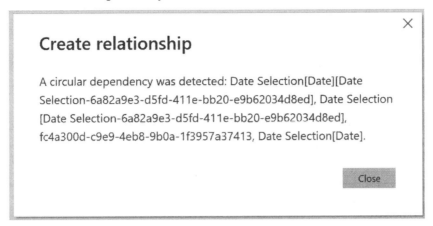

Figure 2.3.16: A circular dependency error

There is another issue that will appear when we start using the Date Selection table: in the Sales Last Year measure discussed earlier in this chapter, we switch between different ways of calculating last year's results based on filters on columns in the ISO Date table. However, a selection option in Date Selection could cause a selection in ISO Date without a direct filter; for instance, the **Last two full weeks** option will cause two weeks to be selected, without a filter on the ISOWeek column. The last year calculation will select an incorrect calculation method.

To address this issue, we add another column in the Date Selection table that indicates which level in the date hierarchy is being selected. The last year calculation will have to test not only the filters on ISO Date, but also the level of selection in Date Selection. Additionally, we need to consider the situation in which the Date Selection is not used at all. We call the additional column Level, with these values:

- **Day**: Level = 1
- **Week**: Level = 2
- **Period**: Level = 3
- **Year**: Level = 4
- **All**: Level = 5

The last level must be in the Date Selection table at all times, and functions as an indicator that nothing is selected. As an example, here is a part of the table with the **Last two full weeks** option, plus the **"All"** level:

Date	Selection	Level
11/9/2021	Last two full weeks	2
11/4/2021	Last two full weeks	2
11/5/2021	Last two full weeks	2
11/6/2021	Last two full weeks	2
11/1/2021	Last two full weeks	2
11/7/2021	Last two full weeks	2
11/8/2021	Last two full weeks	2
11/3/2021	Last two full weeks	2
11/10/2021	Last two full weeks	2
11/11/2021	Last two full weeks	2
11/12/2021	Last two full weeks	2
11/13/2021	Last two full weeks	2
11/14/2021	Last two full weeks	2
11/2/2021	Last two full weeks	2
1/13/2019	All	5
1/14/2019	All	5
1/15/2019	All	5

Figure 2.3.17: Date Selection table including Level column

With the model structure in place, let's see how to create the Date Selection table, including its different selection options, with DAX.

Creating selection options

The Date Selection table is a calculated table in which the current date is used to define the different selection options. The basic idea is to create a list of dates belonging to a selection option, together with a name for the option and its level.

The current date is retrieved with the TODAY function, and we can use the SelectDate table to retrieve other current values we need, like the current WeekCtr value. The formula starts with this:

```
Date Selection =
VAR CurrentWeekCtr =
    CALCULATE(
        MAX(SelectDate[WeekCtr]),
        SelectDate[Date] = TODAY()
    )
```

For our example **Last two full weeks** option, the formula continues with:

```
VAR LastTwoFullWeeks =
ADDCOLUMNS(
    CALCULATETABLE(
        VALUES(SelectDate[Date]),
        SelectDate[WeekCtr] IN
                {CurrentWeekCtr - 1, CurrentWeekCtr - 2}
    ),
    "Selection", "Last two full weeks",
    "Level", 2
)
```

In this code, we select dates for which the WeekCtr value is contained in a list of values corresponding to one and two weeks before the current week. With ADDCOLUMNS, the Selection and Level columns are added.

Let's add the "All" option now:

```
VAR LevelAll =
ADDCOLUMNS(
    VALUES(SelectDate[Date]),
    "Selection", "All",
    "Level", 5
)
```

Of course, for the "All" option, we select all the dates from the SelectDate table. Again, the Selection and Level columns are added with ADDCOLUMNS. We now have two variables containing a part of what must become the Date Selection table.

To combine these parts, we can use the UNION function:

```
RETURN
UNION(
    LastTwoFullWeeks, LevelAll
)
```

The UNION function accepts an arbitrary number of arguments, all of which must be tables with the same number of columns. The rows in all these tables form one big table, which is our Date Selection table.

You can add all the selection options you can imagine, as long as you can derive the definition of the selection from the current date. For example, a selection option to select the whole of the previous year is created with the following code:

```
VAR CurrentYear =
    CALCULATE(
        MAX(SelectDate[ISO Year]),
        SelectDate[Date] = TODAY()
    )
VAR PreviousISOYear =
ADDCOLUMNS(
    CALCULATETABLE(
        VALUES(SelectDate[Date]),
        SelectDate[ISO Year] = CurrentYear - 1
    ),
    "Selection", "Previous year",
    "Level", 4
)
```

After including this code, the PreviousISOYear variable should be added to the UNION function for the rows to appear in the end result. As another example, for selecting the last 5 periods including the current, but only up to today, the code below will do:

```
VAR CurrentPeriod =
    CALCULATE(
        MAX(SelectDate[PeriodCtr]),
        SelectDate[Date] = TODAY()
    )
VAR LastFivePeriods =
ADDCOLUMNS(
    CALCULATETABLE(
```

```
        VALUES(SelectDate[Date]),
        SelectDate[PeriodCtr] >= CurrentPeriod - 4,
        SelectDate[Date] <= TODAY()
    ),
    "Selection", "Last five periods",
    "Level", 3
)
```

 The full `Date Selection` formula including these options can be found in this chapter's model file.

In the next section, we look at changing the `Sales Last Year` measure to deal with date selections.

Using Date selection in measures

Going back to the `Sales Last Year` measure, we used the `ISFILTERED` function to detect what type of selection is made on the `ISO Date` table in order to apply the correct calculation:

```
SWITCH(
    TRUE(),
    ISFILTERED('ISO Date'[Date]),
        <day-level calculation>
    ISFILTERED('ISO Date'[ISOWeek]),
        <week-level calculation>
    ...
```

If you were to use this measure in a report and select the **Last two full weeks** option, you would see results for the last two full weeks, but the `ISFILTERED('ISO Date'[ISOWeek])` clause is not triggered. Indeed, there is no filter on the `ISOWeek` column in this situation. This leads to the wrong calculation being applied.

To correct this, we use the `Date Selection` table's `Level` column as well. With the selection of **Last two full weeks**, the `Level` column contains only the value 2. This can be used to implement the following logic to test whether to use the week-level calculation:

- The largest selected level is 2; or
- The `ISOWeek` column is filtered.

In code, this translates to:

```
Sales Last Year (with date selection) =
VAR MaxLevel = MAX('Date Selection'[Level])
RETURN
SWITCH(
    TRUE(),
    MaxLevel = 2 || ISFILTERED('ISO Date'[Date]),
        ...
    MaxLevel = 3 || ISFILTERED('ISO Date'[ISOWeek]),
        ...
```

We are not done yet: in each calculation in the original measure, the new selection on the date table is applied, and old filters on the date table are removed. For the week-based calculation it looks like this:

```
VAR PYWeeks =
    SUMMARIZE(
        'ISO Date',
        'ISO Date'[ISOWeek],
        'ISO Date'[Previous Year]
    )
RETURN
CALCULATE(
    [Sales],
    TREATAS(
        PYWeeks,
        'ISO Date'[ISOWeek],
        'ISO Date'[ISO Year]
    ),
    ALL('ISO Date')
),
```

We can now, however, have a situation where there are no filters on the date table directly, but a filter on Date Selection filtering the table instead. That filter is not removed, resulting in an empty selection on the date table. What we need to do is change the calculation in such a way that Date Selection filters are removed as well:

```
ISFILTERED('ISO Dates'[ISOWeek]),
    VAR PYWeeks =
        SUMMARIZE(
            'ISO Date',
```

```
            'ISO Date'[ISOWeek],
            'ISO Date'[Previous Year]
    )
RETURN
CALCULATE(
    [Sales],
    TREATAS(
        PYWeeks,
        'ISO Date'[ISOWeek],
        'ISO Date'[ISO Year]
    ),
    ALL('ISO Date'),
    ALL('Date Selection')
),
```

We will not repeat the complete, lengthy formula here; you can find it in the model file. The chart below shows the results for Sales and Sales Last Year in the adapted measure, for the selection **Last five periods**; again, the current date here is November 15, 2021.

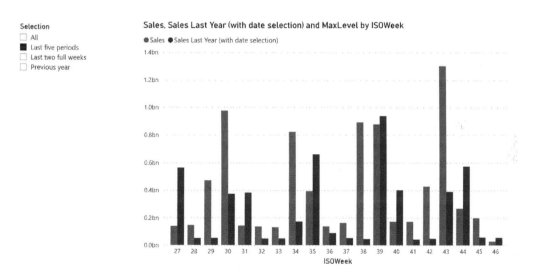

Figure 2.3.18: Results with date selection

As can be seen from this chart, although we have made a date selection on periods (the last five periods), the chart returns results at the week level. So, in this case, it is clear that the formula is triggered by ISFILTERED('ISO Date'[ISOWeek]), not by 'Date Selection'[Level].

Summary

In this chapter, you have learned how to implement time intelligence when your calendar looks different to the standard Gregorian calendar that a Power BI model assumes.

For time intelligence analysis, you need a specific date table containing columns corresponding to the hierarchical levels in your calendar. In this chapter, we have implemented this as a calculated table.

To do actual time intelligence calculations, meticulous filtering over the date table and the various columns in it is needed. In particular, calculating results for "the previous year" requires a lot of different calculations, depending on what selections are made in the query context. All this evokes a renewed appreciation for what the built-in DAX time intelligence functions accomplish!

We closed this chapter off with an alternative to relative date filters in Power BI reports that is more flexible and can handle selections in non-standard calendars as well.

The next chapter focuses on AutoExist, a lesser-known concept in Power BI that, when misunderstood, can lead to bad performance in reports and confusion over the results a Power BI model generates.

2.4

Working with AutoExist

When working with DAX, you should not forget that the whole point of what you are doing is to create useful output from your model. It is therefore useful to have some understanding of how Power BI visualizes results from a model. Without going into everything possible in Power BI visual reports, there are some fundamentals of how visualizations and a Power BI model work together that need to be discussed here. One of these is a lesser-known concept called **AutoExist**, which is the subject of this chapter.

AutoExist is a Power BI feature that aims to speed up reports by only evaluating DAX measures for relevant data points. The challenge here is that Power BI determines which data points are relevant by guessing, and while these guesses are good in many cases, sometimes they are not. Through a practical example, you will learn how AutoExist works, how to leverage it to solve specific problems and optimize the performance of your reports, and how to solve the problems AutoExist sometimes causes.

We are going to cover the following topics:

- How Power BI visualizes the output of a model
- What AutoExist is and what it does
- Example: the case of the missing workdays
- How to solve the missing workdays problem
- Optimizing report performance with AutoExist

The Power BI model

Most of this chapter is based on a small sample model:

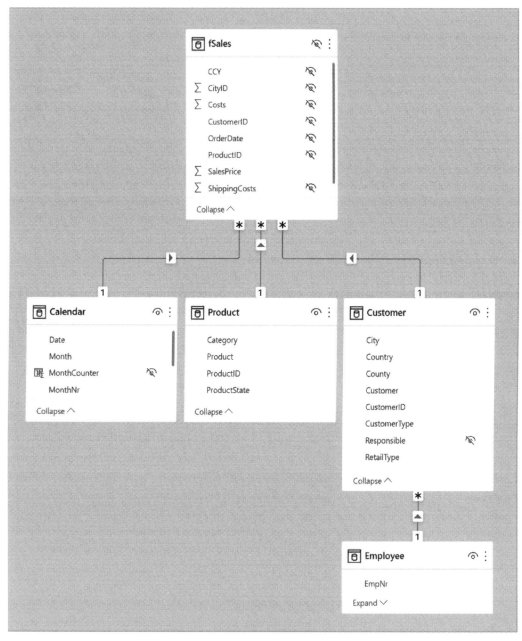

Figure 2.4.1: Diagram of the Power BI model

We have a fact table, fSales, with sales transactions for customers in the Customer table. A Customer has a responsible, who is an employee; the model therefore relates the Responsible column in Customer to the EmpNr column in Employee. So, with this model, we can report sales by customer, but also by employee, or any of either's attributes.

 This model file, 2.4 AutoExist.pbix, can be found at https:// github.com/PacktPublishing/Extreme-DAX/tree/main/ Chapter2.4.

We will mainly work with the results of a single DAX measure for sales:

```
Sales = SUM(fSales[SalesPrice])
```

In addition, we use a measure that only returns sales for some product categories:

```
Sales (core products) =
CALCULATE(
    [Sales],
    KEEPFILTERS(
        Product[Category]
        IN {"Bikes", "Clothing", "Accessories"}
    )
)
```

See *Chapter 1.4, Context and Filtering,* for a discussion on CALCULATE and the use of KEEPFILTERS.

How Power BI visualizes the output of a model

As you will know, a Power BI report's main components are visualization objects. These objects take some fields from a model (either included in the same file, or a remote model) and render a visualization of the information provided by the model.

As with many elements in Power BI, these visualizations work like a beginner user would expect in many situations. When things become more complex, however, you may easily run into unexpected results. In these cases, it is useful to understand a bit more about the technicalities of visualizations. Why do they show what they show, and how do they do it?

Visual filters and context

A core concept in Power BI is that of **filters**. This is specifically true for DAX, but filters do play an important role in visualizations as well. Let's take this simple report as an example:

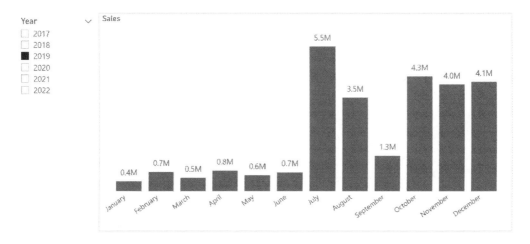

Figure 2.4.2: A simple Power BI report

You can see what the chart represents: sales numbers by month in the year 2019. We have used three fields from the Power BI model to create this simple report:

- Year: Values in this column populate the slicer
- Month: Used as labels on the *x*-axis of the column chart
- Sales: Used as values in the chart

There is a fundamental difference between the Year and Month fields, and Sales: Year and Month are columns of data in the model, while Sales is a measure. The results of the calculations that are implemented in the Sales measure are determined by the selected values of Year and Month. In other words: the *query context* for the Sales calculation is formed by filters on the Year and Month columns. See *Chapter 1.4, Context and Filtering*, for an in-depth discussion of context.

This is how Power BI reports are generally built up: columns in the Power BI model are used as labels in the report's visuals. Each label forms a filter that is applied for the calculation of measures in the report's visuals. Some filters apply to the visual as a whole, like the Year filter, and come from "outside" of the visual.

Others come from "inside," because columns are used to populate a chart axis, row labels, or other visual elements.

Filters coming from outside of the visual are easily detected using the funnel icon in the visual header, which shows a filter tooltip.

Figure 2.4.3: The filter tooltip

In this case, we can see that there is, in fact, another filter on this visual, on the Country column. Whenever you see strange or seemingly incorrect results in a visual, a good starting point is to check which filters apply to the visual!

Filters caused by columns used in the visual itself are harder to detect. You will just have to examine the visual closely to see what labels are visible, and try to deduce which columns may have been used to create the visual. If you are the report author, you can of course just check the fields in the **Visualization** pane.

Note that a filter is not just a selection of values in a column. You can have multiple filters on the same column at the same time; for instance, you may have both a page level filter on the Year column (in the report's **Filters** pane) and a slicer on the same Year column. You will then see both filters in the filter tooltip.

Having multiple filters, some of which are hidden, is often a cause for confusion. Again, check the filter tooltip.

How using measures changes the behavior of visuals

Visual filters determine what data is shown by a visual. This is true not only for the calculated results presented in the visual, but also for the data points themselves. To understand this, you can start using a simple table visual on a column like Category (from the Product table) in the following picture. Note that only the Category column, and no other field from the model, is used for this visual:

Figure 2.4.4: A table of product categories

In this table, all unique values in the Category column are shown. This set of values can be described with a DAX table expression:

```
DISTINCT('Product'[Category])
```

When you apply a filter to this visual, via a slicer, for instance, the filter determines which values are presented in the visual. That is, only if that filter is relevant for the column where the values are taken from. For example, consider:

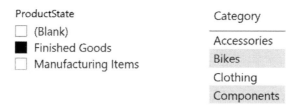

Figure 2.4.4: Product categories filtered through a slicer

Here, you have a slicer on ProductState, which is a column from the same Product table as Category. In the table visual, you now only have categories corresponding to the product state Finished Goods. Apparently, the product category Unknown does not contain any Finished Goods products! When you use a column from another table in your slicer, it all depends on the structure of your model whether or not the values in the table visual will be filtered.

When filters are applied to the visual, the resulting set of values can be described in DAX. For the filter above, this would be:

```
CALCULATETABLE(
    DISTINCT('Product'[Category]),
    'Product'[ProductState] = "Finished Goods"
)
```

When you add a *measure* to a visual, this behavior changes: now, only values for which the measure returns a non-blank result are presented. This is a fundamental difference that is often overlooked. Also, this is why BLANK is such an important value in DAX: if it is the result of a measure, the label corresponding to it will not be shown. Note that BLANK is different from 0 (zero). A zero value *will* be presented in the visual.

In the following image, we added the Sales (core products) measure, which returns sales for only the Bikes, Clothing, and Accessories categories:

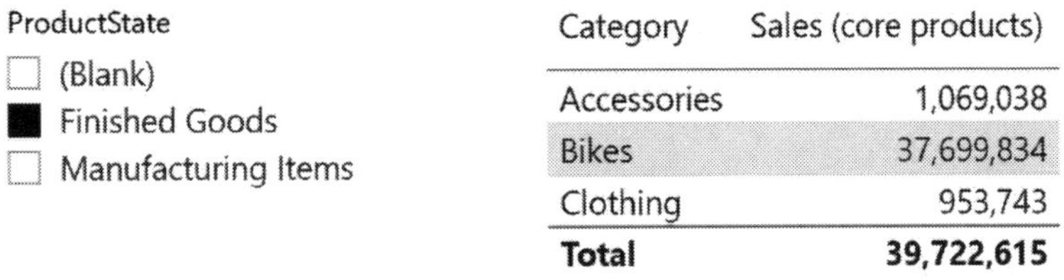

ProductState		Category	Sales (core products)
☐ (Blank)			
■ Finished Goods		Accessories	1,069,038
☐ Manufacturing Items		Bikes	37,699,834
		Clothing	953,743
		Total	**39,722,615**

Figure 2.4.5: Adding a measure to the visual

As you would guess, the Components category does not appear in the visual anymore. You may ask how Power BI knows that Components must not be in the visual. The answer is: the measure is evaluated for *all* category values, and only the categories that yield a non-blank result are shown in the table. You may then ask: is the measure evaluated for the Unknown category, which only contains products with the Manufacturing Items product state? In this case, it is not; but the general answer is more complicated. This is where AutoExist comes into play. To understand what AutoExist is, let us first dive into the way a Power BI visual is populated at a more technical level.

Understanding a visual's DAX query

Each visual in a Power BI report is populated through a single DAX query to the underlying data model. Think of a DAX query as a DAX formula that returns a table of data from the Power BI model. Most of the time, you don't need to worry about what this query is exactly.

But it is possible to inspect it, and it is insightful to take a look at some queries – especially if you want to know what calculations are being done, or why a visual takes a long time to render.

Inspection of the DAX query is somewhat hidden in Power BI Desktop. You can find it through the **Performance analyzer**, which you can open from the **View** ribbon.

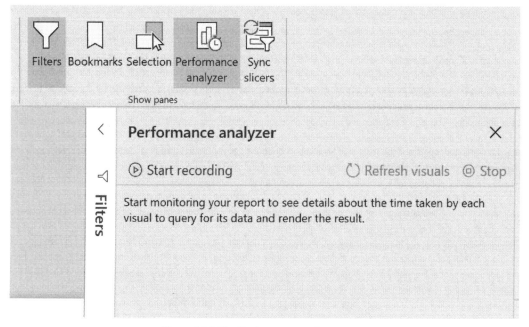

Figure 2.4.6: The Performance analyzer pane

From the **Performance analyzer** pane, you can monitor the performance of the visuals in your report. To do this, follow these steps:

1. Click **Start recording**.
2. Click **Refresh visuals**, or change or interact with the visuals.

Whenever a visual retrieves new results from the data model, it is recorded and reported in the Performance analyzer on a visual-by-visual basis. You can expand the basic numbers for a visual to get a deeper insight into what happens:

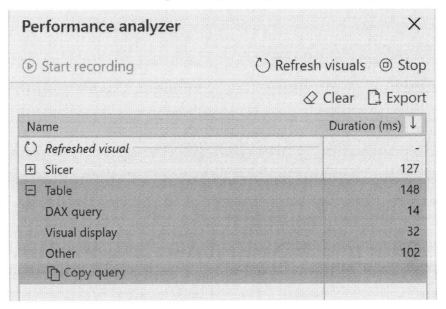

Figure 2.4.7: Performance analyzer results

When you expand the information, you will see a **Copy query** link. Clicking this copies the visual's DAX query to the clipboard.

As an example, the DAX query of our filtered table of product categories, without a measure, starts by declaring two variables:

```
// DAX Query
DEFINE
  VAR __DS0FilterTable =
    TREATAS({"Finished Goods"}, 'Product'[ProductState])

  VAR __DS0FilterTable2 =
    TREATAS({"Germany"}, 'Customer'[Country])
```

These variables implement the two filters that act upon the table visual in a rather generic way. The function TREATAS can be used to treat any list of values as the selected items in a column, resulting in a subset of the column values. The variable __DS0FilterTable implements the filter in the ProductState slicer, while the variable __DS0FilterTable2 implements the hidden filter we saw earlier in the filter tooltip.

The next variable is our list of category values, filtered by the two filters implemented by the first two variables:

```
VAR __DS0Core =
  CALCULATETABLE(
    DISTINCT('Product'[Category]),
    KEEPFILTERS(__DS0FilterTable),
    KEEPFILTERS(__DS0FilterTable2)
  )
```

The remainder of the DAX query retrieves the data:

```
VAR __DS0PrimaryWindowed =
  TOPN(501, __DS0Core, 'Product'[Category], 1)

EVALUATE
  __DS0PrimaryWindowed

ORDER BY
  'Product'[Category]
```

The variable __DS0PrimaryWindowed implements the behavior that not all data is retrieved right away, by selecting the first 501 rows. This has no impact on our small table, of course, but for long tables you can use the Performance analyzer to see that new DAX queries are sent to the data model when you scroll down the table. In our case, however, the first "window" already contains all the rows. It is retrieved from the data model at once, ordered by the category name.

When you add a measure (the core products sales measure, in our case) and inspect the DAX query, you will notice that the previous CALCULATETABLE function is now replaced by SUMMARIZECOLUMNS:

```
VAR __DS0Core =
  SUMMARIZECOLUMNS(
    'Product'[Category],
    __DS0FilterTable,
    __DS0FilterTable2,
    "Sales__core_products_", 'Results'[Sales (core products)]
  )
```

This adds a column with the measure results, of course, but more importantly, one of the specifics of SUMMARIZECOLUMNS is that no rows are returned for which the expression (in our case, the [Sales (core products)] measure) returns BLANK.

So, by looking at the DAX queries, you can see that adding measures to a visual makes a fundamental difference in the underlying DAX query.

What AutoExist is, and what it does

In the previous section, we discussed how visuals are populated with data and calculated results. Typically, when using measures in a visual, more calculations are performed than what you get to see in the visual. Calculations are also needed to determine which data points should be presented.

This raises the question: how many calculations are being done? And is it possible to control that number? AutoExist is a Power BI feature that optimizes the number of calculations needed to populate a visual. In this section, you will learn how this is done.

Using multiple filters in a visual

To explain AutoExist, we create a table visual using two columns from the Customer table:

Country	RetailType
Australia	Not Applicable
Australia	Specialty Bike Shop
Australia	Value Added Reseller
Australia	Warehouse
Canada	Limited
Canada	Not Applicable
Canada	Specialty Bike Shop
Canada	Value Added Reseller
Canada	Warehouse
France	Not Applicable
France	Specialty Bike Shop
France	Value Added Reseller
France	Warehouse
Germany	Not Applicable
Germany	Specialty Bike Shop

Figure 2.4.8: Table with Country and RetailType

As you can see from the table, there are some customers in Canada with the Limited retail type. In Australia, however, there are none. We know that when we add a measure to this table, we will not necessarily see all combinations of Country and RetailType but only those combinations for which the measure returns a non-blank value.

Suppose now that we have a trivial measure that always returns the value 1:

```
One = 1
```

Using this measure in the visual means that we will see all combinations of labels for which the measure is evaluated. An interesting question is: will we see the combination Australia and Limited? After all, the measure will return a non-blank value for this combination, even though there are no customers in Australia with the retail type Limited.

Here is the result:

Country	RetailType	One
		1
Australia	Not Applicable	1
Australia	Specialty Bike Shop	1
Australia	Value Added Reseller	1
Australia	Warehouse	1
Canada	Limited	1
Canada	Not Applicable	1
Canada	Specialty Bike Shop	1
Canada	Value Added Reseller	1
Canada	Warehouse	1
France	Not Applicable	1
France	Specialty Bike Shop	1
France	Value Added Reseller	1
France	Warehouse	1
Germany	Not Applicable	1

Figure 2.4.9: The table with a measure added

You can see the changed behavior of the visual as a result of using a measure from the appearance of an (apparent) blank row in the customer table. But the combination Australia and Limited does not appear. This is AutoExist in action.

How AutoExist optimizes DAX evaluation

The goal of AutoExist is to not evaluate DAX measures for combinations of labels that are not relevant for the report. Power BI guesses which combinations are relevant and, fortunately, these guesses follow simple rules. Specifically, AutoExist means that Power BI will not bother to evaluate combinations of values from columns in the same table that do not exist in the table. In our example, the Country Australia and the RetailType Limited do not appear in the same row in the Customer table, and Power BI will therefore not evaluate this combination.

In most cases, this is a sound thing to do. If you were to create a table visual with customer name and customer number, for instance, it typically wouldn't make sense to evaluate *all* combinations of customer numbers and customer names. In a customer table with, say, 50,000 customers, AutoExist prevents Power BI from doing $(50,000)^2$ or 2.5 billion calculations, and limits the work to only 50,000 calculations.

Whenever you use combinations of columns from *different* tables, every combination of values is evaluated. Consider, for instance, the following table visual containing Customer[Country] and Employee[Division]:

Division	Country
Asia	Australia
Americas	Canada
Europe	France
Europe	Germany
Europe	United Kingdom
Americas	United States

Figure 2.4.10: A table visual with columns from two separate tables

In this visual, only combinations of values are presented for which customers exist in that country, and whose responsible employee is in that division. This is the behavior when no DAX measures are used in the visual. When you add a measure to the visual, *all* combinations of division and country are evaluated, even though there are no customers with those combinations of properties:

Division	Country	One
		1
Americas		1
Asia		1
Board		1
Europe		1
	Australia	1
Americas	Australia	1
Asia	Australia	1
Board	Australia	1
Europe	Australia	1
	Canada	1
Americas	Canada	1
Asia	Canada	1
Board	Canada	1
Europe	Canada	1

Figure 2.4.11: A table visual with columns from two tables and a measure

If you were to inspect the DAX queries for the preceding table visuals, you would find that even in the visual without a measure, all combinations are evaluated. Power BI makes up a measure to determine which rows should be shown in the visual, in this case `COUNTROWS(Customer)`, or: whenever a customer exists for a combination, the combination is shown.

Power BI is quite smart when it comes to choosing a measure to use when there are columns from different tables in one visual. Suppose, for instance, that you combine a column from the `Product` table with a column from the `Customer` table. There is no relationship between these tables, but they are somewhat connected as there is a relationship from the `fSales` fact table to both tables. In this case, Power BI chooses `COUNTROWS(fSales)` as the measure to use to populate the visual.

This works even when you have more than one fact table between both tables. In this situation, Power BI simply creates a measure for each table and shows all combinations for which at least one of the measures returns a non-blank value.

Only if Power BI cannot find a relationship or intermediate table and therefore is not able to come up with an appropriate measure does it fail and throw an error:

Figure 2.4.12: Error message on a failed relationship

When you add a measure to the visual yourself, Power BI will use that measure to determine how to populate the visual and the error will disappear.

In short, Power BI applying AutoExist means that:

- From columns in the same table, only combinations of values that exist in rows of the table are evaluated (in other words, the columns are auto-existed).

- From columns in different tables, all combinations of values are evaluated.

And so, there are two aspects of Power BI populating a visual with results:

- **Which calculations are done**: Power BI uses AutoExist to determine which combinations of label values are evaluated.

- **What results the calculations provide**: The label values provide filters that form a query context, which determines the result of the calculations.

There is one issue, though. Your Power BI model will apply these rules, but it doesn't know what your DAX measures are supposed to calculate. In other words, you may have very good reasons to have a measure that returns a non-blank result for a combination of label values that isn't found in the data. In the next few sections, we describe a scenario where this happens.

Example: The case of the missing workdays

Having something like AutoExist sounds like a wonderful idea. Indeed, minimizing the number of calculations to be done is always helpful for performance. But there are situations where AutoExist gets in the way of what you want your Power BI model to achieve. In this section and the next, we will discuss a scenario where you have to circumvent AutoExist for things to work correctly. As with most of the cases in this part of the book, this one is based on a real customer's analytical challenges.

The business case

Let's assume that the company QuantoBikes, which sells bikes, parts, and accessories, has a business-to-business (B2B) sales channel where sales representatives actively pursue prospects, close deals, and book orders. As a B2B business, sales take place mostly on workdays. Here is a chart of typical sales in July 2020:

Daily Orders

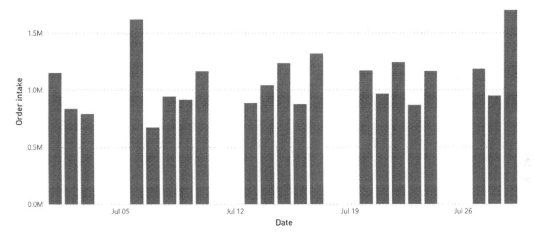

Figure 2.4.13: Daily sales chart for QuantoBikes

As a month progresses, we are interested in whether or not the sales will meet targets, but we want to compare results to business in previous months as well. In this case, we will focus on the latter.

Model structure

For this scenario, all we need to work with is a simple Power BI model:

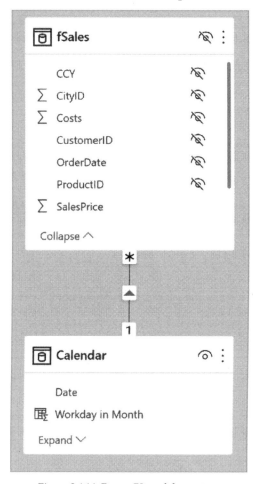

Figure 2.4.14: Power BI model structure

We have a fact table, fSales, containing sales orders. This table is related to a Calendar table on the field OrderDate. This means we can analyze numbers based on the days when orders are received. The fSales table contains other data, like keys for customer and product, but we won't need these here. The Calendar table contains the usual columns, like Year and Month, but we will take a closer look at this table later on.

The important column in fSales is SalesPrice. This column contains the sales amount for each order. We can therefore calculate the order intake with a simple measure:

```
Order intake = SUM(fSales[SalesPrice])
```

This measure is the basis for all other measures in this scenario.

Order intake analysis

Let's start with a measure to calculate the cumulative order intake during a month. You can use the TOTALMTD function for this or, alternatively, use DATESMTD:

```
Order intake MTD =
CALCULATE(
    [Order intake],
    DATESMTD('Calendar'[Date])
)
```

When put in a line and column combo chart, you get the following results. Note that we don't yet have any order intake in the last two workdays.

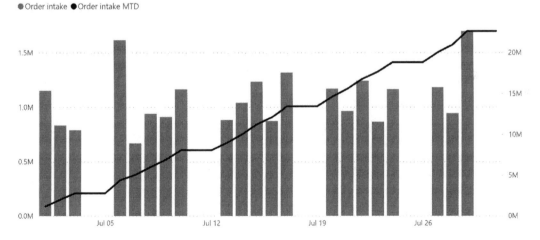

Figure 2.4.15: Daily and month-to-date order intake

You will probably notice something problematic: the month-to-date line staggers as a result of (almost) no orders coming in during the weekend. In addition to that, it doesn't really make sense to report the weekends in the chart, as nothing really happens then.

The easiest way to make this chart better is to only include workdays on the *x*-axis. You can do this by having a `Workday` column in the `Calendar` table, with the value 1 for workdays and 0 for weekend days. (You could also exclude bank holidays this way.) Note that you also have to change the *x*-axis type for this to work. When you add a date column on the *x*-axis, the axis type is set to **Continuous**, which means that the dates are spaced according to their value, even if you have filtered out some. When you change it to **Categorical**, you will see that the weekend days disappear from the axis:

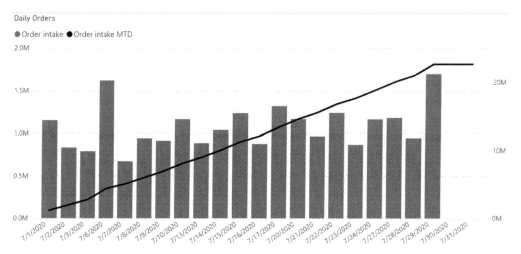

Figure 2.4.16: Order intake for workdays only

Next, we would like to compare this month's order intake to the previous month. You could first try this with a standard time intelligence function, `DATEADD`:

```
Order intake LM =
CALCULATE(
    [Order intake MTD],
    DATEADD('Calendar'[Date], -1, MONTH)
)
```

In this formula (`LM` for *last month*), `DATEADD` takes the current context on the `Calendar` table, shifts it back in time one month, and calculates the cumulative order intake in the new context.

When you add this measure to the chart (and remove the daily order intake columns for readability), you get this:

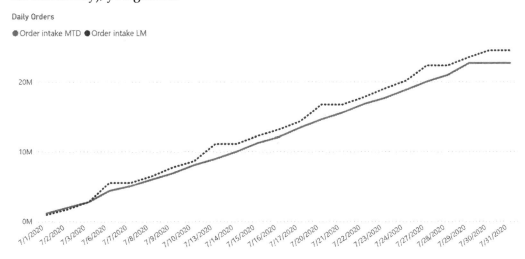

Figure 2.4.17: Month-to-date order intake for current and previous months

Notice the bumps in the dotted LM line. These are, again, caused by the structure of our data. Consider, for example, July 21, 2020; a Tuesday. If we shift this back one month, we get the results for June 21, 2020. But this was a Sunday, which is not a workday. The LM result is therefore the same as for the 20th, which was a Saturday in June, and for the 19th, which was a Friday in that month. That is why the dotted line becomes level on these days. However, note that July 19, 2020 was a Sunday and therefore not included on the axis, and as a consequence, the LM result for June 19, 2020 is not visible either.

Similarly, the dotted line increases strongly from, for example, July 17 to the next data point, which is July 20. The 18th and 19th are a Saturday and Sunday, respectively, and are therefore not included on the axis. However, the 18th and 19th of June are a Thursday and a Friday. This means that the LM result for July 20 contains three additional days of order intake instead of one.

Extending the Calendar table

It is clear that we can do a better job of comparing month-over-month numbers. A more sensible analysis would be to compare on a workday-to-workday basis. When you do that, the native time-intelligence functions no longer help. You will have to build your own calculation, and some extra columns in the Calendar table will help.

There are many ways to add columns, of course, depending on where you get your Calendar table from; you could do this in Power Query, in your data source (if you have one), or as part of the DAX code used to generate the Calendar table. To clearly show the additional columns, below we provide DAX formulas for calculated columns, although we do not recommend calculated columns in general.

First, make sure you have a YearMonthNr column containing the year and month as one number. The DAX formula for such a column is:

```
YearMonthNr = 100 * YEAR([Date]) + MONTH([Date])
```

This way, July 2020 would be 202007, October 2021 would be 202110, and so on.

Another useful column is MonthCounter, containing a continuous sequence of numbers from the start of your Calendar, that increases every month. With this, it is easy to move back and forth through the months without having to worry about ending up in the previous or next year. If you wanted to create this column as a calculated column with DAX, you would use this formula:

```
MonthCounter =
VAR ThisYearMonthNr = 'Calendar'[YearMonthNr])
RETURN
COUNTROWS(
    FILTER(
        DISTINCT('Calendar'[YearMonthNr]),
        'Calendar'[YearMonthNr] <= ThisYearMonthNr
    )
)
```

For each date in the Calendar table, MonthCounter looks at the YearMonthNr value and counts all YearMonthNr values smaller than or equal to the current value.

The third column you need is a column that tells you which workday in the month a date corresponds to. For a sound comparison, we want to compare the first workday in the current month with the first workday in the previous month (or earlier months, of course), compare the second workday with the second workday in the previous month, and so on. What we need, therefore, is a counter for workdays in a month. If you create this column as a calculated column, this is the DAX formula:

```
Workday in Month =
VAR ThisYearMontNr = [YearMonthNr]
VAR ThisDate = [Date]
VAR WorkdayNum =
COUNTROWS(
```

```
    FILTER(
        'Calendar',
        'Calendar'[YearMonthNr] = ThisYearMonthNr
        && 'Calendar'[Date] <= ThisDate
        && 'Calendar'[Workday] = 1
    )
)
RETURN
COALESCE(WorkdayNum, 1)
```

In each row of the Calendar table, we note the YearMonthNr and the Date in that row in the variables ThisYearMonthNr and ThisDate, respectively. We then filter the Calendar table to only rows that have the same YearMonthNr and a Date before or on ThisDate, and that correspond to workdays. Counting the number of rows provides the workday number for that date.

Note that for days in the weekend, this calculation returns the same number as the preceding Friday; after all, the same number of workdays precede a Saturday or Sunday as that of the Friday before it. This is fine in this case, as we can simply count orders that come in during the weekend as order intake on Friday. You may have a different requirement, of course; and you may change the formula in such a way that the weekend days have the same workday number as the Monday after them. Whatever the logic, it is advisable not to leave the workday number blank for weekends as you may want to report order intake by day, and you would miss the orders that have, by exception, come in during the weekend.

The last part of the formula, COALESCE(WorkdayNum, 1), is used to deal with the situation where the first day or first two days of the month are not workdays. In that case, the calculation returns BLANK, as there are no preceding workdays in that month. To avoid having blank values, we set the workday number to 1 in this case. The COALESCE function returns the first non-blank value among its arguments. Note that orders taken in during the first weekend are counted with the following Monday now! Again, you may want to do this in a different way by changing the logic of the DAX formula.

Workday analysis

Our "naïve" last month order intake measure used DATEADD to change the Calendar context to the previous month. With the new Calendar columns, we can build our own logic to move to the previous month, while still looking at the same set of workdays.

Remember that we are creating a "previous month, month to date" measure. To understand what we need to do, it is helpful to take a close look at what the DATESMTD function exactly does. DATESMTD determines the latest date in the current context, and returns a range of dates ending with that date, and starting on the first day of the month of that date. This means that it doesn't really matter if your context consists of one day, or a range of days: all that matters is what the last date is. Knowing this, we can mimic this logic in a new measure:

```
Order intake LM (workdays) =
VAR LatestDate = MAX('Calendar'[Date])
```

We are, however, not interested so much in the last date as in the month and workday number of that date. You can use CALCULATE to determine the month counter and workday number values of the latest date:

```
VAR LatestMonth =
CALCULATE(
    MAX('Calendar'[MonthCounter]),
    'Calendar'[Date] = LatestDate
)
VAR LatestWorkday =
CALCULATE(
    MAX('Calendar'[Workday in Month],
    'Calendar'[Date] = LatestDate
)
```

With LatestMonth and LatestWorkday, you can now change the context to what is needed to get the same workday in the previous month:

```
RETURN
CALCULATE(
    [Order intake MTD],
    'Calendar'[MonthCounter] = LatestMonth - 1,
    'Calendar'[Workday in Month] = LatestWorkday,
    ALL('Calendar')
)
```

All you have to do is subtract 1 from the month counter (which was specifically designed to enable that without worrying about ending up in another year) and set the workday number to the latest workday number you determined. As this may lead you outside of the current context, you should remove all other filters using `ALL('Calendar')`.

The result of this new calculation is the following:

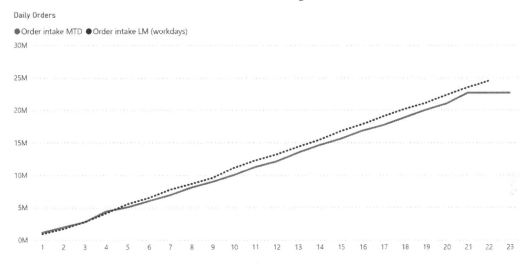

Figure 2.4.18: Last-month workday sales – without bumps

You can now make a clear comparison between the cumulative order intake by day and last month's order intake. For clarity, it would be better to put the workday number on the *x*-axis of the chart instead of the date; after all, we now compare the result on a specific day (say, July 28) not with the same day in the previous month (the June 28), but with the same workday in the previous month. When doing that, you wouldn't need to include the workday indicator as a filter anymore, and the *x*-axis type can be set back to **Continuous**.

Note that another, more subtle difference was introduced by our new measure: it seems from the graph that there is no equivalent to the last workday in July (July 31) in June. Indeed, July 31 is the 23rd workday in July, while June had only 22 workdays. As we change the context to be the same workday number but in the previous month, the resulting context is empty, and the calculation returns a blank value.

Where's my workday gone?

There is a problem in this workday-to-workday analysis that is not directly obvious or easy to notice. Let's take a look at the numbers for May 2020:

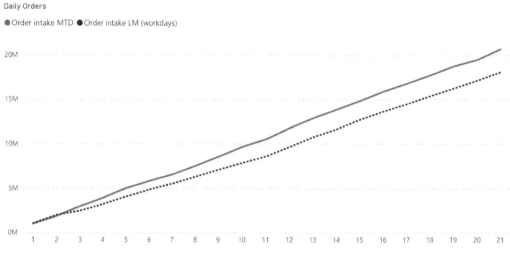

Figure 2.4.19: Workday analysis for May 2020

Here, you can see that in this month, we've had 21 workdays. For each workday, we have a result both for the current month (May) and for the previous month (April). Now, look at the same chart for April 2020:

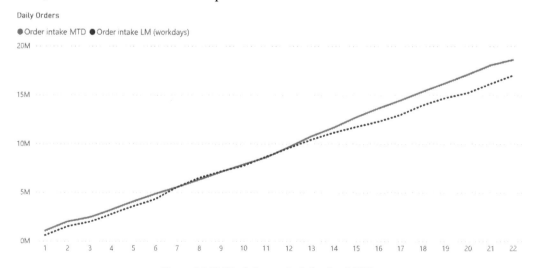

Figure 2.4.20: Workday analysis for April 2020

Again, we have results for the current month (now April) and the previous month (March), each for 22 workdays. But wait: we now learn that April 2020 had 22 workdays, whereas in the May 2020 chart, only 21 workdays are presented. What happened to April's workday number 22?

How to solve the missing workdays problem

The case of the missing workdays is a not-so-exotic situation that appears to bring up rather deep issues. It can happen in any situation where you change the context to calculate something other than what's available in the original context. In other words, whenever you use CALCULATE to change context, you may run into this problem without even noticing it. As filtering and context transformation is core to working with DAX, it is a fundamental issue. And as you may have guessed, it has everything to do with AutoExist.

The root of the problem

Let's take a very close look at the context in the last datapoint in May 2020's order intake chart. We haven't included all report elements in the image, but you can guess that there are a number of filters in this context:

- 'Calendar'[Year]: 2020
- 'Calendar'[Month]: May
- 'Calendar'[Workday in Month]: 21

What we would like Power BI to do is to also show a result for workday 22. There, the Order intake MTD measure would return no result, but the Order intake LM (workdays) measure would return the cumulative order intake for workday 22 in April.

The filters on Year and Month come from outside of the visual, and the core of the visual's DAX query is:

```
VAR __DS0Core =
  SUMMARIZECOLUMNS(
    'Calendar'[Workday in Month],
    __DS0FilterTable,
```

```
        __DS0FilterTable2,
       "Order_intake_MTD", 'Results'[Order intake MTD],
       "Order_intake_LM__workdays_",
       'Results'[Order intake LM (workdays)]
   )
```

Here, __DS0FilterTable and __DS0FilterTable2 implement the filters on Year and Month.

The SUMMARIZECOLUMNS function applies these filters on the 'Calendar'[Workday in Month] column, meaning that we get all the values in the column from rows that correspond to Year 2020 and Month May. As May 2020 has 21 workdays, workday 22 is never even considered for evaluation!

Remember the rule of thumb for AutoExist: for columns from the same table, only combinations of values that occur together in rows in the table are evaluated. Our workday analysis is the victim of AutoExist's optimization.

Changing model structure to get around AutoExist

Now that we know that AutoExist is the cause of the missing workdays, the solution is clear: the only way you can get around AutoExist is to remove the Workday in Month column from the Calendar table and move it to another table.

As you do not need anything other than the workday number in the new table, it is going to be a single-column table. Let's call it Workday. You can implement it as a calculated table based on a DAX formula:

```
Workday = DISTINCT('Calendar'[Workday in Month]
```

You still need the workday number to filter the dates, so a relationship is needed between the Calendar table and the new table:

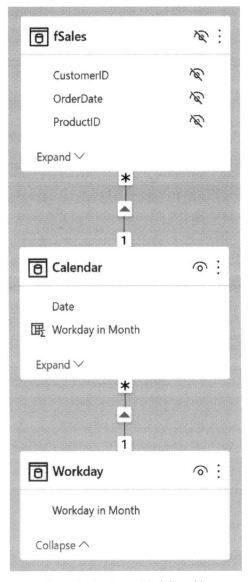

Figure 2.4.21: A new Workday table

With the new table in place, you can change the report by using the [Workday in Month] column from the Workday table instead of the Calendar table. By doing this, you will effectively cancel out AutoExist and cause each workday number to be evaluated.

You may wonder if the cross filter property of the new relationship should be set to **Single** or to **Both**. This makes no difference for AutoExist. AutoExist looks at which tables the columns come from, but does not consider filtering relationships between the tables. The setting does, however, impact the calculation of measures.

Always consider the context!

If you follow along with this example and update your report, you will notice that the solution doesn't seem to work. We're still not getting other workdays than those available in the selected month. This is, however, a different problem from what we solved dealing with AutoExist. To see this, let's add the One measure we used earlier in this chapter and look at the output in table format. In the following images, the original output with workday numbers from the Calendar table is shown in *Figure 2.4.22*, while the new version using the Workday table is shown in *Figure 2.4.23* (both showing data for May 2020).

Workday in Month	Order intake MTD	Order intake LM (workdays)	One
1	969,134	1,046,040	1
2	1,861,245	1,990,665	1
3	2,984,600	2,453,943	1
4	3,919,610	3,221,883	1
5	5,024,878	4,064,485	1
6	5,832,173	4,861,616	1
7	6,559,185	5,531,331	1
8	7,519,382	6,306,719	1
9	8,539,383	7,083,843	1
10	9,652,071	7,854,820	1
11	10,519,804	8,579,550	1
12	11,784,864	9,656,680	1
13	12,871,467	10,765,083	1
14	13,830,158	11,652,683	1
15	14,814,316	12,709,396	1
16	15,865,189	13,627,753	1
17	16,739,043	14,443,229	1
18	17,698,067	15,341,937	1
19	18,726,965	16,216,068	1
20	19,459,298	17,107,587	1
21	20,656,979	18,054,367	1

Figure 2.4.22: Table output without the Workday table

Workday in Month	Order intake MTD	Order intake LM (workdays)	One
1	969,134	1,046,040	1
2	1,861,245	1,990,665	1
3	2,984,600	2,453,943	1
4	3,919,610	3,221,883	1
5	5,024,878	4,064,485	1
6	5,832,173	4,861,616	1
7	6,559,185	5,531,331	1
8	7,519,382	6,306,719	1
9	8,539,383	7,083,843	1
10	9,652,071	7,854,820	1
11	10,519,804	8,579,550	1
12	11,784,864	9,656,680	1
13	12,871,467	10,765,083	1
14	13,830,158	11,652,683	1
15	14,814,316	12,709,396	1
16	15,865,189	13,627,753	1
17	16,739,043	14,443,229	1
18	17,698,067	15,341,937	1
19	18,726,965	16,216,068	1
20	19,459,298	17,107,587	1
21	20,656,979	18,054,367	1
22			1
23			1

Figure 2.4.23: Table output with the Workday table

As is clear from these tables, when using the workday number from the new Workday table, all workday numbers are evaluated, even workdays 22 and 23, which do not exist in May 2020. The problem is, the Order intake LM measure should return a result for workday 22, as April 2020 has 22 workdays, while it clearly does not.

This problem is not so much related to AutoExist, but comes from the context of the calculation. Remember the two elements of presenting output that we discussed earlier:

- AutoExist defines *which* combinations of label values are evaluated.
- The query context created through the label filters determines *what* the result of the calculation is.

This means that combinations of filters may be evaluated that constitute an empty selection in a fact table that the calculation is performed on. This is what happens here. Let's take a close look.

In our problematic context, we have basically three filters:

- `Calendar[Year] = 2020`
- `Calendar[Month] = May`
- `Workday[Workday in Month] = 22`

Let us revisit the `Order intake LM (workdays)` measure in this context. The measure starts with the variable `LatestDate`:

```
Order intake LM (workdays) =
VAR LatestDate = MAX('Calendar'[Date])
```

What is `MAX('Calendar'[Date])` in this context? The filters on `Year` and `Month` cause the selection of all rows in the `Calendar` table in May 2020. The filter on `Workday in Month` selects number 22 from the `Workday` table. The relationship between the `Workday` and `Calendar` tables propagates this selection to the `Calendar` table; in other words, only rows in `Calendar` are selected that satisfy all three filters. This means that in this context, only rows in `Calendar` are selected that are both in May 2020, and have workday number 22. And as we already know, there is no workday 22 in May 2020, so the selection is empty! As a consequence, the result of `MAX('Calendar'[Date])` is BLANK.

The variable `LatestDate` is used to calculate two other variables:

```
VAR LatestMonth =
CALCULATE(
    MAX('Calendar'[MonthCounter]),
    'Calendar'[Date] = LatestDate
)
VAR LatestWorkday =
CALCULATE(
    MAX('Calendar'[Workday in Month]),
    'Calendar'[Date] = LatestDate
)
```

In both declarations, we use a filter argument `'Calendar'[Date] = LatestDate`, or `'Calendar'[Date]` equals BLANK. Since no date in the `Calendar` table is blank, both `LatestMonth` and `LatestWorkday` are blank as well.

The remainder of the calculation, in turn, uses the variables to compute the final result:

```
RETURN
CALCULATE(
    [Order intake MTD],
    'Calendar'[MonthCounter] = LatestMonth - 1,
    'Calendar'[Workday in Month] = LatestWorkday,
    ALL('Calendar')
)
```

With the values of LatestMonth and LatestWorkday known, and knowing that DAX will translate BLANK into zero when doing subtraction, you can derive that this calculation comes down to:

```
RETURN
CALCULATE(
    [Order intake MTD],
    'Calendar'[MonthCounter] = -1,
    'Calendar'[Workday in Month] = 0,
    ALL('Calendar')
)
```

It is not hard to see that, with these filter arguments, the selection on Calendar is empty (there's no month with MonthCounter -1, let alone a day in that month that has workday number 0), and the result of the final calculation is blank. And, as a visual does not show blank values by default, we'll miss out workday 22 from the chart altogether.

Fixing the workday calculation

In the previous section, we have seen that our DAX formula for Workday analysis does not work well with some query contexts provided. The good news is that this problem is not that difficult to solve, as long as you keep thinking carefully about the steps in the calculation.

We know that we cannot just calculate the latest date using MAX('Calendar'[Date]). But we do not really need the latest date; we only used it to determine the latest month (month counter, to be precise) and the latest workday number. Are there other ways to calculate these? In fact, there are.

Let's start with the latest month:

```
Order intake LM (workdays 2) =
VAR LatestMonth =
    CALCULATE(
        MAX('Calendar'[MonthCounter]),
        ALL(Workday)
    )
```

The workday number is not needed to calculate the latest month. We can therefore circumvent problematic contexts by removing the filter on Workday with ALL(Workday).

Similarly, we do not need the latest date to compute the workday number. It's really the opposite: the workday number determines the latest date. So, instead of calculating the latest workday number from the Calendar table, we can simply retrieve it from the Workday table:

```
VAR LatestWorkday = MAX(Workday[Workday in Month])
```

In our problematic context of workday 22 and May 2020, LatestMonth is the MonthCounter value corresponding to May 2020, and LatestWorkday is 22. And with this, the remainder of the calculation can remain the same:

```
RETURN
CALCULATE(
    [Order intake MTD],
    ALL('Calendar'),
    'Calendar'[MonthCounter] = LatestMonth - 1,
    Workday[Workday in Month] = LatestWorkday
)
```

The result of this is indeed the month-to-date order intake for workday 22 of April 2020. When put in a visual, we now get the correct results:

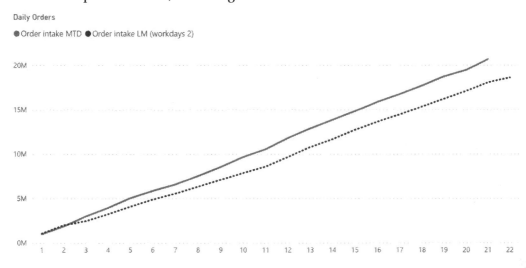

Figure 2.4.24: Correct workday analysis chart

As you can see, we were able to solve the missing workdays problem by considering both the AutoExist behavior of Power BI and the (sometimes weird) query contexts that are evaluated.

Optimizing report performance with AutoExist

When you know how AutoExist works, you can use this knowledge to solve common performance issues in Power BI reports. In this section, we discuss a number of things for you to consider.

Granularity in fact tables

As we discussed in *Chapter 1.2, Model Design*, the typical structure of a Power BI model consists of fact tables and filter (or dimension) tables. In most real-life cases, multiple fact tables exist in a model. By connecting these to the same filter tables, you can compute aggregate results over these fact tables simultaneously.

Things get a bit more complicated when your fact tables have different granularity. With this, we mean when some facts are gathered on a more detailed level than other facts. Take, for instance, a sales model for a company that sells blocks. Blocks come in different colors and shapes, as well as different sizes, types, and so on.

 This model can be found as `2.4 AutoExist - Product Hierarchy.pbix` at https://github.com/PacktPublishing/Extreme-Dax/tree/main/Chapter2.4.

The items that are actually sold to customers, or, you may say, appear on sales invoices, are the stock keeping units, or SKUs. There are 15,000 different SKUs. Sales reps need to provide sales forecasts; these are not provided by SKU, but by product. Products group multiple SKUs (you may think of a product as a physical block, and an SKU being a localized description of that block, like in cm or inches). The total number of products is 3,000. The company also works with targets; targets are not set on the level of SKUs or products, but on the product category level. In total, there are 100 product categories.

A straightforward way to model this would be to have three fact tables: fSales, fForecast, and fTarget. Each row in fSales relates to one SKU, but a row in fForecast relates to one product, and a row in fTarget relates to one category.

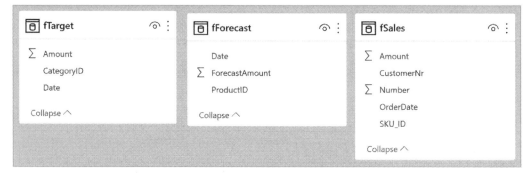

Figure 2.4.25: Fact tables with varying granularity

Filtering on multiple fact tables

The preferred relationship type to join a fact table to a filter table is many-to-one. In the block sales model, this suggests having separate SKU, Product, and Category tables, like in the following diagram:

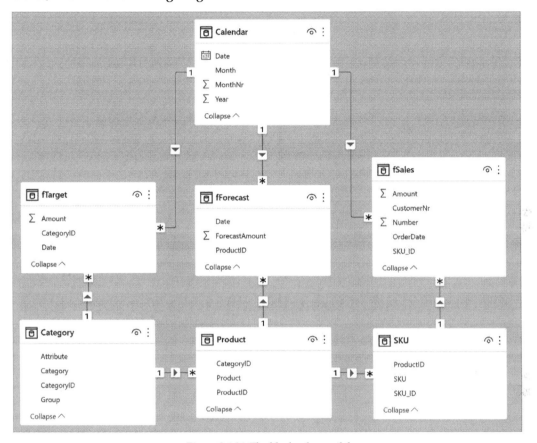

Figure 2.4.26: The block sales model

As you can see, not only do we have many-to-one relationships between each fact table and its filter tables, but we have relationships between the three product hierarchy tables as well. By doing this, you can not only report sales by SKU, but also by Product and Category.

You cannot report things like forecast by SKU through this model. This makes sense, as forecast is not registered on the SKU level, but the Product level. If you were to create a visual with forecast by SKU, the visual would, for each SKU, show the total forecast for all products together.

You could also set the Product-SKU relationship's cross filter property to **Both**, in which case the visual would, for each SKU, present the forecast for the product that SKU belongs to.

It is really a business decision how you want this to work. For instance, you can create a measure to calculate the percentage sales versus forecast:

```
Sales vs Forecast =
DIVIDE(
    SUM(fSales[Amount]),
    SUM(fForecast[ForecastAmount])
)
```

When using this measure in a visual by SKU, you will typically get small percentages, as the forecast is set on the product level and there are five SKUs per product on average. This may be fine, however. But you could also decide to detect whether the measure is called in a context for a single SKU, and not return any result in that case.

There is another potential issue in this model structure that is related to AutoExist. Suppose you want to create a list of categories and their products and SKUs as a table visual:

Category	Product	SKU
Colored A-blocks	Colored A-block AE1	Colored A-block AE1-R50278
Colored A-blocks	Colored A-block AE1	Colored A-block AE1-S89913
Colored A-blocks	Colored A-block AE1	Colored A-block AE1-T34112
Colored A-blocks	Colored A-block AE1	Colored A-block AE1-U32136
Colored A-blocks	Colored A-block AE1	Colored A-block AE1-Y27356
Colored A-blocks	Colored A-block AE10	Colored A-block AE10-R23773
Colored A-blocks	Colored A-block AE10	Colored A-block AE10-S52392
Colored A-blocks	Colored A-block AE10	Colored A-block AE10-T69941
Colored A-blocks	Colored A-block AE10	Colored A-block AE10-U17138
Colored A-blocks	Colored A-block AE10	Colored A-block AE10-Y95090

Figure 2.4.27: Categories, products, and SKUs in a table visual

As we saw earlier in this chapter, Power BI nicely retrieves the right combinations of Category, Product, and SKU from the model. You will get a table of 15,000 combinations, which are pulled from the model in batches while you scroll down in the table.

Now add a simple measure to the table, like SUM(fSales[Amount]). You may again get 15,000 rows as output, but it could be fewer, as not every SKU is necessarily sold:

Category	Product	SKU	Amount
Colored A-blocks	Colored A-block AE1	Colored A-block AE1-R50278	450
Colored A-blocks	Colored A-block AE2	Colored A-block AE2-S66398	2
Colored A-blocks	Colored A-block AE2	Colored A-block AE2-U56913	0
Colored A-blocks	Colored A-block AE3	Colored A-block AE3-S50400	12,500
Colored A-blocks	Colored A-block AE3	Colored A-block AE3-T57074	25,500
Colored A-blocks	Colored A-block AE3	Colored A-block AE3-Y19422	30
Colored A-blocks	Colored A-block AE4	Colored A-block AE4-U74494	65,992
Colored A-blocks	Colored A-block AE5	Colored A-block AE5-T29406	15,472
Colored A-blocks	Colored A-block AE7	Colored A-block AE7-R73207	19,754
Total			**608,712,361**

Figure 2.4.28: Categories, products, SKUs, and their sales

But what about the number of evaluations needed to populate this visual? This is much *larger* than the 15,000 in the table without a measure. As each of the Category, Product, and SKU fields is in its own table, the model evaluates each combination. The total number of evaluations is therefore 100 (categories) x 3,000 (products) x 15,000 (SKUs), or 4.5 billion!

The behavior described here is the main reason we generally advise against using tables in Power BI reports. People who come from Excel reports, or paginated reports in a database-focused reporting tool, are used to reports in the form of tables with many columns. When moving to Power BI, you may be inclined to stay close to the old style of reports, but having tables with many attribute columns from different tables in the model usually leads to an explosion of combinations that need to be evaluated.

Instead, aim for "non-tabular" visuals with drill-through interactions. Only when drilling into a small subset of data may you show broad tables with many details. Otherwise, restrict yourself to only one or two attribute columns.

To be clear, the DAX engine is so powerful that even a huge number of evaluations like this isn't slow by definition. (For instance, the initial DAX query for the table above only took 62 milliseconds on our machine.) It may, however, become a problem when your DAX calculations become more complex, and are written in a less efficient way. Or, even worse, when one of your measures isn't compatible with the labels, causing all or most of the combinations to yield a result. The engine will definitely have an issue calculating billions of results, only to be able to retrieve the first batch to show! (As a test, we added the One measure discussed earlier to the table visual. It returned a memory error after running for almost 10 minutes.)

Optimizing model structure

The solution to avoid the potential problems discussed in the previous section comes down to limiting the number of different tables that you draw the labels in your visuals from. You can do this in two ways:

- Use fewer labels in visuals, or only labels from the same table.
- Combine tables in the model.

The first one is clear, we assume, so let's dive into the second approach. As discussed in *Chapter 1.2, Model Design*, a star schema is often considered the go-to model structure. Now, having a star schema will not prevent the problems discussed here, as you may use columns from different "points of the star" and still have the same issues. However, it is wise not to split up the entities of your model into too many small pieces, but to look for "broader" tables wherever it makes sense.

Considering the example block sales model, however, saying *"use a star schema"* will not help you much either. It's obvious that Category, Product, and SKU are closely related entities, or even different aspects of a single entity. But forcibly combining them into one table causes problems in itself, due to the different granularities of the fact tables in this model. Having a single Product Hierarchy filter table would force you to have many-to-many relationships on the fSales and fForecast fact tables.

There is, however, a different approach you can take. After all, what matters is that we take attributes from a single table where possible; it doesn't matter so much what the model structure looks like.

You can, therefore, move the describing columns from the `Category` and `Product` tables to the `SKU` table, while keeping all IDs in place:

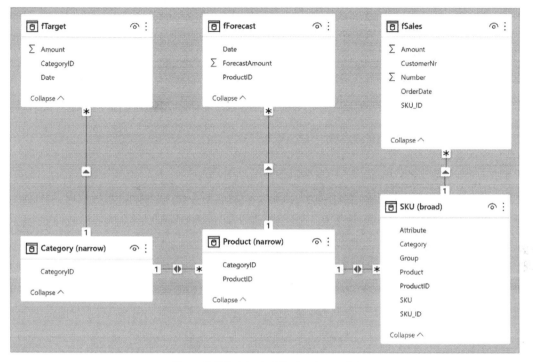

Figure 2.4.29: Adapted block sales model

Note that we set the cross filter direction to **Both** on the relationships between `Category (narrow)`, `Product (narrow)` and `SKU (broad)` now, as selecting a category from the `SKU (broad)` table should filter the `fTarget` and `fForecast` tables.

As the `Category (narrow)` and `Product (narrow)` tables only contain ID columns for relationships, they can be hidden, and you could give the SKU table a name to better reflect the product hierarchy.

With this model structure, the engine doesn't have any problem whatsoever with visuals combining category, product, and SKU, even using our One measure. As you can see in the following figure, only applicable combinations of the three labels are now evaluated:

Category	Product	SKU	Amount	One
Colored A-blocks	Colored A-block AE1	Colored A-block AE1-R50278	450	1
Colored A-blocks	Colored A-block AE1	Colored A-block AE1-S89913		1
Colored A-blocks	Colored A-block AE1	Colored A-block AE1-T34112		1
Colored A-blocks	Colored A-block AE1	Colored A-block AE1-U32136		1
Colored A-blocks	Colored A-block AE1	Colored A-block AE1-Y27356		1
Colored A-blocks	Colored A-block AE10	Colored A-block AE10-R23773		1
Colored A-blocks	Colored A-block AE10	Colored A-block AE10-S52392		1
Colored A-blocks	Colored A-block AE10	Colored A-block AE10-T69941		1
Colored A-blocks	Colored A-block AE10	Colored A-block AE10-U17138		1
Total			**608,712,361**	**1**

Figure 2.4.30: Output from the adapted block sales model

Optimizing the visual

In the previous section, we changed the structure of the Power BI model to avoid getting caught by AutoExist in table visuals. There is another solution you can apply that does not involve adapting the model structure.

In the block sales example, it should be clear that for each SKU, there is exactly one product and one category. Instead of adding these to the visual as labels, you can decide to create a DAX measure that returns the product name for an SKU, and another measure that returns the category name. By doing this, the Category and Product columns are populated with the results of the measures, which are calculated for each of the 15,000 SKUs.

It is a lesser-known fact that DAX measures can have text as a result. But there is a group of DAX functions that return text, like CONCATENATE, which, you've guessed it, concatenates values in a column, or FORMAT, which transforms a value into a text string with a specific format.

The product measure you would need here returns the value of the Product column in the product table that corresponds to a selected SKU. You need to consider possible contexts again; specifically, what should the measure return when multiple SKUs are selected?

We'll keep it simple here and say that only one Product is returned:

```
SKU_Product =
CALCULATE(
    FIRSTNONBLANK('Product'[Product], 1),
    CROSSFILTER('Product'[ProductID], SKU[ProductID], Both)
)
```

The FIRSTNONBLANK function takes a column reference as its first argument. For each value in the column, the expression in the second argument is evaluated until the result is non-blank. The corresponding column value is returned. As we use the simple expression 1 here, FIRSTNONBLANK simply returns the first product. As the relationship between the Product and SKU tables does not propagate a filter from SKU to Product, we use CROSSFILTER to change the filter propagation direction to BOTH.

A measure for Category works in a similar way but, this time, we have to change the filter propagation direction for two relationships:

```
SKU_Category =
CALCULATE(
    FIRSTNONBLANK(Category[Category], 1),
    CROSSFILTER('Product'[ProductID], SKU[ProductID], Both),
    CROSSFILTER(Category[CategoryID], 'Product'[CategoryID], Both)
)
```

While this solution avoids the need to change the model structure, additional DAX measures are needed for specific visuals. What the best option is depends on your specific Power BI model and reporting needs.

Summary

While most of the DAX challenges you will face, and most of this book's chapters, are fundamentally about context, or *what* is being calculated, this chapter focused on *which* calculations are done to populate a visual from a Power BI model.

Power BI applies AutoExist to guess the combinations of label values to evaluate. The simple rule is:

- When columns from the same table are used in a visual, only combinations of column values that are found in rows of the table are evaluated.
- When columns from different tables are used, all combinations of values are evaluated.

Understanding how AutoExist works will help you to find out why you sometimes do not see results in a visual when, logically, you would expect them. It also helps to avoid performance problems in reports that are the result of using too many columns from too many tables in one visual. An important lesson is this: be careful with table visuals!

The next chapter returns mainly to DAX context challenges when we look at the complexities you face when analyzing across boundaries, like business between subsidiaries within a company, and business across longer periods of time.

2.5

Intercompany Business

Larger organizations are normally organized into multiple legal entities. These entities may be separated along product lines, countries, or other business attributes. Whenever this happens, you will have to deal with data crossing the boundaries between entities: the subsidiary in, say, Japan, may do business with Japanese customers, but may also provide products or services to the subsidiary in India. Invoices sent to India may be counted in sales numbers for Japan, but should be consolidated when reporting the worldwide sales numbers. That is, assuming that the India subsidiary booked the purchases from Japan correctly.

A similar challenge arises when business crosses other boundaries. For instance, a company that executes multi-year projects for customers, or sells multi-year support contracts, has to answer questions about what part of the total sales on each project or contract is counted as sales in a specific year. With this, you can provide more detailed insights into sales, even when the sales invoice hasn't been sent yet.

In this chapter, we discuss some of these cross-boundary problems. In each situation, you will learn that understanding the concept of **context** is crucial in understanding how to solve these problems. The subject of this chapter is, again, the multinational company QuantoBikes with its many subsidiaries.

The problems discussed in this chapter are:

- Business between subsidiaries
- Future sales

Modeling the QuantoBikes sales process

Many business systems record different stages in a business process. A typical **enterprise resource planning (ERP)** system allows us to define the stages, for an invoice to be sent, for example. It is important to note that recording these stages assumes that a business process works in that specific way. The reality is almost always different.

In fact, analyzing the difference between a designed process and the actual process is a field of its own, named *process mining*. When you consider a large number of invoices, you will commonly find many deviations from the process as it is designed. Optimizing the business process starts with knowing which variants of the process occur. Some odd variants may have a large impact on throughput or even profitability; eliminating these variants by specific corrective actions can significantly improve business process performance. Analysts who apply process mining can also apply machine learning to predict which process variant a specific case will follow, making it possible to intervene for that case to follow a more optimal process variant.

This book is not about process mining. When thinking about the sales process of QuantoBikes, however, we should be aware that not every sale will follow the designed process. In a Power BI model, you need to be very careful and aware of the assumptions you make to avoid making errors in your analysis. These errors may be very hard to detect!

The sales process

For the QuantoBikes example, we use a fairly straightforward sales process. For a sale to come into effect, two steps are taken:

1. A *sales order* is set up.
2. A *sales invoice* is sent to the customer, for the amount of the sales order.

QuantoBikes works both with **one-off** sales orders and with sales orders that cover a certain period of time, for instance for a support or service contract; let's call these **long-term** sales orders. A one-off sales order is issued on a certain date, and provides the date the corresponding sales invoice will be sent. A long-term sales order can have a duration of 1 to 5 years. During this time, a sales invoice will be sent each month, evenly distributing the total sales order amount over the months covered by the sales order.

Figure 2.5.1 depicts the decrease of open sales order amounts (or, the amount that has not been invoiced yet) over time, for sales orders with different durations.

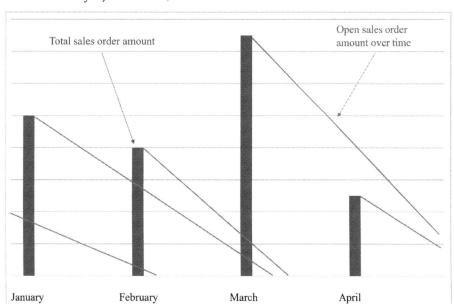

Figure 2.5.1: Open sales order amounts over time

For QuantoBikes' business, purchases need to be made as well. These follow the same basic process:

1. A *purchase order* is set up.
2. A *purchase invoice* is received from the supplier.

Like sales orders, purchase orders may cover some period of time in which a purchase invoice is received each month.

QuantoBikes works with *projects*, grouping both sales and purchases for a single customer. A customer can have multiple projects.

Internal sales and purchases, or transactions between QuantoBikes subsidiaries, are ordinary sales and purchase orders and invoices in this model. Internal transactions can be detected through the customer or the supplier: in each subsidiary's customer and supplier list, other subsidiaries may show up as internal customers and suppliers.

This is only the sales process as it is designed. In reality, anything may happen and will happen: invoices will be sent without a sales order, sales amounts will differ from order to invoice, and invoices on sales orders covering multiple months will not be evenly distributed.

And with internal transactions, the sales amount of one subsidiary may differ from the purchase amount of the other subsidiary, or may not exist at all.

Model structure

The basic structure of the data model is in the figure below:

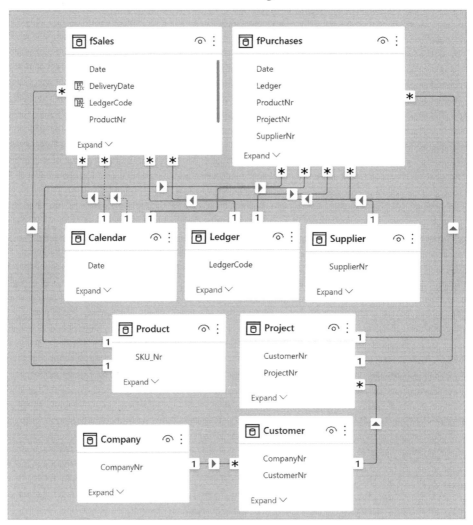

Figure 2.5.2: The QuantoBikes Power BI model

The model contains two fact tables: fSales, for sales orders and invoices, and fPurchases, for purchase orders and invoices. The fact table thus contains both orders and invoices, which are distinguished by a column Type.

Both fact tables are linked to filter tables: Product, Calendar, Project, and Ledger. The Ledger table contains the duration of long-term sales orders and purchase orders. The fPurchases table is linked to a Supplier filter table as well.

As you can see from the diagram, the Project table is linked to a Customer table, which in turn is linked to a Company table containing the QuantoBikes subsidiaries. This means that a project is always connected to a single customer, and each customer has a unique company.

 The Project, Customer, and Company tables may be combined into one in this model. In a larger model, however, there could be additional fact tables that must be linked to the Customer table (like a customer-based forecast) or the Company table as well, in which case having separate tables would be better.

Notice that the Supplier table is not linked to the Company table; each supplier can be used by each subsidiary.

 You can find the Power BI file for this chapter, 2.5 Intercompany business.pbix, at https://github.com/PacktPublishing/ Extreme-DAX/tree/main/Chapter2.5.

Business between subsidiaries

For the purpose of internal transactions, QuantoBikes subsidiaries are listed in the global supplier list and therefore appear in the Supplier table. A QMB Subsidiary column denotes these special suppliers with the value 1, whereas all normal suppliers have a value of 0 in this column:

SupplierNr	Supplier	QMB Subsidiary
359	QMB CANADA	1
297	QUANTOBIKES UK	1
284	QMB FRANCE	1
257	QMB DEUTSCHLAND	1
80	QUANTO MOTORBIKES INDIA	1
45	QUANTOBIKES JAPAN	1
19	QMB UNITED STATES	1

Figure 2.5.3: QuantoBikes subsidiaries

Similarly, each subsidiary that sells to another subsidiary needs to add the subsidiary to its customer list. In the Customer table, an Internal column is used to distinguish between internal and external customers:

Customer	CustomerNr	CompanyNr	Internal
QMB UK	2915	3	1
QMB USA	1384	3	1
QMB JAPAN	191	3	1
QMB UK	4973	7	1
QMB FRANCE	4870	7	1
QMB GERMANY	4685	7	1
QMB INDIA	3921	7	1

Figure 2.5.4: Internal customers have an Internal value of 1

We can now create DAX measures that do or do not include internal customers using the Internal column. In other words, we can either calculate a **subsidiary view** (including internal customers) or a **consolidated view** (excluding internal customers).

Subsidiary view versus consolidated view

When analyzing sales, it is important to consider the level at which you do this analysis. For instance, for a view for the QMB Japan subsidiary only, sales numbers should include sales to other subsidiaries. But global QuantoBikes sales should use a consolidated view, excluding all sales between subsidiaries. The same is true for purchases. In this section, we look at DAX measures to do these calculations as well as to pick the correct calculation.

The basic measure needed to report sales is straightforward:

```
BaseSales =
CALCULATE
    SUM(fSales[Amount]),
    fSales[Type] = "Sales Invoice"
)
```

For a consolidated view, all transactions to internal customers should be excluded. You can do this with a simple CALCULATE formula:

```
SalesConsolidated =
CALCULATE(
    [BaseSales],
    KEEPFILTERS(Customer[Internal] = 0)
)
```

We apply KEEPFILTERS here as a report could be filtered on Internal customers only; it would be confusing to see consolidated sales to these customers! See *Chapter 1.4, Context and Filtering*, for a more detailed discussion on KEEPFILTERS.

The challenge here is, of course, that from the perspective of DAX we don't know which version of sales should be calculated, the consolidated one or the basic calculation. We need to create a measure that detects whether the user is looking at the whole company or a single subsidiary. The DAX function to use here is HASONEVALUE:

```
Sales =
IF(HASONEVALUE(Company[CompanyNr]),
    [BaseSales],
    [SalesConsolidated]
)
```

We use HASONEVALUE on the unique CompanyNr column to avoid triggering the BaseSales measure when two companies with the same name are selected. This may seem highly unlikely, as it would be very confusing to have different subsidiaries with the same name. However, it is still important to think about which column to use. In the real world, the Company table may contain different "versions" of subsidiaries identified by CompanyNr; in this case, the versions would be grouped together based on name, and HASONEVALUE(Company[Company]) would be the better option.

On the other side of the equation, you will need the same kinds of measures for purchases:

```
BasePurchases =
CALCULATE(
    SUM(fPurchases[Amount]),
    fPurchases[Type] = "Invoice"
)
```

```
PurchasesConsolidated =
CALCULATE(
    [BasePurchases],
    KEEPFILTERS(Supplier[QMB Subsidiary] = 0)
)
```

Again, the overall measure determines which purchase calculation is selected:

```
Purchases =
IF(HASONEVALUE(Company[CompanyNr]),
    [BasePurchases],
    [PurchasesConsolidated]
)
```

The Sales and Purchases measures now enable both global and subsidiary reporting on income and costs.

Matching internal sales and purchases

Having a consolidated view of sales and purchases is important. Just as insightful is focusing specifically on internal sales and purchases. For this, you can use a straightforward variation on the consolidated measures:

```
SalesInternal1 =
CALCULATE(
    [BaseSales],
    KEEPFILTERS(Customer[Internal] = 1)
)
```

And:

```
PurchasesInternal1 =
CALCULATE(
    [BasePurchases],
    KEEPFILTERS(Supplier[QMB Subsidiary] = 1)
)
```

With these measures, you can answer questions like: how much did QMB Japan sell to other subsidiaries? And how much did QMB Japan purchase from other subsidiaries? But there are two more questions to ask: how much did other subsidiaries purchase from QMB Japan? And how much did other subsidiaries sell to QMB Japan?

Theoretically, these things should match: internal sales by QMB Japan should equal internal purchases from QMB Japan by all other subsidiaries. In the real world, we can only hope that this is the case, and it is better to monitor it. It would be good to have a measure to calculate the difference between the sales from one subsidiary and the corresponding purchases in other subsidiaries.

The main challenge here is that you will have to deal with some complicated context transformations. This is best illustrated with some sample output. A Power BI report could contain a matrix visual with sales from QMB Japan to QMB India, purchases by QMB India from QMB Japan, and the difference between the sales and purchases amounts:

	QMB India		
	Sales	**Purchases**	**Difference**
QMB Japan	1,000	900	100

Figure 2.5.5: QMB India and QMB Japan matrix

In this visual, you can see that one subsidiary is selected as a row label (QMB Japan) and another as a column label (QMB India). In other words, in the context for these calculations, we have two filters:

- `Company[Company] = "QMB Japan"`
- `Customer[Customer] = "QMB India"`

The `SalesInternal1` measure will correctly calculate the sales from QMB Japan to QMB India. If you were to use `PurchasesInternal1` in this context, however, you would find that the result is not what you want. In fact, what the measure returns is purchases done by QMB Japan from an unspecified supplier, where QMB India acts as the customer. What we are looking for, however, is purchases done by QMB India for which QMB Japan is the supplier. To solve this, we will have to transform the context and reverse the roles of QMB Japan and QMB India:

- `Company[Company] = "QMB India"`
- `Supplier[Supplier] = "QMB Japan"`

In other words, we need to use the selected customer as the company, and the selected company as the supplier. Or stated in yet another way, we need to transition the selection in the `Customer` table to the `Company` table, and transition the selection in the `Company` table to the `Supplier` table.

To do this kind of context transformation, you must use the TREATAS function:

```
PurchasesFromCompany1 =
CALCULATE(
    [PurchasesInternal1],
    TREATAS(DISTINCT(Customer[Customer]), Company[Company]),
    TREATAS(DISTINCT(Company[Company]), Supplier[Supplier]),
    ALL(Company),
    ALL(Customer),
    ALL(Supplier)
)
```

In this formula, DISTINCT is used to retrieve the unique values from the respective columns. TREATAS feeds these values as filters on the column provided in the second argument. Do not forget that the existing filters on the Company and Customer tables must be removed; and while we're at it, we'll remove filters from the Supplier table as well, to get rid of possible filters that stand in our way there. (Because of the relationship between Customer and Company, ALL(Customer) will also remove filters from the Company table, so ALL(Company) is not really needed here.)

There is one major problem with this approach: it depends on the names of the subsidiaries. Note that the name of a subsidiary appears at three places in the model: in the Company table, the Customer table, and the Supplier table. The name of a subsidiary must be exactly the same in each of the three tables. This is a dangerous assumption to make and, as a matter of fact, in our example data, the names are not identical.

The better approach would be to use a unique subsidiary identifier. We cannot use the Customer or Supplier numbers, as they are not identical either; the best candidate is the Company number. So, we should add information to the Customer and Supplier tables to identify the subsidiaries with their Company number. You could add a specific column containing the company number, but in fact, the perfect columns to do this are already there! The Customer[Internal] and Supplier[QMB Subsidiary] columns contain the value 1 to denote internal customers and suppliers, but the only thing that really matters is that this value is different from 0, to distinguish them from external customers and suppliers. So, instead of using the value 1, you can work with the corresponding Company number.

Our internal sales and purchases measures need to be slightly adapted:

```
SalesInternal2 =
CALCULATE(
    [BaseSales],
```

```
        KEEPFILTERS(Customer[Internal] > 0)
)
```

And:

```
PurchasesInternal2 =
CALCULATE(
    [BasePurchases],
    KEEPFILTERS(Supplier[QMB Subsidiary] > 0)
)
```

The `PurchasesFromCompany2` measure can now work with the `Company` number columns. For readability, let's use some variables:

```
PurchasesFromCompany2 =
VAR SubsidiariesAsCustomers = DISTINCT(Customer[Internal])
VAR SubsidiariesAsCompanies = DISTINCT(Company[CompanyNr])
RETURN
CALCULATE(
    [PurchasesInternal2],
    TREATAS(SubsidiariesAsCustomers, Company[CompanyNr]),
    TREATAS(SubsidiariesAsCompanies, Supplier[QMB Subsidiary]),
    ALL(Company),
    ALL(Customer),
    ALL(Supplier)
)
```

Note that `DISTINCT(Customer[Internal])` may also contain the value 0 when external customers are selected (for instance, because no filtering has been done at all). This is not a problem, however: `TREATAS` applies these values to the `Company[CompanyNr]` column, but there is no value 0 in that column so only the non-zero values will lead to a subsidiary being selected.

There is yet another thing to improve here. We can now correctly calculate both internal sales and internal purchases in the same context for a `Company`. However, the name of the other subsidiaries is taken from the `Customer` table; and as each subsidiary has its own customer list, the same subsidiary can appear in the `Customer` table multiple times, and with different names. This will be confusing and that is not what we want.

What we want to do is make sure that, when reporting on intercompany business, the proper names from the Company table are used. This means that the Company[Company] column could be needed twice in a single visual, for instance, providing both row labels and column labels, while having a different context in each. This is impossible. The only way to solve that is to duplicate the Company table altogether. Let's call this new table Company (to).

The new table does not need to have relationships with other tables, as we will use the TREATAS function to transition filter context from the table to other appropriate tables. The SalesInternal3 measure becomes a bit more complex as, this time, we need to take into account that selecting customers is now done on the Company (to) table:

```
SalesInternal3 =
VAR InternalCustomers = DISTINCT('Company (to)'[Companynr])
RETURN
CALCULATE(
    [BaseSales],
    TREATAS(InternalCustomers, Customer[Internal]),
    ALL(Customer),
    -- Customer[Internal] > 0
    VALUES(Company[CompanyNr])
)
```

When you think about it, you will conclude that the Customer[Internal] > 0 filter, commented out in the formula, is obsolete now; company numbers, each of which is larger than zero, are fed into this column and thus no external customers are selected. As ALL(Customer) removes filters from the Company table as well, we need to feed the selected companies back into the calculation using VALUES.

The internal purchases measure now takes the Company numbers from the new Company (to) table instead of the Customers table:

```
PurchasesFromCompany3 =
VAR InternalCustomers = DISTINCT('Company (to)'[Companynr])
VAR SubsidiariesAsCompanies = DISTINCT(Company[CompanyNr])
RETURN
CALCULATE(
    [BasePurchases],
    TREATAS(InternalCustomers, Company[CompanyNr]),
    TREATAS(SubsidiariesAsCompanies, Supplier[QMB Subsidiary]),
    ALL(Company),
```

```
    ALL(Customer),
    ALL(Supplier)
)
```

A more subtle change in the formula is that we no longer call the
[PurchasesInternal] measure, but the [BasePurchases] measure instead. The
difference between the two is the application of the Supplier[QMB Subsidiary] > 0
filter; and like in the sales measure, this filter is implicitly applied by TREATAS from
the Company[CompanyNr] column.

Visualizing intercompany business

Now that we have proper measures for internal sales and internal purchases
working with the Company and Company (to) tables, we can calculate the *internal
balance* with a simple measure:

```
Internal Balance = [SalesInternal3] - [PurchasesFromCompany3]
```

But wait – with this measure, you can check whether there is a balance between, say,
QMB Japan's sales invoices to QMB India, and QMB India's purchase invoices with
QMB Japan as the supplier. The QuantoBikes executive team may want these to be in
balance; however, there is another way business between QMB Japan and QMB India
can be in balance: when QMB India sells something to QMB Japan, they may opt to
send a lower sales invoice instead of booking a purchase invoice. Business between
subsidiaries may be largely informal, and it is likely that no actual invoices are sent
to and fro.

Note that this is a business issue, not a technical issue. There is no single right way
to tackle this from a technical perspective; instead, business owners need to decide
what calculation they want to be done.

But for now, let's assume that we are not so interested in the formal balance, but
rather in the informal balance; that means that we need to calculate the balance
between four financial streams:

- Sales invoices from A to B
- Purchase invoices from B to A
- Sales invoices from B to A
- Purchase invoices from A to B

The `Internal Balance` measure calculates the balance in two of the four streams. For the other two, we need to calculate a similar balance but in a reversed direction: instead of the balance between `Company` and `Company (to)`, we need the balance between `Company (to)` and `Company`. But to be able to add the two measures and complete our balance calculation, the second measure must be calculated in the same context as the first. In other words, we must, once again, flip the context on the two tables. We may as well do this directly on the internal sales and purchases measures that make up the internal balance measure:

```
SalesInternal (reversed) =
VAR CompaniesFrom = DISTINCT(Company[CompanyNr])
VAR CompaniesTo = DISTINCT('Company (to)'[CompanyNr])
RETURN
CALCULATE(
    [SalesInternal3],
    TREATAS(CompaniesTo, Company[CompanyNr]),
    TREATAS(CompaniesFrom, 'Company (to)'[CompanyNr]),
    ALL(Company),
    ALL('Company (to)')
)

PurchasesFromCompany (reversed) =
VAR CompaniesFrom = DISTINCT(Company[CompanyNr])
VAR CompaniesTo = DISTINCT('Company (to)'[CompanyNr])
RETURN
CALCULATE(
    [PurchasesFromCompany3],
    TREATAS(CompaniesTo, Company[CompanyNr]),
    TREATAS(CompaniesFrom, 'Company (to)'[CompanyNr]),
    ALL(Company),
    ALL('Company (to)')
)
```

Again, we use the TREATAS function to insert the selection in one table as a filter on the other table, applying ALL to get rid of the original filters. Note that we still allow multiple companies to be selected on either side; this way, we can calculate the total balance for the whole QuantoBikes company (which ideally should be zero).

The measure to calculate the overall balance must combine the four internal sales and purchases measures:

```
Internal Balance (total) =
[SalesInternal3]
- [PurchasesFromCompany3]
- [SalesInternal (reversed)]
+ [PurchasesFromCompany (reversed)]
```

The picture below shows the output of this measure for the year 2020 in a matrix visual.

Company	QMB Japan	QMB USA	QMB India	QMB Germany	QMB France	QMB UK	QMB Canada	**Total**
QMB Japan	0			28,430			-442,511	**-414,081**
QMB USA			-276,683			-1,073	-66,815	**-344,571**
QMB India		276,683				-66,756	286,348	**496,274**
QMB Germany	-28,430				-130,611	-5,891	12,914	**-152,018**
QMB France				130,611			-454,927	**-324,316**
QMB UK		1,073	66,756	5,891				**73,721**
QMB Canada	442,511	66,815	-286,348	-12,914	454,927			**664,992**
Total	**414,081**	**344,571**	**-496,274**	**152,018**	**324,316**	**-73,721**	**-664,992**	**0**

Figure 2.5.6: View on internal balance for QuantoBikes

You may notice a couple of things here. First, the grand total (the result in the **Total** row and **Total** column) is zero. Does this mean that there is a perfect balance between sales and purchases? The answer is no; rather, because we are comparing all subsidiaries here, the results of the [SalesInternal3] and [SalesInternal (reversed)] measures are exactly the same, as are the results of the [PurchasesFromCompany3] and [PurchasesFromCompany (reversed)] measures. It does not mean that [SalesInternal3] and [PurchasesFromCompany3] are in balance.

Another thing you may notice is that all results appear twice in the visual, albeit negated and mirrored across the diagonal. As this adds nothing to the insights provided by this analysis, it would be better to hide half of the numbers. You can do this by adding an additional filter to the internal balance calculation:

```
Internal Balance (final) =
VAR Companies =
    FILTER(
        CROSSJOIN(
            DISTINCT(Company[CompanyNr]),
            DISTINCT('Company (to)'[CompanyNr])
        ),
        Company[CompanyNr] >= 'Company (to)'[CompanyNr]
    )
```

```
RETURN
CALCULATE(
    [Internal Balance (total)],
    Companies
)
```

In this formula, the CROSSJOIN function creates a table containing all combinations of values of [CompanyNr] from both Company tables (that is, only those values that are selected in the query context for this measure). With the FILTER function, the combinations for which [CompanyNr] in the Company (to) table is smaller than that in the Company table are removed. The filtered table is used as a filter in CALCULATE, effectively reducing the selection in both the Company and Company (to) table.

For the result to look nice, you will also have to set the sort order on the [Company] columns in both tables to follow the [CompanyNr] column. This will cause all results to be shown below the diagonal in the matrix. The result now looks like this (we set the **Show items with no data** option on both the row and the column fields):

Company	QMB Japan	QMB USA	QMB India	QMB Germany	QMB France	QMB UK	QMB Canada	**Total**
QMB Japan	0							**0**
QMB USA								
QMB India		276,683						**276,683**
QMB Germany	-28,430							**-28,430**
QMB France				130,611				**130,611**
QMB UK		1,073	66,756	5,891				**73,721**
QMB Canada	442,511	66,815	-286,348	-12,914	454,927			**664,992**
Total	**414,081**	**344,571**	**-219,592**	**123,588**	**454,927**			**0**

Figure 2.5.7: Cleaned-up internal balance view

As you can see, the duplicates are gone and, as a result, the totals also show a different value. The overall result is still zero.

As with any insight, new questions will arise from what you see here. We can now see there is an imbalance between many subsidiaries (frankly, it's quite a mess at QuantoBikes!) and you may wonder what is actually happening. And where does that zero at QMB Japan come from? It would be a good addition to this visual to add a tooltip, for instance, with the breakdown of the internal balance. After all, we have already created measures for sales and purchases in all directions.

To make this tooltip easily readable, we will add some dynamic titles to avoid forcing the user to guess what goes where. After all, it is easy to lose track of which subsidiary is playing which role at what time.

We give you the formulas to do this without further ado:

```
From Company = SELECTEDVALUE(Company[Company], "(Multiple)")

To Company = SELECTEDVALUE('Company (to)'[Company], "(Multiple)")

Title_Sales_AtoB =
    "Sales from " & [From Company] & " to " & [To Company]

Title_Purchases_BfromA =
    "Purchases by " & [To Company] & " from " & [From Company]

Title_Sales_BtoA =
    "Sales from " & [To Company] & " to " & [From Company]

Title_Purchases_AfromB =
    "Purchases by " & [From Company] & " from " & [To Company]
```

It is a good idea to give measures that are solely aimed at creating dynamic titles a name starting with `Title`. When these titles are specific to a report and you build your reports as "live connection" (meaning in a different file to the model), it is advisable to create these measures in the report file and not in the model. In doing this, you avoid having a large number of report-specific measures that will cause more maintenance on the model.

A tooltip created with these dynamic titles adds additional clarity to the output:

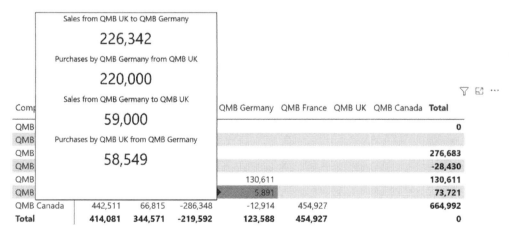

Figure 2.5.8: Adding details to the internal balance view

In this example, we can see that although the total internal balance between QMB UK and QMB Germany is less than 6,000, it comes from an imbalance in sales from the UK to Germany that is partly offset by an imbalance in sales from Germany to the UK.

With this tooltip, we can also discover where the zero at QMB Japan comes from: it turns out that Japan issued a purchase from themselves! This is a somewhat unexpected insight coming from our calculations, but the world is indeed messy, and often, the first outcome of a Power BI analysis is discovering all these weird things that are happening, or are wrongly reflected in the data.

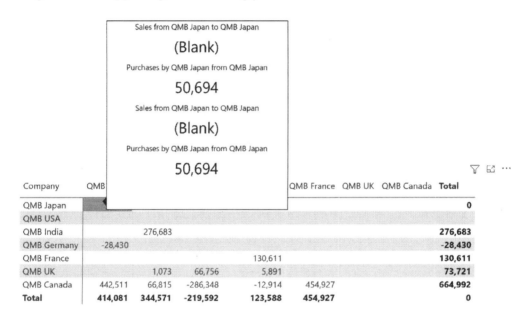

Company	QMB			QMB France	QMB UK	QMB Canada	Total
QMB Japan							0
QMB USA							
QMB India		276,683					276,683
QMB Germany	-28,430						-28,430
QMB France				130,611			130,611
QMB UK		1,073	66,756	5,891			73,721
QMB Canada	442,511	66,815	-286,348	-12,914	454,927		664,992
Total	**414,081**	**344,571**	**-219,592**	**123,588**	**454,927**		**0**

Figure 2.5.9: Insight into weird results at QMB Japan

You can, of course, extend this report with further drillthrough options. After all, in our measures we did nothing with dates, products, or projects, so the calculations will still work when additional filters from the `Calendar`, `Product`, or `Project` table are added. This makes it possible to zoom in further and see exactly where things are not in balance.

Future sales

For our next analysis, let's turn back to the QuantoBikes sales process, focusing on two simple steps: booking a sales order, and sending an invoice based on the sales order.

You can calculate the actual sales (and purchases, for that matter) from the invoices in our model. A common question to ask is: how will sales develop through the rest of the year? One part of the answer to this question deals with sales forecasting and the sales pipeline. These are very useful things to analyze, although they come with inherent uncertainty.

A much more specific part of the answer comes from looking at sales orders that have not been (fully) invoiced yet. After all, a sales order is typically booked when the customer agrees to the sale, but the corresponding invoice is sometimes sent on a later date. So, what could be easier than determining what sales orders have not been invoiced yet, or at least, not completely?

Well, a lot of things are easier than that, but we'll cover how to do it here. In addition, we'll talk about a more sophisticated analysis that takes long-term sales orders and calculates the invoice amount that can be sent on those sales orders.

Sales on one-off sales orders

When you look at the fSales table, you will find both sales orders and sales invoices among its rows. How can you determine which invoice goes with which order? This is done with two columns: DocumentNr and OrderNr:

Date ▼	Amount ▼	Type ▼	DocumentNr ▼	OrderNr ▼
2/26/2021	2,956.69	Sales Invoice	89030	82845
2/26/2021	4,453.94	Sales Invoice	89030	82845
2/26/2021	5,940.76	Sales Invoice	89030	82845
2/26/2021	16,842.12	Sales Invoice	89030	82845
2/26/2021	263.18	Sales Invoice	89030	82845
2/26/2021	18,245.63	Sales Invoice	89030	82845
4/19/2021	15,269.33	Sales Invoice	91919	88990
4/23/2021	17,043.31	Sales Invoice	92661	82845
4/23/2021	1,500.48	Sales Invoice	92668	82845
4/23/2021	3,625.00	Sales Invoice	92668	82845

Figure 2.5.10: How orders and invoices are linked

As you can see from the picture, multiple `fSales` rows can have the same `DocumentNr` value. These could be different lines on the same invoice. Sales orders have a `DocumentNr` as well. Invoices that are bound to a sales order have the `DocumentNr` value of that sales order stored in the `OrderNr` column.

As it happens, sometimes invoices are sent without a sales order. Obviously, you may want to report on these, but they do not play a role in invoices that are yet to be sent. A more interesting analysis is to determine which sales orders have not been invoiced yet; this is somewhat complicated by the fact that the normal process allows for sales orders that will only be invoiced at a later delivery date.

So, what we need to do is to find sales orders that could have been invoiced in a period of time, but have not been. We only deal with one-off sales orders for now; these can be detected by the fact they have a duration of zero (while long-term sales orders have a non-zero duration). From a DAX perspective, we need a few steps:

- Determine which sales orders have a delivery date in the selected period of time
- Determine the invoice amount that has not yet been invoiced

You may conclude from this that we will have to go through the set of sales orders one by one and find the corresponding invoices. But we can do this in a simpler way by calculating the total number of invoices related to the set of sales orders found. It doesn't really matter which invoice belongs to which sales order. The *assumption* that supports this approach is that the total amount invoiced does not exceed the sales order amount. In a real business setting, this assumption should, of course, be validated!

Keep in mind that the relationship between `fSales` and `Calendar` is on the date of the order or invoice, not on the delivery date.

First, we find our sales orders:

```
To Invoice (project) =
VAR SalesOrders =
    CALCULATETABLE(
        DISTINCT(fSales[DocumentNr]),
        fSales[Type] = "Sales Order",
        KEEPFILTERS(Ledger[Duration] = 0),
        USERELATIONSHIP(fSales[DeliveryDate], 'Calendar'[Date])
    )
```

Using USERELATIONSHIP, we tell DAX to filter the fSales table on the DeliveryDate column, through which we get exactly the sales orders with a delivery date in the selected period of time. Next, we calculate the invoice amount for these sales orders:

```
VAR InvoicedAmount =
    CALCULATE(
        SUM(fSales[Amount]),
        fSales[Type] = "Sales Invoice",
        ALL('Calendar'),
        TREATAS(SalesOrders, fSales[OrderNr])
    )
```

The main filter here is the one using TREATAS. This filter applies our list of sales orders to the OrderNr column, effectively selecting invoices linked to those orders. The normal situation would be that these invoices have a date within the selected period of time, but we are not sure everything is normal, so we look for other dates as well by removing filters from the Calendar table.

We can now compute the total sales order amount of these sales orders, and compare that to the amount invoiced; the difference is what's left to invoice:

```
VAR OrderedAmount =
    CALCULATE(
        SUM(fSales[Amount]),
        fSales[Type] = "Sales Order",
        KEEPFILTERS(Ledger[Duration] = 0),
        USERELATIONSHIP(fSales[DeliveryDate], 'Calendar'[Date])
    )
RETURN
OrderedAmount - InvoicedAmount
```

By applying the exact same filters as for the SalesOrders variable, we are sure that we get the corresponding order amount.

There is another assumption made implicitly in this calculation: it returns the *current* amount still to be invoiced. You may want to do historical calculations as well; this analysis can provide insights into how the organization's discipline in sales order depletion is improving or worsening over time. We will not cover historical analysis in this chapter.

Sales on long-term sales orders

Let us now turn to long-term sales orders. These sales orders have a duration that typically spans multiple years, which means that you cannot simply compare the sales order amount and the total amount invoiced so far. Instead, a period of time needs to be selected, and then we can calculate the amount that can be invoiced during this period; this is only equal to the full open amount when the duration of the sales order ends within the selected time period. The period of time to select could be, for instance, the rest of the current year, to calculate the planned sales from support contracts that will contribute to this year's results.

The figure below shows, once again, the typical decrease in open sales order amount for a sample of long-term sales orders. The dark-colored sales orders have a duration of 2 years, or 24 months, to invoice, whereas the light-colored sales order has a duration of 1 year, or 12 months.

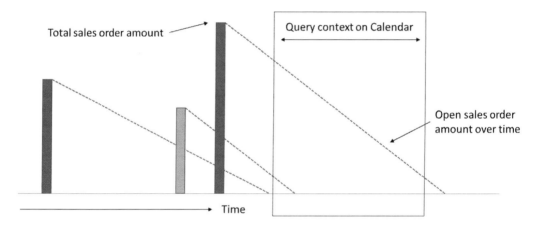

Figure 2.5.11: Expected invoice amounts during a selected time period

In the figure, the rectangle depicts the period of time selected. We can see different situations regarding the three sales orders in the picture, based on where the dotted lines end:

- One sales order has been fully invoiced (dotted line ends before the selection; an **old sales order**)
- One sales order still has an open amount, but will be invoiced in full during the selected time period (dotted line ends within the selection; a **current sales order**)

- One sales order will still have an open amount after the selected time period (dotted line ends after the selection; also a **current sales order**)

This is only the expected, ideal flow of events; the reality is probably different. And that is what we want to detect with this analysis.

Before we dive into the calculations, let's take a look at how the durations are modeled. The fSales fact table has a relationship with a Ledger table containing a Duration column.

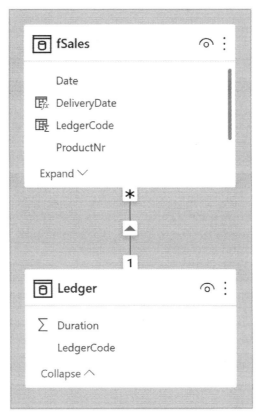

Figure 2.5.12: fSales and Ledger

Looking at a sample of data in the Ledger table, you will learn that durations are stored as a number of months:

LedgerCode	Duration
211500	60
211400	48
211300	36
211200	24
211100	12
111500	60
111400	48
111300	36
111200	24
111100	12
194500	60

Figure 2.5.13: Durations in the Ledger table

The status of a sales order – whether it should be invoiced in full, will be invoiced in full during our selected period, or will still have an open amount – can be derived from the duration in combination with the delivery date of the sales order.

Dealing with old sales orders

The model will contain a lot of historical records, including long-term sales orders that have been invoiced in full a long time ago. We want to deal with these sales orders as efficiently as possible. The problem is, there may be old sales orders that are *not* fully invoiced yet.

We can treat these sales orders in the same way as one-off sales orders: all open amounts can – and should – be invoiced right away. The challenge comes down to selecting these sales orders.

To start, we determine the date from which to determine the old sales orders. This is, of course, the first day in the selected period: any sales order without scheduled invoicing after that date is old. But there is a caveat: we want to make sure that we only look to the future.

After all, we cannot expect invoices to be sent during months that have already passed:

```
Old sales orders =
VAR MinDate = MIN('Calendar'[Date])
VAR FirstDayOfSelection = EOMONTH(MAX(MinDate, TODAY()), 0)
RETURN
```

By taking the largest of either `MinDate` or `TODAY()`, we know for certain that we are working with a date that is not in the past. We push this to the end of the month using `EOMONTH` to make our life a little easier.

What are the "old" sales orders? These are the sales orders with a delivery date that is at least the number of months before `FirstDayOfSelection` that is equal to the duration of the sales order. To better understand the logic, it helps to do the calculation by duration:

```
SUMX(
    FILTER(
        DISTINCT(Ledger[Duration]),
        Ledger[Duration] > 0
    ),
    VAR ThisDuration = Ledger[Duration]
    VAR CutOffDate =
        EOMONTH(FirstDayOfSelection, -1 * ThisDuration)
    VAR SalesOrders =
        CALCULATETABLE(
            DISTINCT(fSales[DocumentNr]),
            fSales[Type] = "Sales Order",
            fSales[DeliveryDate] <= CutOffDate,
            ALL('Calendar')
        )
```

We first determine the set of distinct durations. One-off sales orders have a ledger with duration zero, so we need to filter out the zeroes. `SUMX` iterates over this set, and we like to store the current value in a variable, `ThisDuration` in this case, mainly for readability.

The `CutOffDate` variable subtracts the correct number of months from `FirstDayInSelection`. It is easiest to take a simple example to understand this: when the first date in the `Calendar`'s selection is, say, September 1, `FirstDayInSelection` is September 30 and, with a duration of 6 months, the cut-off date is March 31.

That means that for a sales order with a delivery date before that, there are 6 months (starting from April) in which invoices could have been sent, including September. Even when the last invoice is scheduled for September but is not yet sent, we can still compare the full sales order amount with the total invoice amount to get the correct open order amount.

The SalesOrders variable can now collect the DocumentNr values for the sales orders from before the cut-off date. With the list of sales orders, the total sales order amount and actual invoice amount can now be calculated using TREATAS in the way we discussed earlier in this chapter, using the [DocumentNr] column for sales orders and [OrderNr] for invoices:

```
VAR InvoicedAmount =
    CALCULATE(
        SUM(fSales[Amount]),
        fSales[Type] = "Sales Invoice",
        ALL('Calendar'),
        TREATAS(SalesOrders, fSales[OrderNr])
    )
VAR OrderedAmount =
    CALCULATE(
        SUM(fSales[Amount]),
        fSales[Type] = "Sales Order",
            ALL('Calendar'),
        TREATAS(SalesOrders, fSales[DocumentNr])
    )
RETURN

    OrderedAmount - InvoicedAmount
)
```

The key step in this calculation is to determine the correct list of sales orders. Is it possible to do this without iterating over the durations?

As a matter of fact, it is. We will use the [YearMthCtr] column in the Calendar table for this, as it is a convenient counter we can add to and subtract from to move through the months. In the code snippet below, first the FirstYearMthCtr variable is evaluated as the YearMthCtr value corresponding to the FirstDayOfSelection date.

The MonthsDurations variable creates a list of Duration/YearMthCtr pairs that correspond to delivery dates before the cut-off date for the duration. This list is then used as a sophisticated *two-column* filter in the calculation of the SalesOrders variable:

```
    VAR FirstYearMthCtr =
        CALCULATE(
            MIN('Calendar'[YearMthCtr]),
            ALL('Calendar'),
            'Calendar'[Date] = FirstDayOfSelection
        )
    VAR MonthsDurations =
        GENERATE(
            FILTER(
                DISTINCT(Ledger[Duration]),
                Ledger[Duration] > 0
            ),
            VAR ThisDuration = Ledger[Duration]
            RETURN
            CALCULATETABLE(
            DISTINCT('Calendar'[YearMthCtr],
                'Calendar[YearMthCtr] <=
                FirstYearMthCtr - ThisDuration,
                ALL('Calendar')
                )
        )

    VAR SalesOrders =
        CALCULATETABLE(
            DISTINCT(fSales[DocumentNr]),
            fSales[Type] = "Sales Order",
            MonthsDurations,
            ALL('Calendar'),
            USERELATIONSHIP(fSales[DeliveryDate], 'Calendar'[Date])
        )
```

The MonthsDurations variable shows a rare use of the GENERATE DAX function.
GENERATE takes two arguments, both tables. The second argument is typically a
table expression, which is evaluated in row context for each row in the table in
the first argument. We store the duration in the ThisDuration variable and use
CALCULATETABLE with a straightforward filter that implements the cut-off date.

The SalesOrders variable determines the list of DocumentNr values for sales orders
that have an "old" delivery date relative to their duration. Note that we need to use
USERELATIONSHIP here to filter on the delivery date, as the MonthsDurations filter
is a filter on the Calendar table and the Ledger table. In our previous approach, we
filtered on the fSales table directly (on the DeliveryDate column), so we didn't have
to worry about the Calendar relationship.

We show you this approach mainly to demonstrate that iterators or table aggregations can often be circumvented. In this particular case, the distinct number of durations is very small and you won't win much, if at all, by implementing the calculation without the SUMX; with larger sets, however, it can make a huge difference in performance, as we will see later in this chapter.

To recapitulate, here is the complete DAX formula for old sales orders:

```
Old sales orders =

VAR MinDate = MIN('Calendar'[Date])
VAR FirstDayOfSelection = MAX(MinDate, TODAY())
VAR FirstYearMthCtr =
    CALCULATE(
        MIN('Calendar'[YearMthCtr]),
        ALL('Calendar'),
        'Calendar'[Date] = FirstDayOfSelection
    )

VAR MonthsDurations =
    GENERATE(
        FILTER(
            DISTINCT(Ledger[Duration]),
            Ledger[Duration] > 0
        ),
        VAR ThisDuration = Ledger[Duration]
        RETURN
        CALCULATETABLE(
            DISTINCT('Calendar'[YearMthCtr],
            'Calendar[YearMthCtr] <=
                FirstYearMthCtr - ThisDuration,
            ALL('Calendar')
            )
    )

VAR SalesOrders =
    CALCULATETABLE(
        DISTINCT(fSales[DocumentNr]),
        fSales[Type] = "Sales Order",
        MonthsDurations,
        ALL('Calendar'),
        USERELATIONSHIP(fSales[DeliveryDate], 'Calendar'[Date])
    )
```

```
VAR InvoicedAmount =
    CALCULATE(
        SUM(fSales[Amount]),
        fSales[Type] = "Sales Invoice",
        ALL('Calendar'),
        TREATAS(SalesOrders, fSales[OrderNr])
    )

VAR OrderedAmount =
    CALCULATE(
        SUM(fSales[Amount]),
        fSales[Type] = "Sales Order",
            ALL('Calendar'),
        TREATAS(SalesOrders, fSales[DocumentNr])
    )

RETURN

OrderedAmount - InvoicedAmount
```

Note that this calculation is not particularly suited to be used in a monthly chart or a similar visual. For example, if you were to evaluate this measure for every month of the year 2045, you would get the amounts to be invoiced for all old sales orders as of today, *in every month*. You could create a version of this calculation that only returns a result for the first day in context, but we will not cover that here. Instead, let's look at current sales orders.

Dealing with current sales orders

We can now focus on calculating the amounts still to be invoiced on current sales orders. The logic for the expected flow of events is rather straightforward: take the total amount for a sales order, divide it by the duration in months, and you will get the monthly invoice amount. Count the number of months in the selected time period and you will have the amount that can be invoiced.

We will go one step further and take the realities into account. A number of things can happen:

- Not enough was invoiced before the selected time period
- Invoices are sent exactly on schedule (or, just enough was invoiced)
- Too much was invoiced before the selected time period

The question is how to deal with these situations. This is definitely a business decision. Suppose we have a five-year support contract, and in the first year we invoiced twice the amount expected. Are we not going to send invoices in year two? Or do we continue invoicing until the fourth year, after which no further invoices will be sent? These are obviously not technical questions, but for now we'll just pick one option and say that when too much has been invoiced, we compensate for that in calculating expected future sales. In other words, the amount that was invoiced too much is subtracted from the scheduled invoice amount.

A similar question arises in the case of sales orders that are behind their invoice schedule. In that situation, let's say we assume normal invoicing will continue without catching up the backlog. Only at the end of the duration of a sales order is the remaining amount invoiced. In doing this, we take the cautious stance in both cases and we avoid being too optimistic as much as possible.

When designing the DAX formula for this calculation, we have to consider the query context and determine the logical steps to take. The most relevant part of the query context is, of course, the selected time period. This can be anything, but as with the old sales orders calculation, we need to consider only the future. Again, we will work on the basis of months to align with the monthly invoicing cadence. This means that we need to construct a list of months to work with. The next steps are:

1. Determine the list of relevant sales orders.

2. For each sales order, check whether too much has already been invoiced.

3. If so, subtract the amount that has been invoiced too much from the scheduled amount to be invoiced.

4. If not, calculate the amount that can be invoiced (either the monthly invoice amount multiplied by the number of months in our list, or the remaining open order amount; depending on whether the duration of the sales order ends during the time period).

To create the month list, we use a straightforward CALCULATETABLE calculation:

```
Current Sales Orders =
VAR MonthList =
    CALCULATETABLE(
        DISTINCT('Calendar'[MonthYearCtr]),
        KEEPFILTERS('Calendar'[Date] >= TODAY())
    )
```

To determine what the relevant sales orders are, the easiest thing to do is to reuse the logic we already developed: current sales orders are all those that are not old. Note that we have an easier way to find `FirstYearMthCtr` now that we already have `MonthList`.

There is one important thing to consider, however, and that is the possibility that our selected time period is completely in the past. In this case, `MonthList` will be empty and `FirstYearMthCtr`, as derived below, will be blank. We want the `MonthsDurations` table to be empty as well and we will do this by adding a test for the `FirstYearMontNr` value in the definition of `MonthsDurations`:

```
VAR FirstYearMthCtr =
    MINX(
        MonthList,
        'Calendar'[MonthYearCtr]
    )
VAR LastYearMthCtr =
    MAXX(
        MonthList,
        'Calendar'[MonthYearCtr]
    )

VAR MonthsDurations =
    GENERATE(
        FILTER(
                DISTINCT(Ledger[Duration]),
                Ledger[Duration] > 0
                && NOT(ISBLANK(FirstYearMthCtr))
        ),
        VAR ThisDuration = Ledger[Duration]
        RETURN
        CALCULATETABLE(
            DISTINCT('Calendar'[YearMthCtr]),
            'Calendar'[YearMthCtr] > FirstYearMthCtr - ThisDuration
            && 'Calendar'[YearMthCtr] <= LastYearMthCtr,
            ALL('Calendar')
            )
    )
```

```
VAR SalesOrders =
    CALCULATETABLE(
        DISTINCT(fSales[DocumentNr]),
        fSales[Type] = "Sales Order",
        MonthsDurations,
        ALL('Calendar'),
        USERELATIONSHIP(fSales[DeliveryDate], 'Calendar'[Date])
    )
```

With the set of current sales orders in the `SalesOrders` variable, we have established *step 1* in the calculation's flow. We can now continue with the other steps of the calculation:

```
SUMX(
    SalesOrders,
    VAR ThisSalesOrderNr = fSales[DocumentNr]

    VAR InvoicedAmount =
        CALCULATE(
            SUM(fSales[Amount]),
            fSales[Type] = "Sales Invoice",
            ALL('Calendar'),
            fSales[OrderNr] = ThisSalesOrderNr,
            ALL(fSales[DocumentNr])
        )
    VAR SalesOrderAmount =
        CALCULATE(
            SUM(fSales[Amount]),
            ALL('Calendar')
        )
```

The `InvoicedAmount` variable is quite straightforward: calculate the total invoice amount for the current sales order. The only caveat here is that we're in a row context on a list of `DocumentNr` values, and `CALCULATE` causes a filter on this column. We want the `OrderNr` to be the current value, but setting this does not automatically erase the filter on `DocumentNr`, hence the `ALL(fSales[DocumentNr])`. The formula for the sales order amount is easier because we are already looking at the correct `DocumentNr` and know that it is a sales order.

We must now calculate the amount that should have been invoiced until today. This is equal to the total sales order amount, divided by the duration in months, multiplied by the number of months between the initial delivery date of the sales order and today. Let's start off by defining variables for the duration and the monthly invoice amount:

```
VAR ThisDuration =
    CALCULATE(
        MIN(Ledger[Duration]),
        CROSSFILTER(
            fSales[Ledger], Ledger[LedgerCode], Both
        ),
        ALL('Calendar')
    )
VAR InvoicePerMonth = DIVIDE(SalesOrderAmount, ThisDuration)
```

The ThisDuration calculation looks overly complicated: all we want is the related Duration value for this sales order. However, remember that we are not looking at a single row in fSales, but at a single row in the list of DocumentNr values; and one value may correspond to multiple lines in fSales. So, although we are in a row context here, we cannot use the RELATED function as you may expect. Instead, we let the fSales-Ledger relationship filter from fSales to Ledger using the CROSSFILTER function. We must use an aggregation here, although we will only find one Duration value, so it doesn't really matter which aggregation we choose: MIN, MAX, or even AVERAGE or SUM would work – AVERAGE and SUM would be very confusing though! Note also that existing filters on Calendar are still there, while we are looking at a sales order from the past. So again, we need to remove these filters with ALL (and you will see the same thing over and over again below).

To calculate the number of months from the delivery date until today, we have to first find the delivery date and then count the number of months. With these, we can calculate the scheduled invoice amount:

```
VAR ThisDeliveryDate =
    CALCULATE(
        MIN(fSales[DeliveryDate]),
        ALL('Calendar')
    )
```

```
    VAR ThisDeliveryDateCtr =
        CALCULATE(
            MIN('Calendar'[YearMthCtr]),
            'Calendar'[Date] = ThisDeliveryDate,
            ALL('Calendar')
        )
    VAR NumberOfMonths =
        CALCULATE(
            DISTINCTCOUNT('Calendar'[YearMthCtr]),
            'Calendar'[Date] >= ThisDeliveryDate,
            'Calendar'[Date] < TODAY(),
            ALL('Calendar')
        )
  VAR ScheduledInvoiceAmount = InvoicePerMonth * NumberOfMonths
```

In calculating `ThisDeliveryDate`, again we must use an aggregation while knowing that we will find only one value. `CALCULATE` turns the row context into a filter context, causing `fSales` to be filtered down to only rows with the current `DocumentNr` value.

As the calculation is month-based, we also calculate the `YearMthCtr` value of the delivery date and use that for calculating the number of months passed since then until the first month of the `Calendar` context. Note that this defines the logic we assume on the invoice schedule: the first invoice is assumed to be sent in the month of the delivery date and, after that, one invoice is sent each month. `ScheduledInvoiceAmount` thus is the invoice amount we expect to have been invoiced *before* our selected time period.

We now have done all preparations to compute the amount that can be invoiced in the selected time period. First, let's determine the invoice surplus, or the amount that is invoiced on top of what should have been invoiced. This is *step 2* in the calculation flow.

```
    VAR InvoiceSurplus =
        MAX(InvoicedAmount - ScheduledInvoiceAmount, 0)
```

If the actual amount invoiced is *less* than scheduled, we set the surplus to zero. The next thing to do is to compute the scheduled invoice amount during our selected time period. This is either the monthly invoice continued, or the remainder of the sales order amount (when the duration ends during our time period). In the former case, we need to subtract the invoice surplus from this (*step 3* in the calculation flow) and may find that there is nothing to invoice anymore. In the latter case, we do not have to deal with the invoice surplus, as we have assumed that no more is invoiced than the sales order amount.

Note that *step 4* of our flow is implemented through this as well: when the amount invoiced is not too much, the invoice surplus is zero; and when the duration of the sales order ends, we invoice the remaining amount and catch up with any late invoicing.

How do we determine whether the duration ends during the time period? Well, our `YearMthCtr` counter comes in handy here. We can compute the last month of scheduled invoicing by starting with the delivery date counter (that we already have), adding the duration in months, and subtracting 1. If this last month is in our selection, the invoice schedule of the sales order ends here. The `CONTAINS` function is perfect to check this:

```
CONTAINS(
    MonthList,
    'Calendar'[YearMthCtr],
    ThisDeliveryDateCtr + ThisDuration - 1
)
```

When this is false, we need to determine the number of months for which the monthly invoice schedule will continue. Typically, this is the number of rows in `MonthList`; however, we may be looking at a sales order with a delivery date in our selected time period, and we don't want to count months before that date. So, we need to filter `MonthList`. The total formula for the expected invoice amount then becomes:

```
VAR Toinvoice =
    IF(
        CONTAINS(
            MonthList,
            'Calendar'[YearMthCtr],
            ThisDeliveryDateCtr + ThisDuration - 1
        ),
        SalesOrderAmount - InvoicedAmount,
        MAX(
            COUNTROWS(
                FILTER(
                    MonthList,
                        'Calendar'[YearMthCtr] >=
                    ThisDeliveryDateCtr
                )
```

```
            ) * InvoicePerMonth
            - InvoiceSurplus,
            0
        )
    )
    RETURN
    ToInvoice
)
```

And that's it: for every current sales order, we now calculate the expected invoice amount in the selected time period.

Optimizing the current sales order calculation

There is one issue with the current sales order calculation: after determining which sales orders are current, we iterate over these sales orders individually. The number of sales orders can be quite high (we are iterating over a high-cardinality column in a fact table) and we do a lot of work for each sales order. This constitutes a potential performance problem.

Now that we've thoroughly worked through the logic required for the calculation by sales order, it would be good to explore whether we can achieve the same results with a lower number of iterations (or ideally, no iterations at all). To get a good overview of our logic, let's write the calculation in pseudocode:

```
Current Sales Orders =
VAR SalesOrders = <determine current sales orders>
SUMX(SalesOrders,
    Calculate:
        actual invoiced amount
        sales order amount
        scheduled invoice amount
        invoice surplus ( = actual - scheduled invoice)
        invoice amount in selected time period:
            either relevant number of months
                * monthly invoice,
                and if surplus > 0, subtract it
                but keep it at >= 0
            or remaining amount on sales order
)
```

Now, ask yourself: which steps in this calculation need to be calculated by individual sales order?

- `Actual invoiced amount` and `sales order amount` can easily be computed for all sales orders together.

- `Scheduled invoice amount` depends on the number of months passed for the sales order, which is derived from the delivery date and the duration. It could therefore be calculated by a delivery month/duration combination.

- `Invoice surplus` is derived from actual and scheduled, and can therefore also be calculated by a delivery month/duration combination.

- `Invoice amount in selected time period`: We have two situations here:

  - The first one, `relevant number of months * monthly invoice`, can be calculated by duration: the monthly invoice amount is the sales order amount divided by the duration. Which sales orders this should be computed for can be derived from the delivery date and duration: this situation applies to all sales orders for which the invoice schedule does not end within the selected time period. We can conclude that this can be calculated at once for all sales orders that satisfy the delivery date/duration criteria.

  - The second situation, `remaining amount on sales order`, again depends on delivery date and duration: it can be derived from the number of months in the sales order's invoice schedule that fall within the selected time period. Once again, the delivery month/duration combination appears to be the appropriate granularity.

The observations above strongly suggest that we can iterate over delivery month/duration combinations. The happy coincidence is that we already have these combinations: remember that we created a `MonthsDurations` variable to determine the set of current sales orders! Remember what this variable contains: it is a list of each duration, in combination with the possible months in which sales orders can be (first) delivered and still be current within the period selected in the query context.

The pseudocode version of the DAX formula now becomes:

```
Current Sales Orders =
VAR MonthDurations =
    <all relevant delivery month/duration combinations>
SUMX(MonthDurations,
    Calculate for the sales orders for this month/duration:
        total actual invoiced amount
```

```
        total sales order amount
        total scheduled invoice amount
        total invoice surplus ( = actual - scheduled invoice)
        invoice amount in selected time period:
            either relevant number of months
                * monthly invoice,
                and if surplus > 0, subtract it
                but keep it at >= 0
            or total remaining sales order amount
)
```

The devil is in the detail, though, and we have some final steps to go. We need to specifically focus on the Invoice amount in selected time period part, which contains two clauses: relevant number of months * monthly invoice, and remaining amount on sales order. The former needs to deal with invoice surplus, which we will deal with in the next section.

Dealing with invoice surplus

In the calculation by individual sales order, we subtract the invoice surplus, when it is larger than zero, from the full scheduled amount (the number of months multiplied by the monthly invoice); but do not let the end result fall below zero. Now, we calculate by individual month/duration combination; this means we work with the total scheduled amount for all sales orders for this combination, and with the total invoice surplus for the same sales orders.

This is all fine when the individual surplus for each sales order is larger than zero. But it may also occur that the surplus for one sales order is negative, say -500, but the surplus for another sales order is positive and larger, say 700. In this case, the total surplus is 200 and we would subtract this from the scheduled amount; in reality, however, we should subtract 700! We are in serious trouble here, as to do a correct calculation, we would need to go over each sales order individually, which is the very thing we are trying to get away from.

The best we can do is to select the sales orders with a positive invoice surplus as efficiently as possible. This is a good case for having a calculated column, as we can directly filter on values in that column. The only restriction here is that the calculation for creating the column should not be dependent on the query context for the DAX measure; after all, a calculated column contains static data.

As the Current Sales Orders measure is only calculated for future periods of time, we can compute the current invoice surplus for each sales order: the surplus as of today.

However, as our query context may select a future time period, we need to be able to relate today's surplus to the remaining surplus at the start of the selected time period. We can solve this by expressing the invoice surplus in *number of monthly invoices*. We will discuss the formula to create this column below, but let us first look at the logic to implement in the measure (with a numeric example):

a.   Determine today's date (say, January 15, 2022).

b.   Determine the number of months in context (say, 5).

c.   Determine the first month in context, and how many months this is away from a) (say, July 2022, and 6). This is how many monthly invoicing occurrences could have been used to compensate for a surplus.

d.   Select sales orders with a surplus (in monthly invoices) larger than c) (for example, order 1: 12 months, order 2: 10.5 months).

e.   Subtract c) from d) (order 1: 6, order 2: 4.5). This is the surplus still to compensate for at the start of the selection (July 2022).

f.   Take the minimum of b) and e) (order 1: 5, order 2: 4.5). This is what can be corrected during the selection.

g.   To calculate the correction, multiply f) by each sales order's monthly invoice amount.

The figure below shows this logic:

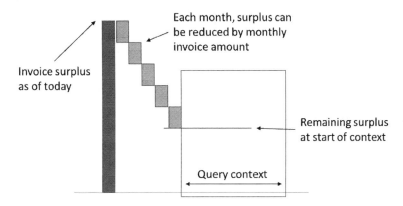

Figure 2.5.14: Determining the invoice surplus

The formula for the calculated column is this:

```
Current invoice surplus =
VAR ThisOrder = [DocumentNr]
VAR ThisDuration = RELATED(Ledger[Duration])
VAR ThisProduct = [ProductNr]
VAR ThisDeliveryDate = [DeliveryDate]
VAR Invoiced =
    CALCULATE(
        SUM(fSales[Amount]),
        fSales[Type] = "Sales Invoice",
        fSales[OrderNr] = ThisOrder,
        fSales[ProductNr] = ThisProduct,
        ALL(fSales)
    )
VAR DeliveryYearMthCtr =
    CALCULATE(
        MIN('Calendar'[YearMthCtr]),
        'Calendar'[Date] = ThisDeliveryDate
    )
VAR TodayYearMthCtr =
    CALCULATE(
        MIN('Calendar'[YearMthCtr]),
        'Calendar'[Date] = TODAY()
    )
VAR MonthlyInvoice = DIVIDE([Amount], ThisDuration)
VAR InvoicedSchedule =
    (TodayYearMthCtr - DeliveryYearMthCtr) * MonthlyInvoice
RETURN
DIVIDE(
    Invoiced - InvoicedSchedule,
    MonthlyInvoice
)
```

The Invoiced variable calculates the total amount invoiced for the current (sales order) document. Other relevant filters, in this case ProductNr, should be taken into account for a correct result. The InvoicedSchedule variable calculates the scheduled invoice amount, based on the starting month (from delivery date), current month (from today), and the monthly invoice amount (from total sales order amount and duration). Finally, the difference between the Invoiced and InvoicedSchedule amounts is divided by the MonthlyInvoice amount to express it in months.

Note that this formula is evaluated for every row in the fSales table, including invoice lines and one-off sales orders. As we will only use results for long-term sales orders, the results for other rows don't really matter.

When you look at steps a) to g) above, you can see that the duration and delivery month of the sales orders involved do not play any role, except for computing the monthly invoice amount in the last step. This means that we can take the invoice surplus logic out of the main MonthDurations iteration, and even put it in a separate measure.

The DAX measure for surplus correction is:

```
Surplus Correction =
VAR MonthList =
    CALCULATETABLE(
        DISTINCT('Calendar'[YearMthCtr]),
        KEEPFILTERS('Calendar'[Date] >= TODAY())
    )
VAR MonthsInContext = COUNTROWS(MonthList)
VAR FirstYearMthCtr =
    MINX(
        MonthList,
        'Calendar'[YearMthCtr]
    )
VAR TodayYearMthCtr =
    CALCULATE(
        MIN('Calendar'[YearMthCtr]),
        ALL('Calendar'),
        'Calendar'[Date] = TODAY()
    )
VAR MonthsGap = FirstYearMthCtr - TodayYearMthCtr
VAR SalesOrders =
    CALCULATETABLE(
        fSales,
        fSales[Type] = "Sales Order",
        fSales[Current Invoice Surplus] > MonthsGap,
        Ledger[Duration] > 0 && MonthsInContext > 0,
        ALL('Calendar')
    )
```

We start by setting up our basic variables for steps a), b), and c). The `SalesOrders` variable implements step d), using the calculated `Current invoice surplus` column. Note that filters from the `Calendar` table need to be removed here as the `fSales` table is related to the `Calendar` table on the `Date` column.

The filter argument `Ledger[Duration] > 0 &&`
`MonthsInContext > 0` needs some clarification. For query contexts in the past, the `MonthList` variable is an empty table, and `FirstYearMthCtr` is blank. That means the `MonthsGap` variable equals the value of `TodayYearMthCtr`. Although exceptional, this could mean that in `SalesOrders`, sales orders are selected that have a large current invoice surplus, when what we really want is not to select any sales order at all.

In other words, we want to do something like
`IF(MonthsInContext > 0, CALCULATETABLE(....` However, when `MonthsInContext` equals zero, this will return a blank value when we really need an empty table for the `SUMX` iterator to function later on. The `MonthsInContext > 0` clause cannot be used as a separate filter argument in `CALCULATETABLE` as it does not refer to any column; instead, we add the clause to another filter argument. This filter argument checks, for each `Duration` value, whether the value is larger than zero *and* whether `MonthsInContext` is larger than zero.

The remaining steps are done for each sales order in this list:

```
RETURN
SUMX(
    SalesOrders,
    VAR MonthsToCompensate =
        fSales[Current invoice surplus] - MonthsGap
    VAR CompensationMonths =
        MIN(MonthsToCompensate, MonthsInContext)
    RETURN
    CompensationMonths
        * DIVIDE(fSales[Amount], RELATED(Ledger[Duration]))
)
```

The `MonthsToCompensate` variable computes how many months of monthly invoices must still be compensated at the start of the selected period (step e)). The `CompensationMonths` variable calculates how many months can be compensated during this time (step f)). The final result multiplies this number by the monthly invoice amount.

With the `Surplus Correction` measure, we have a calculation for the amount that needs to be subtracted from the "normal" monthly invoicing. In the next section, we will look at how to calculate the normal invoice amount. After that, we will deal with another scenario: sales orders that are behind invoicing schedule and need a correction at the end of their duration. As these are easy to detect with the calculated column we created (these sales orders have a negative `Current invoice surplus` value), they can be taken out of the main calculation flow to eliminate any conditional logic.

Dealing with sales orders on schedule

In the pseudocode for the `Current Sales Orders` measure, we no longer need to worry about surplus now that we have a separate measure for the surplus compensation. That means that we need a measure that just returns the scheduled invoice amounts for the selected period of time in the query context. Let's start again by setting up some variables:

```
Sales Orders on schedule =
VAR MonthList =
    CALCULATETABLE(
        DISTINCT('Calendar'[YearMthCtr]),
        KEEPFILTERS('Calendar'[Date] >= TODAY())
    )
VAR FirstYearMthCtr =
    MINX(
        MonthList,
        'Calendar'[YearMthCtr]
    )
VAR LastYearMthCtr =
    MAXX(
        MonthList,
        'Calendar'[YearMthCtr]
    )
VAR MonthsDurations =
    GENERATE(
        FILTER(
            DISTINCT(Ledger[Duration]),
            Ledger[Duration] > 0
        ),
        VAR ThisDuration = Ledger[Duration]
        RETURN
        FILTER(
```

```
          ALL('Calendar'[YearMthCtr]),
          'Calendar'[YearMthCtr] + Duration - 1
              >= FirstYearMthCtr
          && 'Calendar'[YearMthCtr] <= LastYearMthCtr
      )
   )
```

We first determine the list of `YearMthCtr` values, as well as the first and last value. After that, the `MonthsDurations` variable sets up a list of durations with the possible delivery months that a sales order can have, while still having a part of its duration within the selected time period. This means that the last month of the schedule must be the first `YearMthCtr` value or later (note that the invoice schedule of a sales order starts in the delivery month, therefore the last month of the schedule is the delivery month plus the duration minus 1), and the delivery month must not be after the selected time period to avoid including future sales orders.

Each month/duration combination now corresponds to a number of months in the invoice schedule that fall within our selected time period. This makes it fairly easy to compute the amount to invoice. The DAX formula continues:

```
RETURN
SUMX(
    MonthsDurations,
    VAR ThisDuration = Ledger[Duration]
    VAR ThisDeliveryMonth = 'Calendar'[YearMthCtr]
    VAR NumberOfMonths =
        COUNTROWS(
            FILTER(
                MonthList,
                'Calendar'[YearMthCtr] >= ThisDeliveryMonth
                && 'Calendar'[YearMthCtr] <=
                    ThisDeliveryMonth + ThisDuration - 1
            )
        )
    VAR SalesOrderAmount =
        CALCULATE(
            SUM(fSales[Amount],
            fSales[Type] = "Sales Order",
            ALLEXCEPT('Calendar', 'Calendar'[YearMthCtr]),
            USERELATIONSHIP(
                fSales[DeliveryDate],
                'Calendar'[Date]
            )
        )
```

```
    VAR MonthlyInvoiceAmount =
        DIVIDE(SalesOrderAmount, ThisDuration)
    RETURN
    MonthlyInvoiceAmount * NumberOfMonths
)
```

The `NumberOfMonths` variable determines the correct number of months by filtering the `MonthList`: we only want to include months that are the delivery month or later, and which are the last month of the invoice schedule at the latest. The `SalesOrderAmount` variable calculates the total amount of all sales orders that correspond to the current duration and delivery month. Likewise, `MonthlyInvoiceAmount` is the total monthly invoice amount for all these sales orders. Note that we use `ALLEXCEPT` to remove all existing filters on the `Calendar` table, except for the filter on the `YearMthCtr` column that comes from the current row in `MonthsDurations`.

Corrections for sales orders behind schedule

The only thing remaining is that we need to add an amount at the end of the duration for every sales order that is behind schedule. Two things will help to create an efficient calculation:

- These sales orders are easy to detect, as they have a negative value in the `Current invoice surplus` column.
- The correction is applied in the last month of the sales order's schedule, which means that we can work with a very specific (and small) set of month/duration combinations.

Let us start by setting up the relevant list of month/duration combinations:

```
End Correction =
VAR MonthList =
    CALCULATETABLE(
        DISTINCT('Calendar'[YearMthCtr]),
        KEEPFILTERS('Calendar'[Date] >= TODAY())
    )
VAR MonthsDurationsEnd =
    GENERATE(
        FILTER(
            Ledger[Duration] > 0
        ),
        VAR ThisDuration = Ledger[Duration]
        RETURN
```

```
        FILTER(
            ALL('Calendar'[YearMthCtr]),
            'Calendar'[YearMthCtr] + ThisDuration - 1
                IN MonthList
        )
    )
```

Again, we take that part of the query context that is in the future. The GENERATE function creates, for every duration larger than zero, the list of YearMthCtr values that a sales order can have as its delivery date, while ending in the selected period in the MonthList variable. In other words, the last month of the invoice schedule must be one of the months in the selected period. We can use a simple IN operator here, as MonthList is a table with only one column.

The calculation continues with an iteration over the MonthsDurationsEnd rows:

```
RETURN
SUMX(
    MonthsDurationsEnd,
    VAR ThisDuration = Ledger[Duration]
    VAR SalesOrderAmount =
        CALCULATE(
            SUMX(
                fSales,
                fSales[Amount] * fSales[Current invoice surplus]
            ),
            fSales[Type] = "Sales Order",
            ALLEXCEPT('Calendar', 'Calendar'[YearMthCtr]),
            USERELATIONSHIP(
                fSales[DeliveryDate], 'Calendar'[Date]
            ),
            fSales[Current invoice surplus] < 0
        )
    RETURN
    -1 * DIVIDE(SalesOrderAmount, ThisDuration)
)
```

The SalesOrderAmount variable selects each sales order that corresponds to the current duration and delivery month and that has a negative Current invoice surplus value. For these sales orders, we calculate the sales order amount multiplied by the current invoice surplus. This may seem strange, but remember that we need to calculate the end-of-schedule correction; Current invoice surplus is the surplus in the number of monthly invoice amounts. To compute the correction required, we must multiply this number by the monthly invoice amount, which is the sales order amount divided by the duration.

As the duration is the same for all sales orders selected here (we are in an iteration over `MonthsDurationsEnd`, after all), we can decide to multiply by the sales order amount first and divide the total by the duration later. And this is what happens after the `RETURN`.

With the `Surplus Correction`, `Sales Orders on Schedule`, and `End Correction` measures, we now have everything in place to calculate the correct amounts to be invoiced. The picture below shows example output for a small set of sales orders. In this example, `TODAY()` is a date in October, 2021. Note that by definition, for a single sales order the `Surplus Correction` and `End Correction` measures cannot both return a result; after all, we use mutually exclusive filters on the `Current invoice surplus` column for these calculations.

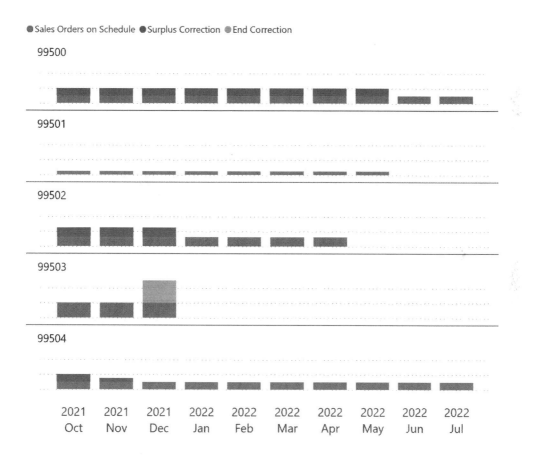

Figure 2.5.15: Output for some sample sales orders

Different cases are visible in the chart:

- Sales order 99500 has a current invoice surplus of 8 months, which means that the monthly invoice is corrected for 8 months, after which the normal invoicing can continue until the end of the schedule in July, 2022.
- Sales order 99501 is on schedule, and invoicing will continue until May, 2022.
- Sales order 99502 has a 3-month invoice surplus.
- Sales order 99503 is behind schedule, and this can be corrected in December, 2021, which is the last month of this sales order's schedule.
- Sales order 99504 has a surplus of about 1.5 months.

The all-up future invoice measure is a simple combination of the three measures:

```
Invoice Outlook =
    [Sales Orders on Schedule]
    - [Surplus Correction]
    + [End Correction]
```

All we need to do now is calculate the regularly scheduled invoice amount and correct for positive invoice surplus (which is done by subtracting from the monthly schedule for as long as needed) and for negative invoice surplus (which is done in the last month of the invoice schedule).

Further optimization

By moving from iterating over individual sales orders to combinations of delivery months and duration, we potentially save many thousands of iterations. But is that true in all cases? Unfortunately, no. When a report zooms in to, say, one customer, or even one sales order, the "unoptimized" version of our calculation will probably need fewer iterations than our optimized one. This is because we look at all delivery month/duration combinations, without considering whether there are any sales orders for that combination.

It is not difficult to further restrict the number of iterations by specifically taking into account the data we already have on sales orders. You can use the SUMMARIZE function to do just that. SUMMARIZE can be used to retrieve unique combinations of values from multiple columns in a table (just like DISTINCT does the same for a single column). But SUMMARIZE supports retrieving values from columns in related tables as well, like this:

```
SUMMARIZE(fSales, 'Calendar'[YearMthCtr], Ledger[Duration])
```

As we have relationships between the fSales and Calendar tables, and between the fSales and Ledger tables, this SUMMARIZE statement returns the unique combinations of YearMthCtr values and Duration values that have corresponding rows in the fSales table.

We need a bit more than this, as the active relationship is on date, not delivery date, and we still need to filter on current sales orders. This can be done by activating the relationship on delivery date with USERELATIONSHIP as a filter argument in a CALCULATETABLE statement:

```
CALCULATETABLE(
    SUMMARIZE(fSales, 'Calendar'[YearMthCtr], Ledger[Duration]),
    USERELATIONSHIP(fSales[DeliveryDate], 'Calendar'[Date])
)
```

The different MonthsDurations variables used in the measures in the previous sections can now be defined using the code above, resulting in tables with only rows for which sales orders are found. For instance, the MonthsDurationsEnd code used in the End Correction measure was:

```
VAR MonthsDurationsEnd =
    GENERATE(
        FILTER(
            DISTINCT(Ledger[Duration]),
            Ledger[Duration] > 0
        ),
        VAR ThisDuration = Ledger[Duration]
        RETURN
        FILTER(
            ALL('Calendar'[YearMthCtr]),
            'Calendar'[YearMthCtr] + ThisDuration - 1
                IN MonthList
        )
    )
```

This definition can be rewritten as:

```
VAR MonthsDurationsEnd =
    FILTER(
        CALCULATETABLE(
            SUMMARIZE(fSales,
                Ledger[Duration], 'Calendar'[YearMthCtr]
            ),
```

```
            USERELATIONSHIP(
                fSales[DeliveryDate],
                'Calendar'[Date]
            ),
            ALL('Calendar')
            ),
            VAR ThisDuration = Ledger[Duration]
            RETURN
            'Calendar'[YearMthCtr] + ThisDuration - 1 IN MonthList
    )
```

The `CALCULATE(SUMMARIZE(...` statement retrieves the combinations of duration and delivery months that correspond to sales orders in our data. With the `FILTER` function, this table is filtered down to only those combinations for which the invoice schedule ends within `MonthList`.

Where the first version returns *all* durations and all delivery months per duration for which the invoice schedule ends within `MonthList`, the second version only returns those durations and delivery months for which actual sales orders exist.

Testing complex calculations

You may aspire to master DAX in such a way that you can write calculations like the ones in this chapter correctly at once. In reality, errors are easily made, of course, so it is important to test your calculations. With a complex set of calculations that iterate over a set of items, this is no easy task.

What can help is to create a number of copies of the formula, each of which returns the value of one of the variables used along the way. For instance, if you wanted to test the `Sales Orders on Schedule` measure, the first test measure could be:

```
1 - MonthList =
VAR MonthList =
    CALCULATETABLE(
        DISTINCT('Calendar'[YearMthCtr]),
        KEEPFILTERS('Calendar'[Date]) >= TODAY())
    )
RETURN
COUNTROWS(MonthList)
```

As a DAX measure must always return a scalar value, you will need to adapt the code in such a way that it does; in the formula above, this means using `COUNTROWS` to count the number of rows of `MonthList`. Using this test measure in different contexts provides clarity on how the code behaves.

If you want to see the actual contents of a table variable like `MonthList`, you can create a calculated table with the same code (this time without `COUNTROWS`). It is a bit harder to evaluate the code in a specific context; however, query contexts can be simulated using `CALCULATETABLE`. The example below returns the `MonthList` contents in a context for the year 2021:

```
MonthList table =
CALCULATETABLE(
    VAR MonthList =
    CALCULATETABLE(
        DISTINCT('Calendar'[YearMthCtr]),
        KEEPFILTERS('Calendar'[Date] >= TODAY())
    )
    RETURN
    MonthList,
    'Calendar'[Year] = 2021
)
```

You will have to consider that `SUMX` returns the sum of multiple values, which can make it difficult to see what happens. The best way is to first view output for single cases, like an individual sales order.

The figure below shows our test output for sales order 99503 that we saw earlier in *Figure 2.5.15*. This sales order has a delivery date of January 22, 2020, and a duration of 24 months. We set "today" to be a date in October 2021, and restricted output to `YearMthCtr` values 69 to 73.

Year	2021				2022
	69	70	71	72	73
1 - MonthList		1	1	1	1
2 - FirstYearMthCtr		70	71	72	73
3 - LastYearMthCtr		70	71	72	73
4 - MonthDurations count	5	180	180	180	180
5 - NumberOfMonths		180	180	180	180
6 - SalesOrderAmount		480,000	480,000	480,000	
7 - MonthlyInvoiceAmount		20,000	20,000	20,000	
Sales Orders on Schedule		20,000	20,000	20,000	

Figure 2.5.16: Test output for sales order 99503

Note that we retrieve output in five different contexts here. For YearMthCtr values 70, 71, and 72, the end result is exactly what we expect. We do see, however, that the number of iterations over the MonthDurations table is 180, even though we selected only a single sales order. Clearly, the optimization in the previous section was not applied here!

Another thing that stands out is that in month 69, which is in the past, we still have five rows in MonthDurations. You will not notice this when looking at the end result, which is blank as expected. However, it means that the DAX engine has to do calculations that lead to nothing. After further analysis, it turns out that these five rows come from a blank row in the Calendar table. This is the code for the MonthDurations variable in the Sales Orders on Schedule measure:

```
VAR MonthsDurations =
    GENERATE(
        FILTER(
            DISTINCT(Ledger[Duration]),
            Ledger[Duration] > 0
        ),
        VAR ThisDuration = Ledger[Duration]
        RETURN
        FILTER(
            ALL('Calendar'[YearMthCtr]),
            'Calendar'[YearMthCtr] + Duration -1 >=
                FirstYearMthCtr
            && 'Calendar'[YearMthCtr] <= LastYearMthCtr
        )
    )
```

Indeed, when our selection is fully in the past, MonthList is empty and both FirstYearMthCtr and LastYearMthCtr are blank. A blank value for YearMthCtr (in the blank row in Calendar) satisfies the filter criteria in the FILTER function above.

We can solve this inefficiency by making sure that a possible blank row in the Calendar table is not included. This can be achieved by using ALLNOBLANKROW instead of ALL in the code. Like the name says, ALLNOBLANKROW returns all values, except the one from the blank row:

```
VAR MonthsDurations =
    GENERATE(
        FILTER(
            DISTINCT(Ledger[Duration]),
            Ledger[Duration] > 0
        ),
        VAR ThisDuration = Ledger[Duration]
        RETURN
        FILTER(
            ALLNOBLANKROW('Calendar'[YearMthCtr]),
            'Calendar'[YearMthCtr] + Duration -1 >=
                FirstYearMthCtr
            && 'Calendar'[YearMthCtr] <= LastYearMthCtr
        )
    )
```

As you can see from this example, not only will testing steps of a calculation help you to get correct results, it can also add to further optimization of your DAX code.

Summary

In this chapter, we discussed two main business challenges: intercompany business and consolidated views, and invoices to be sent on open sales orders.

In analyzing intercompany business, you have seen that thoroughly keeping track of context is the key to sophisticated results. In analyzing the balance between sales and purchases between two subsidiary companies, we needed to switch roles; the selling companies for one revenue stream were the purchasing companies for another revenue stream, and vice versa. DAX provides rich capabilities to perform the context transformations needed for these kinds of calculations.

In the intercompany business example, you have also seen that in some cases, DAX measures must be specifically tailored to the visualizations used to produce understandable results.

The second business challenge, specifically invoicing on long-term sales orders, provides a good example of how to approach this kind of advanced analysis: first, make sure that the calculation is correct from a business perspective; and second, look for ways to improve the efficiency of the DAX code to achieve the best performance possible. Minimizing the number of iterations when using DAX table functions, as well as replacing conditional logic by filters (as we did in the End Correction measure), are both good strategies to apply to achieve well-performing DAX measures.

The invoicing analysis again showed the importance of understanding DAX context. This will be a recurring theme in the next chapter as well, where we look at forecasting and extrapolation.

2.6

Exploring the Future: Forecasting and Future Values

Forecasting is a commonly used method to estimate the future value of investments. Power BI is a great tool for visualizing forecasts in an effective way based on DAX calculations. Financial functions in DAX allow for analyzing multiple scenarios to investigate the result of investments.

The business case in this chapter focuses on insights into the value of an investment over time. As a specific example, think of acquiring a property to rent out: after an initial investment, incoming and outgoing cash flows are to be expected in the future. The value of a single dollar in the future is different from a dollar in the present; this is due to inflation, but is also related to the option to invest the dollar from the present to earn a return over time. Future cash flows therefore need to be adjusted to make them comparable to today's investment and ultimately to answer the question: *is this a good investment to make?*

As these are quite specific concepts, this chapter starts with an overview of financial terms and definitions to work with. The topics covered in this chapter are:

- Financial calculations
- Financial DAX functions
- The business case and model

- Calculating Future Value (FV)
- Calculating Net Present Value (NPV)
- Calculating the Internal Rate of Return (IRR)
- Calculating cost-covering rent

We will use a real-estate scenario as an example throughout this chapter, a portfolio of properties with costs and income over time. However, these calculations are applicable to any investment scenario where future cash flows are in play.

Financial calculations

If you want to buy a house, most of the time you will need to take out a loan. You then have to pay interest over the course of the loan, in combination with regular payback. But when doing the math on this, inflation is a factor to take into account as well: if you had a loan of, say, $100,000, and you only paid interest, in 20 years your debt would still be $100,000 nominally, but the *worth* of it would be much less.

The same is true when making an investment. If you have $100,000 and you plan to invest it by acquiring a property, multiple financial elements will be part of the equation:

- The initial investment (of acquiring the property)
- Future incoming cash flows (tenants paying rent)
- Future outgoing cash flows (maintenance, taxes, and other expenses)
- The residual value (the worth of the property at the end of your period of investigation)

The question is, given these four elements and expectations about future devaluation of cash and assets, *am I making a good investment*? This is what we want to analyze.

For simplicity, let's assume that we do the analysis on a year-by-year basis. This means that all cash flows are calculated by year, as is the devaluation of cash and assets. Conceptually, you can do these kinds of analyses at any granularity you want, although you do need data at the appropriate granularity. For example, doing the analysis at the week level only makes sense if your tenants pay weekly rent and you have weekly devaluation rates available!

The **initial investment** is the amount needed to start the project. Keep in mind that you may own the property long before the start date of your analysis; it is not necessarily a payment made, but an assessment of the current value of the property. The initial investment is the total financial picture for year 0 (no other cash flows are taken into account in this year) and it is valued at the current price level.

The future **cash flows** can be highly predictable (rent payments) or not (emergency maintenance). In any case, for a valuable analysis, there needs to be data about the expected cash flows. Additionally, to be able to compare the value of future cash flows, the nominal amounts must be adjusted by a *discount rate* during the expected life cycle of the property or the amount of time analyzed. The problem, of course, is that we do not know what the future brings; inflation may rise or fall, having a significant impact on the adjusted amounts. You will have to make assumptions here.

The **residual value** is the expected worth of the property in the last year of its life cycle (or the end of our analysis), for instance, the expected proceeds from selling the property. What is true for future cash flows is even more true for the residual value: the discount rate that should be applied to this value to compare it with amounts in the present is highly uncertain. But you have to have something to work with.

In short, while you may have some idea of the nominal or *future value* of cash, this cannot be used directly as the basis of a decision in the present. This is where *present value* comes into play.

Present Value and Net Present Value

The discounted future value of a cash flow is known as the **Present Value (PV)**. The PV expresses the nominal value of the cash flow in today's worth. The PV of a cash flow with future value FV in year n can be described with the formula below:

$$PV = \frac{FV}{(1 + r)^n}$$

In this formula, r is the (yearly) discount rate. For example, with a discount rate of 5%, a value of $100 in 2 years has a PV of 100 divided by 1.05^2, or $90.70.

The total of (undiscounted) initial investment, discounted future cash flows, and discounted residual value is known as the **Net Present Value (NPV)**. The NPV is a single value that indicates the current value of the property, taking all (discounted) income and expenses over time into account. If this single value is positive, you expect to make a profit, otherwise you have a loss. The NPV can also be used to compare this particular investment to other investment options, like bringing your money to the bank.

To calculate the NPV of an investment project, you need the duration of the project, the expected cash flows that will occur during the project execution, and the discount rates. The NPV returns one value: the total return of all positive and negative cash flows, calculated to a single value based on the current position in time.

This is the formula:

$$NPV = \sum_{n=0}^{N} \frac{FV_n}{(1+r)^n}$$

This formula sums the PVs of cash flows for each year of the project. Here, N is the duration of the project in years and FV_n is the future value of cash flows in each year n. The initial investment is FV_0 (which is a negative cash flow) and the residual value is FV_N. For example, when you invest \$95 now and receive \$100 back in two years (see the PV example above), the NPV of this investment is -\$95 + \$90.70, or -\$4.30. This is clearly not a good deal!

Internal Rate of Return

In the calculation of NPV, the initial investment is an important factor. After all, this is often the largest investment in the project and, in addition, it is not discounted at all. Because of this, the NPV, though a good measure for determining the attractiveness of a single investment project, is not very suitable for comparing different investment options.

For this, you can use the **Internal Rate of Return (IRR)**. The technical definition of IRR is that it is the discount rate at which the NPV is zero:

$$\sum_{n=0}^{N} \frac{FV_n}{(1+IRR)^n} = 0$$

IRR is not an easily comprehensible metric. What it roughly indicates is the (annual) return rate of investments made at the beginning and during the project. More importantly, however, the IRR makes it possible to compare different projects.

There is no exact mathematical formula to calculate the IRR. Instead, approximative methods must be used that approach the IRR iteratively. In Excel, the function IRR does this; we will later see that you can do this with DAX as well. Our simple example returns an IRR of 2.59%, meaning that you have a compound return of 2.59% per year on your \$95.

While you may be able to do these calculations on a single investment, it becomes highly complex when multiple properties to invest in, and different types of cash flows, are involved. Different properties may have different "life expectancies," discount rates for one property may differ from those for another property, and so on. The ideal case for a Power BI model!

Financial DAX functions

DAX has borrowed many financial functions straight from Excel. Of these, two are applicable to this chapter's case study in particular: XNPV and XIRR. The X in the name of these functions suggests that they are table aggregations, and indeed, the first argument of each is a table.

XNPV can be used to calculate the NPV of a table of cash flows:

```
XNPV(CashFlowTable, <value>, <date>, Rate)
```

Note that the cash flows do not need to be in the table: you provide the values of the cash flows as an expression that is evaluated in row context on the CashFlowTable. Similarly, an expression returning a date is evaluated for each row. This means that discounting is done on a daily basis, and the (annual) n value from the formulas in the previous section is calculated (for the mth row in the table) as:

$$n = \frac{d_m - d_1}{365}$$

The XIRR value tries to approximate the IRR for a table of cash flows:

```
XIRR(CashFlowTable, <value>, <date>)
```

Like with the XNPV function, a value expression and date expression are evaluated for each row in CashFlowTable. As an optional fourth argument, a guess can be provided to suggest to the XIRR function where to start looking for a feasible rate. An optional fifth argument can be included with a value that is returned when XIRR cannot find a solution.

Both XNPV and XIRR must receive at least one negative cash flow value and one positive value to function. To illustrate both functions, let's consider the following table:

Date	CashFlows1	CashFlows2
12/31/2020	-1,000,000	-1,000,000
12/31/2021	64,000	32,000
12/31/2022	64,000	32,000
12/31/2023	60,000	30,000
12/31/2024	60,000	30,000
12/31/2025	52,000	26,000
12/31/2026	48,000	24,000
12/31/2027	64,000	32,000
12/31/2028	52,000	26,000
12/31/2029	56,000	28,000
12/31/2030	952,000	926,000

Figure 2.6.1: Sample data for investment calculations

We have created a very simple model with just one table, called Investment. It contains a Date column and two columns with distinct sets of cash flows. The first column is a good investment, while the second is not. You will see why. In both cases:

- The initial investment is $1,000,000
- We use a discount rate of 3%
- After the initial investment, all years generate a positive cash flow
- We expect the property to last for 10 years with a residual value of $900,000

 You can download this small model, 2.6 NPV XIRR example. pbix, from https://github.com/PacktPublishing/Extreme-DAX/tree/main/Chapter2.6.

The future value of the cash flows is simply a DAX measure calculating the sum of the individual cash flows. For scenario 1:

```
FV = SUM(Investment[CashFlows1])
```

The NPV for scenario 1 is calculated using the XNPV function:

```
NPV1 =
XNPV(
    Investment,
    Investment[CashFlows1],
    Investment[Date],
    0.03
)
```

Note that the cash flow values and dates are evaluated in row context on the Investment table; we can therefore directly use the values in the appropriate columns.

For calculating the IRR, we use the XIRR function:

```
IRR1 =
XIRR(
    Investment,
    Investment[CashFlows1],
    Investment[Date]
)
```

For scenario 2, the DAX measures are the same except for the use of the CashFlows2 column.

The results for scenario 1 are below:

FV1	472,000
NPV1	159,975
IRR1	4.97%

Figure 2.6.2: Results for scenario 1

So, everything looks great. Note the difference between the FV total of the cash flows and the NPV result: although the nominal return is almost half a million, with the 3% discount rate, this return is worth only about 160,000 in today's (well, 2020's) money. But the NPV is still positive, and with an IRR of almost 5%, this investment is worth making.

If we look at scenario 2, the results are different:

FV2	186,000
NPV2	-85,225
IRR2	1.95%

Figure 2.6.3: Results for scenario 2

In this scenario, the cash flows generate a positive future value of $186,000. But the NPV is negative and the IRR is below 2%! This means the positive cash flow is not enough to cover the 3% rate in 10 years and you should be able to find better investments, assuming the 3% discount rate is accurate.

The business case and model

In the remainder of this chapter, we look at a portfolio of real estate properties. Different properties may have different life cycle durations. Each property has:

- An investment in year 0, cash flows, and a residual value.
- Cash flows with a recurring pattern during the life span of the property, either positive (income) or negative (expenses).
- Positive or negative cash flows with an irregular pattern, like maintenance.

 You can download this model, 2.6 Exploring the future. pbix, from https://github.com/PacktPublishing/Extreme-DAX/tree/main/Chapter2.6.

The model contains three fact tables: fPosCashFlows for positive recurring cash flows, fNegCashFlows for negative recurring cash flows, and fIrregular for irregular cash flows.

There can be many different cash flow drivers; to be able to analyze them separately, there is a filter table with the type of cash flow for each fact table:

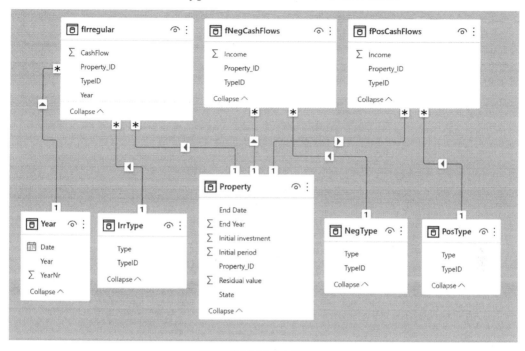

Figure 2.6.4: Model diagram

You may notice that in this model, there are no relationships from the fNegCashFlows and fPosCashFlows tables to the Year table. The reason for that is that we will not just use cash flow values for each year; instead, the recurring cash flows are modeled as a single value (per cash flow type) that is *indexed* for each year. Think of this as a yearly increase in rent. As an example, with an initial positive cash flow of $1,000 and a yearly index of 2%, or 1.02, the cash flow in year 1 would be $1,020, in year 2 it would be $1,040.40, and so on. The initial values of these cash flows are always in year 0 and therefore a relationship with the Year table does not help in any way.

For irregular cash flows, we do not use indexed values; instead, for each year, a cash flow value is loaded and the fIrregular table is related to the Year table.

The Year table is used to map different cash flows to the corresponding year, and to calculate the discounts on these cash flows. The table contains one row per year, with columns for the year, the year as a date value, and a year number. In our analysis, the year 2020 is year 0:

Year	Date	YearNr
2020	12/31/2020	0
2021	12/31/2021	1
2022	12/31/2022	2
2023	12/31/2023	3
2024	12/31/2024	4
2025	12/31/2025	5
2026	12/31/2026	6

Figure 2.6.5: Data in the Year table

With this model, we want to analyze several aspects of the investment portfolio to help decision-making. The analysis should provide answers to questions like:

- Is the portfolio profitable? Which properties are most profitable, and which properties provide a loss over the expected lifetime?
- What is the expected rate of return on each of the properties?
- How does varying the index of cash flow growth affect the return on the portfolio?
- To what extent does a changing discount rate impact the profitability of the portfolio?
- What is the minimum rent (recurring positive cash flow) required to make the investment viable?

In answering these questions, the NPV and IRR play a major role. But while we introduced these metrics with a fixed discount rate, we want to be able to use varying discount rates and cash flow indexes to gain insights in multiple scenarios. This will help us to get a thorough understanding of the investment portfolio. We therefore need to extend the basic model to enable working with different rates. In Power BI, this can be done with "what-if" parameters, which we explore below.

Creating adjustable rates and indexes

Power BI Desktop allows the creation of **what-if** parameters to enable dynamic adjustment of analysis variables. To create a what-if parameter, click the **New parameter** button in the ribbon:

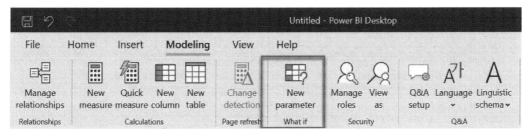

Figure 2.6.6: Creating a what-if parameter

A parameter can have a fixed, limited number of values, which are set through the **What-if parameter** window:

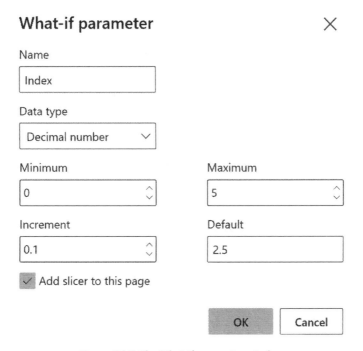

Figure 2.6.7: The What-if parameter window

You provide the lowest, highest, and default value of the parameter, as well as the increment, which determines the values between the lowest and highest that are available.

Once created, a what-if parameter enables a special slicer style for selecting a single parameter value using a slider:

Figure 2.6.8: Single-value slicer for what-if parameters

In addition, the what-if parameter leads to a calculated table being created in the model with the same name as the parameter. The table contains a single column, again with the parameter's name, with every possible value the parameter can have. A DAX measure is generated automatically to retrieve the selected value of the parameter:

```
Index Value = SELECTEDVALUE('Index'[Index], 2.5)
```

In this measure, the default value you provide for the what-if parameter is used as the value to return when no selection is made.

> To keep your model nice and tidy, move the auto-generated measure to a measure table.

In our portfolio analysis, we want to be able to choose a specific index to grow recurring cash flows in years 1, 2, and 3. As it is hard to predict possible growth rates for later years, we choose to use the index of year 3 for later years as well. We need three what-if parameters to accomplish this; let's call them Index, IndexY1, and IndexY2. The settings for these parameters are as shown in *Figure 2.6.7*: we can vary between 0% and 5% with increments of 0.1% and a default of 2.5%. In the same way, we want to consider various discount rates.

For this, we create a what-if parameter called Discount, varying between 0% and 10% with a default of 6%, again with a 0.1% increment.

 It is common to not have too much freedom in choosing a discount rate, as it is mainly an external variable: it is the rate of return an investment is expected to generate in the general market. Selecting a discount rate that is very different from that should result in complaints from your accountant!

As all our what-if parameters are percentages, we change the default value measures to make them return a proper percentage value:

```
Index value = SELECTEDVALUE('Index'[Index], 2.5) / 100
```

With these what-if parameters in place, we can start calculating the various requested metrics.

Calculating Future Value (FV)

As the first step in the calculations, we need to calculate the nominal or future value of all cash flows. Remember that we have multiple parts to calculate: initial investment, recurring cash flows, irregular cash flows, and residual value. We will start with the easy part.

Initial investment and residual value

In our model, both the initial investment and residual value are attributes of a property. We could simply total up the values in the corresponding columns in the Property table, but for our analysis, the values should be mapped onto the correct year: the initial investment in year 0, and the residual value in the last year of the property's life cycle.

To help with mapping the initial investment to year 0, an additional column, Initial period, is in the Property table. This column always contains the value 0. The initial investment is calculated with the DAX measure below:

```
FV Initial Investment =
CALCULATE(
    SUM('Property'[Initial investment],
    TREATAS(VALUES('Year'[YearNr]), 'Property'[Initial period])
)
```

At first sight, the filter argument in this CALCULATE expression may look equivalent to Property[Initial period] = 0. However, this filter makes sure that the initial investment is only returned when year 0 is in the query context. For example, when only the year 2023 is selected, TREATAS leads to only rows in the Property table being selected for which Initial period equals 2; but the table contains only rows with the value 0 in this column.

A similar formula can be used for the residual value. This time, we use an End year column in the Property table, which contains the last year of the property's life cycle (not the year number):

```
FV Residual Value =
CALCULATE(
    SUM('Property'[Residual value]),
    TREATAS(VALUES('Year'[Year]),'Property'[End Year])
)
```

This time, TREATAS makes sure that for each year, only the residual values are calculated for properties for which the life cycle ends in that year.

The chart below shows the results of both measures:

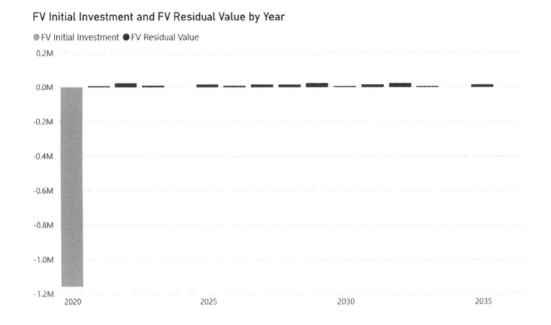

Figure 2.6.9: FV of initial investment and residual values

As expected, we have a large negative value in year 0, and smaller positive values in most years corresponding to properties at the end of their life cycle.

Irregular cash flows

To allow for one-off and other non-recurring cash flows, the fIrregular table contains future cash flows by year. Like with initial investment and residual value, we want these cash flows to be calculated in the corresponding year. As we have a Year column in the fIrregular table, the easiest way to accomplish this is to simply have a relationship between fIrregular and Year.

 The fIrregular table could be used to store emergency expenses, but in a multi-year analysis, it is difficult to account for these. Rather, you could schedule a multi-year plan for the physical maintenance of a property, or reserve cash for contingencies.

To allow a more detailed analysis, we create separate measures for positive and negative irregular cash flows. First:

```
FV Irregular positive =
CALCULATE(
    SUM(fIrregular[CashFlow]),
    fIrregular[CashFlow] >= 0
)
```

Calculating positive irregular cash flow comes down to simply filtering on the value of the CashFlow column. The negative cash flow is, of course, calculated by filtering on only negative CashFlow values:

```
FV Irregular negative =
CALCULATE(
    SUM(fIrregular[CashFlow]),
    fIrregular[CashFlow] < 0
)
```

The relationship between fIrregular and Year will cause the cash flow amounts to land in the corresponding years automatically.

Recurring cash flows

The most complex aspect of calculating the future value is the recurring cash flows. Not only do we have to work with values that must be indexed but, in addition, each property can have a different life cycle. We need to take care that we are not calculating recurring cash flows after the end of each property's life cycle.

We will focus on positive cash flows only and calculate values without indexing first:

```
FV Recurring positive (not indexed) =
SUMX(
    FILTER('Year', 'Year'[YearNr] > 0),
    VAR ThisYear = 'Year'[Year]
    RETURN
    CALCULATE(
        SUM(fPosCashFlows[Income]),
        'Property'[End Year] >= ThisYear
    )
)
```

As we can have a different set of properties that are still "active" in each year, we need to do the calculation on a by-year basis. For each year after year 0, we calculate the positive cash flows for properties that are not yet at the end of their life cycle. Note that the filter here requires End Year to be larger than or equal to the current year, meaning that we calculate the recurring cash flow for all years, including the last year of the property's life cycle.

Below is the result for a small set of properties:

Property_ID	2021	2022	2023	2024	2025	2026	2027	Total
35	9,193	9,193	9,193	9,193	9,193			45,965
79	10,778	10,778	10,778	10,778	10,778	10,778		64,668
81	9,559	9,559	9,559	9,559	9,559	9,559	9,559	66,913
82	11,421	11,421						22,842
Total	40,951	40,951	29,530	29,530	29,530	20,337	9,559	200,388

Figure 2.6.10: FV of positive recurring cash flows

From this table of results, it is clear that each property ends in a specific year; for instance, property 35 has its End Year attribute set to 2025.

To calculate the indexed recurring cash flows, we need to multiply the base amount in each year by a power of 1 plus the index value:

$$(1 + r)^n$$

Here, n is the number of the year. As we have a different index for years 1 and 2, we do a separate calculation for these years:

```
FV Recurring positive =
CALCULATE(
    [FV Recurring positive (not indexed)]
        * (1 + [IndexY1 value]),
    KEEPFILTERS('Year'[YearNr] = 1
)
```

The KEEPFILTERS function makes sure this calculation is only done for year 1. For the amount in year 2, we need to use the square of the multiplication factor:

```
+
CALCULATE(
    [FV Recurring positive (not indexed)]
        * POWER(1 + [IndexY2 value], 2),
    KEEPFILTERS('Year'[YearNr] = 2
)
```

Instead of the POWER function, you can use the ^ operator as well:

```
(1 + [IndexY2 value]) ^ 2
```

For later years, we use the default Index value with higher powers:

```
+
SUMX(
    FILTER('Year', 'Year'[YearNr] >= 3),
    [FV Recurring positive (not indexed)]
        * POWER(1 + [Index value], 'Year'[YearNr])
)
```

The indexed cash flows for properties shown in *Figure 2.6.10* is below:

Property_ID	2021	2022	2023	2024	2025	2026	2027	Total
35	9,423	9,658	9,900	10,147	10,401			**49,529**
79	11,047	11,324	11,607	11,897	12,194	12,499		**70,568**
81	9,798	10,043	10,294	10,551	10,815	11,086	11,363	**73,950**
82	11,707	11,999						**23,706**
Total	**41,975**	**43,024**	**31,801**	**32,596**	**33,410**	**23,585**	**11,363**	**217,753**

Figure 2.6.11: Indexed values of future recurring cash flows

The calculation for recurring negative cash flows is similar, but as the values of the negative cash flows are stored as positive amounts, we need to multiply by -1:

```
FV Recurring negative (not indexed) =
SUMX(
    FILTER('Year', 'Year'[YearNr] > 0),
    VAR ThisYear = 'Year'[YearNr]
    RETURN
    -1 *
    CALCULATE(
        SUM(fNegCashFlows[Expenses]),
        'Property'[End Year] >= ThisYear
    )
)
```

The indexed negative cash flow is again calculated using the index values:

```
FV Recurring negative =
CALCULATE(
    [FV Recurring negative (not indexed)]
        * (1 + [IndexY1 value]),
    KEEPFILTERS('Year'[YearNr] = 1)
)
+
CALCULATE(
    [FV Recurring negative (not indexed)]
        * POWER(1 + [IndexY1 value], 2),
    KEEPFILTERS('Year'[YearNr] = 2)
)
+
```

```
SUMX(
    FILTER('Year', 'Year'[YearNr] >= 3),
    [FV Recurring negative (not indexed)]
        * POWER(1 + [Index value], 'Year'[YearNr])
)
```

Positive and negative cash flows

We now have all components in place to calculate the total future value. The positive cash flows consist of positive recurring and irregular cash flows, and the residual value:

```
FV positive =
[FV Recurring positive]
+ [FV Irregular positive]
+ [FV Residual Value]
```

These values can be viewed in a chart for the four example properties:

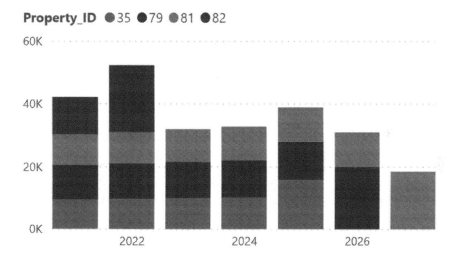

Figure 2.6.12: Positive FV

The negative future value is the negative recurring and irregular cash flows, plus the initial investment:

```
FV negative =
    [FV Recurring negative]
    + [FV Irregular negative]
    + [FV Initial Investment]
```

Sample output for the negative FV:

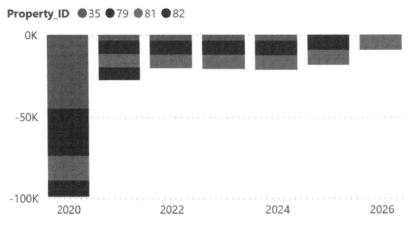

Figure 2.6.13: Negative FV

Note that in both charts above, the amounts tend to decrease over the years despite the indexing of the recurring cash flows. This is an effect of properties reaching the end of their life cycle: in later years, fewer properties add to the total FV.

Finally, the overall FV is calculated by combining the two measures above:

```
Future Value = [FV positive] + [FV negative]
```

With this, we have everything in place to start working on the Present Value analysis.

Calculating Net Present Value (NPV)

The NPV is the sum of the present values of all cash flows over the years. Remember the definition of PV:

$$PV = \frac{FV}{(1+r)^n}$$

So, to calculate the PV of a cash flow in year *n*, we need to take the discount rate and divide the FV by a power of the discount rate. As an example, if you wanted to create a calculated column in the `Property` table with the PV of the residual value of each property (we are sure you don't want to do that by now!), you could do that with the formula below:

```
PV Residual Value =
VAR EndYearNr =
    LOOKUPVALUE('Year'[YearNr], 'Year'[Year], Property[End Year])
VAR DiscountFactor =
    (1 + [Discount value]) ^ EndYearNr
RETURN
DIVIDE(Property[Residual Value], DiscountFactor)
```

In normal language: we take the property's end year, find the corresponding year number, calculate the discount factor with the year number as power, and divide the residual value by the discount factor. The discount factor is 1 plus the discount rate, which we take from the what-if parameter `Discount`.

The complexity in this formula is mainly in retrieving the correct year number. When designing PV measures, we have to deal with the same complexity. However, we designed the FV measures in such a way that each FV is already connected to the correct year. We can therefore simply iterate over the years to compute the PV. For example, for the PV of the residual value, the formula below will suffice:

```
PV Residual Value =
SUMX(
    'Year',
    VAR DiscountFactor = (1 + [Discount value]) ^ 'Year'[YearNr]
    RETURN
    DIVIDE(
        [FV Residual Value],
        DiscountFactor
    )
```

All other PVs can be calculated in the same way. We will not list them all here; you can find PV measures in the model accompanying this chapter. As an illustration of the effect of discounting, in the chart below are the positive recurring cash flow values for a sample property:

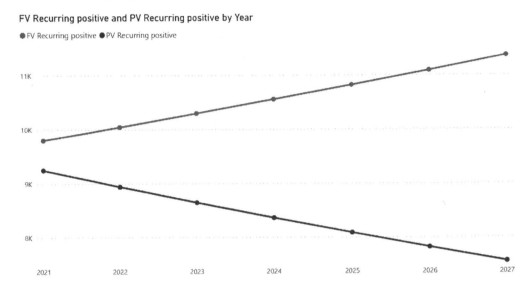

Figure 2.6.14: FV and PV

While the FV of the recurring cash flow increases each year (it is indexed, after all), the PV of this cash flow decreases. The reason for this is that in this case, the discount rate is higher than the index.

There is one PV calculation that is particularly interesting: the PV of the overall FV calculation. By definition, this is the NPV!

```
Net Present Value =
SUMX(
    'Year',
    VAR DiscountFactor = (1 + [Discount value]) ^ 'Year'[YearNr]
    RETURN
    DIVIDE(
        [Future Value],
        DiscountFactor
    )
)
```

With this measure, it is now possible to view the NPV for each property:

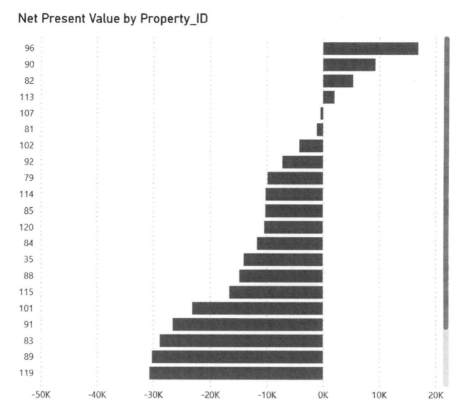

Net Present Value by Property_ID

Figure 2.6.15: Net Present Value

You can draw a clear conclusion from this chart: most of the properties are not profitable with the current settings!

But wait: didn't we have a special NPV function in DAX? We can use the XNPV function to calculate the NPV as well:

```
Net Present Value 2 =
XNPV(
    'Year',
    [Future Value],
    'Year'[Date],
    [Discount value]
)
```

And indeed, we get mostly the same results with both NPV calculations. There are slight differences, due to the fact that the XNVP function works on the basis of days; the power for the discount factor is calculated as:

$$n = \frac{d_m - d_1}{365}$$

This is fully correct most of the time, but for leap years, the factor slightly deviates from what it should be. You could say we outsmarted DAX here! In most cases, these differences are not something to worry about. However, the way we calculated the NPV from low-grained calculations has the added benefit that you can get much more detailed insights about why the NPV has a certain value.

Calculating the Internal Rate of Return (IRR)

Now that we know how to calculate the NPV in our model, calculating the IRR is easy, as it is just an application of the XIRR function. Before we do that, it is worthwhile to look more closely at what the IRR is.

In the chart below, the NPV is plotted for a single property against different possible values of the discount rate:

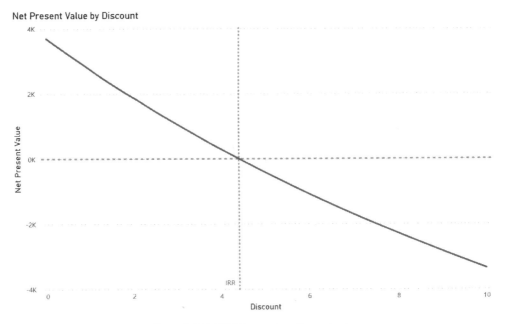

Figure 2.6.16: NPV for varying discount rates

It is not easy to see in this chart, but the line has a slight curve; which is to be expected as the NPV is some complex polynomial function of the discount rate. Remember that the definition of IRR is the discount rate at which the NPV equals zero. The chart contains a (horizontal) constant line at zero to allow for visually determining where the IRR must be. The vertical, dotted line is an approximation of the IRR. As can be seen in the chart, for some discount rates, the NPV for this property is positive, but for other discount rates, it is negative. In this case, the IRR is about 4.5.

The meaning of this is (roughly) that when you have another investment opportunity that will give you more than 4.5% return on the investment and all returns, you'd better choose that opportunity. Or, if the bank will give you more than 4.5% interest, you would be better off leaving your money at the bank instead of investing in this property.

To calculate the IRR, you have to solve the complex NPV function for the zero point. The XIRR function does that for us by approximation:

```
Internal Rate of Return =
XIRR(
    'Year',
    [Future Value],
    'Year'[Date]
)
```

Indeed, the IRR result for the property in *Figure 2.6.16* is close to 4.5:

4.41%

Internal Rate of Return

Figure 2.6.17: IRR

Looking at the chart, you may suspect that we could also find an approximate IRR by calculating the NPV for many different discount rates and picking the best one:

```
IRR approximation =
MAXX(
    FILTER(
        Discount,
        [Net Present Value] > 0
    ),
    Discount[Discount]
)
```

The result of this measure is below:

4.40

IRR approximation

Figure 2.6.18: IRR approximation

While this result looks good, we have cheated to get here. First, we have used the knowledge that the NPV chart declines with increasing discount rate. Second, we have approached the zero-line from the best side possible; if we had filtered the Discount table on values with an NPV smaller than zero and taken the minimum rate, the result would have been 4.5: much further from the actual IRR. And third, we only considered discount rate values that are in the Discount table. We selected the property used in this section specifically to show you the zero line, but many properties only reach a zero NPV at discount rates outside of the Discount what-if parameter.

While the assumption of a downward slope in the NPV chart seems plausible, we would have to check many more discount rate options than we did to arrive at acceptable results. For calculating the IRR, the XIRR function is simply the most convenient tool available. In the next section, however, we focus on a metric for which no standard DAX function is available, and for that, an approximative approach in DAX will show itself to be valuable.

Calculating cost-covering rent

The last topic in this chapter is about **cost-covering rent**, or **CCR** for short. This is the answer to the question: *what is the minimum rent to charge property tenants to make the investment break even?*

Let's go back to the NPV formula once again:

$$NPV = \sum_{n=0}^{N} \frac{FV_n}{(1+r)^n}$$

The IRR is calculated by solving this formula for the rate r at zero NPV:

$$\sum_{n=0}^{N} \frac{FV_n}{(1+IRR)^n} = 0$$

The cost-covering rent also comes from solving the NPV formula, but now for (roughly) the future values:

$$\sum_{n=0}^{N} \frac{CCR_n}{(1+r)^n} = 0$$

To be more precise, while our future values are composed of multiple components, we only want to solve for the (initial) recurring positive cash flows in this case. The question is therefore: instead of the positive recurring cash flows in the fPosCashFlows table, and specifically those with Type 2 (rent), which values can we use to get a zero NPV?

Like with the IRR, there is no direct way of calculating this. And worse, there is no DAX function that will solve this equation. We therefore need to apply an approximative method instead.

 Instead of *approximative method*, you may also read *brute force*: we just do a lot of calculations to pick the best results. While we try to work a bit more smartly than that, as you will see later in this section, the measures created will not be the fastest ever, especially with larger portfolios; they simply have to do a lot of work. However, the business value of these calculations is substantial and it may be worth the wait.

Determining cost-covering rent by approximation

As we will calculate the NPV for many different values of rent (positive recurring type 2), it makes sense to start with a measure that calculates the NPV part for all cash flows except the rent. This is the formula to use:

```
NPV no rent =
SUMX(
    'Year',
    VAR DiscountFactor = (1 + [Discount value]) ^ 'Year'[YearNr]
    RETURN
    DIVIDE(
        [FV Negative]
        + [FV Irregular positive]
        + [FV Residual Value]
        + CALCULATE(
```

```
            [FV Recurring positive],
            PosType[TypeID] <> 2
        ),
        DiscountFactor
    )
)
```

This formula has the same structure as the all-up NPV measure, but now we only add FV results not including the rent cash flows. The zero NPV we are looking for is equivalent to:

$$PVPR(rent) = -1 * NVP \text{ no rent}$$

where *PVPR(rent)* is the PV of the positive recurring cash flow associated with a specific *rent* value. As we may plausibly assume that the higher the positive cash flows, the higher the NPV will be, what we are looking for is the lowest rent value for which:

$$PVPR(rent) \geq -1 * NVP \text{ no rent}$$

The result we are looking for only makes sense for individual properties. A CCR measure will therefore need to iterate over the Property table. We also need a set of values to try; this will be created as a variable. The NPV no rent value is also stored in a variable to use later on:

```
Cost-covering Rent 1 =
VAR PossibleValues = GENERATESERIES(0, 10000, 1)
SUMX(
    'Property',
    VAR NPVNoRent = -1 * [NPV no rent]
```

The GENERATESERIES function creates a table with one Value column, filled with values between a lower bound (0, in this case) and an upper bound (10,000 for us) with a fixed interval between them (we take 1 for now). As we want to try each value, the formula must iterate over this table; if we use FILTER to leave only the values for which the PVPR is high enough, we can then select the smallest. In pseudocode, this is what we do:

```
    RETURN
    MINX(
        FILTER(
            PossibleValues,
            VAR ThisRent = [Value]
```

```
        RETURN
            <PVPR> >= NPVNoRent
    ),
    [Value]
)
```

Note that [Value] in the code above refers to the column in the PossibleValues table; as this is a virtual table that is not derived from an existing table in the model, it does not have a name that we can include before the column name.

The problem to solve now comes down to calculating the PVPR for a specific property and rent value in PossibleValues. For this, we will go back to our earlier calculation of the FV and, after that, the PV of recurring cash flows. We cannot use an external measure here, as we do not have a way to inject the rent value into another measure; so we need to replicate the logic right here. As both the FV and PV calculations iterate over the years, we will combine both calculations in one iteration. You may remember that we used different index values in year 1, year 2, and later years; we will work with more DAX variables to keep track of what we are doing:

```
VAR PVPRYear1 =
    SUMX(
        FILTER('Year',
                'Year'[YearNr] = 1
                && 'Year'[Year] <= 'Property[End Year]
        ),
        ThisRent * (1 + [IndexY1 Value])
    )
```

The FILTER part in the PVPRYear1 variable makes sure the rent for year 1 is only calculated when the current property has not reached the end of its life cycle, and only for year 1. In a similar way, we can compute the PV for rent in year 2 and later:

```
VAR PVPRYear2 =
    SUMX(
        FILTER('Year',
                'Year'[YearNr] = 2
                && 'Year'[Year] <= 'Property[End Year]
        ),
        ThisRent * POWER(1 + [IndexY1 Value], 2)
    )
VAR PVPRYear3Plus =
    SUMX(
```

```
        FILTER('Year',
                'Year'[YearNr] >= 3
                && 'Year'[Year] <= 'Property[End Year]
        ),
        ThisRent * POWER(1 + [IndexY1 Value], 'Year'[YearNr])
)
```

The sum of these three PVPR variables can now be compared with NVPNoRent to eventually select the best rent option. The full formula looks like this:

```
Cost-covering Rent 1 =
VAR PossibleValues = GENERATESERIES(0, 10000, 1)
SUMX(
    'Property',
    VAR NPVNoRent = -1 * [NPV no rent]
    RETURN
    MINX(
        FILTER(
            PossibleValues,
            VAR ThisRent = [Value]
            VAR PVPRYear1 =
                SUMX(
                    FILTER('Year',
                        'Year'[YearNr] = 1
                        && 'Year'[Year]
                            <= 'Property[End Year]
                    ),
                    ThisRent * (1 + [IndexY1 Value])
                )
            VAR PVPRYear2 =
            SUMX(
                FILTER('Year',
                    'Year'[YearNr] = 2
                    && 'Year'[Year]
                        <= 'Property[End Year]
                ),
                ThisRent * POWER(1 + [IndexY1 Value], 2)
            )
            VAR PVPRYear3Plus =
            SUMX(
                FILTER('Year',
```

```
                    'Year'[YearNr] >= 3
                    && 'Year'[Year]
                        <= 'Property[End Year]
            ),
            ThisRent * POWER(1 + [IndexY1Value],
                                'Year'[YearNr])
        )
        VAR PVPR = PVPRYear1 + PVPRYear2 + PVPRYear3Plus
        RETURN
        PVPR >= NPVNoRent
    ),
    [Value]
    )
)
```

To visualize the result, we created a chart with possible rent values and a measure that computes the NPV for each rent value for a single property:

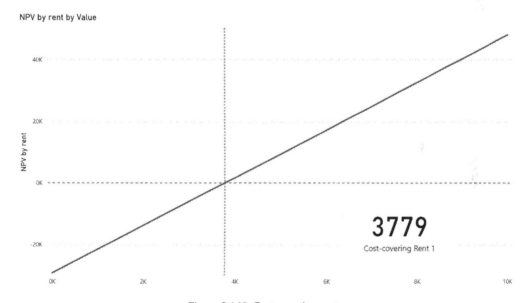

Figure 2.6.19: Cost-covering rent

The zero NPV line intersects with the **NPV by rent** line exactly at the cost-covering rent returned by the Cost-covering Rent 1 measure, $3,779 in this case.

Optimizing the approximation

While the calculated optimal rent is a good approximation, the calculation has a few drawbacks: first, the result is restricted to whole numbers, and second, for each property we have to do 10,000 NPV calculations, and that is assuming that all cost-covering rents are between 0 and 10,000.

It is possible to optimize this approach. In *Figure 2.6.20*, a smaller section of the above chart is plotted. From this, it is clear that the value 3,779 is only an approximation. This may be good enough, but whether we need more precision, more possible values, or better performance, it is good to consider if we can reach the same result with fewer calculations.

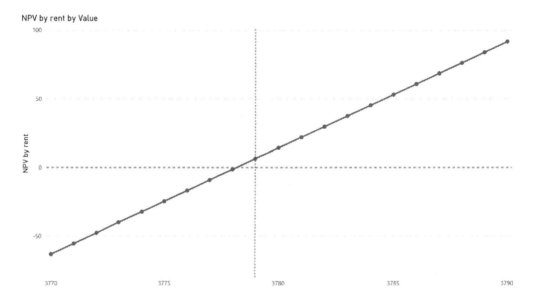

Figure 2.6.20: A detailed view of cost-covering rent

In *Figure 2.6.21*, a similar NVP chart is shown on values with an interval of 100. Between 0 and 10,000, this yields a list of only 101 values, which therefore needs far fewer calculations to traverse.

Necessarily, the approximation is much less accurate.

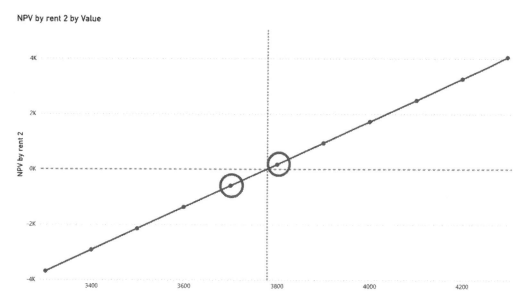

Figure 2.6.21: Approximation with only a few data points

The two highlighted data points are the ones with an NPV closest to zero out of this range. The approach is now to create a second series of possible rent values between these two; when we take 1/100 of the difference between the two rent values as the interval, we have again 101 possible values; but now, the interval is only 1 and we reach the same precision as before. This time, however, only 202 calculations need to be done to get there.

We need quite some code to do this, primarily because the PVPR calculation must be done inside the formula. We have to implement it twice now: once to find the best two values from the "coarse" list, and again to calculate the values from the "fine" list. We start with the same setup as before:

```
Cost-covering Rent 2 =
VAR PossibleValuesCoarse = GENERATESERIES(0, 10000, 100)
RETURN
SUMX(
    'Property',
    VAR NPVNoRent = -1 * [NPV no rent]
```

Instead of searching for the value with the smallest PVPR that is still above NPVNoRent, we are now interested in two values where PVPR is closest to NPVNoRent.

```
VAR Top2Values =
TOPN(
    2,
    PossibleValuesCoarse,
    VAR ThisRent = [Value]
    VAR PVPRYear1 =
    SUMX(
        FILTER('Year',
            'Year'[YearNr] = 1
            && 'Year'[Year] <= 'Property[End Year]
        ),
        ThisRent * (1 + [IndexY1 Value])
    )
    VAR PVPRYear2 =
    SUMX(
        FILTER('Year',
            'Year'[YearNr] = 2
            && 'Year'[Year] <= 'Property[End Year]
        ),
        ThisRent * POWER(1 + [IndexY1 Value], 2)
    )
    VAR PVPRYear3Plus =
    SUMX(
        FILTER('Year',
            'Year'[YearNr] >= 3
            && 'Year'[Year] <= 'Property[End Year]
        ),
        ThisRent * POWER(1 + [IndexY1Value],
                            'Year'[YearNr])
    )
    VAR PVPR = PVPRYear1 + PVPRYear2 + PVPRYear3Plus
    RETURN
    ABS(PVPR - NPVNoRent),
    ASC
)
```

Above, the TOPN function is used to retrieve the two best values from the
PossibleValuesCoarse list. The complex part is in the third TOPN argument: the
expression that is evaluated for each row in the list. This is where the PVPR calculation
goes. To find the best two values, the values for which the NPV is closest to zero, we
take the absolute value of the difference between the PVPR and the other part of the
NPV: ABS(PVPR - NPVNoRent). Note that we use ASC as the fourth argument for TOPN
to find the values with the smallest result.

We now have a list with the two best possible values, and we are going to use these
values to create the fine list of possible values. We cannot use a basic aggregation
to retrieve the values from the Top2Values list: a function like MIN needs a column
reference, and the Top2Values variable does not have a table name. But we can use
table aggregations:

```
VAR Value1 = MINX(Top2Values, [Value])
VAR Value2 = MAXX(Top2Values, [Value])
VAR PossibleValuesFine =
GENERATESERIES(
    Value1,
    Value2,
    (Value2 - Value1) / 100
)
```

We take the smallest Value in Top2Values for Value1 and the largest for Value2. The
fine possible values list is created with GENERATESERIES again, now using 1/100 of the
difference between the two values to create another 101 values on a finer scale.

With the finer scale, we can now continue as before:

```
RETURN
MINX(
    FILTER(
        PossibleValuesFine,
        VAR ThisRent = [Value]
        VAR PVPRYear1 =
            SUMX(
                FILTER('Year',
                    'Year'[YearNr] = 1
                    && 'Year'[Year]
                        <= 'Property[End Year]
                ),
```

```
            ThisRent * (1 + [IndexY1 Value])
    )
    VAR PVPRYear2 =
    SUMX(
        FILTER('Year',
                'Year'[YearNr] = 2
                && 'Year'[Year]
                    <= 'Property[End Year]
        ),
        ThisRent * POWER(1 + [IndexY1 Value], 2)
    )
    VAR PVPRYear3Plus =
    SUMX(
        FILTER('Year',
                'Year'[YearNr] >= 3
                && 'Year'[Year]
                    <= 'Property[End Year]
        ),
        ThisRent * POWER(1 + [IndexY1Value],
                            'Year'[YearNr])
    )
    VAR PVPR = PVPRYear1 + PVPRYear2 + PVPRYear3Plus
    RETURN
    PVPR >= NPVNoRent
    ),
    [Value]
)
)
```

When you look at the code, you will see that we traverse twice a list of 101 possible rent values to calculate the result. This is much better than the 10,000 items we had to check before!

If you are willing to write even more code, you could further optimize the measure by, for instance, creating lists of 10 possible values four times, zooming in from an interval between values of 1,000, to 100, to 10, to 1. Or even go further and add a precision of 0.1, while still only doing about 50 evaluations.

Note that we haven't used the upward slope of the **NPV by rent** chart in this approach: even with a complex, non-linear function, you can use this approach to approximate the lowest or highest value. There is a restriction, of course: the function should have an optimum within the range you consider.

With multiple (local) optima, you risk finding a suboptimal one. But by then, you are doing more advanced maths.

Another note: there are only a few constants in this formula, being the lower and upper limit of the coarse possible values list, and the number of points to consider within a range. You may choose to create what-if parameters to set these limits dynamically. This would enable you to create a dashboard where the user can try another range when the cost-covering rent is on the edge of the investigated range, which suggests that the real value is outside of that range.

Summary

In this chapter, you have learned about financial metrics for analyzing the future of investments. We have discussed Future Value, Present Value, Net Present Value, and Internal Rate of Return, all of which are common metrics that are used by investment analysts around the world. They are so common that DAX offers some specific functions to calculate them: XNPV and XIRR.

In creating a model for dynamic financial analysis, you have learned how to use what-if parameters in complex calculations. We have seen that the NPV metric can be computed without the XNPV function as well, which opens up additional possibilities to view results at a lower level of detail than the all-up NPV.

The IRR is a metric that is not easily calculated, and an approximative method is needed to find a "good enough" result. This is what the XIRR function implements. We have presented an alternative approach through DAX which, although without much added value in calculating IRR, proved to be very useful in calculating another metric: the cost-covering rent. This approach is applicable to many other scenarios in which exact solutions are not possible to calculate.

In the next chapter, we are going to focus on analyzing status-oriented data, with inventory management as the main example.

2.7

Inventory Analysis

This chapter is all about analyzing inventory levels and changes in inventory. This is a specific kind of analysis, as we are interested in the *status* of something, in this case inventory quantity or value, at a specific point in time.

An inventory report could provide insights into how inventory levels vary over time, and which products risk running out of inventory. And, on the other side of the spectrum, you may have simply too much inventory for a product relative to its turnover speed – although the question "*how much inventory is too much?*" is not a simple one to answer. As an example, in this chapter, we will calculate the number of products that are likely to be still in stock twelve months from now, given a sales forecast. It may seem obvious that products that are on the shelves for a year could have been produced or purchased later, saving the company money.

Although this chapter uses product inventory for our beloved QuantoBikes company as an example, the kind of calculation discussed here is not just useful for inventory. You can apply the same kind of analysis on any metric for which the status at a specific point in time is relevant, like patients in a hospital, cars in a city's network of parking lots, a financial balance, or even water levels in a river delta. A more advanced analysis could incorporate the use of AI to *predict* changes in the statuses instead of working with a forecast, but that will not be covered in this book.

This chapter will cover these topics:

- Data modeling for status-oriented data
- Basic inventory calculations
- Inventory forecasting

Data modeling for status-oriented data

First, a discussion is needed on different ways to model data for which status is the determining factor. In the real world, how data is modeled is typically a trade-off between what is best for the Power BI model and what is achievable from a data preparation point of view. Here, we focus on what would be best for the model; if you apply this for your organization, you may find that data preparation efforts weigh in more heavily.

In deciding what the facts in the model will be, you have two basic options:

1. Store the *status* for each unit of time, usually each day.
2. Store the *changes* in the status.

The first option may seem the most straightforward. We just store one data point per day, per product:

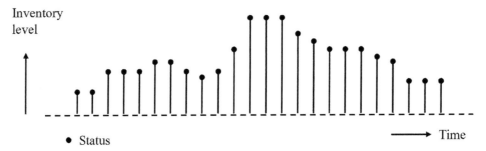

Figure 2.7.1: Storing the status of inventory

There are, however, a number of issues with this option that you need to take care of if you choose to model this way:

*   Most source systems store inventory transactions rather than the inventories themselves, which means that you need to put a lot of work into preparing your data. Either you have to compute the current inventory for every point in time needed, or, if the source system does provide inventories, you must use an intermediate data store to build up a history of inventory levels.

*   This way of modeling the data is heavily dependent on the unit of time chosen. If, say, it is decided that inventory levels only need to be known once a month, it will be difficult to change that into once a day. And similarly, if the data is stored at once-a-day granularity, it is virtually impossible to change that into one-hour granularity.

- Depending on the time interval chosen, a lot of data may be stored while nothing is really happening. For products that do not have any transactions for some time, identical copies of status data will be stored during that period.

- From the perspective of a Power BI model, the fact table is typically related to a calendar table. With this modeling approach, you cannot simply select a month, for instance, and retrieve the inventory level: you need to take care to only select one point in time for which to retrieve the inventory.

The second option, using changes in status, like inventory transactions as facts, solves many of the issues with the first approach. In the data, we would have two types of data points: data that represents the initial status (the dot in the figure below) and data that represents any transaction that takes from or adds to inventory (the results of which are visualized by the dotted line):

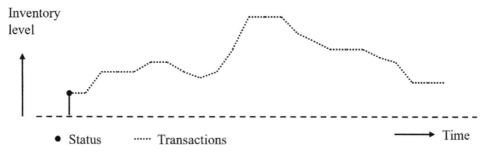

Figure 2.7.2: Storing the status once, and changes after that

This approach comes with its own issues, though:

- You cannot just use transactions to find a specific inventory level: you need to have a reference level to work from. In some scenarios, this reference is readily available; a financial balance sheet, for instance, is typically computed at the end of the fiscal year and can then be used as the starting point for the new year. But for products in warehouses, things are less straightforward.

- Assuming you have a reference level, you still need to do some work to calculate the inventory level at a specific point in time: you need to start with the reference and add or subtract all transactions up to the point you are interested in. Luckily, this is something DAX is particularly good at.

Based on the issues above, we commonly choose to use inventory *transactions* as facts in a Power BI model. But we still need to deal with the reference level somehow. Again, we have several options for how to solve this:

- Store the initial inventory level for each product, or (plausibly) assume it to start at zero. This is the option depicted in *Figure 2.7.2*. There are two major problems with this: first, you would be forced to store all transactions for each product, even when a product was introduced 20 years ago; second, the reference level would be found at a different point in time for each product. The consequence of this is that you could only calculate the total inventory by iterating over the products and calculating inventory by individual product. So, this option would not only lead to a humongous model, but also to inefficient DAX code.

- Store the initial inventory level at fixed points in time for each product, like at the start of each year; see *Figure 2.7.3*. This is a much better approach, as we can select the reference level for all products at once and use efficient aggregations to compute actual inventory levels. The drawback of this approach is that you will probably store multiple copies of reference levels (one for each year, for example), and your DAX code will need to determine where the relevant reference level can be found, and ignore other references and transactions before the right reference level.

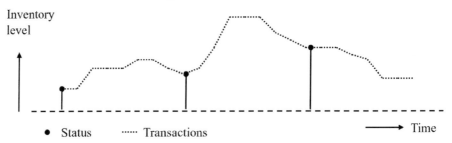

Figure 2.7.3: Storing the status regularly, and changes in between

- The third option, and this is the one we will use, is to store reference levels for all products at *the most recent* point in time; see *Figure 2.7.4*. From a DAX perspective, this is an attractive way to model the data, as it is easy to calculate inventory levels at any point in time.

We discuss this after the figure:

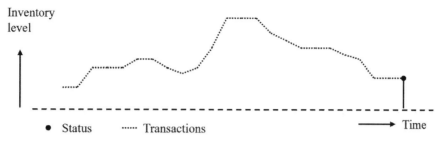

Figure 2.7.4: Storing the latest status, and transactions leading up to it

To calculate an inventory level at point-in-time T, you need to take the reference level and *subtract* all transactions from point T onward. For instance, if the reference is 200, new inventory was added yesterday, say 100 units, and 30 units were sold four days ago (this would be modeled as a transaction of -30 units), the inventory one week ago was 130 units. To make calculations even easier, you can multiply each transaction's numbers by -1; incoming transactions would then be negative (-100 in the example above) and outgoing transactions positive (30). The inventory one week ago can then be calculated by simply adding everything after that: -100, plus 30, plus 200.

This way of modeling the inventory has the added benefit that reference levels of old products, which are no longer in stock, do not have to be stored: they will show up in the result automatically when you look back far enough to hit a transaction on such a product. After all, the current inventory for these products will be zero (or blank); if, for instance, the last outgoing transaction was two years ago for 25 units (stored as -25), the result of the calculation for a point in time just before two years ago would be 25 units.

As mentioned earlier, this modeling option may not be the optimal choice when it comes to data preparation efforts: it can be quite a challenge to retrieve current inventory levels when the source systems do not readily provide these. That said, an argument can be made that an optimal model structure should be prioritized. After all, an efficient Power BI model is best for the users of the reports.

Based on the calculations in this chapter, you could try another option yourself: store the most recent reference level and add transactions after that with negative amounts. This will allow for calculating inventory levels after the most recent reference level, but will add complexity to the calculations.

With the above considerations, the model for QuantoBikes' inventory analysis looks like the figure below. Commonly, inventory is managed by **SKU**, or **stock-keeping unit**, the official name for what is actually lying on the shelf, while "product" may be a grouping of several SKUs in your case. As grouping is a straightforward concept in DAX, we will use *SKU* and *product* interchangeably in this chapter.

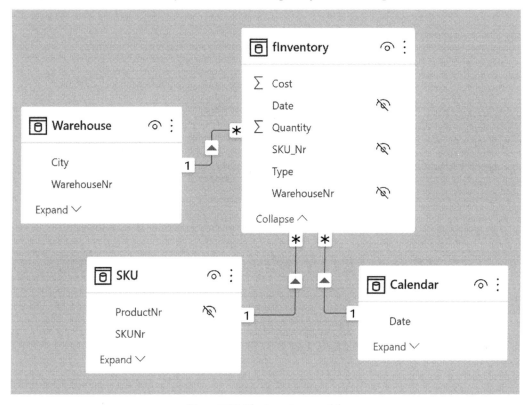

Figure 2.7.5: The inventory model

The central fact table, fInventory, contains both the reference levels and inventory transactions. To distinguish the two, the Type column contains a 0 for reference levels and a 1 for transactions. In both cases, the Quantity column contains the number of products in stock or partaking in the transaction, respectively.

The fact table is linked to relevant filter tables: Warehouse, SKU, and Calendar. You may have additional filters on this level, like transaction types that provide more detail on the transactions, vendors for purchased products, customers for inventory transactions that involve shipping products to customers, and so on.

To manage inventory, additional fact tables can be added. For instance, if we add a fSalesForecast table containing forecasted sales by product, these can be used as forecasted outward inventory transactions. We may also have inventory targets, like minimum stock levels, in fInventoryTargets.

 You can download the model used in this chapter, 2.7 Inventory.pbix, from GitHub at https://github.com/ PacktPublishing/Extreme-DAX/tree/main/Chapter2.7.

Inventory granularity

Before we dive into the analysis, we need to discuss the issue of **granularity**, or detail level, of our facts. We have stored our actual inventory at a fairly low detail level: transactions on individual SKUs in individual warehouses. Additional facts may or may not be available on the same level of SKU/warehouse.

The same is true, of course, for the time dimension: it is not likely that we have sales forecasts on a daily level, while we do have daily inventory data. It doesn't make much sense to make daily comparisons to a monthly forecast; and in our analysis, both in DAX measures and visual reports, we will have to deal with this discrepancy. In a Power BI model, facts with a lower granularity than days are usually mapped to a day in the Calendar table anyway. So, you may map the sales forecast for February to February 1. As long as your report shows results by month as the most detailed view, you will not notice this. You still need to be aware that you did this, though, as some calculations may work with data on the day level even when they are retrieved in a month-based context.

For SKUs, it works in exactly the same manner. You may have sales forecasts on the SKU level, but it is more probable that forecasts are provided at a coarser granularity, like product or product category. This can be dealt with in the same way as with the Calendar table, although it is less common to map the higher-level fact to a single SKU.

It is the Warehouse granularity that we need to take extra care of, from a functional perspective. Here, we have a business decision to make, as multiple warehouses may be in the same physical location or in close proximity to each other. This means that when one warehouse runs out of stock for a specific SKU, another warehouse may step in and fulfill orders for that SKU. From the perspective of our analyses, it means that choosing the level at which to calculate, for instance, forecasted stock levels, is fundamental to the outcome.

And, as inventory analysis is inherently not suited for aggregating everything (we will need to do most of our calculations on a by-warehouse basis), the level chosen impacts the fundamental structure of the DAX code. It is the difference between, say:

```
SUMX(
    VALUES(Warehouse[Warehouse]),
    ...
```

And:

```
SUMX(
    VALUES(Warehouse[City]),
    ...
```

In dealing with these detail levels, you may opt to let the report users choose the detail, by providing a level slicer or just different pages in the report, or you may try to derive the level needed from the context; for instance, when a single warehouse is selected, you could conclude that it doesn't make sense to do the calculation on the level of City.

Basic inventory calculations

Let us start by answering the most basic question: what is the actual inventory? Because of the way we have modeled our data, this one is easy to do:

```
Actual Inventory =
CALCULATE(
    SUM(fInventory[Quantity]),
    fInventory[Type] = 0
)
```

All we need to do is retrieve the rows with [Type] = 0, as it is in those where the actual inventory is stored.

There is one issue with this calculation, however: it assumes that we have selected the whole of the Calendar table, or at least made a selection that includes the date with the Type 0 rows. After all, when we select last year, the rows containing the current inventory will not be selected. It would be better to create a measure that returns a result for any selection on Calendar.

If we assume that we have some selection in Calendar, the first question to ask is: which exact date do we pick to return the status for? After all, the inventory status is strictly date-specific.

The common practice is to take the latest date in the selection for this:
`MAX('Calendar'[Date])`. But this raises a problem for selections that extend beyond
the reference date with the latest inventory status (typically today's, or yesterday's,
inventory). Let us put this in a diagram:

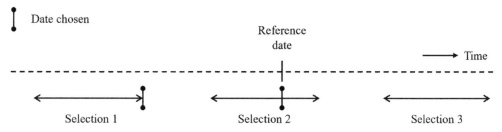

Figure 2.7.6: Three Calendar selections

In this diagram, three different `Calendar` selections are depicted:

1. When the complete selection is before the reference date, taking the latest
   date will work fine.

2. When the reference date falls within the selection, we should not take the
   latest date but the reference date instead; after all, the inventory status will be
   calculated by aggregating all transactions *after* the status's date (including the
   reference status), so taking a date after the reference date will return nothing.

3. When the complete selection falls after the reference date, we cannot
   effectively return inventory (it's the future, typically), so taking the latest date
   in the selection will do: the result will be blank.

In addition to these options, we have to deal with another, special case, which
may occur more often than you think: an *empty* `Calendar` selection. Taking
`MAX('Calendar'[Date])` would return a blank value, and aggregating all transactions
after it does effectively return the aggregation of the complete transaction table. This
is because DAX translates blank to zero when doing comparisons.

The DAX formula for inventory thus starts with setting up some variables for
important dates in the calculation:

```
Inventory Qty =
VAR MaxDate = MAX('Calendar'[Date])
VAR RefDate =
CALCULATE(
    MAX(fInventory[Date]),
    ALL('Calendar'),
    fInventory[Type] = 0
)
```

Note that we need to use ALL('Calendar') to remove filters from Calendar, as we need to retrieve the reference date, which may fall outside of the current selection. We also filter on Type = 0, although you may omit this when you have modeled your date in such a way that no inventory transactions are included with a date after the reference date, ever.

In the remainder of the code, we use the SWITCH function to detect which of the four scenarios we are dealing with. As the criteria are not uniform, we use the SWITCH(TRUE(),...) construct we have seen before, which makes SWITCH select the first statement that is true:

```
RETURN
SWITCH(
    TRUE(),
    -- empty selection
    ISBLANK(MaxDate),
        BLANK(),
    -- reference date falls within selection
    CONTAINS(VALUES('Calendar'[Date]), 'Calendar'[Date], RefDate),
        CALCULATE(
            SUM(fInventory[Quantity]),
            ALL('Calendar'),
            fInventory[Type] = 0
        ),
    -- else
    CALCULATE(
        SUM(fInventory[Quantity]),
        ALL('Calendar'),
        'Calendar'[Date] > MaxDate
    )
)
```

The function CONTAINS determines if a value (RefDate, in our case) is found in a column ('Calendar'[Date]) of a table (VALUES('Calendar'[Date])), and is therefore particularly suitable for what we need here. Note that in this case, we don't need to take any transactions into account, but can focus only on the reference status.

There is a subtle distinction to be made here. You may have expected to see this calculation in the "else" clause of the SWITCH:

```
CALCULATE(
    SUM(fInventory[Quantity]),
    ALL('Calendar'),
    'Calendar'[Date] = RefDate
),
```

After all, we just retrieved the reference date and we know that that is where the reference status is found, right? The catch is that there may also be inventory transactions on the same day. So, filtering on the date will aggregate both the reference status and the transactions for that day, returning the inventory status *at the start of the day* (or the end of the previous day). It is important to apply the same logic as in the case that the selection is completely in the past; when we, for instance, retrieve inventory status for April 15, 2021:

```
'Calendar'[Date] > DATE(2021, 4, 15)
```

What we actually compute is the status at the end of that day. A simple example makes it clear: if I sold 50 items today, and my current inventory is 100 (at the end of today), I must have started the day with an inventory of 150, which is by definition the inventory at the end of yesterday.

Another thing to learn from this is that we must store the reference inventory status as the inventory at the end of the day.

The figure below shows sample output for a set of warehouses, with reference levels stored at July 14, 2021:

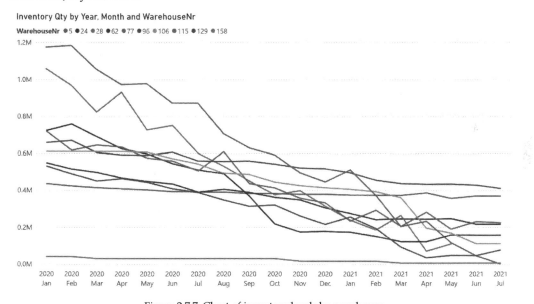

Figure 2.7.7: Chart of inventory levels by warehouse

As an exercise, try to understand why the formula does not return results for August 2021 and later. Hint: in which clause of the SWITCH expression does selection 3 (in *Figure 2.7.6*) land?

Inventory targets

When your business depends on being able to sell products from your inventory, you do not want products to run out of stock. This means that you need to find a way to make sure you have enough inventory. At the same time, products on shelves cost money, and having too much inventory harms your business as well. You must therefore find a way to balance your inventory versus your sales.

The simplest way to do this is to have an inventory target. With this, you provide a target quantity for each product in each warehouse, wherever relevant. In this section, we discuss a straightforward way to compute targets and compare the actual inventory levels with the targets. Later in this chapter, we will take a more sophisticated approach, taking into account sales forecast and/or product run rate.

Inventory management typically works with minimum stock levels and restock levels; when inventory comes below the minimum level, stock is replenished so that it returns to the restock level. As this chapter is not purely about inventory management, we will stick with the generic term *target*. The principles implemented in the calculations in this chapter can be adapted to specific scenarios without too much effort.

Let us assume we have a yearly inventory target for our products. In other words, for each year, and each product/warehouse combination that is relevant to us, we register the target level. As discussed earlier, the common way to model this is to map the year onto a specific date in that year, like January 1. We store the targets in a fact table, fInvTarget. Like the fInventory table, fInvTarget has relationships with the Warehouse, SKU, and Calendar table.

Warning: When your analysis takes into account working days, excluding weekends and holidays, choosing January 1 may cause you to lose the targets altogether! In this case, choose a date that is certain to be a working day – which may be a bit harder to accomplish.

Here is what the extended model looks like:

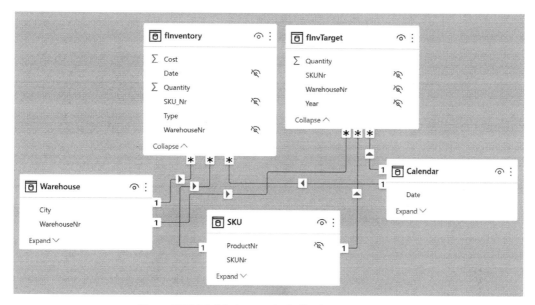

Figure 2.7.8: Model structure including inventory targets

The target quantity can be computed with the formula below:

```
Target Qty =
CALCULATE(
    SUM(fInvTarget[Quantity]),
    ALL('Calendar'),
    VALUES('Calendar'[Year])
)
```

Keep in mind that our context may include a filter on a different column in Calendar than Year, like YearMonth. If the selection through this filter comes down to, for instance, September 2021, there is no way to get to a selection of the whole year (including the date the targets are mapped to) other than to remove all filters from Calendar and to "feed" the selected Year values back into the context. This is done here with the VALUES function.

Moving on to comparing the inventory levels with the targets, your first guess might be a calculation like this:

```
Inventory balance = [Inventory Qty] – [Target Qty]
```

Unfortunately, this will not yield useful results. This calculation compares the *total* inventory with the *total* target, and while we may have enough stock on a global level, that doesn't mean that individual warehouses, or entire cities or regions, have enough.

What we need to do is compare actual inventory with targets on a more detailed level, and aggregate that in some way that doesn't obscure the details. When you think about it, it is not even enough to do the calculation on the individual warehouse level; instead, we need to do it on the individual SKU level. (We assume that our targets are set on the SKU level as well, although it is probable that a higher level in the product hierarchy is used. That would only call for a simple change in the formulas, though.)

Another consideration is that when we aggregate these results, we do not want warehouses that have a surplus in inventory to compensate for warehouses that have a deficiency. The best way to deal with this is to use two separate measures: one that computes the surplus, and another that calculates the quantities below target. These measures are easy variations on a single theme.

To calculate the difference between actual and target inventory by warehouse and product, you may use this formula:

```
Actual vs Target Qty 1 =
SUMX(
    Warehouse,
    SUMX(
        SKU,
        [Inventory Qty] – [Target Qty]
    )
)
```

Alternatively, we can do the same thing with just one iterator by using CROSSJOIN:

```
Actual vs Target Qty 2 =
SUMX(
    CROSSJOIN(Warehouse, SKU),
    [Inventory Qty] – [Target Qty]
)
```

Both formulas suffer from the same issue: we let DAX do a lot of calculations that may not be needed. When we compute the overall result, SUMX needs to iterate over a table of the number of warehouses times the number of SKUs. Another, more subtle issue is: what happens with inventory on SKUs that we don't have a target for? In this case, [Target qty] is BLANK, which is treated as zero in the subtraction, so the complete actual quantity is taken in the aggregation. This is probably not what we want.

Both issues can be addressed by only taking warehouse/SKU combinations into account for which a target is available. You can do this with the following expression:

```
FILTER(
    CROSSJOIN(Warehouse, SKU),
    [Target qty] > 0
)
```

However, using FILTER here still forces DAX to compute the target quantity for each warehouse/SKU combination, only to determine which combinations should be selected! The better option is to use SUMMARIZE:

```
SUMMARIZE(
    fInvTarget,
    Warehouse[WarehouseNr],
    SKU[SKUNr]
)
```

SUMMARIZE can be used to retrieve the unique combinations of values from multiple columns in a table, but allows for using columns from related tables as well. In our case, SUMMARIZE returns the unique warehouse/SKU combinations that appear in the fInvTarget table: exactly what we want. It has the additional benefit that we now have a table of only two columns, instead of the crossjoin of two *entire* tables.

But be warned! Using SUMMARIZE to retrieve the combinations will take into account all other filters affecting fInvTarget. As our yearly targets are mapped onto January 1, the result of SUMMARIZE will be empty when, for instance, only February is selected. You have already seen how to solve that:

```
CALCULATETABLE(
    SUMMARIZE(
        fInvTarget,
        Warehouse[WarehouseNr],
```

```
        SKU[SKUNr]
    ),
    ALL('Calendar'),
    VALUES('Calendar'[Year])
)
```

We will store this table in a variable. The calculation for inventory surplus versus target then looks like this:

```
Surplus vs Target Qty =
VAR WarehouseSKUCombinations =
    CALCULATETABLE(
        SUMMARIZE(
            fInvTarget,
            Warehouse[WarehouseNr],
            SKU[SKUNr]
        ),
        ALL('Calendar'),
        VALUES('Calendar'[Year])
    )
RETURN
SUMX(
    WarehouseSKUCombinations,
    MAX([Inventory Qty] - [Target Qty], 0)
)
```

The MAX expression provides a zero when the inventory is below target, by which the measure effectively returns only the surplus. To compute the total deficiency, you reverse the calculation by excluding the positive outcomes (returning a negative value for deficiency):

```
MIN([Inventory Qty] - [Target Qty], 0)
```

Or alternatively, to return the deficiency as a positive value:

```
MAX([Target Qty] - [Inventory Qty], 0)
```

The chart below shows the inventory surplus and deficiency over time, as well as the target level and the actual inventory (note that these are plotted on a second *y*-axis at the right).

As the target is a single value for the whole year, it is shown as a horizontal line in the chart.

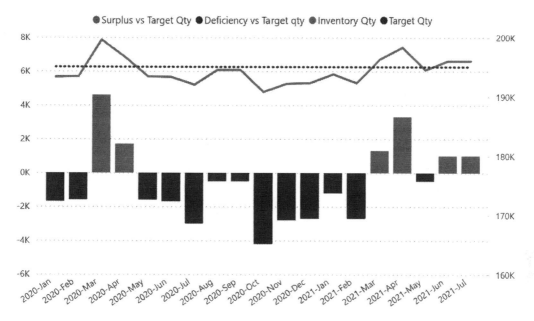

Figure 2.7.9: Chart of inventory versus target

The measures described here calculate the surplus and deficiency at the individual warehouse level. We may assume that warehouses in close proximity of each other can help compensate for stock shortages; if this is the case, it makes sense to do the calculation not on the warehouse level, but on the city level. After all, when the total inventory is above the total inventory target for the city, all warehouses could jointly provide the products needed.

Changing the calculation to the level of cities is a simple change in the SUMMARIZE expression:

```
SUMMARIZE(
    fInvTarget,
    Warehouse[City],
    SKU[SKUNr]
)
```

We should, however, take into account that the context may be a selection of just one warehouse. In any case, the measure should return the surplus for the city as a whole.

So, we must force the context to be whole cities, in the same way we changed context to whole years earlier:

```
Surplus vs Target qty by City =
CALCULATE(
    VAR CitySKUCombinations =
    CALCULATETABLE(
        SUMMARIZE(
            fInvTarget,
            Warehouse[City],
            SKU[SKUNr]
        ),
        ALL('Calendar'),
        VALUES('Calendar'[Year])
    )
    RETURN
    SUMX(
        CitySKUCombinations,
        MAX([Inventory qty] - [Target qty], 0)
    ),
    ALL(Warehouse),
    VALUES(Warehouse[City])
)
```

Now, the measure will return the city results for both individual warehouses and cities.

Inventory forecasting

You have now seen some examples of inventory calculations. In some way, the measures describe a static view of inventory: the quantities at a specific point in time, and the differences compared to a fixed inventory target level. In reality, inventory is constantly in flux: products are shipped from our warehouses, and new products come in from manufacturing. It is therefore more interesting to take turnover speed into account when we analyze inventory. And as the real business value comes from balancing our inventory levels as exactly as possible with our sales, we want to have some way of looking into the future of our inventory. In other words, what we want is an inventory forecast.

Two types of forecast

There are, of course, many ways to get a prediction of the future state of inventory. We will cover two options here: first, using a sales forecast that is provided by salespeople, and second, extrapolating changes in the inventory that have occurred in the past. You may also use AI modeling to make predictions, and in addition to a sales forecast, you may work with a manufacturing forecast as well.

In a real situation, chances are that you can even use a hybrid approach: use a sales forecast for shipments to larger customers or strategic products, and make extrapolations for bulk customers or less strategic products.

Using a sales forecast to predict inventory changes

To work with a sales forecast, we need to have, of course, a table in our model containing the sales forecast: fForecast. There are many choices to make; let us assume that we have a monthly forecast by city, by product (being an aggregation of one or more SKUs). For simplicity, we will also assume that we only store forecasts for months after the reference date for the inventory (remember, that is the date for which we have stored the actual inventory status). Additionally, we map a month's forecast to the 1st of that month. See the table below for an example of forecast data:

City	ProductNr	Month	Quantity
Tokyo	1745	01/08/2021	10000
Tokyo	2690	01/08/2021	1200
Tokyo	503	01/08/2021	15000
Tokyo	1745	01/09/2021	10000
Tokyo	2690	01/09/2021	2700
Tokyo	503	01/09/2021	15000
Tokyo	1745	01/10/2021	25000
Tokyo	2690	01/10/2021	1000
Tokyo	503	01/10/2021	15000
Tokyo	1745	01/11/2021	15000

Figure 2.7.10: Sales forecast data

Because of the different granularity of this fact table compared to the inventory and target tables, we add the City and Product tables to the model. These are related to Warehouse and SKU, respectively, with relationships that have a cross filter direction of **Both**. This way, we can hide the new tables altogether and keep filtering, for instance, cities through the City column in the Warehouse table:

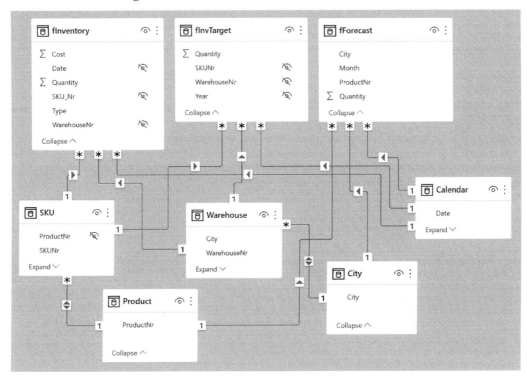

Figure 2.7.11: Model diagram including sales forecast

To compute the predicted inventory level in the future, we need to take the reference level and subtract all sales forecast data until the last day of the Calendar selection. As an example, if our reference inventory is on September 21, and we want to know the predicted inventory for November, we subtract the sales forecast for October and November from the reference level. This gives us the predicted inventory at the end of November:

```
Inventory Forecast Qty 0 =
VAR RefLevel =
    CALCULATE(
        SUM(fInventory[Quantity]),
        ALL('Calendar'),
```

```
        fInventory[Type] = 0
    )
VAR MaxDate = MAX('Calendar'[Date])
VAR SalesForecast =
    CALCULATE(
        SUM(fForecast[Quantity]),
        ALL('Calendar'),
        'Calendar'[Date] <= MaxDate
    )
RETURN
RefLevel - SalesForecast
```

If only it were so easy! In reality, we can run into situations where the forecasted sales cannot be fulfilled because the inventory level is too low for a specific SKU. The all-up `RefLevel - SalesForecast` calculation above would obscure these problems, as they could be offset by other SKUs that have more than enough inventory. Once again, the calculation must be done on the warehouse/SKU level, or on a higher level if we allow warehouses to borrow products from each other to fulfill sales. Let us work on the level of cities for now.

Moreover, we need to deal with a sales forecast that is set on the higher product level. We can only assume that a forecasted sale for a product could be fulfilled with any of the SKUs grouped into that product. In the formula, we use `SUMMARIZE` again, this time to create a summary over the `fInventory` table. After all, we do want to have a forecasted inventory level, even when there is no sales forecast available for the city/product combination:

```
SUMMARIZE(
    fInventory,
    Warehouse[City],
    SKU[Product]
)
```

One thing to keep in mind here is that we are calculating a forecasted inventory. Almost by definition, the context for this calculation will involve a *future* selection in the `Calendar` table. But this means that the selection in the `fInventory` table is empty! What we need to do is to summarize the reference levels in `fInventory` instead:

```
CALCULATETABLE(
    SUMMARIZE(
        fInventory,
        Warehouse[City],
```

```
        SKU[Product]
    ),
    ALL('Calendar'),
    fInventory[Type] = 0
)
```

With this, we can do the proper calculation:

```
Inventory Forecast Qty =
VAR MaxDate = MAX('Calendar'[Date])
VAR CityProductCombinations =
    CALCULATETABLE(
        SUMMARIZE(
            fInventory,
            Warehouse[City],
            SKU[Product]
        ),
        ALL('Calendar'),
        fInventory[Type] = 0
    )

RETURN
SUMX(
    CityProductCombinations,
    VAR RefLevel =
        CALCULATE(
            SUM(fInventory[Quantity]),
            ALL('Calendar'),
            fInventory[Type] = 0
        )
    VAR SalesForecast =
        CALCULATE(
            SUM(fForecast[Quantity]),
            ALL('Calendar'),
            'Calendar'[Date] <= MaxDate
        )
    RETURN
    MAX(RefLevel - SalesForecast, 0)
)
```

Note that we use DAX variables in two places in the formula: the variables MaxDate and CityProductCombinations are computed once, while the variables RefLevel and SalesForecast are computed for every row in the CityProductCombinations table.

And of course, the difference between `RefLevel` and `SalesForecast` is capped at zero, which was the whole point of this endeavor.

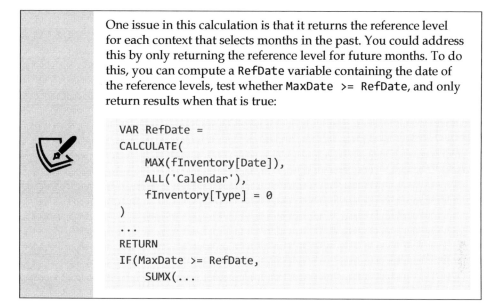

One issue in this calculation is that it returns the reference level for each context that selects months in the past. You could address this by only returning the reference level for future months. To do this, you can compute a `RefDate` variable containing the date of the reference levels, test whether `MaxDate >= RefDate`, and only return results when that is true:

```
VAR RefDate =
CALCULATE(
    MAX(fInventory[Date]),
    ALL('Calendar'),
    fInventory[Type] = 0
)
...
RETURN
IF(MaxDate >= RefDate,
    SUMX(...
```

The figure below shows sample output for this calculation:

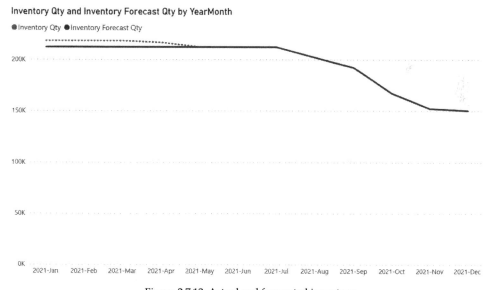

Figure 2.7.12: Actual and forecasted inventory

Using extrapolation to predict inventory changes

The second approach we discuss here is to use extrapolation as a means to predict future inventory. This means that instead of working with a sales forecast, which may not be available, we could look back and see what the typical shipping rate of products has been. This rate can then be used to extrapolate to the future.

Before we dive into the DAX code needed, we have to first set the stage and think about the business assumptions we can make in this analysis. To name a few:

- Again, we need to think about the granularity that can be applied. As in the previous section, let us assume that warehouses in the same city can use each other's inventory for shipments.

- Technically, we can do the extrapolation on the individual SKU level, but you should realize that the lower the detail level, the higher the chance that one-off shipments and outliers affect the extrapolation. Let us work at the product level instead.

- Another decision to make is how much to look back. There is no single right decision here, as it really depends on the characteristics of the business, which may even vary between products. When there is a strong seasonality in sales (which is plausible for a company selling motorbikes like QuantoBikes), it makes sense to work with a full year to base the extrapolation on.

- Finally, we have to make an assumption about *how* to extrapolate future shipments from the past. We will keep it simple here and just take the average shipment, assuming that shipments have been stable overall during the period considered. You may want to go one step further and consider whether shipments are generally increasing or decreasing. This can be done via linear regression on monthly shipments, which can be performed in DAX (at the end of this chapter, we briefly discuss how). Go two steps further and you will find yourself in machine learning territory, which is beyond what DAX can do.

Important to note is that, for now, we will only look at shipments from warehouses, and not at replenishments. You can, of course, apply the same principles to forecast products coming into the warehouses, or use a manufacturing forecast; we leave it to you to do this.

In short, we want to calculate average shipments per month in the year before the reference date. This time, we are not interested in the reference inventory level, but in the outgoing transactions. These have `Type = 1` and `Quantity > 0`.

The total shipments can be calculated using the reference date:

```
VAR RefDate =
    CALCULATE(
        MAX(fInventory[Date]),
        ALL('Calendar'),
        fInventory[Type] = 0
    )
VAR TotalShipments =
    CALCULATE(
        SUM(fInventory[Quantity]),
        fInventory[Type] = 1,
        fInventory[Quantity] > 0,
        DATESINPERIOD('Calendar'[Date], RefDate, -12, MONTH)
    )
```

The DATESINPERIOD function provides the one-year (or twelve-month) period that we want to consider. Because time intelligence functions like DATESINPERIOD perform an implicit ALL('Calendar'), we don't need to include it explicitly here.

How do we get from the total shipments to the average per month? The obvious answer is to divide by 12. In some cases, however, this may not be correct, like in the case of newly introduced products or even new warehouses. It is not a simple task to correctly compute the correct number of months to divide by in every case. One thing you can do is retrieve the months from the fInventory table itself:

```
VAR NumberOfMonths =
    COUNTROWS(
        CALCULATETABLE(
            SUMMARIZE(
                fInventory,
                'Calendar'[YearMonthNr]
            ),
            DATESINPERIOD(
                'Calendar'[Date],
                RefDate,
                -12, MONTH
            )
        )
    )
```

When computing this, you will find that, in general, you overstate the number of months by one, as the reference date is almost always at some point in the middle of a month and you will count 13 different `YearMonthNr` values when you go one year back. A perhaps more serious problem is that you may have products that only ship every now and then, leaving gaps in the list of months. This can be addressed by not simply counting the months, but computing both the first and the last month (which is the month of the reference date) and taking the difference between the two. For this to work, you need a counter column, say `YearMonthCtr`, that is a continuous sequence. The number of months can then be calculated with:

```
VAR RefMonthCtr =
    CALCULATE(
        MAX('Calendar'[YearMonthCtr]),
        ALL('Calendar'),
        'Calendar'[Date] = RefDate
    )
VAR FirstInventoryDate =
    CALCULATE(
        MIN(fInventory[Date]),
        fInventory[Type] = 1,
        fInventory[Quantity] > 0,
        DATESINPERIOD('Calendar'[Date], RefDate, -12, MONTH)
    )
VAR FirstMonthCtr =
    CALCULATE(
        MIN('Calendar'[YearMonthCtr]),
        ALL('Calendar'),
        'Calendar'[Date] = FirstDate
    )
VAR NumberOfMonths = RefMonthCtr - FirstMonthCtr
```

The average shipments per month is a simple division now:

```
VAR AvgShipmentsMth =
    DIVIDE(TotalShipments, NumberOfMonths)
```

Note that most of these variables need to be evaluated for city/product combinations, although some, like `FirstInventoryDate`, are generic.

To compute a proper inventory prediction, we should start with the reference level, and subtract the monthly run rate for every month between the reference date and the last day of the `Calendar` selection.

In other words, we need to not only count the number of months in the past, to calculate the run rate, but also in the future. This time, we are merely counting across the `Calendar` table, so we do not need to jump through hoops to translate a date to a `YearMonthCtr` value, but we can retrieve it directly:

```
VAR MaxMonthCtr = MAX('Calendar'[YearMonthCtr])
VAR NumberOfMonthsFuture = MaxMonthCtr - RefMonthCtr
VAR PredictedShipments = NumberOfMonthsFuture * AvgShipmentsMth
```

Note that as the reference date is at some point in the middle of a month, no shipments are predicted for the rest of that month. It is up to you to decide if that is OK or not. You can compensate for it by also computing the fraction of the month that is missed, and add a prediction for that fraction.

Another approach would be to work from the last day of the month preceding the reference date. You will then effectively calculate the average shipments from the last twelve full months, and predict shipments for the current month as a whole. You should subtract the actual shipments in the current month to get a good result.

Let us now use all the variables above to build a proper DAX measure:

```
Inventory Prediction Qty =
VAR RefDate =
    CALCULATE(
        MAX(fInventory[Date]),
        ALL('Calendar'),
        fInventory[Type] = 0
    )
VAR RefMonthCtr =
    CALCULATE(
        MAX('Calendar'[YearMonthCtr]),
        ALL('Calendar'),
        'Calendar'[Date] = RefDate
    )
VAR MaxMonthCtr = MAX('Calendar'[YearMonthCtr])
VAR NumberOfMonthsFuture = MaxMonthCtr - RefMonthCtr

VAR CityProductCombinations =
    CALCULATETABLE(
```

```
        SUMMARIZE(
            fInventory,
            Warehouse[City],
            SKU[ProductNr]
        ),
        ALL('Calendar'),
        fInventory[Type] = 0
    )

RETURN
```

These are all variables that can be evaluated once for the calculation. The `CityProductCombinations` variable is the list of cities and products for which a reference level is available. The rest of the calculation is done on a per-city/product combination basis:

```
SUMX(
    CityProductCombinations,
    VAR TotalShipments =
        CALCULATE(
            SUM(fInventory[Quantity]),
            fInventory[Type] = 1,
            fInventory[Quantity] > 0,
            DATESINPERIOD('Calendar'[Date], RefDate, -12, MONTH)
        )
    VAR FirstInventoryDate =
        CALCULATE(
            MIN(fInventory[Date]),
            fInventory[Type] = 1,
            fInventory[Quantity] > 0,
            DATESINPERIOD('Calendar'[Date], RefDate, -12, MONTH)
        )
    VAR FirstMonthCtr =
        CALCULATE(
            MIN('Calendar'[YearMonthCtr]),
            ALL('Calendar'),
            'Calendar'[Date] = FirstInventoryDate
        )
    VAR NumberOfMonths = RefMonthCtr - FirstMonthCtr
    VAR AvgShipmentsMth = DIVIDE(TotalShipments, NumberOfMonths)
    VAR PredictedShipments = NumberOfMonthsFuture * AvgShipmentsMth
```

```
VAR RefLevel =
    CALCULATE(
        SUM(fInventory[Quantity]),
        ALL('Calendar'),
        fInventory[Type] = 0
    )
RETURN
```

For each city/product combination, the `TotalShipments` variable is the total of the outgoing units in the last 12 months. The `FirstInventoryDate` and `FirstMonthCtr` variables, discussed before, are used to compute the correct `NumberOfMonths` value. With these, we can compute the average shipments per month in the `AvgShipmentsMth` variable. And, of course, we need the reference level for the city/product combination as well.

The remainder of the formula is really simple: all we need to do is subtract the prediction from the reference level, keeping it at zero when it ends up below:

```
    MAX(RefLevel - PredictedShipments, 0)
)
```

The figure below shows sample output for this calculation. Note that we deal with the same issue as the forecast calculation earlier: the measure returns results for past months as well.

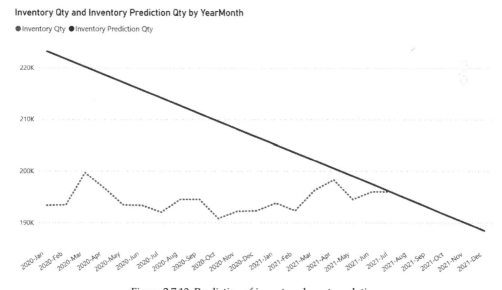

Figure 2.7.13: Prediction of inventory by extrapolation

This concludes our approach to predicting inventory through either a sales forecast or extrapolation. You could use a hybrid approach, with a sales forecast for some strategic products and extrapolation for others. The most straightforward way to do this is through the `CityProductCombinations` variable used in the DAX formulas discussed earlier. For instance, limiting this list to products with the status `"Strategic"` would not be hard to implement when there is a `Status` column in the `SKU` table:

```
VAR CityProductCombinations =
    CALCULATETABLE(
        SUMMARIZE(
            fInventory,
            Warehouse[City],
            SKU[Product]
        ),
ALL('Calendar'),
        fInventory[Type] = 0,
        SKU[Status] = "Strategic"
    )
```

Using this variable declaration instead of the one we defined earlier in `Inventory Forecast Qty` would lead to a result for only the strategic products. In the same way, the list used in the `Inventory Prediction Qty` measure could be limited to non-strategic products to use extrapolation for those products only. You can then add both measures to obtain a hybrid inventory outlook.

With a similar approach to what we used to forecast or predict shipments, you can build DAX measures for either forecasted or extrapolated replenishments of inventory.

Calculating long-lasting inventory

We now have the means to calculate the expected inventory at any time in the future. This gives an overall impression of whether our inventory level is too high or too low. We can also take another view by computing the quantity of stock we have now that will probably still be in stock after some time, say, a year. By doing this calculation not in quantity but in value, by taking the costs of our products into account, we will learn how much money is stuck in long-lasting inventory. Businesswise, you would want to find a balance between minimizing inventory value and keeping customer service at appropriate levels.

You can probably guess that this calculation is just another one within the same framework as the previous measures we discussed in this chapter. The approach is:

1. Compute the current (reference) level of inventory.
2. Predict the shipments between now and a year.
3. Calculate what remains of the current inventory after that year.

Again, we need to decide on which level to do the calculation. We will keep things simple and stay with the same city/product combination level as we used in the previous section. Let's begin by creating a calculation of long-lasting inventory *quantity*, which starts again with the declaration of some variables:

```
Long-lasting Inventory Qty =
VAR RefDate =
    CALCULATE(
        MAX(fInventory[Date]),
        ALL('Calendar'),
        fInventory[Type] = 0
    )
VAR CityProductCombinations =
    CALCULATETABLE(
        SUMMARIZE(
            fInventory,
            Warehouse[City],
            SKU[ProductNr]
        ),
        ALL('Calendar'),
        fInventory[Type] = 0
    )
```

Again, the formula starts with setting up the general things we need and that you have seen before: the reference date and the table of city/product combinations. We proceed by iterating over this table, and for each combination, we will need to calculate the reference level and either the `SalesForecast` or `PredictedShipments` variable, whichever approach you choose. Let's stick with using a sales forecast:

```
RETURN
SUMX(
    CityProductCombinations,
    VAR RefLevel =
        CALCULATE(
            SUM(fInventory[Quantity]),
```

```
                ALL('Calendar'),
                fInventory[Type] = 0
            )
    VAR SalesForecast =
        CALCULATE(
            SUM(fForecast[Quantity]),
            DATESINPERIOD(
                'Calendar'[Date],
                RefDate,
                12, MONTH
            )
        )
    )
```

Note that DATESINPERIOD returns a period of 12 months, starting on the reference date. You should take special care here: when the sales forecast is mapped to, say, the first day of the month, and the reference date happens to be the second of the month, the sales forecast for that month will not be included in the result. It is a business question whether this is OK or whether you would prefer to include the whole month's sales forecast; in the latter case, you could shift the start date for DATESINPERIOD with:

```
EOMONTH(RefDate, -1) + 1
```

The EOMONTH function returns the last day of the month *before* RefDate (because of the -1); we add one day to arrive at the first day of RefDate's month.

The remainder of the formula is straightforward. We subtract the forecast from the reference level but avoid going below zero. What remains is the inventory that is not expected to be shipped in the coming 12 months:

```
    RETURN
    MAX(RefLevel - SalesForecast, 0)
)
```

We now have a DAX measure to compute the quantity of long-lasting inventory. The next step is to assign a value to this inventory. We haven't discussed how to model value in the Power BI model, which is highly dependent on what the costs of a product (or SKU) are. The company may have a standardized, fixed cost for a SKU that can be used for all warehouses, but costs may also differ between warehouses, and may even change over time.

One way to model product costs would be to have a Cost column in each fact table. If this is the case, you could simply replace each occurrence of Quantity with Cost in the Long-lasting Inventory Qty measure to create a Long-lasting Inventory Value measure. This can only be done, of course, when it is possible to provide these columns in a way that makes sense, business-wise.

Here, we will cover the option to have a Cost column in the SKU table; this means that our company has a fixed SKU cost globally. As we do our calculations on the level of city/product combinations, this means that when we compute the total value of inventory, we must aggregate multiple SKUs for each city/product combination. After all, a product is a grouping of multiple SKUs.

The challenge (whichever way you model things) is that the inventory quantity for a product in 12 months, which we calculated in the Long-lasting Inventory Qty measure, is based on the actual (reference) level and the sales forecast. The sales forecast, however, is only available at the product level, which means that we have no way of knowing how many of each specific SKU will be in stock in 12 months. How then can we compute the value when different SKUs have different costs?

We must decide upon a way to estimate the average SKU cost as accurately as possible. For this calculation, we will take the weighted average SKU cost, taken against the reference inventory. This is the total cost of all SKUs in the reference inventory, divided by the total quantity of that inventory.

The measure again starts by declaring variables:

```
Long-lasting Inventory Value =
VAR RefDate =
    CALCULATE(
        MAX(fInventory[Date]),
        ALL('Calendar'),
        fInventory[Type] = 0
    )
VAR CityProductCombinations =
    CALCULATETABLE(
        SUMMARIZE(
            fInventory,
            Warehouse[City],
            SKU[ProductNr]
        ),
        ALL('Calendar'),
        fInventory[Type] = 0
    )
```

Like before, the calculation is done by iterating over the `CityProductCombinations` table:

```
RETURN
SUMX(
    CityProductCombinations,
    VAR RefLevel =
        CALCULATE(
            SUM(fInventory[Quantity]),
            ALL('Calendar'),
            fInventory[Type] = 0
        )
    VAR SalesForecast =
        CALCULATE(
            SUM(fForecast[Quantity]),
            DATESINPERIOD(
                'Calendar'[Date],
                RefDate,
                12, MONTH
            )
        )
)
```

Next to the `RefLevel` and `SalesForecast` variables used before, which we need to compute the quantity in 12 months, we now compute the weighted average costs:

```
    VAR RefTotalCosts =
        CALCULATE(
            SUMX(
                VALUES(SKU[Cost]),
                SKU[Cost] *
                CALCULATE(
                    SUM(fInventory[Quantity]),
                    ALL('Calendar'),
                    fInventory[Type] = 0
                )
            )
        )
    VAR AvgSKUCost = DIVIDE(RefTotalCosts, RefLevel)
```

The `RefTotalCosts` variable deserves some extra attention here. Note that this variable is evaluated in a row context on the `CityProductCombinations` table, which means that the SKUs are not automatically filtered down to those belonging to the current `Product`. We therefore need to add `CALCULATE` to make sure we only see the correct SKUs.

You can also notice that a SUMX is done over the list of Cost values, not over the list of SKUs. The reason is twofold: if we were to use VALUES(SKU[SKUNr]), the Cost column would not be available for the calculation; and additionally, when multiple SKUs for the current product have the same cost, we have fewer iterations to do by using VALUES(SKU[Cost]). The second CALCULATE in this variable's declaration turns the row context on the table of costs into a filter context, making sure that for each Cost value, the calculation is only done over transactions on a SKU with that cost.

The last part of the formula is straightforward:

```
    RETURN
    MAX(RefLevel – SalesForecast) * AvgSKUCost
)
```

We multiply the quantity of long-lasting inventory by the weighted average cost per SKU in the current (reference) inventory, which should be a fairly accurate value assessment.

Working with forecast-based inventory targets

Earlier in this chapter, we worked with simple inventory targets, stating that inventory for some product in some warehouse should always be at a certain level. In the real world, inventory targets can have a more sophisticated logic. For example:

- For each product, enough items must be in stock to cover 90 days of business run rate.

- For each product, enough items must be in stock to cover the expected business during a product-specific "target horizon."

- For each product, the current level minus the expected shipments in 90 days must be above a certain, product-specific target.

- For each product, the current level minus the expected shipments in a product-specific "target horizon" must be above a certain target.

Now that we know how to calculate expected shipments for any period we choose, it is not difficult to implement these targets. You can either compute the total quantity of products that are below target, the value of missing inventory (and, therefore, the business risk coming from out-of-stock items), or the number of products that are below target. You could also attach a color code: green for products with enough inventory, yellow for products that have enough inventory when warehouses in the same city may help to fulfill demand, and red for products without enough inventory.

As an example, we give the formula for the first target type, for products that are below this target. The formula contains some variables that can be altered to implement other target types. We begin with a definition of the variables `RefDate` and `WarehouseProductCombinations` (using a lower detail level now, as the targets may be warehouse-specific):

```
Inventory vs Target (90 days) low =
VAR RefDate =
    CALCULATE(
        MAX(fInventory[Date]),
        ALL('Calendar'),
        fInventory[Type] = 0
    )
VAR WarehouseSKUCombinations =
    CALCULATETABLE(
        SUMMARIZE(
            fInventory,
            Warehouse[WarehouseNr],
            SKU[ProductNr]
        ),
        ALL('Calendar'),
        fInventory[Type] = 0
    )
```

Within the `SUMX` iterator, we define the variables `RefLevel`, and either `SalesForecast` (which we choose here) or `AvgShipmentsMth` (similar to the extrapolation discussed earlier in this chapter):

```
RETURN
SUMX(
    WarehouseProductCombinations,
    VAR RefLevel =
        CALCULATE(
            SUM(fInventory[Quantity]),
            ALL('Calendar'),
            fInventory[Type] = 0
        )
```

```
    VAR TargetHorizon = 90
    VAR SalesForecast =
        CALCULATE(
            SUM(fForecast[Quantity]),
            DATESINPERIOD(
                'Calendar'[Date],
                RefDate,
                TargetHorizon, DAY
            )
        )
```

We put the 90-day horizon in a variable, and use that variable in the DATESINPERIOD function (with DAY as the unit now). If you needed to implement a product-specific target horizon, you would include a calculation here to retrieve the target horizon for the product at hand. The formula concludes with:

```
    VAR Threshold = 0
    RETURN
    MIN(RefLevel - SalesForecast, Threshold)
```

Here, a Threshold variable is added to easily be able to change from a fixed target (*"expected inventory at target horizon must be larger than zero"*) to a product-specific target (*"expected inventory at target horizon must be larger than this product's threshold"*).

Using linear regression for extrapolating inventory

When using extrapolation to predict future shipments, we have assumed that a constant, average number of shipments per month can be used. The reality could be more complex than that: hopefully, business is growing, but it may be slowing down as well. Rather than working with a constant shipment rate, it would be beneficial to take growth or shrinkage into account.

To do this, you can use linear regression, as shown in the figure below. In Excel, linear regression is a common feature, and a regression line can sometimes be added in Power BI charts too, through the **Analytics** pane for a visual.

There is, however, no built-in way to do linear regression and use the values of the regression line in a DAX calculation.

Figure 2.7.14: A regression line in an Excel chart

Fortunately, for the case of *simple linear regression*, which is linear regression using only one variable, exact mathematical formulas exist to calculate the regression line. In mathematical terms, given a collection of (x, y) pairs, the challenge is to find a function

$$y = a + bx$$

such that the line defined by this function is "closest" to the collection of (x, y) pairs. Without going into the mathematical details, assumptions, and constraints, the values for a and b can be exactly computed from the (x, y) pairs:

$$a = \frac{\sum y - b \sum x}{n}$$

$$b = \left(\sum xy - \frac{\sum x \sum y}{n} \right) / \left(\sum x^2 - \frac{(\sum x)^2}{n} \right)$$

These formulas apply the **least squares** method to optimize the regression line, where n is the number of (x, y) pairs used for the regression.

What are the (*x*, *y*) pairs in our case? We want to do an extrapolation of shipments based on the shipments per month in the last twelve months. We happen to have a YearMonthCtr column in the Calendar table, which can provide the *x* values (it is important that we can do arithmetic on these values). The corresponding *y* values are the shipments in each month.

We will use the same approach as in our simple extrapolation discussed earlier, starting with some variables to retrieve the YearMonthCtr value for the reference inventory, and the list of city/product combinations:

```
Shipments Regression =
VAR RefDate =
CALCULATE(
    MAX(fInventory[Date]),
    ALL('Calendar'),
    fInventory[Type] = 0
)
VAR RefMonthCtr =
CALCULATE(
    MAX('Calendar'[YearMonthCtr]),
    ALL('Calendar'),
    'Calendar'[Date] = RefDate
)
VAR CityProductCombinations =
CALCULATETABLE(
    SUMMARIZE(
        fInventory,
        Warehouse[City],
        SKU[ProductNr]
    ),
    ALL('Calendar'),
    fInventory[Type] = 0
)
```

Note that we strictly do not need to only select city/product combinations that have a reference inventory, as we do here; but we will leave this as it is, as the regression results will be used to predict future inventory in the end, which does not make sense for combinations that do not have a reference inventory.

As usual, we iterate over CityProductCombinations to continue our calculation for one combination at a time. The RefMonthCtr variable and the FirstMonthCtr variable declared in the code below allow us to construct the list of YearMonthCtr values that we want to use for the linear regression; it is simply the list of all YearMonthCtr values between FirstMonthCtr and RefMonthCtr:

```
RETURN
SUMX(
    CityProductCombinations,
    VAR FirstInventoryDate =
    CALCULATE(
        MIN(fInventory[Date]),
        fInventory[Type] = 1,
        fInventory[Quantity] > 0,
        DATESINPERIOD('Calendar'[Date], RefDate, -12, MONTH)
    )
    VAR FirstMonthCtr =
    CALCULATE(
        MIN('Calendar'[YearMonthCtr]),
        ALL('Calendar'),
        'Calendar'[Date] = FirstInventoryDate
    )
    VAR Months =
    FILTER(
        ALL('Calendar'[YearMonthCtr]),
        'Calendar'[YearMonthCtr] >= FirstMonthCtr
        && 'Calendar'[YearMonthCtr] <= RefMonthCtr
    )
```

Note that using DATESINPERIOD with -12 months, the list will normally contain 13 values (as RefDate is somewhere in the middle of a month).

To create our (x, y) pairs, we can add a column to the Month table variable. ALLEXCEPT is needed here, as we need to remove existing filters on Calendar that are still in place but do not want to lose the filter on YearMonthCtr that has just been introduced in the filter context created by CALCULATE. Another thing to deal with is the possibility that there are no shipments in a certain month. If we leave this month in the list, the Shipments value will be treated as zero, which would not be correct.

We therefore use `FILTER` to clean up the (x, y) pairs list:

```
VAR XYPairs =
FILTER(
    ADDCOLUMNS(
        Months,
        "Shipments",
        CALCULATE(
            SUM(fInventory[Quantity]),
            fInventory[Type] = 1,
            fInventory[Quantity] > 0,
            ALLEXCEPT('Calendar', 'Calendar'[YearMonthCtr])
        )
    ),
    NOT(ISBLANK([Shipments]))
)
```

We now have our list of (x, y) pairs as a table with columns `YearMonthCtr` and `Shipments`. When you look at the formulas for the coefficients a and b, it is clear that we need to compute several values from the set of (x, y) pairs: the sum of x, the sum of y, the sum of x times y, the sum of x squared, and the number of pairs. Let us calculate those first:

```
VAR Sum_X = SUMX(XYPairs, [YearMonthCtr])
VAR Sum_Y = SUMX(XYPairs, [Shipments])
VAR Sum_XY = SUMX(XYPairs, [YearMonthCtr] * [Shipments])
VAR Sum_XX = SUMX(XYPairs, [YearMonthCtr] * [YearMonthCtr])
VAR n = COUNTROWS(XYPairs)
```

Now that we have these variables, the regression line coefficients can be computed:

```
VAR b =
DIVIDE(
    Sum_XY - DIVIDE( Sum_X * Sum_Y, n ),
    Sum_XX - DIVIDE( Sum_X * Sum_X, n )
)
VAR a =
DIVIDE(
    Sum_Y - b * Sum_X,
    n
)
```

With *a* and *b* in place, we can compute the extrapolated shipments in any future selection of months by applying the *ax+b* function to values of YearMonthCtr. When multiple YearMonthCtr values are in the selection, the results for these values should be summed:

```
VAR ExtrapolatedShipments =
SUMX(
    VALUES('Calendar'[YearMonthCtr]),
    a + 'Calendar'[YearMonthCtr] * b
)
RETURN
ExtrapolatedShipments
)
```

In the figure below, we have plotted the calculated regression line in comparison with actual shipments for a sample warehouse and product. In this example, the reference date is in July 2021; the regression is therefore done on the shipments between July 2020 and July 2021. From the chart, you can see that there are 8 months with shipments during this period:

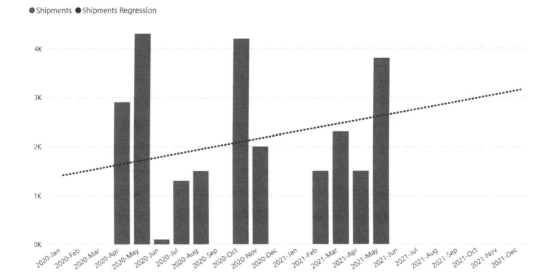

Figure 2.7.15: A regression line calculated in DAX

Remember that in a complete report, the linear regression would be done on a Warehouse/SKU level or higher, depending on your business assumptions. This means that this single measure would perform a lot of linear regression calculations, which may take a while.

Summary

In this chapter, we have dealt with analyzing inventory data, although the kind of analysis in this chapter can be applied to all sorts of status-oriented data.

We have discussed different ways to model this kind of data, how to calculate inventory status at some point in time, and how to compare actuals with targets.

You have also seen different ways to look into the future. As inventory is typically needed to fulfill sales orders, being able to estimate future stock levels is a valuable capability. We have covered creating a future inventory outlook through sales forecasts and through extrapolation based on average shipment volumes. We have also shown you how to do linear regression in DAX, providing a slightly more sophisticated method to predict future shipments and extrapolate current inventory levels to the future.

More advanced ways to extrapolate or predict future inventory than the ones covered in this chapter are possible as well; you could create extrapolations based not only on simply average shipments, but with seasonality taken into account. Or, you could build AI models to incorporate many more variables in predicting future shipments.

In the next and final chapter of this book, we focus on planning personnel based on future workloads with DAX.

2.8
Personnel Planning

For a company selling large projects involving a great number of project members with different roles, it is important to be able to plan how many people are needed at which time. This is, of course, not about the number of individuals; we do the analysis in **FTEs (full-time equivalents)** instead. (Besides, needing 2.5 FTEs sounds a lot better than needing 2.5 people, right?)

This chapter discusses an example of personnel planning for a project-based business. As you will see, only a few DAX measures are needed to compute the global need for personnel. The main complexity is in the large number of context transformations occurring during the calculation.

This chapter covers the following topics:

- The Power BI model for personnel planning
- Calculating sales, both order intake and projected sales over time
- Calculating FTEs needed for projects sold
- Optimizing the Power BI model
- Considering aggregation levels

The Power BI model

The analysis in this chapter is based on the model below.

 You can download the Power BI model for this chapter, 2.8 Personnel Planning.pbix, from this link: https://github. com/PacktPublishing/Extreme-DAX/tree/main/Chapter2.8.

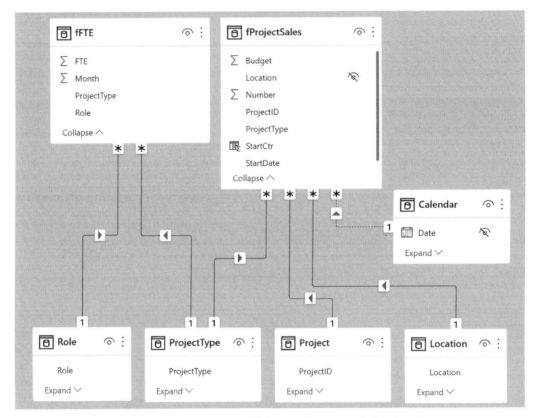

Figure 2.8.1: Power BI model diagram for personnel planning

The model contains two main fact tables:

- fProjectSales contains projects sold. The primary information in the table is the project type, which is the main characteristic of a project. The table also contains a Number column, which denotes the size of the project in terms of the project type. For example, a project can have type A and number 3, meaning that the project is comparable to three typical type A projects. The table contains the project budget as well.

- fFTE is a fact table with information about project types. It is an atypical fact table, as it does not contain any data that is strictly time-related. Instead, for each project type it contains a list of roles and the number of FTEs needed in that role for each month during the project (where we start counting at month 0). The figure below shows a sample of the data in fFTE; note that, implicitly, a project type determines the duration of a project of that type in months.

ProjectType	Month	FTE	Role
A1	9	0,50	Project Manager
A1	10	0,50	Project Manager
A1	11	0,50	Project Manager
A1	12	0,50	Project Manager
A1	13	0,50	Project Manager
A1	14	0,50	Project Manager
A1	15	0,50	Project Manager
A1	2	1,00	Analyst
A1	3	1,00	Analyst
A1	4	1,00	Analyst
A1	5	1,00	Analyst
A1	6	1,00	Analyst
A1	1	0,20	Controller
A1	2	0,20	Controller
A1	3	0,20	Controller

Figure 2.8.2: Sample data from fFTE

The combination of the two fact tables allows the determination of how many FTEs a project needs in a specific month. For example, if a project with project type A1 and Number 2 starts in February 2022, two full-time analysts are needed for the project from March 2022 onward until July 2022.

The fFTE fact table is related to filter tables Role and ProjectType. The fProjectSales fact table is related to ProjectType as well, but can have other relationships like, in our example, Project and Location. The model could be extended with all kinds of filter tables related to fProjectSales, such as Sales Unit, Customer, and others. When we calculate the total number of FTEs needed, we should be able to filter the result on role and on month but also on location, project, project type, and any other filter that selects specific projects.

Note that we made the relationship between fProjectSales and Calendar *inactive*. This is done because most calculations will probably not group projects by their start date, but spread results over a period of time *beginning* with the start date of a project. The inactive relationship will save us a lot of ALL('Calendar') clauses in our DAX code.

The model allows for complex project configurations; for example, a project may be equivalent to three type A1 projects in Amsterdam, plus two B1 projects in London. The DAX calculations in this chapter will have to be designed to support project configurations like these; but as you will see, we will need nothing specific to achieve this.

Calculating sales

To start with a straightforward measure, let us calculate the total sales amount:

```
Total Sales =
CALCULATE(
    SUM(fProjectSales[Budget]),
    USERELATIONSHIP(fProjectSales[StartDate], 'Calendar'[Date])
)
```

As USERELATIONSHIP activates the relationship between the fProjectSales table and the Calendar table on the StartDate column, this measure returns the amount sold in each month. While this is valuable information in terms of order intake, when working with projects that may span multiple years, another valuable insight would be to have the project budget spread out over the duration of the project.

There are several ways to do this. The easiest would be to divide the project budget by the duration of the project, and take that amount for each month that the project will run. This assumes that the income from the project will be evenly spread over the months.

While the duration of a project could be derived from the fFTE table, a more convenient approach would be to have a duration column in the ProjectType table; after all, the duration is a fixed attribute of a project type. As the fFTE table starts counting months from zero, let us just take the highest month number, which is then one less than the actual duration of the project type. To avoid confusion, we will name this column MaxMonth:

```
MaxMonth = CALCULATE(MAX(fFTE[Month]))
```

Note that we have to use CALCULATE here to make sure we get the largest Month value for the corresponding project types, not for all project types.

Let us assume that all calculations can be done on a month-by-month basis. The first month of the project, which is the month in which the start date of the project falls, is month zero; the last month is month zero plus MaxMonth.

 For the calculations in this chapter, it is important to understand the consequences of this assumption. As an example, consider a project with February 15, 2022, as the start date, and a MaxMonth value of 3. This MaxMonth value means that we have four months of fFTE data, for February, March, April, and May, 2022. The project budget will be spread over these four months. You could be tempted to think that the *duration* of this project is four months, meaning that the project would run until June 15; however, the month of June does not count for our calculations.

This means that, given a selection on the Calendar, a project is active during (part of) that time period when:

- The first month of the project starts before the last date in the Calendar selection;
- *And* the project's last month ends after the first date in the selection.

The figure below illustrates this schematically for a few projects with MaxMonth = 2.

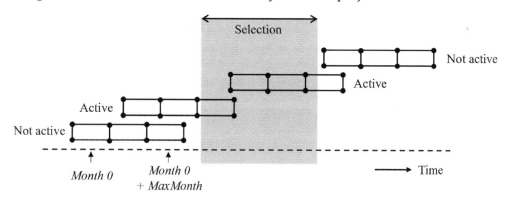

Figure 2.8.3: Active projects

Our first challenge is to determine the projects that are active during the selection on the Calendar table. The DAX formula below starts by filtering the fProjectSales table, implementing the logic outlined above:

```
Sales (over time) =
VAR MaxDate = MAX('Calendar'[Date])
VAR MinDate = MIN('Calendar'[Date])
RETURN
SUMX(
    FILTER(
        fProjectSales,
        EOMONTH(fProjectSales[StartDate], -1) + 1
        <= MaxDate
        && EOMONTH(
            fProjectSales[StartDate], RELATED(ProjectType[MaxMonth]
        ) >= MinDate
    ),
```

Let us pause here for a while and see what is happening. After storing the first and last days of the Calendar selection in variables, we traverse the fProjectSales table and apply the logic to retrieve the projects active within the selected period. The EOMONTH function adds a number of months to a date value, in this case fProjectSales[StartDate], then moves that date to the end of the month. The first EOMONTH expression returns the last day of the month preceding the start date, and adding 1 day gives us the first day of month zero. Adding MaxMonth in the second EOMONTH expression brings us to the last day of the last month of the project.

Now that we have selected the right projects, we can continue calculating the desired results:

```
    VAR ProjectBudget = fProjectSales[Budget]
    VAR ProjectStartDate = fProjectSales[StartDate]
    VAR ProjectMaxMonth = RELATED(ProjectType[MaxMonth])
    VAR MonthlyBudget =
        DIVIDE(
            ProjectBudget,
            ProjectMaxMonth + 1
        )
    VAR ActiveMonths =
    CALCULATETABLE(
        DISTINCT('Calendar'[YearMonthCtr]),
        KEEPFILTERS(
```

```
                'Calendar'[Date] >= ProjectStartDate
                && 'Calendar'[Date] <=
                EOMONTH(ProjectStartDate, ProjectMaxMonth)
            )
        )
        RETURN
        COUNTROWS(ActiveMonths) * MonthlyBudget
    )
```

After declaring the variables containing the values we need for the calculation, the `ActiveMonths` variable is the list of months (or `YearMonthCtr` values – this being a continuously increasing counter at the month level) in the `Calendar` selection that are within the duration of the project: between the start date and the end date. Note the use of `KEEPFILTERS` here to avoid losing any filters on the `Calendar` table; in this way, we get the overlap between the `Calendar` selection and the project duration.

The end result by project is the number of active months multiplied by the monthly project budget, which is the part of the total project budget expected to be spent during the selected period.

The figure below shows the difference between the `Total Sales` and `Sales (over time)` measures, for two sample projects:

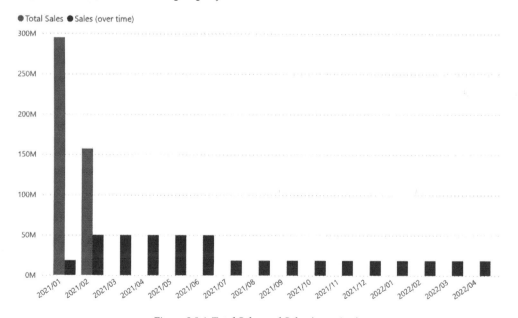

Figure 2.8.4: Total Sales and Sales (over time)

In the chart, one project can be seen that starts in January 2021. The last month of this project is April 2022, and an evenly distributed amount is reported in every month between. A second project starts in February 2021, with a smaller total budget. The duration of the project is shorter, though; the budget is distributed over 5 months, indicating a MaxMonth value of 4.

Optimizing the sales calculation

The flaw in the Sales (over time) measure is, as you may have spotted already, that we iterate over a fact table. While you may assume that the number of multi-million projects sold is not super high, it is still worthwhile to see if we can change that.

The clear indicator here is the use of RELATED to retrieve information from a filter table in the process. Whenever your table aggregation contains the RELATED function, you should think about whether you can iterate over the filter table instead. In our case, the question is whether we can do the same calculation while iterating over the ProjectType table, and more specifically, the (unique) values of ProjectType[MaxMonth].

If we were to iterate over VALUES(ProjectType[MaxMonth]), we could calculate the total budget for all projects with that duration at once. Unfortunately, that does not help us completely: the calculation of the overlap between selected months and project duration months is not possible with only the duration.

For this alternative approach to work, we would also need to take the Calendar selection into account. Instead of doing the calculation for all months in the selection at once, we can go through the selection month by month. So, we iterate over the combinations of MaxMonth and YearMonthCtr values that are found in the query context. The table with combinations can be created using the CROSSJOIN function:

```
Sales (over time, optimized) =
VAR MonthDurationCombinations =
    CROSSJOIN(
        DISTINCT(ProjectType[MaxMonth]),
        DISTINCT('Calendar'[YearMonthCtr])
    )
RETURN
SUMX(
    MonthDurationCombinations,
```

```
    VAR ThisMaxMonth = ProjectType[MaxMonth]
    VAR ThisYearMonthCtr = 'Calendar'[YearMonthCtr]
    VAR MaxDate =
    CALCULATE(
        MAX('Calendar'[Date]),
        ALL('Calendar'),
        'Calendar'[YearMonthCtr] = ThisYearMonthCtr
    )
    VAR MinDate =
    CALCULATE(
        MIN('Calendar'[Date]),
        ALL('Calendar'),
        'Calendar'[YearMonthCtr] = ThisYearMonthCtr - ThisMaxMonth
    )
    VAR TotalBudget =
    CALCULATE(
        SUM(fProjectSales[Budget]),
        fProjectSales[StartDate] <= MaxDate
        && fProjectSales[StartDate] >= MinDate
    )
    RETURN
    DIVIDE(TotalBudget, ThisMaxMonth + 1)
)
```

For each combination in the `MonthDurationCombinations` table, we first store the values in the `ThisMaxMonth` and `ThisYearMonthCtr` variables. Next, we need to select the projects active in this particular month. We can do that using their start date, for which we have to derive the earliest, `MinDate`, and latest, `MaxDate`, possible start dates for a project to be active. The latest possible start date is, of course, the last day in this month; any project starting later is not yet active in this month. As for the earliest start dates, we can subtract `ThisMaxMonth` from the `YearMonthCtr` to find the earliest month possible. Any project starting earlier will have finished before this month starts.

To illustrate this, the example in the figure below shows, for month 66 and `MaxMonth` 2, that the earliest possible start date of an active project is the first day of month 64. Any day earlier, like the upper project, and the month zero of the project is month 63 and there is no budget left for month 66.

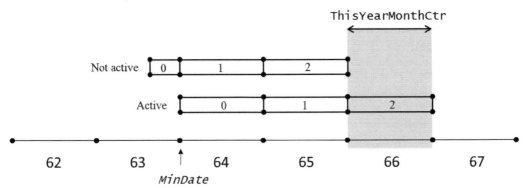

Figure 2.8.5: Finding the earliest possible start date

With this, we can compute the total budget of all active projects at once and, as the calculation is done by `MaxMonth` value, it is easy to divide this by the current duration and retrieve the budget projected for the current month.

 The calculations involving `MaxMonth` are the reason why we use the month counter here, and not simply a month number: with the counter, we don't have to worry about year boundaries.

The number of iterations that `SUMX` has to do is equal to the number of different durations multiplied by the number of months in the query context. This will typically be only a small number and may be far better than traversing through all projects.

Calculating FTEs needed

Now that we have a view of the financial flows over time, let us turn toward analyzing the resources needed to staff the projects. As with the sales calculations, we will do this on a per-month basis, as the `fFTE` table provides this information by month.

The result we are aiming for should make it possible to create output like in the figure below:

Year	2021											
Location	1	2	3	4	5	6	7	8	9	10	11	12
⊟ **Amsterdam**	**1.5**	**2.1**	**5.1**	**5.1**	**8.1**	**20.1**	**29.1**	**26.1**	**26.1**	**26.1**	**26.1**	**26.1**
⊟ **P233-X18**	**1.5**	**2.1**	**5.1**	**5.1**	**8.1**	**20.1**	**29.1**	**26.1**	**26.1**	**26.1**	**26.1**	**26.1**
Analyst			3.0	3.0	3.0	3.0	3.0					
Controller		0.6	0.6	0.6	0.6	0.6	0.6	0.6	0.6	0.6	0.6	0.6
Engineer 1					3.0	9.0	9.0	9.0	9.0	9.0	9.0	9.0
Engineer 2						6.0	15.0	15.0	15.0	15.0	15.0	15.0
Project Manager	1.5	1.5	1.5	1.5	1.5	1.5	1.5	1.5	1.5	1.5	1.5	1.5
⊟ **Dublin**					**4.5**	**6.3**	**15.3**	**15.3**	**24.3**	**60.3**	**87.3**	**78.3**
⊟ **P116-S**					**4.5**	**6.3**	**15.3**	**15.3**	**24.3**	**60.3**	**87.3**	**78.3**
Analyst							9.0	9.0	9.0	9.0	9.0	
Controller						1.8	1.8	1.8	1.8	1.8	1.8	1.8
Engineer 1									9.0	27.0	27.0	27.0
Engineer 2										18.0	45.0	45.0
Project Manager					4.5	4.5	4.5	4.5	4.5	4.5	4.5	4.5
Total	**1.5**	**2.1**	**5.1**	**5.1**	**12.6**	**26.4**	**44.4**	**41.4**	**50.4**	**86.4**	**113.4**	**104.4**

Figure 2.8.6: FTEs needed by location, project, role, and month

For a few projects, you see the number of FTEs per role that are needed in each specific month. The calculation to achieve this is quite complicated, though the formula itself is not that long. We will go through it step by step.

Let us first start with two basic aggregations:

```
TotalFTE = SUM(fFTE[FTE])
```

```
TotalNumber = SUM(fProjectSales[Number])
```

Remember that the Number column denotes the size of a project relative to its type: for a project with Number = 3, we expect three times the FTEs associated with its project type.

The query context for the visual above contains filters on Year, Month, Location, Project, and Role (except for totals and subtotals). Of these, Year and Month are fundamental: for each project active in that month, we need to determine which month it is within the duration of the project, and how many FTEs are needed in that month.

The other filters simply select a subset of projects or FTEs. The measure therefore starts by iterating over the different months, again through the YearMonthCtr value:

```
FTEs needed =
SUMX(
    VALUES('Calendar'[YearMonthCtr]),
    VAR ThisYearMonthCtr = 'Calendar'[YearMonthCtr]
    RETURN
```

We will not bother with the actual table aggregation (SUMX or something else) for now; rather, we will work in a single-month context to test the outcomes of the measure.

The rest of the calculation heavily depends on the project type: it determines the FTE profile over the months of the project, as well as the duration of the project. Let's iterate over the project types as well, and after we have zoomed in to one project type, we could go over all projects of that type, determine whether they are active in the current (in the iteration) month, and determine which month within the duration of the project we are looking at. With that, we can retrieve the FTE number from the fFTE table:

```
    SUMX(
        ProjectType,
        SUMX(
            fProjectSales,
            VAR ThisStartDate = fProjectSales[StartDate]
            VAR ThisStartCtr =
                CALCULATE(
                    MAX('Calendar'[YearMonthCtr]),
                    ALL('Calendar'),
                    'Calendar'[Date] = ThisStartDate
                )
            VAR ProjectMonth = ThisYearMonthCtr - ThisStartCtr
```

We iterate over fProjectSales and, for each project, store the start date in a variable. The ThisStartCtr variable is the month counter corresponding to the start date. The ProjectMonth variable computes which month in the project's duration the current month is, by simply subtracting ThisStartCtr from the counter of the current month. Note that ProjectMonth can be a negative value; this means that the project has not started yet. It can also be a number larger than the duration of the project. In both cases, no FTE number should be returned. Continuing with the last part of the calculation:

```
                VAR FTEsNeeded =
                    CALCULATE(
                        [TotalFTE],
                        fFTE[Month] = ProjectMonth
                    )
                    RETURN
                    FTEsNeeded * fProjectSales[Number]
            )
        )
    )
```

With the FTEsNeeded variable, we compute the sum of FTE values for the project month, which we then multiply by the Number value from fProjectSales for the end result.

There is one critical flaw in this formula so far, which you may have spotted (if so, well done!). The problem is this: the SUMX(fProjectSales,... part is evaluated *in row context* of the ProjectType table. And in this row context, the relationships do not have any filters to propagate. In other words, the fProjectSales table here is the complete table, rather than only the rows that are associated with the current project type!

The effect of this is that for each project type, projects are evaluated that are not linked to that project type. When you follow the code, you will see that the ThisStartDate, ThisStartCtr, and ProjectMonth variables are all evaluated correctly for these projects. However, the definition of the FTEsNeeded variable involves CALCULATE, which turns the row context into a filter context. The result is the FTEs needed for this project, even though it may not have the current project type. In other words: the results for a project are returned for all project types.

Below is some sample output using this flawed measure. The results are four times as high as they should be, corresponding to the four project types in our model:

| Year | 2021 | | | | | | | | | | | |
Location	1	2	3	4	5	6	7	8	9	10	11	12
⊟ **Amsterdam**	**6.0**	**8.4**	**20.4**	**20.4**	**32.4**	**80.4**	**116.4**	**104.4**	**104.4**	**104.4**	**104.4**	**104.4**
⊟ **P233-X18**	**6.0**	**8.4**	**20.4**	**20.4**	**32.4**	**80.4**	**116.4**	**104.4**	**104.4**	**104.4**	**104.4**	**104.4**
Analyst			12.0	12.0	12.0	12.0	12.0					
Controller		2.4	2.4	2.4	2.4	2.4	2.4	2.4	2.4	2.4	2.4	2.4
Engineer 1				12.0	36.0	36.0	36.0	36.0	36.0	36.0	36.0	36.0
Engineer 2					24.0	60.0	60.0	60.0	60.0	60.0	60.0	60.0
Project Manager	6.0	6.0	6.0	6.0	6.0	6.0	6.0	6.0	6.0	6.0	6.0	6.0
⊟ **Dublin**						**18.0**	**25.2**	**61.2**	**61.2**	**97.2**	**241.2**	**349.2**	**313.2**
⊟ **P116-S**						**18.0**	**25.2**	**61.2**	**61.2**	**97.2**	**241.2**	**349.2**	**313.2**
Analyst							36.0	36.0	36.0	36.0	36.0	
Controller						7.2	7.2	7.2	7.2	7.2	7.2	7.2
Engineer 1									36.0	108.0	108.0	108.0
Engineer 2										72.0	180.0	180.0
Project Manager						18.0	18.0	18.0	18.0	18.0	18.0	18.0	18.0
Total	**6.0**	**8.4**	**20.4**	**20.4**	**50.4**	**105.6**	**177.6**	**165.6**	**201.6**	**345.6**	**453.6**	**417.6**

Figure 2.8.7: Incorrect FTE results

The solution for this problem is straightforward: all we have to do is to move from a row context to a filter context while iterating over the ProjectType table. This can be done by simply adding CALCULATE around the expression evaluated:

```
FTEs Needed 2 =
SUMX(
    VALUES('Calendar'[YearMonthCtr]),
    VAR ThisYearMonthCtr = 'Calendar'[YearMonthCtr]
    RETURN
    SUMX(
        ProjectType,
        CALCULATE(
            SUMX(
                fProjectSales,
                VAR ThisStartDate = fProjectSales[StartDate]
```

```
            VAR ThisStartCtr =
                CALCULATE(
                    MAX('Calendar'[YearMonthCtr]),
                    ALL('Calendar'),
                    'Calendar'[Date] = ThisStartDate
                )
            VAR ProjectMonth = ThisYearMonthCtr - ThisStartCtr
            VAR FTEsNeeded =
                CALCULATE(
                    [SumFTE],
                    fFTE[Month] = ProjectMonth
                )
            RETURN
            FTEsNeeded * fProjectSales[Number]
        )
      )
    )
  )
```

With this formula, the FTE results are now calculated correctly. In fact, we created *Figure 2.8.6* using this measure.

 Generally, adding CALCULATE comes with its own issues. Wherever you have directly referenced a column value from the table to iterate over, which is a common thing to do, you will get an error after adding CALCULATE. This is because while you can directly retrieve the value of a column in a row context, in a filter context this is not possible, even if there is only one value there. You will have to aggregate the column using a basic aggregation.

Considering totals

We now have a working FTE calculation that returns valid results by month. What about the totals this measure returns?

As you can see in the output in the figure below, the total by month is nicely computed to be the sum of the FTEs per location, project, or role. The total of the results by month, however, does not make much sense, being the sum of the monthly FTEs.

This comes from the first SUMX in the formula, which calculates by month and adds up all results for the total.

Year	2021													Total
Location	1	2	3	4	5	6	7	8	9	10	11	12	**Total**	
⊟ **Amsterdam**	**1.5**	**2.1**	**5.1**	**5.1**	**8.1**	**20.1**	**29.1**	**26.1**	**26.1**	**26.1**	**26.1**	**26.1**	**201.6**	**201.6**
⊟ **P233-X18**	**1.5**	**2.1**	**5.1**	**5.1**	**8.1**	**20.1**	**29.1**	**26.1**	**26.1**	**26.1**	**26.1**	**26.1**	**201.6**	**201.6**
Analyst			3.0	3.0	3.0	3.0	3.0						**15.0**	**15.0**
Controller		0.6	0.6	0.6	0.6	0.6	0.6	0.6	0.6	0.6	0.6	0.6	**6.6**	**6.6**
Engineer 1					3.0	9.0	9.0	9.0	9.0	9.0	9.0	9.0	**66.0**	**66.0**
Engineer 2						6.0	15.0	15.0	15.0	15.0	15.0	15.0	**96.0**	**96.0**
Project Manager	1.5	1.5	1.5	1.5	1.5	1.5	1.5	1.5	1.5	1.5	1.5	1.5	**18.0**	**18.0**
⊟ **Dublin**					**4.5**	**6.3**	**15.3**	**15.3**	**24.3**	**60.3**	**87.3**	**78.3**	**291.6**	**291.6**
⊟ **P116-S**					**4.5**	**6.3**	**15.3**	**15.3**	**24.3**	**60.3**	**87.3**	**78.3**	**291.6**	**291.6**
Analyst							9.0	9.0	9.0	9.0	9.0		**45.0**	**45.0**
Controller					1.8	1.8	1.8	1.8	1.8	1.8	1.8		**12.6**	**12.6**
Engineer 1									9.0	27.0	27.0	27.0	**90.0**	**90.0**
Engineer 2										18.0	45.0	45.0	**108.0**	**108.0**
Project Manager					4.5	4.5	4.5	4.5	4.5	4.5	4.5	4.5	**36.0**	**36.0**
Total	**1.5**	**2.1**	**5.1**	**5.1**	**12.6**	**26.4**	**44.4**	**41.4**	**50.4**	**86.4**	**113.4**	**104.4**	**493.2**	**493.2**

Figure 2.8.8: FTE result including column totals

To return better total results, we must change this. *How* to change it is more a business decision than a technical problem. You could be interested in the peak capacity, in which case you should replace SUMX(VALUES('Calendar'[YearMonthCtr]) with MAXX(VALUES('Calendar'[YearMonthCtr]). If you wanted to get insight into the general need for personnel, using AVERAGEX(VALUES('Calendar'[YearMonthCtr]) would be a good option as well.

Optimizing the FTE calculation

Like the sales measure earlier in this chapter, the FTE calculation as we have it now suffers from another problem: it iterates over our main fact table. It is worthwhile to ask ourselves if this can be improved.

One easy improvement would be not to iterate over the fProjectSales table as a whole, but to compress the table by only looking at the unique combinations of fields needed. If you analyze the formula, you will find that we use only two fields from the fProjectSales table: fProjectSales[StartDate] and fProjectSales[Number].

The SUMMARIZE function can be used to retrieve only these columns:

```
SUMMARIZE(
    fProjectSales,
    fProjectSales[StartDate]),
    fProjectSales[Number]
)
```

In the measure formula, we can replace the SUMX(fProjectSales, ... with a SUMX over this SUMMARIZE expression.

 You can find the measure using SUMMARIZE in the model file for this chapter as FTEs needed 2 (with SUMMARIZE).

In a context without any filters, the total number of iterations the measure processes now equals the number of months, multiplied by the number of project types, multiplied by the number of unique start dates per project type, multiplied by the number of unique Number values per project type.

You may even go one step further; as the Number column is only used as a multiplier for the FTE value from the fFTE table, we may instead use the total of the Number values for appropriate projects:

```
SUMMARIZE(
    fProjectSales,
    fProjectSales[StartDate],
    "TotalNumber", SUM(fProjectSales[Number])
)
```

Here, we use the option in SUMMARIZE to add a calculated expression to the resulting table. Using this table, we iterate over all unique start dates for projects of the specific project type. The last step in the formula cannot, of course, directly reference the Number column now; indeed, the table does not contain a Number column anymore. Instead, refer to the TotalNumber column, in other words:

```
FTEsNeeded * [TotalNumber]
```

Instead of:

```
FTEsNeeded * fProjectSales[Number]
```

With this change, the maximum number of iterations for the measure is the number of months, multiplied by the number of project types, multiplied by the number of unique start dates per project type.

 In this model file, these changes can be found in the FTEs needed 2 (with TotalNumber) measure.

This is already a huge improvement. But can we optimize any further? In fact, we can. We can leave the fProjectSales table untouched and focus on the fFTE table instead. Stated differently: instead of going over the fProjectSales table, or a summarization of it, and retrieving the corresponding FTE amount (in the FTEsNeeded variable), we can go over the fFTE table and retrieve the corresponding Number amount from fProjectSales. The structure of the formula becomes a bit different:

```
FTEs Needed (through fFTE) =
SUMX(
    VALUES('Calendar'[YearMonthCtr]),
    VAR ThisYearMonthCtr = 'Calendar'[YearMonthCtr]
    RETURN
    SUMX(
        ProjectType,
        VAR FTEMonths = CALCULATETABLE(VALUES(fFTE[Month]))
        RETURN
```

For each project type, we retrieve the list of Month values from fFTE. Note that we need to use CALCULATETABLE here, as we are in row context and fFTE will not be filtered otherwise:

```
        SUMX(
            FTEMonths,
            VAR ThisFTEMonth = fFTE[Month]
            VAR MaxDate =
                CALCULATE(
                    MAX('Calendar'[Date]),
                    ALL('Calendar'),
                    'Calendar'[YearMonthCtr] =
                            ThisYearMonthCtr - ThisFTEMonth
                )
```

```
        VAR MinDate =
            CALCULATE(
                MIN('Calendar'[Date]),
                ALL('Calendar'),
                'Calendar'[YearMonthCtr] =
                        ThisYearMonthCtr - ThisFTEMonth
            )
        VAR TotalNumber =
            CALCULATE(
                SUM(fProjectSales[Number]),
                fProjectSales[StartDate] >= MinDate
                && fProjectSales[StartDate] <= MaxDate
            )
        VAR TotalFTE =
            CALCULATE(
                SUM(fFTE[FTE])
            )
        RETURN
        TotalNumber * TotalFTE
    )
  )
)
```

For each Month value from fFTE, we now need to compute the total of the Number column for the corresponding projects. So, what are the corresponding projects? As an example, for ThisFTEMonth = 3, we need to find the projects for which ThisYearMonthCtr is their third month. This is equivalent to finding projects with a start date in the month with counter value ThisYearMonthCtr - ThisFTEMonth. To easily determine which start dates are in that month, we rework that specific counter value into dates; this is what the MaxDate and MinDate variables are used for.

The simple aggregation of FTE values in the TotalFTE variable takes the current project type and month into account automatically, as CALCULATE creates a filter context including filters for the outer SUMX iterations. Additionally, a filter on the Role table impacts the TotalFTE result as well, while filters that act on the fProjectSales table, like Location, impact the TotalNumber result. This means that we still have a calculation returning results that can be filtered by any attribute available.

The number of iterations the measure has to go through is now the number of months, multiplied by the number of project types, multiplied by the number of months per project type. The best option out of the different optimizations discussed here depends on what the date in the model looks like.

For instance, if there are many project types for very long durations, but only a few projects, the first measure may be the best; this one simply iterates on the projects and will be ready in a few iterations. However, in another scenario, you may expect the number of projects to be significantly higher than the number of project types and other supporting data, and therefore, the optimized measures presented here will make a difference.

Optimizing the Power BI model

While working your way through the measures discussed in this chapter, you may have noticed that we do a lot with the YearMonthCtr column in the Calendar table. Additionally, we do a lot of translations from a project's start date to the corresponding month counter.

Because of this, we have an opportunity to further optimize our solution, while making it easier to understand and maintain, by doing this translation beforehand. This is a case where a calculated column could indeed be appropriate – although it would still be good to consider creating this column using Power Query.

For now, let's create a calculated column in fProjectSales that contains the YearMonthCtr value corresponding to the project's start date:

```
StartCtr =
VAR ThisStartDate = [StartDate]
RETURN
CALCULATE(
    MAX('Calendar'[YearMonthCtr]),
    'Calendar'[Date] = ThisStartDate
)
```

With the new StartCtr column, many of the formulas become a lot easier. The optimized Sales measure would now look like this:

```
Sales (over time, further optimized) =
VAR MonthDurationCombinations =
    CROSSJOIN(
        DISTINCT(ProjectType[MaxMonth]),
        DISTINCT('Calendar'[YearMonthCtr])
    )
RETURN
SUMX(
```

```
        MonthDurationCombinations,
        VAR ThisMaxMonth = ProjectType[MaxMonth]
        VAR ThisYearMonthCtr = 'Calendar'[YearMonthCtr]
        VAR TotalBudget =
        CALCULATE(
            SUM(fProjectSales[Budget]),
            fProjectSales[StartCtr] <= ThisYearMonthCtr
            && fProjectSales[StartCtr] >=
                ThisYearMonthCtr - ThisMaxMonth
        )
        RETURN
        DIVIDE(TotalBudget, ThisMaxMonth + 1)
)
```

Instead of comparing the StartDate column with the first and last date in the current month, we can now simply compare the StartCtr column with the first and last YearMonthCtr values. We no longer have to define the StartDate or EndDate variables.

The FTE calculation becomes easier as well. Instead of (in the FTEs needed 2 (with SUMMARIZE) measure) summarizing the fProjectSales table on StartDate and Number and computing the counter value for each StartDate, we now summarize on StartCtr and Number; we can find the correct set of projects for each YearMontCtr value without having to translate a StartDate to a counter:

```
FTEs Needed 2 (with SUMMARIZE, further optimized) =
SUMX(
    VALUES('Calendar'[YearMonthCtr]),
    VAR ThisYearMonthCtr = 'Calendar'[YearMonthCtr]
    RETURN
    SUMX(
        ProjectType,
        CALCULATE(
            SUMX(
                SUMMARIZE(
                        fProjectSales,
                        fProjectSales[StartCtr],
                        "TotalNumber", SUM(fProjectSales[Number])
                ),
                VAR ThisStartCtr = fProjectSales[StartCtr]
                VAR ProjectMonth = ThisYearMonthCtr - ThisStartCtr
```

```
                    VAR FTEsNeeded =
                        CALCULATE(
                            [SumFTE],
                            fFTE[Month] = ProjectMonth
                        )
                    RETURN
                    FTEsNeeded * [TotalNumber]
                )
            )
        )
    )
```

Likewise, the FTE needed (through fFTE) measure, which iterates over the
fFTE[Month] values, becomes more readable. Again, we don't have to define MinDate
and MaxDate variables to compare a project's StartDate with; instead, the comparison
is performed directly on the counter:

```
FTEs Needed (through fFTE, further optimized) =
SUMX(
    VALUES('Calendar'[YearMonthCtr]),
    VAR ThisYearMonthCtr = 'Calendar'[YearMonthCtr]
    RETURN
    SUMX(
            ProjectType,
            VAR FTEMonths = CALCULATETABLE(VALUES(fFTE[Month]))
            RETURN
            SUMX(
             FTEMonths,
                VAR ThisFTEMonth = fFTE[Month]
                VAR ThisStartCtr = ThisYearMonthCtr - ThisFTEMonth
                VAR TotalNumber =
                    CALCULATE(
                        SUM(fProjectSales[Number]),
                        fProjectSales[StartCtr] = ThisStartCtr
                    )
                VAR TotalFTE =
                    CALCULATE(
                            SUM(fFTE[FTE])
```

```
                )
            RETURN
            TotalNumber * TotalFTE
        )
    )
)
```

Not only is the code shorter, but you can also expect better performance, as the date to counter translation is not needed anymore.

Considering aggregation levels

The FTE calculation, as we have designed it, computes the FTEs needed at the level of project type. This means that we simply add the FTE numbers for all projects with the same type. It is a business consideration as to whether this is what the organization really wants.

For example, if an A1 project in Paris and an A1 project in London will run at the same time and each needs a 0.5 FTE project manager, we need 1 full-time project manager in total. While this is mathematically correct, you may argue that a single project manager will not be able to manage both projects. We may need boots on the ground, which practically excludes having someone travel between Paris and London all the time. The result would be that we need, in fact, two project managers.

The simple solution to this would be to do the calculation on a by-location basis, adding another iteration to the measure. However, even if we compute 0.5 FTE twice, the end result is still 1 FTE. You can change this by rounding the result per location up to a whole number. We reuse the latest, optimized measure:

```
FTEs Needed (by location) =
SUMX(
    Location,
    ROUNDUP([FTEs needed (through fFTE, further optimized)], 0)
)
```

The table below shows the results of the two measures side by side.

Year	2021	
Role	FTEs needed (through fFTE, further optimized)	FTEs needed (by Location)
⊟ **Analyst**	**60.0**	**60**
⊞ Amsterdam	15.0	15
⊞ Dublin	45.0	45
⊟ **Controller**	**19.2**	**20**
⊞ Amsterdam	6.6	7
⊞ Dublin	12.6	13
⊟ **Engineer 1**	**156.0**	**156**
⊞ Amsterdam	66.0	66
⊞ Dublin	90.0	90
⊟ **Engineer 2**	**204.0**	**204**
⊞ Amsterdam	96.0	96
⊞ Dublin	108.0	108
⊟ **Project Manager**	**54.0**	**54**
⊞ Amsterdam	18.0	18
⊞ Dublin	36.0	36
Total	**493.2**	**494**

Figure 2.8.9: FTEs needed by Location

This is truly a business question, as you could do the same thing on any level. For example, would it be possible for someone to act both as a project manager and as an analyst on the same project, or on different projects? If not, you may want to change the calculation to a by-role aggregation and round the results appropriately. The drawback of this, however, is that it becomes more difficult for the report user to understand what the meaning of the result is.

The learning from this is that you should find a balance between calculating sophisticated results and providing insights that the user will understand. A well-designed report will help with that by not only providing the end result, but also allowing the user to dive into the details and see why the result is what it is.

Summary

In this chapter, we have discussed ways to analyze the need for professionals to carry out projects. From a technical perspective, you have learned ways to work with multiple fact tables that must be considered in combination to provide useful results.

The challenge is not only to come up with correct results, but to find the optimal way to compute those results as well. Starting with a calculation per project, with an iteration over the `fProjectSales` fact table in our model, the next step is to consider possible ways to minimize the work done by not iterating over a fact table, but over either filter tables or a summarization of a fact table.

* * *

With this chapter, the book comes to an end. You have come a long way and seen many different business scenarios, as well as a diversity of DAX techniques. If we were to summarize the message of this book as a whole, and *Part 2* in particular, a number of conclusions come to mind:

- The possibilities in what can be done with DAX are endless.

- Using a Power BI model, a well-structured model is foundational, but the power of DAX goes way beyond that. Do not solve in data what you can do in DAX measures!

- Context is everything. Every advanced solution starts with considering the context in which results are needed, the context that will deliver those results, and how to transform one into the other. Virtually any problem with DAX results is solved by studying the context first.

- Most of the scenarios in *Part 2* of this book involve DAX table functions, which is not a coincidence. Though they are among the most complex features of DAX, table functions provide capabilities enabling analyses that are impossible to establish without them.

- Performance is always important when designing and building DAX calculations. When using DAX table functions, the key is to minimize the number of iterations in table aggregations; in other words, only iterate over tables with as few rows as possible. It is even better not to iterate at all, but to use virtual tables as filters instead.

Our hope is to have inspired you to further work on your DAX skills and to go ahead and tackle your business problems using DAX-based analyses. Good luck!

packt.com

Subscribe to our online digital library for full access to over 7,000 books and videos, as well as industry leading tools to help you plan your personal development and advance your career. For more information, please visit our website.

Why subscribe?

- Spend less time learning and more time coding with practical eBooks and Videos from over 4,000 industry professionals

- Learn better with Skill Plans built especially for you

- Get a free eBook or video every month

- Fully searchable for easy access to vital information

- Copy and paste, print, and bookmark content

Did you know that Packt offers eBook versions of every book published, with PDF and ePub files available? You can upgrade to the eBook version at www.Packt.com and as a print book customer, you are entitled to a discount on the eBook copy. Get in touch with us at customercare@packtpub.com for more details.

At www.Packt.com, you can also read a collection of free technical articles, sign up for a range of free newsletters, and receive exclusive discounts and offers on Packt books and eBooks.

Other Books You May Enjoy

If you enjoyed this book, you may be interested in these other books by Packt:

Microsoft Power BI Cookbook – Second Edition

Greg Deckler

Brett Powell

ISBN: 978-1-80181-304-4

- Cleanse, stage, and integrate your data sources with Power Query (M)
- Remove data complexities and provide users with intuitive, self-service BI capabilities
- Build business logic and analysis into your solutions via the DAX programming language and dashboard-ready calculations
- Implement aggregation tables to accelerate query performance over large data sources
- Create and integrate paginated reports
- Understand the differences and implications of DirectQuery, live connections, Import, and Composite model datasets
- Integrate other Microsoft data tools into your Power BI solution

Microsoft Power BI Quick Start Guide – Second Edition

Devin Knight

Mitchell Pearson

Bradley Schacht

Erin Ostrowsky

ISBN: 978-1-80056-157-1

- Connect to data sources using import and DirectQuery options
- Use Query Editor for data transformation and data cleansing processes, including writing M and R scripts and dataflows to do the same in the cloud
- Design optimized data models by designing relationships and DAX calculations
- Design effective reports with built-in and custom visuals
- Adopt Power BI Desktop and Service to implement row-level security
- Administer a Power BI cloud tenant for your organization
- Use built-in AI capabilities to enhance Power BI data transformation techniques
- Deploy your Power BI desktop files into the Power BI Report Server

Packt is searching for authors like you

If you're interested in becoming an author for Packt, please visit authors.packtpub. com and apply today. We have worked with thousands of developers and tech professionals, just like you, to help them share their insight with the global tech community. You can make a general application, apply for a specific hot topic that we are recruiting an author for, or submit your own idea.

Share Your Thoughts

Now you've finished *Extreme DAX*, we'd love to hear your thoughts! Scan the QR code below to go straight to the Amazon review page for this book and share your feedback or leave a review on the site that you purchased it from.

https://packt.link/r/1801078513

Your review is important to us and the tech community and will help us make sure we're delivering excellent quality content.

Index

C

calculated columns **50, 51**

calculated fields **54**

calculated tables **52, 53**

CALCULATE function
used, for filtering 75-82

CALCULATETABLE
using 100, 101

CALCULATETABLE function 107, 219, 220, 227, 228, 239, 242, 243, 296, 301, 303, 304, 306-308, 317-321, 325-327, 383, 384, 386, 389, 390, 393, 395, 398, 399, 401, 404, 407, 418, 430, 434

calculation and date columns
selecting, dynamtically 180-185

CALENDARAUTO function 59, 60

CALENDAR function 59-61, 201, 205

cardinality 37

cash flows 333

COALESCE function 255

collective analytics 7

columnar database 23, 24

complex calculations
testing 326-329

consolidated view
versus subsidiary view 282-284

CONTAINS function 311, 378

context transformation 75

control table 176

cost-covering rent (CCR)
approximation, optimizing 362-367
calculating 356, 357
determining, by approximation 357-361

COUNTROWS function 70, 92, 142, 161, 163, 220, 221, 247, 254, 311, 317, 320, 326, 327, 393, 409, 419

cross filter direction 33-36

CROSSJOIN function 94, 99, 187, 291, 292, 382, 383, 420, 432

cross-report drillthrough 157

current sales orders 305-312
corrections, for sales orders behind schedule 321-324
dealing, with invoice surplus 314-319

dealing with, on schedule 319-321
optimizing 312-314

D

Data Model 8

data modeling
for status-oriented data 370-375

DATATABLE function 53, 177, 181

DATEADD function 252, 255

date selection table 223-226
options, creating 226-229
using, in measures 229-231

DATESINPERIOD function 88, 175, 176, 183-185, 192, 219, 393, 394, 396, 400, 402, 405, 408

DATESMTD function 251, 256

DATESYTD function 86-88, 103, 211

date tables 58, 59
creating 59-61

Date/Time, Date, Time data types 24, 25

DAX-based models
interactive report 11-13
visual reporting 11-13

DAX, best practices
base measures, using as building blocks 62
explicit measures, building 62
measure tables, using 63-65
model elements, hiding 63
table, types 65, 66

DAX context 69
filter context 73
filters, detecting 74
query context 71-73
row context 69-71

DAX evaluation
optimizing, with AutoExist 245-248

DAX, filtering with CALCULATE function
existing filters, removing 78, 79
expression to calculate, evaluating 80-82
filter context, setting up 77, 78
filters, removing with ALL functions 82-85
new filters, applying 79, 80

DAX measures 55
creating, with dynamic labels 188-190
explicit measures 54
implicit measure 54

Made in the USA
Las Vegas, NV
07 September 2022

54816781R00258